1001 Street Fighting SECRETS

The Principles of Contemporary Fighting Arts

PALADIN PRESS · BOULDER, COLORADO

Also by Sammy Franco

The Bigger They Are, the Harder They Fall:
   How to Defeat a Larger and Stronger Adversary in a Streetfight
First Strike: Mastering the Preemptive Strike for Street Combat
Street Lethal: Unarmed Urban Combat
When Seconds Count: Everyone's Guide to Self-Defense

1001 Street Fighting Secrets:
   The Principles of Contemporary Fighting Arts
by Sammy Franco

Copyright © 1997 by Sammy Franco

ISBN 0-87364-887-0
Printed in the United States of America

Published by Paladin Press,
a division of Paladin Enterprises, Inc.
Gunbarrel Tech Center
7077 Winchester Circle
Boulder, Colorado 80301, USA
+1.303.443.7250

Direct inquiries and/or orders to the above address.

PALADIN, PALADIN PRESS, and the "horse head" design
are trademarks belonging to Paladin Enterprises and
registered in United States Patent and Trademark Office.

All rights reserved. Except for use in a review, no
portion of this book may be reproduced in any form
without the express written permission of the publisher.

Neither the author nor the publisher assumes
any responsibility for the use or misuse of
information contained in this book.

Visit our Web site at www.paladin-press.com

Contents

Introduction 1

Chapter One: Street Fighting Fundamentals 9
- The Basics
- The Stances
- Kicking Techniques
- Punching Techniques
- Close-Quarter Techniques
- Defensive Techniques
- Footwork and Mobility

Chapter Two: Training and Conditioning 39
- Goals and Objectives
- Learning and Testing
- Training Preliminaries
- Routines and Workouts
- Equipment
- Sparring
- Supplemental Exercises
- Nutrition
- Reading and Research
- The Instructor
- School Selection

Chapter Three: Attributes of Combatants 65
- Cognitive Attributes
- Physical Attributes

Chapter Four: Tactics and Strategy 79
- General Tactics
- Clothing and Grooming
- Assessment
- De-Escalation Tactics
- Your Adversary

Ranges of Combat
Visual Considerations
Offensive Tactics
Positioning Tactics
Anatomical Considerations
Fighting Multiple Attackers
Makeshift Weapons
Oleoresin Capsicum
Dealing with the Police
The Aftermath of a Street Fight

Chapter Five: Grappling and Ground Fighting **109**
The Basics
Grips
Conventional Submission Techniques
Strategies
Nuclear Tactics
Training

Chapter Six: Bludgeons and Stick Fighting **131**
The Basics
Techniques and Angles
Training

Chapter Seven: Knife Defense and Knife Fighting **143**
Facts
Knife Defense
Knife Fighting Skills
Training

Chapter Eight: Firearms and Combat Shooting **157**
Ownership
Safety
Facts
Nomenclature and Mechanics
Ammunition
Malfunctions
Fundamentals
Positions, Stances, and Grips
Targets
Tactics and Techniques
Home Intrusion
Disarming Techniques
Legal Considerations
Training

Chapter Nine: Philosophy **181**

Glossary **187**

Suggested Reading and Viewing **209**

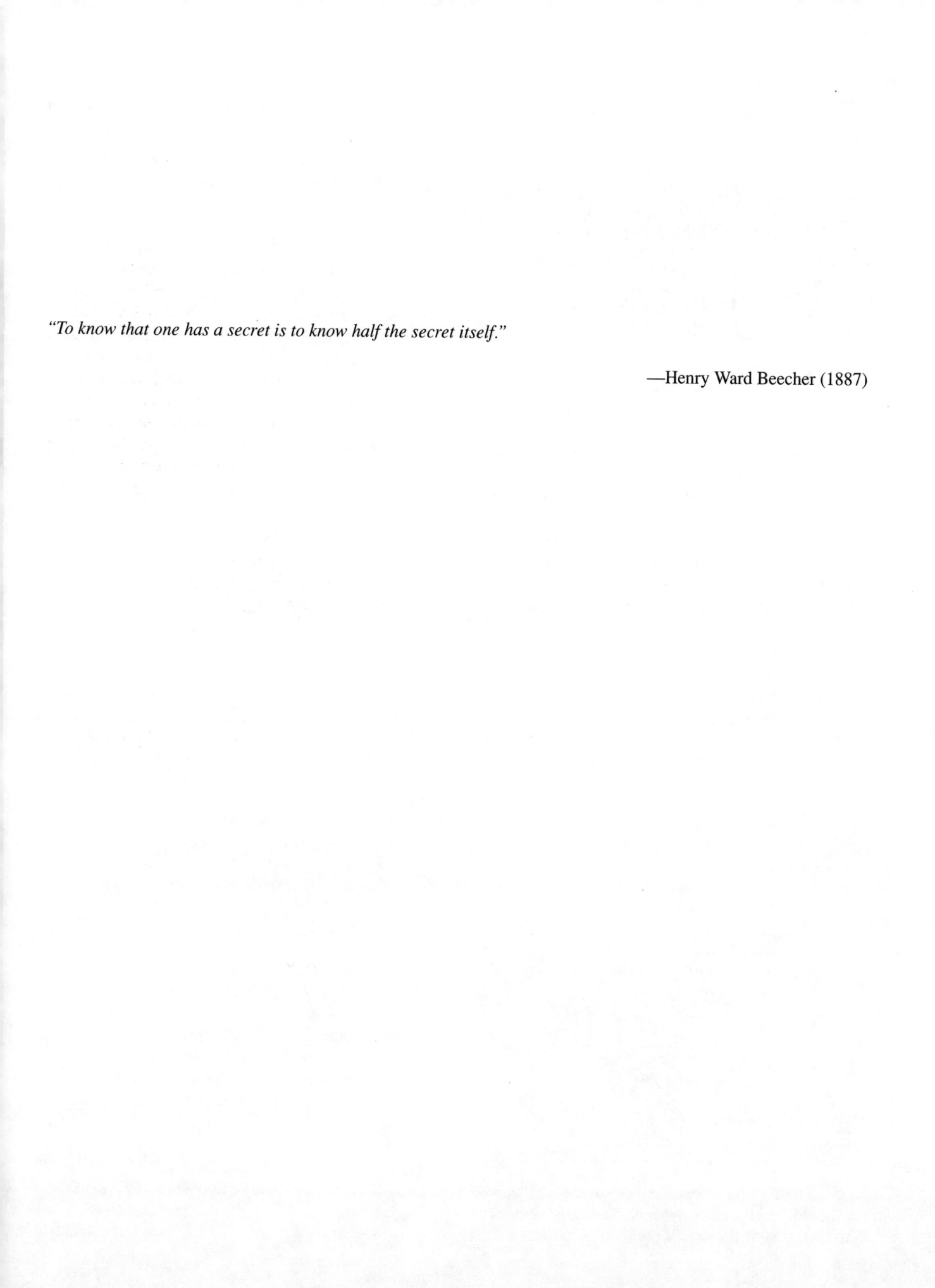

"To know that one has a secret is to know half the secret itself."

—Henry Ward Beecher (1887)

Author's Note

THE FINAL SECRET

You'll notice that the last secret in this book is replaced with question marks. You, the reader, must find the final secret. Here's a clue: this book was written with some secrets placed in a unique order. When you discover this unique formation or pattern, you will be one step closer to finding the final secret to this book. This task, however, is not easy and is reserved for only the most inquisitive and analytical reader. Nevertheless, if you do figure out the final secret, send your answer to Paladin Press, P.O. Box 1307, Boulder, CO, 80306, in care of the author. Good luck!

Preface

1,001 Street Fighting Secrets is an exhaustive compilation of axioms and principles of my system of combat, Contemporary Fighting Arts (CFA). This book will prove to be the most in-depth, detailed, and complete collection of street fighting secrets ever compiled.

Chapter One covers all the foundational elements of street fighting. Topics include stances, offensive skills, natural body weapons, defensive skills and techniques, breathing, common errors, centerline theory, weight distributions, range specialization, stabilizer and mover theory, characteristics of fighting, energy transfer, power generators, combative subtleties, footwork skills, target zones, and ranges of combat.

Chapter Two covers training and conditioning for the rigors of both armed and unarmed combat. You will learn the importance of aerobic conditioning, weight training, training zones, stretching, diet and nutrition, visualization, impact tolerance, sparring drills, training routines, compound attack development, somatotypical training, training dos and don'ts, and shadow fighting.

Chapter Three introduces you to the attributes of both armed and unarmed combat. Some include decisiveness, agility, distancing, explosiveness, pain tolerance, viciousness, speed, power, balance, timing, finesse, accuracy, target recognition, offensive reaction time, evasiveness, confidence, awareness, range proficiency, relaxation, combative uniformity, deceptiveness, the "killer instinct," telegraphic cognizance, histrionics, and adaptability.

Chapter Four teaches you a plethora of street fighting tactics and strategies, including ambush zone avoidance, low-line kicking techniques, methods of attack, combative assumptions, first-strike principle, assessment skills, de-escalation skills, multiple assailant combat, legal considerations, street smart tactics, barroom etiquette, the neutral zone, strategic positioning, environmental exploitation, makeshift weaponry, offensive and defensive range manipulation, and the pitfalls of dependency.

Chapter Five confronts one of the most neglected aspects of martial arts training: grappling and ground fighting. Besides teaching you myriad submission holds, this chapter will teach you ground fighting positions, pummeling skills, the dangers of positional asphyxia, sprawling methods, hand grips, ground fighting with weapons, nuclear and conventional ground fighting tactics, grappling planes, escapes, and reversals.

Chapter Six acquaints you with bludgeons and stick fighting. This chapter will cover some of the following themes: the limitations of zoning, stick grips, deflections, blocks, stick fighting ranges, retention skills, training drills, long arc deficiencies, footwork, stick strangles, swing stages, bludgeon characteristics, disarming techniques, and reverberation paths.

Chapter Seven launches you into the sobering world of edged weapons. In this chapter you will learn about knife defense stances, knife grips, training drills, footwork, secondary weapons, retention skills, the "V" grip, knife fighting tactics, survival principles, drawing skills, cutting angles, withdrawing skills, strategic leaning, insertion points, and knife-palming methods.

Chapter Eight introduces you to the ultimate

force option—firearms. In this chapter you will learn about semiautomatics, revolvers, firearm fundamentals, firearm safety rules, center mass selection, the double-tap principle, one-hand reloading, entry tactics, drawing and retention skills, disarming techniques, shooting positions, cover vs. concealment, ammunition criteria, speed loading, muzzle flash, contact shooting, cartridge malfunctions, ammunition storage, immediate action drills, and the fatal funnel.

Finally, Chapter Nine bridges the gap between the technical and philosophical aspects of combat. In this chapter, you will acquire a greater appreciation and understanding of Contemporary Fighting Arts. This chapter will touch upon the following intellectual themes: pacifism, courage, fear, loyalty, honor, logic, conceptualization, perfectionism, laws of reality, diplomacy, ego, good vs. evil, myth vs. reality, and the belief in a higher power.

One final note to the reader: When reading this text you'll notice that some secrets overlap or replicate others. Don't be alarmed. This is expected since most principles of combat are consanguineous. Like pieces of a jigsaw puzzle, they all have related elements.

Acknowledgments

I would like to express my deepest gratitude to God. He gives me the intelligence and will to carry on. (T.M.F.B.A.K.M.!)

I would also like to thank the following people for their support and encouragement: Carl Henderson for his friendship, sincere loyalty, and devotion to Contemporary Fighting Arts; Laura Lee Stratford for her love, support, and patience; Peter Porosky for his sharp editorial skills; Rick Moody for giving me and CFA a chance; Paula Grano for her keen editorial prowess; Peder Lund, Jon Ford, Karen Pochert, and the entire staff at Paladin Press; Fred Hanna for his computer savvy; and my four-legged pal, Fonto, for his companionship.

Thank you to Carl "Seed" Sosebee, Bradley Alan Meyer, George P. Svejda, Jalil Badran, Richard Stone, Fred Hanna, Corey S. Maillet, Brian Tomes, Mike Desmond, Jr., Jack de Cavagnal, James Massingil, Frank Coviello, Kathleen Tavarez, and Phil Hadeed for posing for the photographs. Thank you, Levon, for all the photographs.

To the many others who have been there throughout the years—Janice Sosebee, the United States Border Patrol (USBP), Joe Jennings of Panther Productions, Dr. Brad Norman, Kevin and Beverly Mont, Shelli Bernstien, Eli Franco, Audrey Franco, and, of course, Mom.

Special thanks to the thousands of people across the United States and throughout the world for their support, interest, and loyalty to Contemporary Fighting Arts.

For my father, Eli Franco.
A man who taught me the meaning of sacrifice.
I love you, Dad.

Introduction

Welcome to Contemporary Fighting Arts (CFA), an innovative self-defense system conceived in 1983. It is the most sophisticated, practical system of self-defense taught in America because it is designed specifically to provide the most efficient and effective methods possible to avoid, defuse, confront, and neutralize both armed and unarmed assailants. Unlike other martial arts, CFA dispenses with the extraneous and the impractical and focuses on real-life fighting.

CFA is the culmination of many years of methodical innovation. Its physical foundation is predicated on stylistic integration. Stylistic integration is the scientific collection of specific elements from various disciplines, which are strategically integrated and dramatically altered to meet three essential criteria for fighting: efficiency, effectiveness, and safety.

In CFA, efficiency means that the techniques allow the practitioner to reach his objective quickly and economically. Effectiveness means that the elements of the system will produce the desired effect. Finally, safety means that the combative elements provide the least amount of danger and risk for the practitioner.

CFA is not about tournaments or competition. It does not practice forms (katas) or any other obsolete rituals. There are no fancy leaping kicks or hip punches. It does not adhere blindly to tradition for tradition's sake. CFA is a pragmatic approach to staying alive on the street.

Most people don't realize that the martial

CFA dispenses with the extraneous and the impractical. In this photo, author and CFA founder Sammy Franco delivers a powerful side kick to his assailant's knee.

CFA training is geared toward real-life encounters.

sciences are only a small percentage of the total integration package necessary for survival on today's mean streets. CFA draws upon the knowledge and wisdom of numerous other sciences and disciplines, including police and military science, criminal justice, criminology, sociology, human psychology, philosophy, histrionics, physics, kinesics, proxemics, kinesiology, emergency medicine, crisis management, and human anatomy. As a result, CFA is a complete system of fighting that can be adapted to anyone or anything.

CFA has been taught to the U.S. Border Patrol, police officers, deputy sheriffs, security guards, military personnel, private investigators, surgeons, lawyers, college professors, airline pilots, and private investigators, as well as black belts, boxers, and kickboxers. CFA's broad appeal results from its no-nonsense approach.

It is essential to mention that the knowledge and skills acquired through CFA are dangerous. Studying this lethal martial art involves tremendous personal and social responsibility. Each and every student must adhere to the highest moral and social values. As a result, CFA reserves the sole right to refuse to teach any person who has a felony conviction or record of mental instability.

HOW DID CONTEMPORARY FIGHTING ARTS GET ITS NAME?

Before discussing the specific elements that make up the CFA system, it is important to explain how CFA acquired its name. The first word, "Contemporary," was selected because it refers to the system's modern, state-of-the-art orientation. Unlike traditional martial arts, CFA is specifically designed to meet the challenges of our modern world.

The second word, "Fighting," was chosen because it accurately describes CFA's combat orientation. After all, why not just call it Contemporary Martial Arts? There are two reasons for this. First, the word "martial" conjures up images of traditional martial art forms that are antithetical to the system. Second, why not use the perfectly functional word "fighting" when it defines the system so succinctly? After all, Contemporary Fighting Arts is about teaching people how to really fight.

Let's look at the third and final word, "Arts." In the subjective sense, "art" refers to the combat skills that are acquired through arduous study, practice, and observation. The bottom line is that effective self-defense skills will require consistent practice and attention. Take, for example, something as seemingly basic as a kick, which will actually require hundreds of hours of practice to perfect.

The pluralization of the word "Art" reflects CFA's multifaceted instruction. The various components of CFA's training (i.e., firearms training, stick fighting, ground fighting, and so on) have all truly earned their status as individual art forms and, as such, require years of consistent study and practice to master.

To acquire a greater understanding of CFA, you need an overview of the system's three vital components: the physical, the mental, and the spiritual.

THE PHYSICAL COMPONENT

The physical component of CFA focuses on the physical development of a fighter, including physical fitness, weapon and technique mastery, and self-defense attributes.

Physical Fitness

If you are going to prevail in a street fight, you must be physically fit. It's that simple. In fact, you will never master the tools and skills of combat unless you're in excellent physical shape. On the average, you will have to spend more than an hour a day to achieve optimal fitness.

In CFA, physical fitness comprises the following three broad components: cardiorespiratory conditioning, muscular/skeletal conditioning, and proper body composition.

The cardiorespiratory system includes the heart, lungs, and circulatory system, which undergo

INTRODUCTION

tremendous stress during the course of a street fight. So you're going to have to run, jog, bike, swim, or skip rope to develop sound cardiorespiratory conditioning. Each aerobic workout should last a minimum of 30 minutes and be performed at least four times per week.

The second component of physical fitness is muscular/skeletal conditioning. In the streets, the strong survive and the rest go to the morgue. In order to strengthen your bones and muscles to withstand the rigors of a real fight, your program must include progressive resistance (weight training) and calisthenics. You will also need a stretching program designed to loosen up every muscle group. You can't kick, punch, ground fight, or otherwise execute the necessary body mechanics if you're "tight" or inflexible. Stretching on a regular basis will also increase the muscles' range of motion, improve circulation, reduce the possibility of injury, and relieve daily stress.

The final component of physical fitness is proper body composition: simply, the ratio of fat to lean body tissue. Your diet and training regimen will affect your level or percentage of body fat significantly. A sensible and consistent exercise program accompanied by a healthy and balanced diet will facilitate proper body composition. Don't neglect this important aspect of physical fitness. (For more information, see *Killer Instinct: Unarmed Combat for Street Survival* by Sammy Franco, available from Paladin Press.)

Weapon and Technique Mastery

You won't stand a chance against a vicious assailant if you don't master the weapons and tools of fighting. In CFA, we teach our students both armed and unarmed methods of combat. Unarmed fighting requires that you master a complete arsenal of natural body weapons and techniques. In conjunction, you must also learn the various stances, hand positionings, footwork, body mechanics, defensive structure, locks, chokes, and holds. Keep in mind that something as simple as a basic punch will actually require hundreds of hours to perfect.

Range proficiency is another important aspect of weapon and technique mastery. Briefly, range proficiency is the ability to fight effectively in all three ranges of unarmed fighting. Although punching range tools are emphasized in CFA, kicking and grappling ranges cannot be neglected. Our kicking range tools consist of deceptive and powerful low-line kicks. Grappling range tools include headbutts, elbows, knees, foot stomps, and biting, tearing, gouging, and crushing tactics.

Although CFA focuses on striking, we also teach our students myriad chokes, locks, and holds that can be used in a ground fight. Although such grappling range submission techniques are not the most preferred methods of dealing with a ground fighting situation, they must be studied for the following six reasons: (1) level of force—many ground fighting situations do not justify the use of deadly force. In such instances, you must apply various nonlethal submission holds; (2) nature of the beast—in order to escape any choke, lock, or hold, you must first know how to apply it yourself; (3) occupational requirement—some professions (police, security officer, etc.) require that you possess a working knowledge of various submission techniques; (4) subduing a friend or relative—in many cases, it is best to restrain and control a friend or relative with a submission hold instead of striking him with a natural body weapon; (5) anatomical orientation—practicing various chokes, locks, and holds will help you develop a strong orientation with the human anatomy; and, finally, (6) refutation requirement—if you are going to criticize the combative limitations of any submission hold, you better be sure that you can perform it yourself.

Defensive tools and skills are also taught. Our defensive structure is efficient, uncomplicated, and impenetrable. It provides the fighter maximum protection while allowing complete freedom to launch a variety of offensive techniques. Our defensive structure is based on distance, parrying,

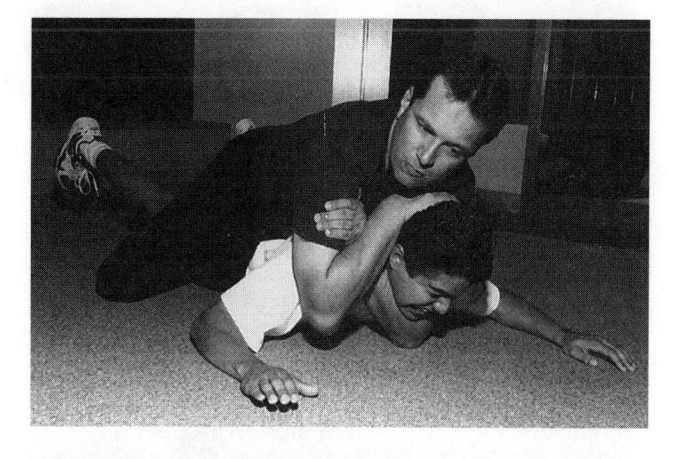

Although CFA emphasizes striking, we teach our students myriad chokes, locks, and holds. In this photo, CFA instructor Carl Henderson (top) applies a popular choke.

In today's modern world, firearms training is essential. CFA's firearm program focuses on owner responsibility and the legal ramifications of the use of deadly force

Powerful low-line kicks can be developed on the foam shield.

blocking, evading, mobility, and stance structure. Simplicity is always the key.

Students are also instructed in specific methods of armed fighting. For example, CFA provides instruction about firearms for personal and household protection. We provide specific guidelines for handgun purchasing, operation, nomenclature, proper caliber, shooting fundamentals, cleaning, and safe storage. Our firearm program also focuses on owner responsibility and the legal ramifications of using deadly force. CFA's weapons program also consists of natural body weapons, knives and edged weapons, single and double sticks, makeshift weaponry, the side-handle baton (for law enforcement only), and oleoresin capsicum (OC) spray.

The focus mitts are unsurpassed training tools in the hands of a skilled handler.

Combat Attributes

Your offensive and defensive tools are useless unless they are used strategically. For any tool or technique to be effective in a real fight, it must be accompanied by specific attributes. Attributes are qualities that enhance a particular tool, technique, or maneuver. Some examples include speed, power, timing, coordination, accuracy, nontelegraphic movement, balance, and target orientation. Many of these combat attributes will be discussed in Chapter 3.

CFA also has a wide variety of training drills and methodologies designed to develop and sharpen these combat attributes. For example, our students learn to ground fight while blindfolded, spar with one arm tied down, and fight while handcuffed.

Reality is the key. For example, in class students participate in full-contact exercises against

INTRODUCTION

Proficiency training can be used for both armed and unarmed skills. In this photo, CFA students work on their side kicks.

fully padded assailants, and real weapon disarming techniques are rehearsed and analyzed in a variety of dangerous scenarios. Students also train with a wide variety of equipment, including heavy bags, double-end bags, uppercut bags, pummel bags, focus mitts, striking shields, mirrors, rattan sticks, foam and plastic bats, kicking pads, chalkable knives, trigger-sensitive (mock) guns, boxing and digit gloves, full-body armor, and hundreds of different environmental props.

There are more than 200 unique training methodologies used in CFA. Each one is scientifically designed to prepare students for the hard-core realities of combat. There are also three specific training methodologies used to develop and sharpen the fundamental attributes and skills of armed and unarmed fighting, including proficiency training, conditioning training, and street training.

Proficiency training can be used for both armed and unarmed skills. When conducted properly, proficiency training develops speed, power, accuracy, nontelegraphic movement, balance, and general psychomotor skill. The training objective is to sharpen one specific body weapon, maneuver, or technique at a time by executing it over and over for a prescribed number of repetitions. Each time the technique or maneuver is executed with "clean" form at various speeds. Movements are also performed with the eyes closed to develop a kinesthetic "feel" for the action. Proficiency training can be accomplished through the use of various types of equipment, including the heavy bag, double-end bag, focus mitts, training knives, real and mock pistols, striking shields, shin and knee guards, foam and plastic bats, mannequin heads, and so on.

Conditioning training develops endurance, fluidity, rhythm, distancing, timing, speed, footwork, and balance. In most cases, this type of training requires the student to deliver a variety of fighting combinations for three- or four-minute rounds separated by 30-second breaks. Like proficiency training, this type of training can also be performed at various speeds. A good workout consists of at least five rounds. Conditioning training can be performed on the bags with full-contact sparring gear, rubber training knives, focus mitts, kicking shields, and shin guards, or against imaginary assailants in shadow fighting.

Conditioning training is not necessarily limited to just three- or four-minute rounds. For example, CFA's ground fighting training can last as long as 30 minutes. The bottom line is that it all depends on what you are training for.

Street training is the final preparation for the real thing. Since many violent altercations are explosive, lasting an average of 20 seconds, you must prepare for this possible scenario. This means delivering explosive and powerful compound attacks with vicious intent for approximately 20 seconds, resting one minute, and then repeating the process.

Street training prepares you for the stress and immediate fatigue of a real fight. It also develops speed, power, explosiveness, target selection and recognition, timing, footwork, pacing, and breath control. You should practice this methodology in different lighting, on different terrains, and in different environmental settings. You can use different types of training equipment as well. For example, you can prepare yourself for multiple assailants by having your training partners attack you with focus mitts from a variety of angles, ranges, and target postures. For 20 seconds, go after them with vicious low-line kicks, powerful punches, and devastating strikes.

When all is said and done, the physical component creates a fighter who is physically fit and armed with a lethal arsenal of tools, techniques, and weapons that can be deployed with destructive results.

THE MENTAL COMPONENT

The mental component of CFA focuses on the cerebral aspects of a fighter, developing killer instinct, strategic/tactical awareness, analysis and integration skills, philosophy, and cognitive skills.

The Killer Instinct

Deep within each of us is a cold and deadly primal power known as the "killer instinct." The killer instinct is a vicious combat mentality that surges to your consciousness and turns you into a fierce fighter who is free of fear, anger, and apprehension. If you want to survive the horrifying dynamics of real criminal violence, you must cultivate and utilize this instinctive killer mentality.

There are 12 unique characteristics of CFA's killer instinct. They are as follows: (1) clear and lucid thinking, (2) heightened situational awareness, (3) adrenaline surge, (4) mobilized body, (5) psychomotor control, (6) absence of distraction, (7) tunnel vision, (8) fearless mind-set, (9) tactical implementation, (10) the lack of emotion, (11) breath control, and (12) pseudospeciation, the assigning of inferior qualities to your adversary.

In CFA, we strive to tap the killer instinct in everyone. Visualization and crisis rehearsal are just two techniques used to develop, refine, and channel this extraordinary source of strength and energy so that it can be used to its full potential. (For more information, see *Killer Instinct* by Sammy Franco, available from Paladin Press.)

Strategic/Tactical Awareness

Strategy is the bedrock of preparedness. In CFA, there are three unique categories of strategic awareness that will diminish the likelihood of criminal victimization. They are criminal awareness, situational awareness, and self-awareness. When developed, these essential skills prepare you to assess a wide variety of threats instantaneously and accurately. Once you've made a proper threat assessment, you will be able to choose one of the following five self-defense options: comply, escape, de-escalate, assert, or fight back. (For more information, see my third book, *When Seconds Count: Everyone's Guide to Self-Defense*, also available from Paladin Press.)

CFA also teaches students to assess a variety of other important factors, including the assailant's demeanor, intent, range, and positioning and weapon capability, as well as such environmental issues as escape routes, barriers, terrain, and makeshift weaponry. In addition to assessment skills, CFA teaches students how to enhance perception and observation skills.

Analysis and Integration Skills

The analytical process is intricately linked to understanding how to defend yourself in any threatening situation. If you want to be the best, every aspect of fighting and personal protection must be dissected. Every strategy, tactic, movement, and concept must be broken down to its atomic parts. The three planes (physical, mental, spiritual) of self-defense must be unified scientifically through arduous practice and constant exploration.

CFA's most advanced practitioners have sound insight and understanding of a wide range of

Every aspect of fighting must be broken down to its atomic parts. In this photo, CFA instructor Carl Henderson (left) evaluates his students' performance.

sciences and disciplines. They include human anatomy, kinesiology, criminal justice, sociology, kinesics, proxemics, combat physics, emergency medicine, crisis management, histrionics, police and military science, the psychology of aggression, and the role of archetypes.

Analytical exercises are also a regular part of CFA training. For example, we conduct problem-solving sessions involving particular assailants attacking in defined environments. We move hypothetical attackers through various ranges to provide insight into tactical solutions. We scrutinize different methods of attack for their general utility in combat. We also discuss the legal ramifications of self-defense on a frequent basis.

In addition to problem-solving sessions, students are slowly exposed to concepts of integration and modification. Oral and written examinations are given to measure intellectual accomplishment. Unlike traditional systems, CFA does not use colored belts or sashes to identify a student's level of proficiency. Instead, its ranking structure consists of colored shirts (no rank, white; rank 1, yellow; rank 2, red; rank 3, blue; expert, black). Serial-numbered certificates are also issued to reflect a student's level of achievement and status in the CFA system.

Philosophy

Philosophical resolution is essential to a fighter's mental confidence and clarity. Anyone learning the art of war must find the ultimate answers to questions concerning the use of violence in defense of himself or others. To advance to the highest levels of combat awareness, you must find clear answers to such provocative questions as, "Could you take the life of another?" "What are your fears?" "Who are you?" "Why are you interested in studying Contemporary Fighting Arts?" "Why are you reading this book?" and "What is good and what is evil?" If you haven't begun the quest to formulate the important answers to these questions, then take a break. It's time to figure out just why you want to know the laws and rules of destruction.

Cognitive Skills

Cognitive exercises are also important for improving one's fighting skills. CFA uses visualization and crisis rehearsal scenarios to improve general body mechanics, tools and techniques, and maneuvers, as well as tactic selection. Mental clarity, concentration, and emotional control are also developed to enhance one's ability to call upon the controlled killer instinct. Meditation is a practical method of developing patience, internal calm, stress reduction, self-awareness, and control over involuntary muscular and related biochemical processes.

THE SPIRITUAL COMPONENT

There are many tough fighters out there. In fact, they reside in every town in every country. However, most are nothing more than vicious animals who lack self-mastery. And self-mastery is what separates the true warrior from the eternal novice.

I am not referring to religious precepts or beliefs when I speak of CFA's spiritual component. Unlike most martial arts, CFA does not merge religion into its spiritual aspect. Religion is a very personal and private matter and should never, ever be incorporated into any fighting system.

CFA's spiritual component is not something that is taught or studied. Rather, it is that which transcends the physical and mental aspects of being and reality. There is a deeper part of each of us that is a tremendous source of truth and accomplishment.

In CFA, the spiritual component is something that is slowly and progressively acquired. During the challenging quest of combat training, one begins to tap the higher qualities of human nature—those elements of our being that inherently enable us to know right from wrong and good from evil. As we slowly develop this aspect of our total self, we begin to strengthen qualities profoundly important to the "truth." Such qualities are essential to your growth through the mastery of inner peace, the clarity of your "vision," and your recognition of universal truths.

One of the goals of my system is to promote virtue and moral responsibility in people who have extreme capacities for physical and mental destructiveness. The spiritual component of fighting is truly the most difficult aspect of personal growth. Yet unlike the physical component, where the practitioner's abilities will be limited to some degree by genetics and other natural factors, the spiritual component of combat offers unlimited potential for growth and development. In the final analysis, CFA's spiritual component poses the greatest challenges for the student. It is an open-ended plane of unlimited advancement.

CHAPTER ONE

Street Fighting Fundamentals

"The fundamentals of combat are the stepping stones to victory."

THE BASICS

1. **DON'T BLINK.**

   Avoid reflexive blinking when a punch or kick is thrown at you. A split-second blink could leave you vulnerable to another blow. Blinking is a natural reflex. As a matter of fact, the eye blinks every two to ten seconds. However, reflexive eye blinking can be eliminated with proper training. For example, during sparring and full-contact sessions, you must make a conscious effort to keep your head forward and your eyes open amid flying blows. Acquiring this skill, of course, will take time and, above all, courage.

2. **BREATHE.**

   Breathing is one of the most important and often neglected aspects of fighting. Proper breathing promotes muscular relaxation and increases the speed and efficiency of your compound attack. The rate at which you breathe will also determine how quickly your cardiorespiratory system can recover from a violent encounter. *NOTE: Always remember to exhale whenever you are executing a striking tool or technique.*

3. **RELAX.**

   Learn to relax and avoid tensing your muscles when you are fighting. Muscular tension will throw off your timing, retard the speed of your movements, and wear you out during a fight. Combative preparation is one of the best methods of preventing unnecessary muscular tension.

4. **EMPLOY EFFICIENT TOOLS AND TECHNIQUES.**

   Every tool, technique, or tactic that you employ in a street fight must be efficient. Efficiency means that the techniques are direct and can be deployed rapidly, allowing you to reach your objective quickly and economically. Efficient techniques are also easy to learn and maintain, and they can be retained under the severe stress of combat. Remember, a technique does not have to be complex to be sophisticated.

5. **EMPLOY EFFECTIVE TOOLS AND TECHNIQUES.**

   Be certain that the tools, techniques, and tactics that you employ in a self-defense situation are effective. Effectiveness means the weapons in your arsenal can produce the desired effects.

6. **EMPLOY SAFE TOOLS AND TECHNIQUES.**

   Never gamble with your life in a street fight. Taking undue or unnecessary risks in a fight is not only stupid, it's suicidal. Every technique and tactic that you employ in a fight must be safe. Safety means that the elements and mechanics of a particular movement present the least amount of danger and risk for you in combat. When you execute a tool or technique, it should offer minimal target openings and minimize your loss of balance.

7. **EMPLOY LOW-MAINTENANCE TOOLS AND TECHNIQUES.**

   Always employ low-maintenance tools in a

fight. Such tools require the least amount of training to maintain their proficiency and generally require no preliminary stretching. The following are some low-maintenance tools: finger jabs, palm heels, head butts, thumb gouges, elbow and knee strikes, hammer fists, and push kicks. Your combat arsenal must be free of high-maintenance tools that require preliminary warm-up or stretching movements. Remember, there is no time to warm up in a fight.

8. **KNOW THE THREE TARGET ZONES.**

The assailant's anatomical targets are located in one of three possible target zones. Zone One (head region) consists of targets related to the assailant's senses, including the eyes, temples, nose, chin, and back of neck. Zone Two (neck, torso, groin) consists of targets related to the assailant's breathing, including the throat, solar plexus, ribs, and groin. Zone Three (legs and feet) consists of anatomical targets related to the assailant's mobility, including the thighs, knees, shins, insteps, and toes.

9. **KNOW THE CHARACTERISTICS OF COMBAT.**

The more you know about fighting, the less fearful and the better prepared you will be. The following are just a few characteristics of "real" combat: (1) combat is fast and explosive, (2) combat is unpredictable and spontaneous, (3) combat is ugly and brutal, (4) combat is extremely dangerous, (5) unarmed combat usually turns into a ground fight, (6) most unarmed combatants head hunt, (7) combat is bloody, (8) kicking is seldom used, (9) compound attacks usually end an unarmed encounter, (10) there are no rules, (11) spectators enjoy watching a fight and may likely join in, (12) combat is almost always unfair, (13) you will not be able to rest until your threat is neutralized, (14) your adversary will most likely be larger and stronger than you.

10. **ACQUAINT YOURSELF WITH YOUR KILLER INSTINCT.**

During a real fight, you must utilize a combat mentality to channel a destructiveness exceeding that of your attacker. This is the killer instinct. The killer instinct is a cold, primal mentality that surges to your conscious mind and turns you into a vicious combatant. Deep within every person is deadly primal power, a virtuous killer instinct that is cold, emotionless, and primed for destruction. The killer instinct is a reservoir of energy and strength. It can channel your destructiveness by producing a mental source of cold, destructive energy. If necessary, it fuels the determination to fight to the death. Everyone has a killer instinct. That's just the way we're made.

The following 14 factors integrate harmoniously to create the killer instinct: (1) clear thinking, (2) heightened situational awareness, (3) adrenaline surge, (4) physical mobilization, (5) psychomotor control, (6) absence of distractions, (7) unified mind (tunnel vision), (8) courage, (9) tactical implementation, (10) lack of emotion, (11) breath control, (12) pseudospeciation, (13) viciousness, and, finally, (14) pain tolerance.

A student demonstrates the lack of emotion that is essential to the killer instinct. The killer instinct is a vast reservoir of vicious energy.

11. **MASTER YOUR NATURAL BODY WEAPONS.**

You must have a working knowledge of your natural body weapons. Body weapons are simply the various body parts that can be used to disable, cripple, or kill an assailant. They include the following: (1) head—used for butting in the grappling range of combat; (2) teeth—used for biting tactics in close-quarter range; (3) voice—used for distracting or startling your assailant; (4) elbows—used as striking tools in the grappling range of combat; (5) fists—used for punching techniques in the punching range; (6) palms—used to deliver palm-heel strikes in the punching range; (7) fingers/nails—used for jabbing, gouging, and clawing the eyes and pulling, tearing, and crushing the throat and testicles;

STREET FIGHTING FUNDAMENTALS

(8) edge of hands—used to deliver knife-hand strikes in both punching and grappling ranges; (9) knees—used to deliver debilitating strikes in the grappling range; (10) shins—used to strike the assailant's thigh, knee, or groin; (11) insteps—used to deliver strikes in the kicking range; (12) heels of feet—used for kicking and stomping techniques; and (13) balls of feet—used for kicking techniques.

12. KNOW THE THREE RANGES OF UNARMED COMBAT.

There are three ranges or distances of unarmed combat, as follows: (1) kicking range—the farthest distance of unarmed combat, at which you would use your legs to strike your adversary; (2) punching range—the midrange of unarmed combat, at which distance you are able to strike your assailant effectively with your hands; and (3) grappling range—the third and final range of unarmed combat, which is divided into two different planes, vertical and horizontal. In the vertical plane, you can generally deliver impact techniques, some of which include elbow and knee strikes, head butts, gouging and crushing tactics, and biting and tearing techniques. In the horizontal plane, you are ground fighting with your adversary and can deliver all of the previously mentioned techniques, including various submission holds, locks, and chokes.

13. BE NONTELEGRAPHIC.

The element of surprise is an invaluable weapon for combat. Successfully neutralizing your adversary requires that you do not forewarn your assailant of your intentions. Telegraphing means inadvertently making your intentions known to your assailant. There are many subtle forms of telegraphing that must be avoided in combat. Here are just a few: (1) cocking your arm back prior to punching or striking; (2) tensing your neck, shoulders, or arms prior to striking; (3) widening your eyes or raising your eyebrows; (4) shifting your shoulders; (5) grinning or opening your mouth; and (6) taking a sudden, deep breath.

Top: The kicking range of unarmed combat.

Middle: The punching range of unarmed combat.

Bottom: The grappling range (vertical plane) of unarmed combat.

One of the most effective ways to prevent telegraphing movement is to maintain a poker face prior to executing any combat movement. Actually you should avoid all facial expressions when faced with a threatening adversary. You can also study your techniques and movements in front of a full-length mirror or have a training partner videotape your movements. These training procedures will assist you in identifying and ultimately eliminating telegraphic movement from your combat arsenal.

THE STANCES

14. BLADE YOUR BODY.

Never stand squarely in front of your assailant. Not only does this stance expose vital targets, it also diminishes your balance, inhibits efficient footwork, and minimizes your reach. Always try to maintain a 45-degree stance from your assailant. This position will help minimize target exposure, enhance your balance, promote mobility, and set up your natural body weapons.

15. ANGLE YOUR CHIN.

Always keep your chin angled slightly down when you assume any type of stance. This movement will make you a more elusive target and help minimize direct strikes to your eyes, nose, jaw, chin, and throat. However, avoid forcing your chin down too low. This will inhibit the mechanical fluidity of your tools and techniques and ultimately slow you down.

16. PROTECT YOUR CENTERLINE.

Your centerline is an imaginary vertical line that divides your body in half. Located on this line are some of your most vital impact targets (eyes, nose, chin, throat, solar plexus, and groin). Your centerline plays a critical role in both armed and unarmed encounters and is best protected through strategic body angulation (stance) and effective mobility.

17. KEEP BOTH HANDS UP.

When squared off with an assailant, avoid the natural tendency to lower your hand guard, which leaves you wide open to a possible counterattack. Remember, when executing a punch or strike, keep your other hand up to either defend or follow up with another strike.

Never drop your hands to your sides.

18. MAINTAIN PROPER WEIGHT DISTRIBUTION.

When squared off with your assailant, always try to maintain a 50-percent weight distribution. This "noncommittal" weight distribution will provide you with the ability to move in any direction quickly and efficiently, while also supplying you with the necessary stability to withstand and defend against various blows and strikes.

19. KEEP YOUR FEET SHOULDER-WIDTH APART.

When assuming any stance, the distance between your feet is a critical factor. If your feet are too close to each other you will lack the necessary

Which stance would you choose?

STREET FIGHTING FUNDAMENTALS

balance to maintain an effective fighting structure. If your feet are too far apart you'll be rigid and static, thus restricting your ability to move quickly. However, by keeping your feet approximately shoulder-width apart, you will provide your stance with sufficient balance and stability without sacrificing mobility.

20. KEEP YOUR FEET PARALLEL.

When assuming a stance, always keep both feet parallel and positioned at a 45-degree angle from the adversary. This position will improve your balance and stability when stationary and when moving.

21. KEEP YOUR FRONT FOOT TURNED INWARD.

When assuming a stance, be certain to keep your front foot turned inward at a 45-degree angle from your adversary. This strategic foot positioning is important for the following two reasons: (1) it protects your groin from a direct kick, and (2) it prevents a possible knee dislocation by allowing your lead knee to bend or "flex" when kicked by your adversary.

22. STABILITY IS ESSENTIAL.

One of the most important elements to an effective stance is stability. If stability is compromised, then so is your stance. Here are four principles to keep in mind when trying to achieve stability in your stance: (1) stability can be achieved by keeping your center of gravity directly over your feet, (2) the lower you drop your center of gravity to its support base, the greater stability you will have, (3) the wider your stance, the greater your stability, (4) the heavier the fighter, the greater his stability.

23. IDENTIFY YOUR STRONG SIDE.

Self-awareness is an important attribute of self-defense. For example, it's important for you to know which side of your body is stronger for both armed and unarmed combat. The term "strong side" refers to the side of your body (hands, arms, and legs) that has the greater amount of strength and psychomotor skill. For example, a right-handed fighter will usually have a dominant right side, while a left-handed fighter will have a stronger left side. In combat (excluding combat with firearms), always try to keep your stronger side forward to enhance the speed, power, and accuracy of your initiating blow. Keep in mind, however, that your ultimate objective in training is to develop and, ultimately, possess two strong sides.

24. PERFECT THE FIGHTING STANCE.

The fighting stance is a strategic and aggressive posture that a fighter assumes when squared off with an assailant. In unarmed combat, the fighting stance is used for both offensive and defensive purposes. It stresses strategic soundness and simplicity over complexity and style. The fighting stance also facilitates maximum execution of body weapons while simultaneously protecting your vital anatomical body targets against possible counterstrikes.

When assuming a fighting stance, blade your feet and body at a 45-degree angle from your assailant. This moves

This wide foot positioning will restrict your mobility.

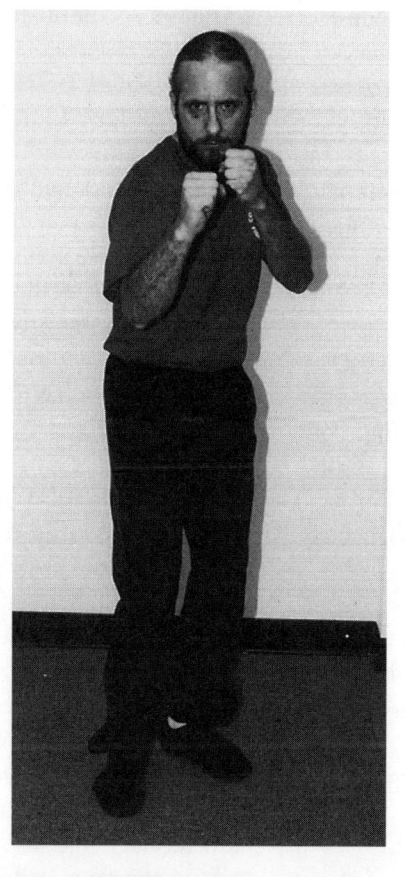

This narrow foot positioning will cause you to lose your balance

The fighting stance maximizes both offensive and defensive capabilities. In this photo, a student demonstrates a right-lead fighting stance.

your body targets back and away from direct strikes but still leaves you strategically positioned. Keep your stronger side forward, facing your adversary. Place your feet approximately shoulder-width apart. Keep both knees bent and flexible. Keep both of your hands up and align your lead hand in front of the rear hand. When holding up your guard in this position, make certain not to tighten your shoulders or arms. Stay relaxed and loose. Finally, keep your chin angled slightly down.

25. POINT YOUR ELBOWS TO THE GROUND.

When assuming the fighting stance, be sure to maintain a proper hand guard. Make certain that your lead arm is bent at approximately a 90-degree angle and that your rear arm is kept back by your chin. Avoid the tendency to let both your elbows flair out to the sides. This type of elbow positioning is dangerous for two key reasons. First, it exposes your waist and ribs to a variety of possible strikes and edged-weapon attacks. Second, it places your hands out of proper body mechanic alignment. You will lose power, and you will expose your centerline unnecessarily when delivering your punching tools.

26. KEEP YOUR HANDS LOOSE.

When assuming a fighting stance, always keep your hands loosely fisted with your fingers curled and your wrists straight. This will help prevent muscular tension and increase the speed of your hand movements (for offense and defense).

27. ALIGN YOUR HANDS.

When assuming a fighting stance, align both your rear and lead hands. This will protect your centerline, temporarily negate the assailant's linear assault, and set up your body weapons. Never open your hands and expose your centerline in an attempt to draw your assailant's attack. You'll get hurt! The open-hand guard is only used for the bludgeon-defense stance.

28. PROTECT YOUR HEAD.

There are many vital targets that you need to protect when fighting; however, the most important one is your head. Your head (this includes top, front, sides, and back) is the computer center that controls the functioning of your entire body. Since most of your vital senses (smell, sight, hearing, and equilibrium) are stored in the head, you must keep it out of harm's way. Assuming the proper combat stance accomplishes this.

29. DON'T STEP FORWARD.

Many fighters make the tactical mistake of stepping forward to assume a fighting stance. This is inherently dangerous for the following reasons: (1) it only moves you closer to your assailant before your protective structure is soundly established, and (2) it dramatically reduces your defensive reaction time, and it looks aggressive from a witness' perspective. Therefore, get into the habit of stepping back to assume a stance. Practice this tactic until it becomes a natural reflex.

30. PERFECT THE KNIFE-DEFENSE STANCE.

The knife-defense stance is a strategic posture that a fighter assumes when confronted by an attacker with an edged weapon. To assume this protective stance, execute the following: (1) blade your feet and torso at approximately a 45-degree angle from the attacker; (2) slightly hunch your shoulders forward and let your stomach sink inward, which will move your vital targets farther away from the knife; (3) stay relaxed and vigilant; (4) keep your head back and away from random slashes or stabs; (5) keep your hands, arms, and elbows close to your body to diminish target opportunities to the assailant;

STREET FIGHTING FUNDAMENTALS

(6) cup your hands with your palms facing you, which will turn soft tissue, veins, and arteries in the arms away from the blade; (6) keep your knees slightly bent and flexible with both legs approximately shoulder-width apart; (7) keep your body weight equally distributed on each leg; and (8) keep your chin angled slightly down.

31. PERFECT THE DE-ESCALATION STANCE.

Successfully de-escalating a hostile situation requires that you maintain a nonaggressive physiology. It is imperative that you assume a stance that is strategically sound yet nonthreatening. The proper de-escalation stance (for kicking and punching ranges) can be acquired by following these steps: (1) blade your body at approximately a 45-degree angle from the adversary; (2) keep both of your feet approximately shoulder-width apart and bend your knees slightly with your weight evenly distributed; (3) keep both of your hands open, relaxed, and up to protect the upper-body targets; (4) be certain to keep your torso, pelvis, head, and back erect; (5) stay relaxed and alert—remain at ease and in total control of your emotions and body; and (6) avoid any muscular tension—don't tighten up your shoulders, neck, arms, or thighs (tension restricts breathing and quick evasive movement, and it will quickly sap your vital energy).

The offensive and defensive capabilities of this de-escalation stance are tremendous.

32. SHOW YOUR PALMS WHEN DE-ESCALATING.

When assuming the de-escalation stance, you must always have both of your palms facing the assailant. This hand positioning is important for the following reasons: (1) it is congruent with the rest of your nonaggressive physiology; (2) it protects a greater area of your centerline; (3) it promotes muscular relaxation, thus enhancing the speed and delivery of both offensive and defensive weapons; (4) it aids in the prevention of onlooker intervention; (5) if you're in a situation that escalates into a fight and you are taken to court later, the judge or jury will look favorably upon the person who appeared nonthreatening prior to the fight; and (6) it is deceptive.

33. PERFECT THE BLUDGEON-DEFENSE STANCE.

The bludgeon-defense stance is a strategic posture that a fighter assumes when confronted by a bludgeon-wielding attacker. To assume this stance, execute the following: (1) keep your stronger side forward, facing your adversary; (2) blade your feet and torso at approximately a 45-degree angle to the attacker; (3) keep both of your hands up (beside each other); (4) keep your hands, arms, and elbows close to your body; (5) keep your head behind your hands and stay relaxed and vigilant; (6) keep your knees slightly bent and flexible with both legs approximately shoulder-width apart; (7) keep your body weight equally distributed on each leg; and (8) keep your chin angled slightly down. When assuming a bludgeon-defense stance, make certain not to tighten your shoulders or arms. Stay relaxed and loose.

34. CHOOSE THE APPROPRIATE STANCE FOR THE SITUATION.

Selecting the appropriate stance for a particular self-defense situation is critical. For example, assuming a de-escalation stance when confronted with a knife-wielding assailant can get you killed, whereas a fighting stance during a de-escalation situation might unnecessarily provoke an attack.

35. PERFECT THE NATURAL STANCE.

The natural stance is a strategic stance that you assume when approached by a stranger who appears nonthreatening—perhaps he is asking for directions. To assume the natural stance, apply the following principles: (1) angle your body 45 degrees from the suspicious individual; (2) keep both of your feet approximately shoulder-width apart and your knees slightly bent with your weight evenly distributed; (3) keep both of your hands in front of your body with some type of natural movement (e.g., rub your hands together, scratch your wrist, or scratch your nose), which will help protect your upper gates from a possible attack; (4) make certain to keep your torso, pelvis, head, and back erect; and (5) stay relaxed but alert, avoiding any muscular tension in your shoulders, neck, arms, or thighs.

36. DON'T DEPEND ON A STANCE.

Although the fighting stance is the foundation of a fighting system, learn to fight your assailant without a combat stance. Practice and train yourself to execute your tools and techniques without any foundational structure. Remember, a stance is often a luxury in a fight.

KICKING TECHNIQUES

37. KICK HIM.

Kicking range is the farthest distance of unarmed combat. There are many advantages to kicking in a fight. Here is a list of some: (1) surprise—since most strikes are delivered with the hands, kicking techniques can surprise an assailant; (2) power—since the legs are more powerful than the hands, kicking techniques can generate more force; (3) time—kicks can buy you some time by temporarily keeping multiple assailants at bay; (4) closing of the distance gap—kicks can be used to close the distance gap between you and the assailant safely; (5) entry into a range of combat—kicks can be utilized as an entry tool into a range of combat; (6) injury—kicks can be used as a tool to injure an assailant; (7) safety—compared to the other ranges of unarmed combat, kicking range is a safer distance from which to launch your attack. *WARNING: All kicking techniques should be used sparingly in combat.*

38. EMPLOY LOW-LINE KICKS.

If you are going to execute kicking techniques in a fight, always employ low-line kicks to targets below the assailant's waist. They are efficient, effective, deceptive, nontelegraphic, and relatively safe. Low-line targets include the groin, quadriceps, common peroneal nerve (approximately 4 inches above the knee area), knee, and shin.

39. KICK WITH YOUR LEAD LEG.

Kicking techniques are an important component of your arsenal. Although most kicks can be delivered from both your lead and rear legs, it's vital to execute 90 percent of your kicks from your lead leg. This is important for several reasons, including the following: (1) it is closer to your assailant's anatomical targets, (2) it accelerates your offensive reaction time, (3) it dramatically reduces telegraphing, (4) it reduces your assailant's defensive reaction time, (5) it improves the accuracy of your strike, and (6) it is safer for you.

Only employ low-line kicks in a fight. Here, a student is placed in an arm lock. Watch how he uses the low-line kick to get out of it.

The student immediately counters with a vicious low-line side kick to his assailant's knee.

STREET FIGHTING FUNDAMENTALS

40. MASTER THE VERTICAL KICK.

The vertical kick is one of the fastest kicks used in combat. This kick is delivered off your lead leg and travels on a vertical path to the assailant's groin and, in some cases, his face. To execute the vertical kick, maintain your balance while quickly shifting your weight back to your rear leg and simultaneously raising your lead leg vertically into the assailant's groin. Once contact is made, quickly force your leg back to the ground. Keep your supporting leg bent for balance. Contact should always be made with the instep of your lead foot. Avoid the tendency to snap your knee as you deliver the kick. Many people don't realize that the vertical kick can be delivered in three different directions—vertically, at a right angle, and at a left angle.

41. HIT WITH YOUR INSTEP.

When delivering a vertical kick, be certain to make contact with your instep. The instep is a good impact tool because it increases the power of your kick, prevents broken toes, and also lengthens the surface area of your natural body weapon.

42. MASTER THE PUSH KICK.

The push kick is another efficient and deceptive kicking range tool that is delivered from your lead leg. To deliver the kick while maintaining your balance, quickly shift your weight to your rear leg and simultaneously raise your lead leg. Thrust the ball of your foot into the assailant's groin, quadriceps, knee, or shin. Quickly drop your leg to the ground. Make certain to keep your supporting leg bent for balance.

43. HIT WITH THE BALL OF YOUR FOOT.

When delivering a push kick into the assailant's quadriceps, it's very important to make contact with the ball of your foot. This action will maximize the penetration of the kick into the assailant's muscle and nerves. You can also quickly snap the ball of the foot into the assailant's shinbone to loosen front grabs. When striking the assailant with the ball of your foot, remember to pull your toes back to avoid jamming or breaking them.

44. MASTER THE SIDE KICK.

The side kick is a powerful linear kick executed from the lead leg. Contact is made with the heel. To execute the kick, shift your weight back, pivot your rear foot, and simultaneously raise and thrust your lead hip and leg into the assailant. Remember that you must pivot your rear foot to facilitate proper skeletal alignment (shoulder, hip, and heel alignment). The side kick is targeted for either the assailant's hip, thigh, knee, or shinbone.

45. KNOW THE THREE VARIATIONS OF THE SIDE KICK.

Most martial artists don't realize that there are three variations of a side kick that can be employed in a street fight. Each variation serves a unique purpose. They include the following: (1) destroyer—used to simply attack and destroy the assailant's anatomical targets, (2) closer—used to close the distance gap between you and the assailant safely and efficiently, and (3) checker—used to keep multiple assailants away and buy you time to either escape or attack. The following chart illustrates some significant characteristics of each kick. For example, the destroyer variation of the side kick requires a maximal chamber, delivers maximum power, generates minimal speed, and has a high potential for telegraphing.

In this photo, a student delivers a vertical kick. Notice that he makes contact with his instep.

SIDE KICK	CHAMBER TYPE	POWER LEVEL	SPEED LEVEL	TELEGRAPHIC POTENTIAL
Destroyer	maximal	maximal	minimal	high
Closer	moderate	moderate	moderate	moderate
Checker	minimal	minimal	maximum	low

46. HIT WITH THE HEEL OF YOUR FOOT.

When delivering a side kick to either the assailant's knee or shin, make contact with your heel. This action will ensure maximum delivery of force by creating proper skeletal alignment. When fighting an assailant in the grappling range (vertical), you can use the heel of your foot to stomp down on his toes.

47. MAINTAIN SKELETAL ALIGNMENT.

One of the most important considerations when executing a side kick is maintaining proper skeletal alignment. Skeletal alignment is the proper alignment or arrangement of your body, which maximizes the structural integrity of your striking tool. Therefore, when executing a side kick, always make certain that the heel, knee, and hip of your kicking leg are properly aligned.

To maximize the power of your side kick, make contact with the heel of your foot.

48. AVOID THESE TWO COMMON ERRORS WHEN EXECUTING THE SIDE KICK.

Here are two common mistakes that occur when executing a side kick: (1) Failure to chamber your leg—your kick will have no force. To remedy this, lift your leg to the bent-knee position (this is known as a moderate chamber position). (2) Your toes lead the extension—you will jam your toes and sprain your ankle. To remedy this, pull your toes back toward your knee. This will ensure that your kick is leading with the heel of your foot.

49. UNDERSTAND THE LIMITATIONS OF A SIDE KICK.

Since most combat stances are predicated on blading your body at a 45-degree angle from your assailant, the side kick does have a limited application. Remember, to execute a side kick properly, you will need to position your body at a 90-degree angle from your target. This obviously presents a problem when you're standing at a 45-degree angle. Executing a side kick from a 45-degree angle can be dangerous because you'll need to pivot your hips and body. This, of course, would telegraph your attack to your adversary.

50. MASTER THE HOOK KICK.

The hook kick is a circular kick that is thrown from your rear leg. Contact is made with either your instep or shinbone. The hook kick is, by far, the most powerful kick you can deliver, because you are torquing your entire body into the target. To execute the hook kick, step at a 45-degree angle and simultaneously twist and drive your rear leg and hip into your target. Make certain to pivot your base foot and follow through your target. When executing the hook kick, either aim for your assailant's knee or drive your shin into the assailant's common peroneal nerve (approximately 4 inches above the knee area). This will collapse and temporarily immobilize the assailant's leg. Keep in mind that if you strike the knee you can cause permanent damage to the cartilage, ligaments, tendons, and bones.

51. HIT WITH YOUR SHIN.

Striking your adversary with your shinbone can quickly cripple him and bring him to his knees in agony. When kicking with your shin, remember to aim for the assailant's thigh (specifically, his common peroneal nerve), side of knee, or groin.

STREET FIGHTING FUNDAMENTALS

When delivering the hook kick, be certain to drive it through your target.

Don't forget to follow through your target and land in a stable stance.

52. LET YOUR KICK SINK IN.

When executing a hook kick, always allow your kick to sink into your assailant's leg briefly. This will maximize the force and penetration of your kick.

53. DON'T THROW HIGH-LINE KICKS.

High-line kicks are kicking techniques directed to targets above the assailant's waist. Never execute a high-line kick in a fight. Here are just a few reasons why: (1) balance—even the great kickers agree that high-line kicks can cause them to lose their balance easily; (2) inefficiency—they are not an efficient method of striking your assailant at this range; (3) no power—the less gravitational pull you put into a kick, the less power you will have; (4) clothing—the clothing you are wearing can drastically limit your ability to execute a high-line kick; (5) terrain—you must have ideal terrain conditions to even consider throwing a high-line kick; (6) flexibility—exceptional flexibility is a prerequisite to execute a high-line kick properly; (7) appendage barriers—high-line kicks must generally be directed to the upper torso and head (why kick where the assailant's arms are?); (8) closest weapon to closest target violation—your legs are closer to the assailant's low-line targets, not his high-line targets; (9) interception—high-line kicks can be intercepted and grabbed by a well-seasoned fighter; (10) lack of speed—high-line kicks take longer to reach their target than low-line kicks; (11) telegraphing—due to the greater travel distance, high-line kicks have a greater tendency to be telegraphed; (12) distance from the ground—high-line kicks take your legs farther away from the ground, thus slowing down your overall compound attack; (13) energy expenditure—high-line kicks require more energy to execute than low-line kicks; (14) target exposure—high-line kicks expose several targets to the assailant during their delivery; (15) high profile—high-line kicks are closer to the assailant's field of vision and are thus easier to see and to defend against.

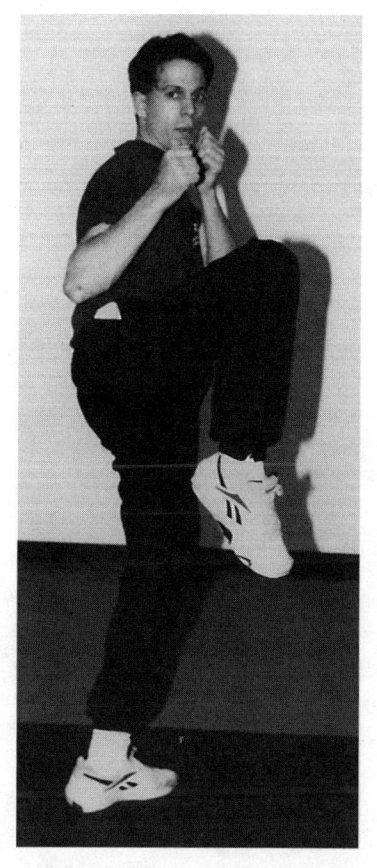

A full-chamber kick such as this one is too risky for real combat.

54. AVOID EXECUTING KICKING COMBINATIONS.

Don't throw a kicking combination in a fight. What most people don't realize is that kicking techniques are a means to an end but not an end in themselves.

55. AVOID EMPLOYING FULL-CHAMBER KICKS.

Chambering a kick means raising or "cocking" the appendage to a maximum height prior to delivering the kick. Full-chambered kicks are dangerous and risky for the following reasons: (1) they are too telegraphic, (2) they are unnecessary for power, (3) they open you up for a counterattack, (4) they can throw you off balance, and (5) they reduce the delivery speed of your kick.

56. DON'T RECHAMBER YOUR KICK.

After executing any kick, drop your extended leg to the ground and complete the rest of your compound attack immediately. Never rechamber your leg in a fight. This is dangerous for the following reasons: (1) it throws you off balance, (2) it exposes your anatomical targets unnecessarily, (3) it breaks your offensive flow, (4) it allows your adversary the opportunity to counterattack immediately, and (5) it prohibits the establishment of a sound fighting structure.

57. KEEP YOUR LEGS ON THE GROUND.

Although kicking techniques are an important part of your repertoire of weapons, the legs are best used for mobility.

PUNCHING TECHNIQUES

58. MAKE A PROPER FIST.

It's ironic how some of the most experienced fighters don't know how to make a proper fist. Improper fist clenching can be disastrous for the following reasons: (1) you can jam, sprain, or break your fingers; (2) you will destroy your wrist alignment, resulting in a sprained or broken wrist; or (3) you'll lose significant power when striking. To make a proper fist, tightly clench the four fingers evenly in the palm of your hand. Make certain that your thumb is wrapped securely around your second and third knuckles and flexed down toward the wrist.

59. MASTER THE SIX PRINCIPLES OF STRIKING.

For any strike to be considered effective, it must possess the following qualities: (1) it must be accurately delivered to the vulnerable targets on the assailant's body, (2) it must be delivered rapidly, (3) it must be delivered with debilitating power (i.e., sufficient energy transfer), (4) it must be economical in delivery—there should be no "energy leaks" in the practitioner's body mechanics, (5) it must minimize danger and risk for the practitioner, and (6) it must be delivered at the proper moment.

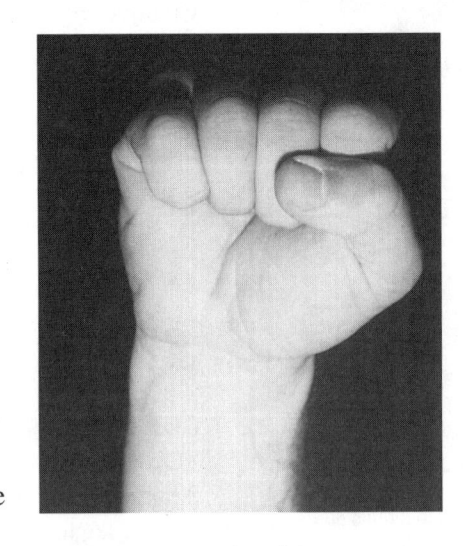

The proper way to make a fist.

60. DELIVER MAXIMUM ENERGY TRANSFER.

Since you may only get one opportunity to strike your adversary, it is important to maximize the force (or impact) of your blow. When delivering your strike, allow the energy to transfer completely into your target. To maximize this energy transfer, you will need to allow your blow to sink into your target for a fraction of a second before your retract it. This is known as the "fluid shock principle." ***WARNING: Avoid jabbing or flicking motions when delivering punches. Such futile movements will only open you up to a variety of possible counterstrikes.***

61. TIGHTEN YOUR FISTS ON IMPACT.

Remember to tighten your fists upon impact with your selected target. This action will allow your natural body weapon to travel with optimum speed and efficiency, and it will also augment the impact power of your strike.

62. AVOID COMMON PUNCHING ERRORS.

When executing punching tools, avoid the following common errors: (1) cocking your arm—this will telegraph your blow to the assailant, (2) dropping your other hand down—your assailant could effectively counterstrike, (3) tensing up—this will slow you down considerably, (4) lifting up your chin—this will expose your chin and throat to a possible strike, (5) dropping your shoulder—this will also open you up to a possible counterstrike, and (6) collapsing your wrist—this will result in a severe wrist sprain.

63. KEEP YOUR WRISTS STRAIGHT.

When throwing punching tools (circular or linear), make certain that your wrists are correctly aligned with your forearm. If your wrist bends or collapses on impact, you will either sprain or break it. A sprained or broken wrist will put you out of commission immediately in most fights. When used properly, the heavy bag will train you to keep your wrists straight when delivering powerful punches.

64. STRIKE WITH YOUR CENTER KNUCKLE.

Punching effectively with your fists is truly an art form, requiring considerable time and training to

STREET FIGHTING FUNDAMENTALS

master. When punching your assailant, strike with the your center knuckle. This is important for the following reasons: (1) it will maximize the impact of your blow, (2) it affords proper skeletal alignment, and (3) it helps prevent unnecessary wrist sprains. *CAUTION: Avoid striking your assailant with your first two knuckles. This impact area diffuses the weight transfer of the blow and can also cause a sprained or broken wrist.*

65. STABILIZE AND MOVE.

When delivering a blow from a stationary position, apply the "stabilizer and mover" theory. This means torquing one side of your body (the striking side) while simultaneously stabilizing the other side. Applying this theory of body mechanics maximizes the power of your blows and minimizes your loss of balance.

66. SNAP YOUR PUNCHES.

Punches should "crack" or snap when they hit a target. Here are a few suggestions to ensure that your punches will snap on impact: (1) try to accurately time the delivery of your blow, (2) properly judge the distance of your impact target, (3) avoid excessive follow-through when striking your target, (4) focus on retracting your blow without sacrificing neutralizing power, (5) avoid fully extending your elbow when punching.

67. DON'T LOCK YOUR ELBOWS.

When throwing linear punches, be certain not to lock your elbows. Elbow locking is a common problem among novices. When delivering a linear blow, your arm should be extended toward the target until the elbow is not more than three inches short of full extension. After contact is made with the target, the fist is returned back to the on-guard position. If your elbow locks upon impact, it will have a pushing effect and rob you of critical power.

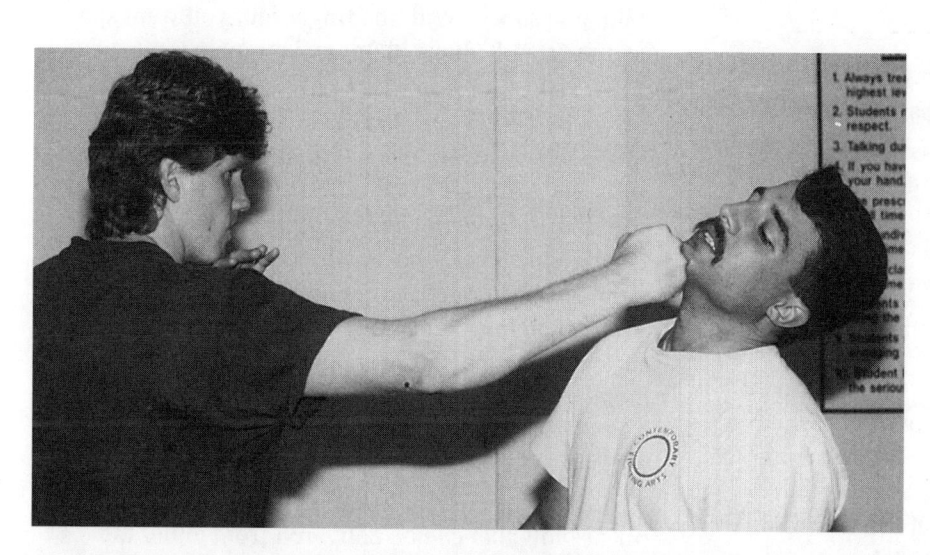

Cocking your arm back is a critical mistake that can cost you a fight.

In this photo, a student delivers a lead straight, making contact with his center knuckle.

68. USE YOUR THREE POWER GENERATORS.

When executing hand techniques from a stationary position, there are three anatomical power generators that will allow you to torque your body maximally. They include the following: (1) shoulders, (2) hips, and (3) feet. Maximally torquing your body into the blow will increase both the force and penetration of the blow. However,

When you are delivering a punch from a stationary position, the stabilizer and mover theory must be applied. In this photo, three advanced students demonstrate the rear cross. Note the proper torquing of the body.

there is a very fine line between power and speed in relation to the three anatomical power generators. Here is an analytical breakdown:

GENERATOR TYPE	POWER LEVEL	SPEED LEVEL
SHOULDER	minimal	maximal
*HIPS	moderate	moderate
**FEET	maximal	minimal

*The hips are used in conjunction with the shoulder.
**The feet are used in conjunction with the hips and shoulder.

Employ all three power generators in the following circumstances: (1) when first introduced to a punching or striking technique; this will help you acquire body mechanic mastery, and (2) when executing a "first strike" from a stationary position. In most street fighting situations, however, it's best to utilize the first two power generators (shoulders and hips) in conjunction with forward movement when delivering a compound attack from the vertical plane.

69. REMEMBER—YOUR LINE OF INITIATION IS YOUR LINE OF RETRACTION.

When executing linear blows (lead straights, rear crosses, finger jabs, palm heels), remember that your line of initiation should always be your line of retraction. Avoid arcing or dropping your blow. Such sloppy body mechanics will throw you off balance, minimize your impact power, and open you up for a possible counterattack. Failure to maintain a straight-line trajectory is usually caused by the following: (1) your elbow not traveling behind your punch, (2) premature wrist torque.

70. MASTER THE FINGER-JAB STRIKE.

The finger jab is a quick, nontelegraphic strike executed from your lead arm. Contact is made with your fingertips. The strike is likened to that of a snakebite. To execute the finger jab properly, quickly shoot your arm out and back. Don't tense your muscles prior to the execution of the strike. Just relax

The finger-jab strike.

and send it out. Targets for the finger-jab are the assailant's eyes. Don't forget that a finger jab strike can cause temporary or permanent blindness, severe pain, and shock. With the finger jab, you want speed, accuracy, and, above all, nontelegraphic movement.

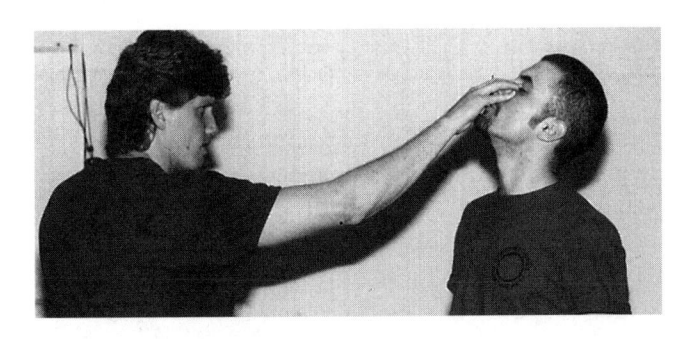

71. MASTER THE LEAD STRAIGHT.

The lead straight is a linear punch thrown from your lead arm, and contact is made with the center knuckle. To execute the lead straight, quickly twist your lead leg, hip, and shoulder forward. Snap your blow into the target and return to the starting position. A common mistake is to throw the punch and let it deflect off to the side. Targets for the lead straight include the nose, chin, and solar plexus.

72. MASTER THE PALM-HEEL STRIKE.

The palm-heel strike is a powerful, open-hand linear blow that can be delivered from either the lead or rear arm. Contact is made with the heel of your

STREET FIGHTING FUNDAMENTALS

In this photo, author Sammy Franco delivers the lead palm-heel strike to his assailant's nose.

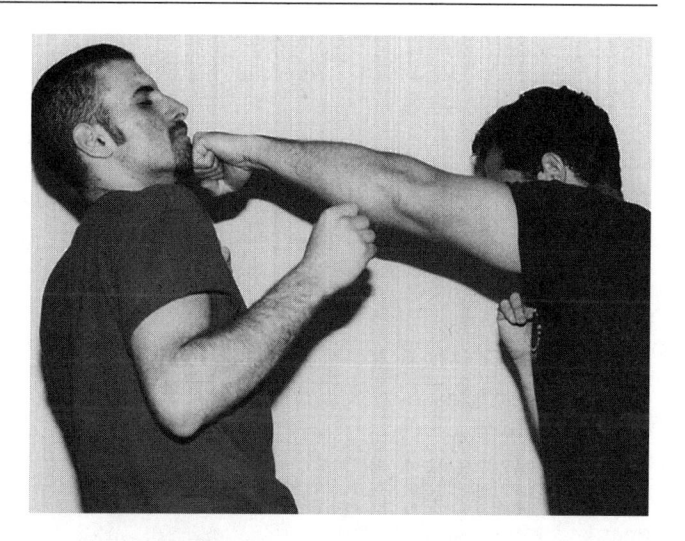

When delivering the rear cross, be certain to protect your head.

palm with the fingers pointing up. Targets include your assailant's nose and chin.

When delivering the blow, be certain to torque your shoulder, hips, and foot into the direction of the strike. Make certain that your arm extends straight and the heel of your palm makes contact with either the assailant's nose or chin, then return to the starting position. Remember to retract your arm along the same line in which you initiated the strike.

73. AVOID THESE TWO COMMON ERRORS WHEN DELIVERING A PALM-HEEL STRIKE.

There are two common errors associated with the palm-heel strike: (1) Leading with the fingertips and not the heel of the palm. This is dangerous because it can cause finger jamming and certainly negate the effectiveness of your strike. To remedy this error, make certain to hyperextend your wrist prior to target impact. (2) Splaying fingers and thumb apart. This problem can also cause finger jamming and rob you of critical impact power. To remedy it, concentrate on keeping your thumb tucked and your fingers pressed together.

74. MASTER THE REAR CROSS.

The rear cross is the most powerful linear tool in your unarmed arsenal. This punch travels in a straight line to your assailant's nose, chin, or solar plexus. Proper waist twisting and weight transfer are of paramount importance to the rear cross. You must shift your weight from your rear foot to your lead leg as you throw the punch. You can generate bone-crushing force by torquing your rear foot, hip, and shoulder into the direction of the blow. To maximize the impact of the punch, make certain that your fist is positioned horizontally. Avoid overextending the blow or exposing your chin during its execution.

75. MASTER THE HOOK PUNCH.

The hook punch is one of the most devastating blows in your arsenal that can be delivered from both the lead and rear sides. However, it's also one of the most difficult to master. To execute the hook punch properly, you must maintain the correct wrist, forearm, and shoulder alignment. When delivering the strike, be certain your arm is bent at least 90 degrees and that your wrist and forearm are kept straight throughout the movement.

To execute the hook punch, quickly and smoothly raise your elbow up so that your arm is parallel to the ground while simultaneously torquing your shoulder, hip, and foot in the direction of the blow. As you throw the punch, be certain that your fist is positioned vertically. Never position your fist horizontally when throwing a hook. This inferior hand placement can cause a sprained or broken wrist. Avoid chambering or cocking the arm and excessive follow-through.

76. KNOW THESE FACTS.

The hook punch (lead and rear) is considered the heavy artillery of punches. However, there are some important facts that you should know about this blow. They include the following: (1) Because of its angle of attack, the hook punch should be used judiciously with minimal telegraphing. Only highly skilled fighters should use the hook punch as an initiation blow in a street fight. (2) The hook punch is most commonly used when the adversary has dropped his hand guard or when the assailant's facial centerline is being flooded with linear blows. (3) The hook punch is a fractal tool that can be applied in both punching- and grappling-range combat.

In this photo, the author demonstrates the lead hook punch. Note the proper wrist and elbow alignment.

When delivering the uppercut, remember to twist and lift your body in the direction of the blow. In this photo, the author delivers a rear uppercut into his assailant's solar plexus.

77. MASTER THE UPPERCUT.

The uppercut is a powerful blow that can be delivered in both the punching and grappling ranges. This fractal tool travels in a vertical direction to either the assailant's chin or body, and it can be delivered from either the lead or rear arm.

To execute the uppercut, quickly twist and lift your body in the direction of the blow. Make certain that the punch has a short arc and that you avoid any "winding up" motions. A properly executed uppercut should feel like an explosive jolt.

78. MASTER THE SHOVEL-HOOK PUNCH.

The shovel hook is a powerful punch that travels diagonally into your assailant. Like the hook punch, this blow can be delivered from both the lead and rear sides. Here is a good way to remember the proper angle of this punch: if the hook punch is positioned at three o'clock and your uppercut is at six o'clock, then your shovel hook is positioned between three and six o'clock. To properly execute the rear shovel hook, dip your shoulder and simultaneously twist your rear leg and hip into your target and then drive your entire body into the assailant. Once again, keep balanced and follow through your selected target.

79. MASTER THE HAMMER FIST.

The hammer fist is a powerful strike that can be delivered vertically and horizontally to either the assailant's nose or neck. To deliver the vertical hammer fist, begin by raising your fist, keeping your elbow flexed. Drive your clenched fist down in a vertical line onto the back of your assailant's neck. Be certain to bend at your hips and knees and follow through your target. To deliver the horizontal hammer fist, begin from the on-guard position, then simultaneously torque your shoulder, hip, and leg

When delivering the shovel hook, be certain to put your body weight into the blow.

STREET FIGHTING FUNDAMENTALS

horizontally into your assailant's nose. Remember to keep your elbow bent on impact and maintain your balance throughout execution. *CAUTION: Never deliver a hammer-fist strike with a straight arm. This will rob you of speed and power and possibly cause a severe elbow strain.*

80. MASTER THE KNIFE-HAND STRIKE.

The knife-hand strike is another fractal tool that can be delivered in both grappling and punching ranges. It can be delivered from both the lead and rear sides as well as from a variety of possible angles—horizontally, vertically, and diagonally.

To deliver the vertical knife hand properly, quickly raise your hand up and vertically drive the edge of your hand onto the back of the assailant's neck. Be certain to bend at your knees and follow through the target.

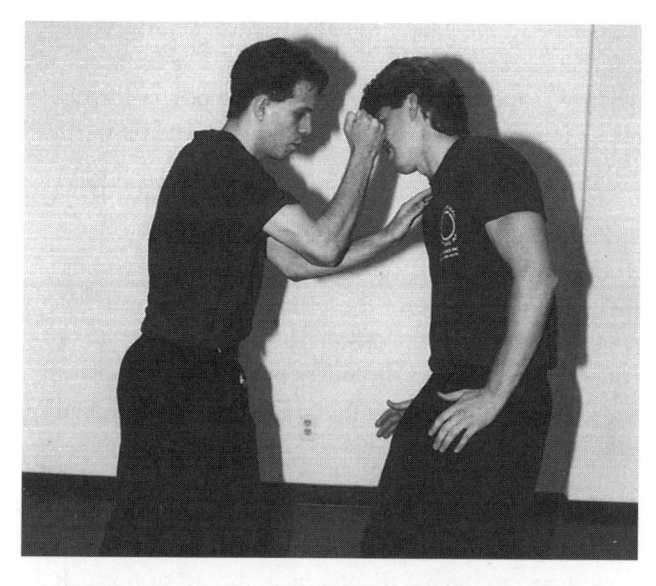

The vertical hammer fist can also be delivered to the assailant's nose. In this photo, a student delivers a deceptive rear vertical hammer fist.

81. DON'T USE A JAB.

The boxer's jab is a common punch used to throw the assailant off balance, set him up for another blow, test his skill, and keep him from moving toward you. Although this punch might be appropriate for the boxing ring, it has no purpose in real combat.

The jab is unsuitable for combat for the following reasons: (1) it lacks neutralizing power, (2) it can expose you to a counterstrike, (3) it agitates your assailant, and (4) it prolongs the fight and allows the assailant the opportunity to counter with viciousness.

The rear vertical knife hand.

82. DON'T USE A BACK FIST.

The back fist is a very popular punch used by many martial artists. Nevertheless, never employ a back fist in a real fight. It lacks neutralizing power and opens you up to a possible counterattack. Also, you can easily smash the delicate bones in the back of your hand if you come in contact with the assailant's head. If you want to attack the assailant with an angular blow, use a hook punch instead.

83. DON'T USE PROBING TECHNIQUES.

Never use a kick or punch to "probe," "test," or "feel" your assailant. Combat is the last place you want to experiment with the assailant. You don't want to employ techniques that probe, test, or stun your assailant. You want powerful, neutralizing blows that end the fight quickly and efficiently.

84. DON'T USE SPINNING PUNCHES.

There is no question that spinning techniques can generate tremendous power from cranking the entire body behind the blow. However, such techniques are suicidal. Spinning punches and kicks are impractical for the following reasons: (1) they are inefficient, (2) they require you to take your eyes off the assailant, (3) they momentarily expose your back to a possible attack, (4) they telegraph your movements, (5) they can cause you to slip and fall to the ground, (6) they disrupt your offensive flow, and (7) they require precise timing with your assailant's movement.

85. DON'T THROW OVERHEAD PUNCHES.

The overhead punch is a popular blow thrown by many street punks. This punch can be delivered using either hand, and it travels up and over your guarding hand. However, you should never throw this punch in a real fight because: (1) the body mechanics necessary to deliver this punch are telegraphic; (2) it lacks the necessary power to neutralize the assailant; (3) the angle of the blow forces your wrist out of skeletal alignment, and there's a very strong possibility that you can strain or break your wrist; (4) the angle of attack can cause you to strike the top of the assailant's head, and because the top of the human skull is so hard, you could easily break your hand upon impact.

The elbow strike is a devastating weapon. In this photo, Franco delivers a lead horizontal elbow to his assailant's temple.

There are too many drawbacks to the overhead punch. Don't use it in a fight.

CLOSE-QUARTER TECHNIQUES

86. MASTER ELBOW STRIKES.

The elbows are devastating weapons that can be used in the grappling range. They are explosive, deceptive, and very difficult to stop. Elbows can generally be delivered horizontally, vertically, and diagonally. Targets include the assailant's temple, throat, chin, cervical vertebrae, ribs, and solar plexus. When delivering elbow strikes, be certain to pivot your hips and shoulder forcefully in the direction of your blow.

(1) Vertical Elbow—The vertical elbow strike travels vertically to the assailant's face, throat, or body. It can be executed from either the right or left side of the body. To perform the strike, raise your elbow vertically (with the elbow flexed) until your hand is next to the side of your head. The striking surface is the point of the elbow. The power for this strike is acquired through the quick extension of the legs at the moment of impact.

(2) Horizontal Elbow—The horizontal elbow strike travels horizontally to the assailant's face, throat, or body. It can also be executed from either the right or left side of the body. To perform the strike, begin from the on-guard hand position, then rotate your hips and shoulders horizontally into your target. Your palms should be facing downward with your hand next to the side of your head. The striking surface is the elbow point.

(3) Diagonal Elbow (traveling downward)—The diagonal elbow strike travels diagonally downward to the assailant's face, throat, or body. It can be delivered from either the right or left side of the body. To execute the strike, rotate your elbow back, up, and over while quickly whipping it downward to your desired target. Bend your knees as your body descends with the strike. Your palm should be facing away from you when making contact. The striking surface is the elbow point.

87. USE YOUR TEETH.

When engaged in grappling range, you can use your teeth for biting anything on the assailant's body (e.g., nose, ears, throat, fingers, or biceps). Although a deep, penetrating bite is extremely painful, it also transmits a powerful psychological message to your assailant. It lets him know that you are willing to do

STREET FIGHTING FUNDAMENTALS

anything to survive. *CAUTION: Biting should only be used as a last resort; you run the risk of contracting AIDS if your attacker is infected and you draw blood while biting him.*

88. MASTER KNEE STRIKES.

The knee strike is another devastating close-quarter grappling-range tool that can bring a formidable assailant to the ground instantly. The knee strike can be delivered vertically and diagonally to a variety of anatomical targets, including the common peroneal nerve, the quadriceps, the groin, the ribs, and, in some cases, the face. When delivering the knee strike, be certain to make contact with your patella and not your lower thigh. To guarantee sufficient power, deliver all your knee strikes with your rear leg.

The mounted position is a critical component of ground fighting. In this photo, a student mounts his assailant.

In this photo, the author demonstrates the proper method of delivering the rear vertical knee strike.

89. POINT YOUR TOES TO THE GROUND.

When delivering the vertical knee strike, keep your rear leg bent with your toes pointed to the ground. This toe position provides the following: (1) it helps maintain proper skeletal alignment, (2) it helps promote muscular relaxation, (3) it helps protect your toes from unnecessary injury, and (4) it facilitates rapid delivery.

90. MASTER THE FOUR CRITICAL ASPECTS OF THE MOUNTED POSITION.

The fighter who establishes the top-mounted position has a tremendous tactical advantage in the ground fight. From this position, you can deliver a variety of blows to your assailant and yet be in a strategic position to avoid most counterstrikes. The mounted position also restricts your assailant's mobility and permits you to generate tremendous power.

If you want to be competent in a ground fight, it is critical that you master the four critical aspects of the mounted position, as follows: (1) attack—you must know how to attack your assailant from the mounted position, (2) defend—you must know how to defend an attack from the mounted position, (3) maintain—you must know how to maintain the mounted position, and (4) escape—you must know how to escape from the mounted position.

91. USE YOUR HEAD.

When engaged in close quarters, use your head for butting your assailant. Head butts are ideal when a strong attacker has placed you in a hold in which your

The head butt can be delivered in a variety of directions. In this photo, Franco delivers a head butt (backward) into his assailant's nose.

arms are pinned against your sides. The head butt can be delivered in the following four directions: (1) forward, (2) backward, (3) right side, and (4) left side.

92. MASTER THE FOOT STOMP.

The foot stomp is a deceptive close-quarter grappling technique that can cause excruciating pain for your assailant. To perform the foot stomp, raise your lead foot approximately 10 inches from the ground and forcibly stomp on the assailant's toes with the heel of your foot. If you doubt the effectiveness of a foot stomp, consider this sobering fact: a woman wearing high-heeled shoes can generate up to 1,600 pounds of pressure per square inch when delivering the foot stomp.

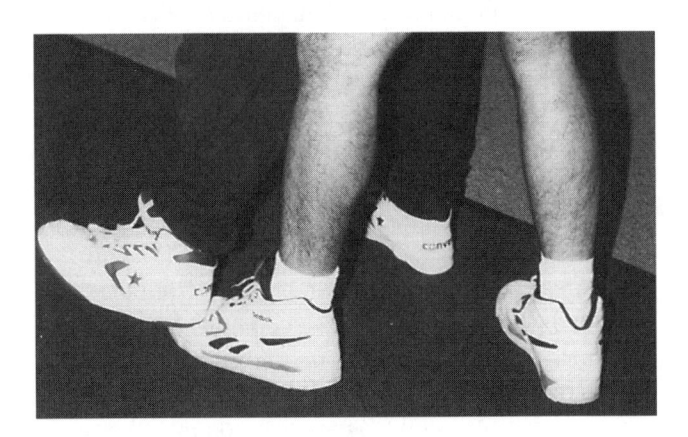

The foot stomp

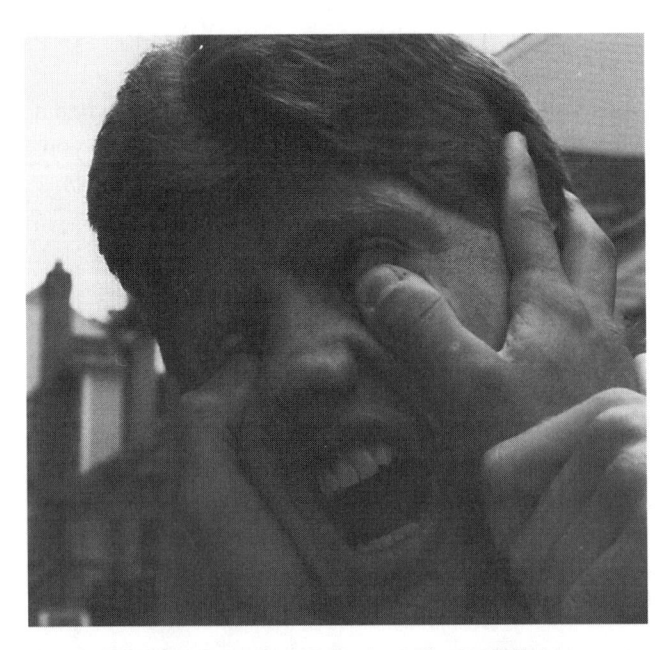

The double-thumb gouge is a nuclear grappling tactic that can produce devastating results.

93. MASTER THE DOUBLE-THUMB GOUGE.

The double-thumb gouge is a nuclear grappling tactic that can produce devastating results. This tactic can be delivered when either standing or fighting on the ground. To perform the gouge, place one hand on each side of the assailant's face. Stabilize your hands by wrapping your fingers around both sides of your assailant's jaw. Immediately drive both your thumbs into the assailant's eye sockets. Maintain and increase forceful pressure. The double-thumb gouge can cause temporary or permanent blindness, shock, and unconsciousness. ***WARNING: The double-thumb gouge should only be used in life-and-death situations! Be certain that it is legally warranted and justified.***

94. MASTER CRUSHING TECHNIQUES.

Crushing techniques are another nuclear ground-fighting tactic that can be used either when standing or ground fighting with your adversary. The two primary crushing targets are your assailant's throat and testicles. When attacking the throat, make certain to drive your fingers deep into the assailant's trachea. Let them envelope the windpipe. Deliberately squeeze the pipe and try to crush it.

When crushing the testicles, grab deep into the assailant's groin region, attempting to isolate the

Crushing techniques are deadly and can be applied from a variety of different angles and positions. In this photo, the author attacks his assailant from behind.

testicles. Squeeze and crush them together as forcefully as you can. ***WARNING: Crushing techniques should only be used in life-and-death situations! Make certain that your actions are legally and morally justified.***

95. POSSESS GROUND-FIGHTING SKILLS.

For most martial art systems, grappling range is the most neglected range of unarmed combat. Too many martial artists make the erroneous assumption that they can avoid or negate a grappling encounter. This faulty logic will get you killed in a real fight. The bottom line is if a fighter is determined to get you on the ground, he will, despite how good your techniques may be. As a matter of fact, statistics show that nine out of ten fights will end up on the ground. So be forewarned!

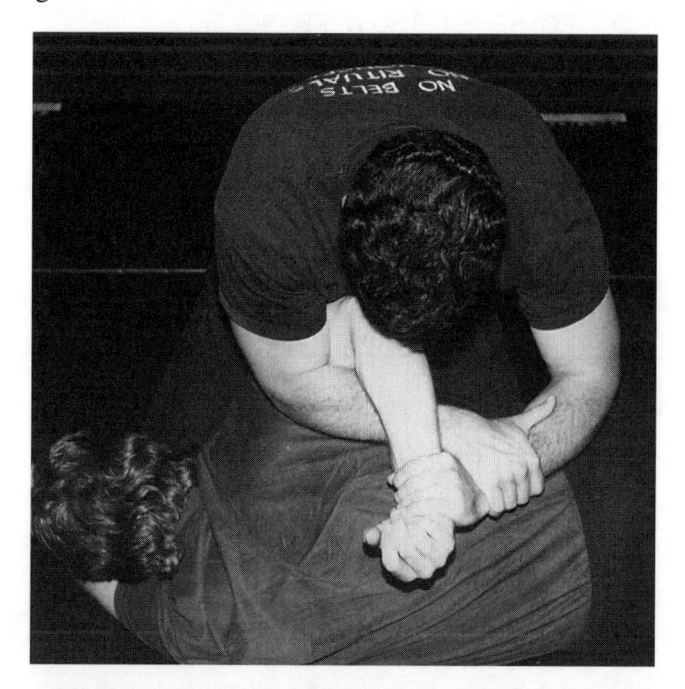

If you want to survive a street fight, you'd better have ground-fighting skills. In this photo, the author demonstrates a kneeling shoulder crank.

96. WHENEVER POSSIBLE, AVOID SUBMISSION HOLDS.

Don't employ submission holds unless they are absolutely necessary. Although submission holds are significant components of your legal use-of-force response when you are required to control and restrain your adversary, always remember that the safest and most efficient method of neutralizing an assailant (in unarmed combat) is through striking techniques.

97. KNOW HOW TO COUNTER VARIOUS GRABS, CHOKES, LOCKS, AND HOLDS.

If you want to be prepared for anything, you'd better know the countertechniques to every conceivable grab, choke, lock, or hold. The following are 10 standing attacks that you should be prepared for: (1) one- and two-hand wrist grabs, (2) one- and two-hand throat chokes from the front and rear, (3) front and rear bear hugs with and without pinned arms, (4) standing side headlocks (both right and left sides), (5) finger pokes, (6) one- and two-hand shoulder grabs, (7) one- and two-hand chest pushes, (8) rear arm locks (both right and left arms), (9) one- and two-hand lapel grabs, and (10) body tackles.

DEFENSIVE TECHNIQUES

98. USE DEFENSE AS A LAST RESORT.

Ideally, your best defense is a strong and powerful offense, but in reality there will be situations and circumstances that demand a defensive response. However, don't misunderstand the necessity of a strong defense by becoming a defensive fighter. A defensive fighter is one who lets his assailant seize and maintain offensive control. This is not what you want. Defense is a temporary setback that will eventually allow you to counter with offensive viciousness. There is a strategic line between offense and defense, victory and defeat, and life and death.

Defense against various wrist grabs is essential. In this photo, a student is grabbed with two hands.

To escape the grab, the student raises his left hand up and over his right hand. He then forcefully pulls his left hand back.

Once his left hand is free, he grabs his assailant's right wrist

The student counters with a rear cross.

99. MASTER THE SEVEN COMPONENTS OF DEFENSE.

The seven components necessary for a sound defensive structure are as follows: (1) distance—the spatial relationship between you and your adversary, (2) stance—the strategic posture you assume prior to or during combat, (3) mobility—the ability to move your body quickly and freely while balanced, (4) blocking—various defensive tools designed to intercept your assailant's oncoming blows, (5) parrying—various defensive tools that redirect your assailant's blows, (6) evading—defensive maneuvers strategically designed to neutralize your assailant's attack without making contact, and (7) attacking—offensive action designed to control, injure, cripple, or kill your assailant.

100. POSSESS GOOD DEFENSE.

A good defensive structure is predicated on a stance that minimizes target exposure, facilitates balance and mobility, and permits quick and evasive movements. Defensive tools and maneuvers should always be efficient, effective, and safe for the fighter.

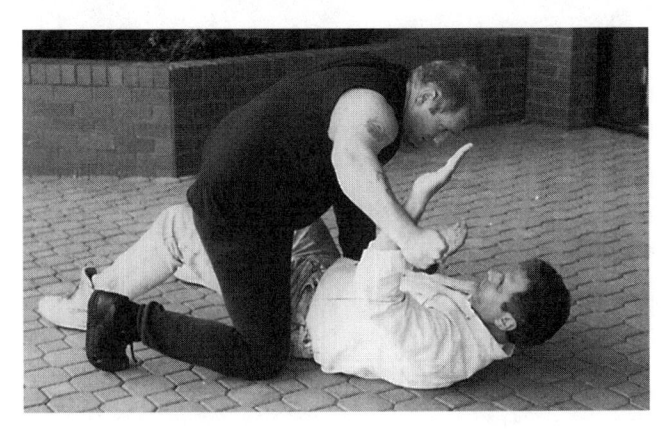

In combat, defense is a temporary setback. In this photo, a student (on the ground) blocks his assailant's swing.

101. BLOCKS.

Blocks are defensive techniques designed to intercept your assailant's circular attacks. Blocks are executed by placing a nonvital body part between the assailant's strike and your anatomical body target. Although blocks require significant deviation from your centerline, they are an essential component of defense.

Blocks are divided into the following two general categories: (1) arm blocks—serve as

STREET FIGHTING FUNDAMENTALS

protective barriers that intercept punches and kicks directed to your head and torso and (2) leg blocks—specifically designed to stop kicks directed to targets below your waist.

There are seven blocks, as follows: high blocks, midblocks, low blocks, elbow blocks, leg blocks, cross blocks, and reinforced low blocks (the last two are used only in rare circumstances).

102. NEVER BLOCK A LINEAR PUNCH.

The quickest and most efficient strikes are those that travel in a straight line (lead straights, rear crosses, palm heels, and finger jabs). Never attempt to block an assailant's linear punch. A block simply does not have the mechanical speed or efficient mechanics to intercept a linear blow. Always use parries to defend against linear punches.

103. BE A ROCK WHEN BLOCKING.

To avoid being knocked off balance when blocking an assailant's blow, apply the following: (1) increase your torso rotation to enhance the power of your blocking structure, (2) make certain to set your feet on the ground, and (3) time your blocking movement properly.

104. MAINTAIN YOUR BALANCE WHEN BLOCKING.

When blocking circular blows, it's essential to maintain a strong center of balance. Balance is the ability to maintain equilibrium while attacking or defending and while stationary or moving. Since most circular punches carry significant force, you must make an extra effort to maintain your position and avoid being knocked off balance. You can establish a strong blocking base by assuming the proper stance and by keeping both of your feet planted on the ground. In some self-defense situations, if you lose your balance you could lose your life.

105. WITHDRAW YOUR BLOCK.

Whenever executing an arm block, make certain to withdraw it to the original on-guard position. This is important for the following reasons: (1) it places you in a better position to effectively counter your assailant, (2) it will prevent you from unnecessarily exposing your centerline to your adversary, (3) it will help prevent your assailant from grabbing or controlling your arm.

106. BLOCKS ARE FOR UNARMED ENCOUNTERS.

Do not forget that blocking techniques are intended for unarmed encounters. Don't make the tragic mistake of attempting to use blocking techniques to stop an attack from a stick, bludgeon, or any edged weapon. Such action can cause you severe injury and even death.

107. INTERCEPT IT AS SOON AS POSSIBLE.

Whenever attempting a block, try to intercept the assailant's attack as soon as possible. In most cases, you should try to intercept the assailant's blow when it reaches approximately two-thirds (75 percent of maximum impact) of the way to its target. This is important for the following reasons: (1) it minimizes balance disruption, (2) it minimizes the contusions on your arm, (3) it quickly arrests the assailant's attack, and (4) it minimizes the assailant's impact power.
WARNING: When blocking, do not let your assailant's blow make contact when it is 100 percent completed.

108. MASTER THE HIGH BLOCK.

The high block is used to defend against powerful overhead punches. To execute the lead high

The high block.

The midblock is probably the most common block that you will use in a fight.

block, simply raise your lead arm up and extend your forearm out and above your head. Be careful not to position your arm where your head is exposed. Make certain that your hand is open and not clenched. This will increase the surface area of your block and provide a quick counterattack. The mechanics for the rear high block are the same for the lead high block. Raise your rear arm up and extend your forearm out and above your head.

109. MASTER THE MIDBLOCK.

One of the most important and commonly used blocks in a street fight is the midblock, which is used to defend against circular blows to your head or upper torso. To perform the block, raise either your right or left arm up at approximately a 90-degree angle while simultaneously pronating it in the direction of the strike. Make contact with the belly of your forearm at the assailant's wrist or forearm. This movement will provide maximum structural integrity for the blocking tool. Make certain that your hand is held open to increase the surface area of your block. When performing the midblock, be certain to time the rotation of your arm with the attack. Don't forget that the midblock has both height (up and down) and a width (in and out) fluctuations that are relative to the characteristics of the assailant's blow. Once you deliver the block, immediately counter.

110. BEWARE OF THESE TWO ERRORS WHEN EXECUTING THE MIDBLOCK.

There are two common errors that are associated with the midblock. They are: (1) Making contact with the back of your forearm—This mistake can injure your arm and significantly weaken your blocking structure. To remedy this error, be certain to rotate your forearm into a palm-out position prior to intercepting the assailant's punch. (2) Inadequate shoulder and trunk rotation—You will fail to generate sufficient force to effectively intercept the oncoming blow. This mistake can cause your assailant's blow to come crashing through your block. To remedy this problem, increase your shoulder and trunk rotation and sweep your arm aggressively in the direction of the attack.

111. MASTER THE ELBOW BLOCK.

The elbow block is used to stop circular blows to your midsection, such as uppercuts, shovel hooks, and hook kicks. To execute the elbow block, drop your elbow down and simultaneously twist your body toward your centerline. Be certain to keep your elbow perpendicular to the floor and your hands relaxed and close to your chest. The elbow block can be used on both the right and left sides.

When employing the elbow block, be certain to keep your elbow perpendicular to the floor and close to your body.

112. MASTER THE LOW BLOCK.

The low block is used to defend against powerful linear shots to your midsection. To execute the lead low block, drop your lead arm so your forearm is parallel to the ground and ensure that your fingers are pointing up to protect against jamming or breaks. With the low block, contact is

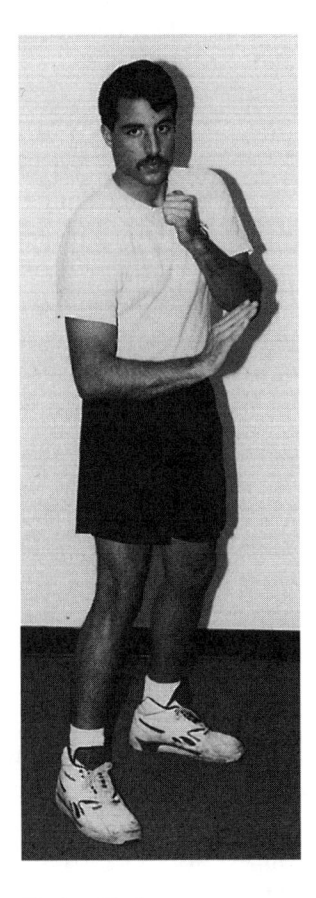

The low block.

STREET FIGHTING FUNDAMENTALS

made with the belly of the forearm and not the palm. The mechanics are the same for the rear low block. Simply drop your rear arm down to meet the assailant's strike.

113. BLOCK LOW-LINE KICKS WITH YOUR LEGS.

Never use your hands or arms to block low-line kicks. Such a defensive response is tactical suicide. If your assailant attacks with low-line kicks or attempts a sweeping technique, you only have one or two possible options: (1) Evasion—you can evade the kick by stepping out of its range or by moving to the right or left. This is accomplished through quick and explosive footwork. (2) Leg block—you can execute a leg block to intercept/ choke/deflect the oncoming kick. The leg block can be delivered from either your lead or rear leg, and it can be positioned at a variety of angles, heights, and vantages. Generally, the leg block should be used only when you can't evade the attack. Realistically speaking, you don't want to absorb the force of any kick if you have the option of evading it.

114. MASTER THE LEG BLOCK.

The leg block is a defensive technique that is used when your assailant executes either a foot sweep or a low-line kick. To perform the leg block, raise your lead leg up to intercept and deflect your assailant's kick. Make contact with the sides of your calves, not your shinbone. Also, make certain that your toe is pointed to the ground to increase the surface area of your defensive tool. The leg block can be executed in the following three general directions: (1) forward, (2) at a right angle, and (3) at a left angle.

115. DON'T DUCK PUNCHES.

Don't duck punches in a fight. Ducking is the process of dropping your body down and forward to avoid the assailant's blows. This defensive maneuver is dangerous for the following reasons: (1) it's a relatively slow defensive move, (2) you can move yourself into knee or elbow strikes easily, and (3) it drastically limits evasive and explosive footwork.

116. DON'T BOB OR WEAVE.

The bob and weave are popular defensive techniques. The bob drops your body down from the waist, and the weave pulls you to the other side. Bobbing and weaving works great for boxers in the ring, but it should not be used in a street fight. The bob and weave are dangerous for the following reasons: (1) they leave you open to knee or elbow strikes, and (2) they lack overall economy of motion.

117. DON'T CROSS BLOCK.

The cross block is a dangerous defensive technique because it requires your arm to cross over your centerline, exposing you to a possible strike. When defending against circular punches, it is much safer and efficient to use mirror-image blocks. Nevertheless, keep in mind that the cross block does have applications in certain circumstances.

118. NEVER USE THE "X" BLOCK.

Although many martial artists still teach and use the "X" block, it is a dangerous and impractical defensive tool for the following reasons: (1) it's too slow to execute, (2) it traps both of your arms together, (3) it exposes anatomical targets to your adversary, and (4) it makes it practically impossible to effectively counter your assailant's attack. In real combat, stick with mirror-image blocks and parrying techniques.

119. DON'T USE STOP-HITS.

A stop-hit is a method of hitting the assailant before his tool reaches full extension. Unfortunately, however, stop-hits are unsafe for combat. Take, for

In this photo, the author demonstrates the leg block. Note his leg and toe positioning.

Although cross blocking is not the ideal defensive response, it can be used in circumstances such as this one.

example, the shoulder stop. This defensive technique is especially dangerous because it moves you closer to the assailant's striking limb. This can be particularly problematic if the assailant has longer appendages than you. Worse yet, the shoulder stop can promote a grappling situation. Most importantly, the shoulder stop will only work if you're confronted with an inferior fighter who dramatically telegraphs his blows.

120. DON'T USE DESTRUCTIONS.

A "destruction" is a combative technique that attacks the assailant's attacking limb on the first beat. Destructions are risky techniques that shouldn't be used in a real combat situation. Here are just a couple reasons why: (1) in unarmed combat, it makes no sense to attack the assailant's striking limb when you have a wide variety of weaker targets available; (2) in almost all cases, you won't have the necessary psychomotor speed to strike the assailant's limbs (biceps or hand) effectively. The bottom line is that destruction techniques are geared for sparring scenarios and not vicious street fights.

121. DON'T USE FEINTS OR FAKES.

Feints and fakes are setup techniques that can draw either offensive or defensive reactions from the adversary, thereby opening him up for a real blow. These and other deceptions are commonly used in tournament competitions and sparring matches to "test" the opponent, wear him down, and score valuable points. In real combat, however, you cannot afford the risk and uncertainty of such techniques. Any initiating tool delivered with less than maximum speed, power, and commitment will be countered with viciousness. In combat, you cannot afford to gamble that your assailant will react in the manner intended. ***WARNING: Experimentation in the face of danger is an invitation for disaster!***

122. DON'T USE THE SHOULDER ROLL.

The shoulder roll is a defensive technique that rocks your body away from a punch in order to nullify its force. Avoid using this technique in a real fight. The shoulder roll technique is based on the assumption that the assailant is going to throw a single blow and wait for you to recover and counter. Furthermore, rolling with any punch turns you out of strategic position, thereby exposing anatomical targets and eliminating your mobility and offensive deployability.

123. MASTER THE PARRY.

The parry is a quick, forceful slap that picks off and redirects your assailant's linear strike (jab, lead straight, or rear cross). There are two general types of parries: horizontal and vertical. Both can be executed from the right and left hands.

(1) Horizontal Parry—to properly execute a horizontal parry, from a stance, move your lead hand horizontally across your body (centerline) to deflect and redirect the assailant's punch. Immediately return to your guard position. Be certain to make contact with the palm of your hand. With sufficient training, you can

The traditional "X" block will get you killed in a real fight.

STREET FIGHTING FUNDAMENTALS

effectively incorporate the horizontal parry with your slipping maneuvers.

(2) Vertical Parry—to execute a vertical parry, from a stance, move your hand vertically down your body (centerline) to deflect and redirect the assailant's blow. Once again, don't forget to counterattack your assailant.

Here, the author demonstrates the proper way to execute a rear horizontal parry. Note that contact is made with the palm of his hand.

124. NEVER PARRY WITH YOUR FINGERTIPS.

A parry is a quick, forceful slap of the palm that redirects a linear punch. When parrying, always make contact with the palm of your hand. ***CAUTION: Do not parry with your fingers. The fingers provide no structural integrity, and they can be jammed or broken easily.***

125. NEVER PARRY A HOOK PUNCH.

A hook punch is a devastating blow that carries tremendous force. Never attempt to parry a hook punch, or any circular blow for that matter. A parry simply does not have the structural integrity to stop the blow. Instead, use a midblock to defend against the hook punch.

126. MASTER EVASIVE TECHNIQUES.

Evasive techniques are maneuvers strategically designed to neutralize your assailant's attack without making contact. Evasive techniques include the following: (1) sidestepping—stepping laterally (right or left) to avoid contact with the adversary, (2) retreating—stepping back to avoid contact with the assailant, (3) slipping—swaying your head and torso (right, left, and back) to avoid the assailant's blow, and (4) escaping—running or escaping from the scene to avoid contact with the adversary.

127. MASTER SLIPPING MOVEMENTS.

Slipping is a quick defensive maneuver that permits you to avoid an assailant's linear blow (jab, lead straight, rear cross, or palm heel) without stepping out of range. Safe and effective slipping requires precise timing and is accomplished by quickly snapping the head and upper torso sideways (right or left) or backwards to avoid the oncoming blow. One of the greatest advantages to slipping is that it frees your hands so that you can simultaneously counter your attacker.

There are three ways to slip. They include the following: (1) Slipping right—start from a stance and quickly sway your head and upper torso to the right to avoid the assailant's blow. Quickly counter or return to the starting position. (2) Slipping left—start from a stance and quickly sway your head and upper torso to the left to avoid the assailant's linear blow. Quickly counter or return to the starting position. (3) Slipping back (also called the snap back)—start from a stance and quickly snap your head back far enough to avoid being hit. Quickly counter or return to the starting position.

FOOTWORK AND MOBILITY

128. KNOW THE STRATEGIC REASONS FOR MOBILITY.

There are seven strategic reasons why mobility is essential for combat, as follows: (1) a moving target is harder to hit, (2) your assailant can misjudge your proximity, (3) it throws the assailant's timing off, (4) it helps prevent multiple assailants from surrounding you, (5) it helps you locate escape routes, (6) it enhances the overall power of your blows (remember that movement is a natural power generator), and (7) it sometimes aids in acquiring superior positioning.

129. MASTER THE FOUR DIRECTIONS OF FOOTWORK.

Basic footwork can be used for both offensive and defensive purposes, and it is structured around the following four general directions: (1) moving forward (advancing)—from your stance, first move

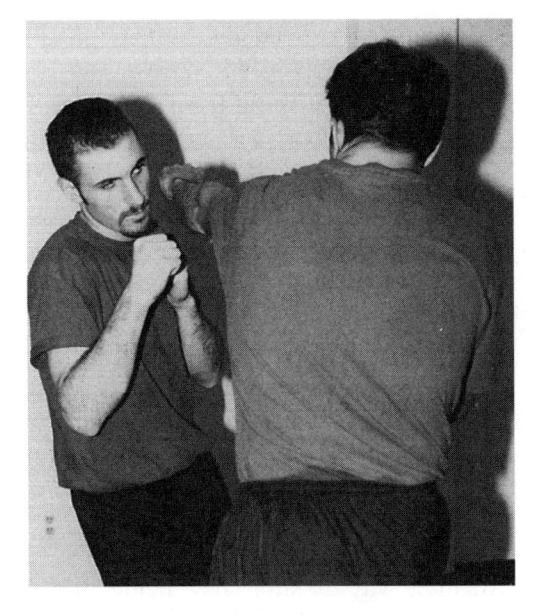

Slipping requires precise timing. In this photo, a student slips to his right.

your front foot forward (approximately 12 inches) and then advance your rear foot an equal distance; (2) moving backward (retreating)—from your stance, first move your rear foot backward (approximately 12 inches) and then move your front foot an equal distance; (3) moving right (sidestepping right)—from your stance, first move your right foot to the right (approximately 12 inches) and then move your left foot an equal distance; and (4) moving left (sidestepping left)—from your stance, first move your left foot to the left (approximately 12 inches) and then move your right foot an equal distance.

130. ACQUIRE EXPLOSIVE FOOTWORK.

Explosive footwork is important for both offensive and defensive purposes. In offense, explosive footwork allows you to maintain compound attacking range. In defense, explosive footwork allows you to disengage quickly from a range of overwhelming assault.

The explosiveness of your footwork is predicated on the following five important factors: (1) basic footwork—you must master the basics of footwork before incorporating explosiveness, (2) proper body posture—maintaining correct body posture through footwork movements will prevent loss of balance, (3) powerful legs—strong and powerful legs allow you to launch your body effortlessly, (4) equal weight distribution—noncommittal weight distribution allows you to move instantly in any direction, (5) raised heel—this creates a springlike effect in your movements.

131. PRACTICE SAFE FOOTWORK.

The safest footwork for combat involves quick, economical steps performed on the balls of your feet while you remain relaxed and balanced. When moving on the balls of your feet, always try to keep your legs shoulder-width apart and your weight evenly distributed. Moving on the balls of your feet does not mean haphazardly dancing around your assailant. This type of showboating will get you into serious trouble. Always move with a strategic purpose in mind.

132. MOVE ON THE BALLS OF YOUR FEET.

Although there are many components of efficient footwork, moving on the balls of your feet is vital. This will make you agile and mobile during the fight. Flat-footed footwork will slow you down considerably, leaving you vulnerable to myriad possible attacks.

133. STEP AND DRAG.

Use the "step and drag" footwork when standing on slippery and unstable terrain. Some examples of unstable terrain include ice, snow, wet grass, wet concrete, wet leaves, wet metal, wet wood, sand, gravel, mulch, mud, and rock.

134. MASTER SIDESTEPPING.

Since many street fighters attack by charging or lunging forward, it's important to master sidestepping. Sidestepping is the process of quickly moving your body laterally (right or left) to evade your charging assailant. When sidestepping, be certain that you don't drop your hand guard. Your hands must be up to protect and counter the assailant. Also, do not bend at your waist. Keep your torso erect and avoid unnecessary shoulder shifting.

135. BEWARE OF THESE TWO ERRORS WHEN SIDESTEPPING.

(1) Your assailant runs over you—this is because you are moving too slowly. To remedy this problem, keep your weight evenly distributed and explode off the balls of your feet. (2) Your assailant tracks you—this is because you are moving too soon. To remedy this problem, avoid premature movements and wait until the very last second before you explode laterally.

136. MASTER STRATEGIC CIRCLING.

Strategic circling is an advanced form of

STREET FIGHTING FUNDAMENTALS

footwork where the fighter uses his lead leg as a pivot point. Strategic circling can be used defensively to evade an overwhelming assault or offensively to strike the adversary from a strategic angle. It can be performed from either the southpaw or orthodox stance: (1) circling right (from a southpaw stance)—from a right lead stance, step 6 to 8 inches to the right with your right foot, then use your right leg as a pivot point and wheel your entire rear leg to the right until the correct stance and positioning is acquired. Remember to keep both of your hands up in case your adversary counters; (2) circling left (from an orthodox stance)—from a left lead stance, step 6 to 8 inches to the left with your left foot, then use your left leg as a pivot point and wheel your entire rear leg to the left until the correct stance and positioning is acquired.

137. BE DYNAMIC IN COMBAT.

No form of combat (armed or unarmed) is ever going to be a static encounter. There is always going to be some type of movement. Be prepared for it!

138. DON'T CROSS-STEP.

Cross-stepping is the process of crossing one foot in front or behind the other when moving. Such sloppy footwork makes you vulnerable to a variety of dangers and risks, including the following: (1) it severely compromises your balance, (2) it restricts tool and technique implementation, (3) it prohibits explosive footwork, (4) it prohibits evasive footwork, (5) it promotes structural breakdown, and (6) it contorts your stance.

The best way to avoid cross-stepping is to follow this basic footwork rule of thumb: always move the foot closest to the direction you want to go

This type of footwork can get you killed in a real fight. Don't cross-step!

first and let the other foot follow an equal distance. In other words, no matter what direction you elect to travel, the foot nearest to your intended direction will always lead the way.

139. DON'T BE AIRBORNE.

Exploding off the balls of your feet is a critical aspect of an effective offensive attack. However, when moving forward, always keep at least one foot in contact with the ground. You never want to be "airborne" in a fight.

CHAPTER TWO

Training and Conditioning

"If you are unfit or out of shape, you won't stand a chance against a vicious assailant. It's that simple."

GOALS AND OBJECTIVES

140. DEFINE YOUR GOALS.

Before you invest a lot of time and money in self-defense training, it is important to first define your goals. What do you hope to accomplish by studying and training for the next 12 months? For example, do you want to get in better shape? Build up your confidence? Handle a vicious street thug? Master combat shooting skills? Or do you want to be capable of fighting multiple assailants? Now is the time to sit down and write down all of the goals that you hope to achieve in the course of your self-defense training.

141. MAKE THE TIME.

All the knowledge in the world is useless unless you put it into action. Although the academic aspects of combat are important, physical practice is critical. If you want to be prepared for a life-threatening encounter, you've got to set aside some time from your busy schedule to practice and refine your skills. This will obviously require a bit of discipline and planning on your part. To really progress in the science of personal combat, you will need to train at least three times per week. However, more frequent training sessions will not only accelerate your progress but also ensure that your current skills and tactics are razor-sharp.

Real-life self-defense training is not just limited to unarmed combat. If you own a firearm, you have the personal responsibility to visit the firing range on a consistent basis. This also applies if you rely on a knife, chemical spray, or defensive baton. You have to practice using it on a regular basis, or you will lose your strategic edge.

142. MAKE A 100-PERCENT COMMITMENT.

Always train with total commitment. The bottom line is that there are no shortcuts to achieving combative mastery.

LEARNING AND TESTING

143. KNOW THE SEQUENCE OF LEARNING.

There is a proper sequence for learning any combat technique. First, you must acquire knowledge of the specific technique. Second, you must develop the proper timing to execute the technique smoothly. The third and final component to the sequence is to apply the attributes (i.e., speed, power, accuracy, etc.) that make the technique effective.

144. THE SEVEN Ps OF TRAINING.

Here is one principle of training that you should never forget: Proper Planning and Preparation Prevent Piss-Poor Performance.

145. PRACTICE.

Practice makes perfect, and perfect makes survivors. The only way to be truly prepared for combat is to practice on a regular basis. You must perform the task, technique, maneuver, or tactic repeatedly to acquire or polish a particular skill. Don't make the common mistake of thinking that expensive equipment will compensate for practice. It won't!

146. DON'T GET COMPLACENT.
The longer you study the combat arts, the greater your chance of falling victim to complacency. Complacency signals a downfall in your training. Always strive to improve your skills and abilities. Stay hungry for knowledge and training and don't lose your drive for personal improvement. Remember, if you think you have arrived, you haven't.

147. TAKE A TEST.
Cognitive and physical testing is a vital component of self-defense training. A complete self-defense exam should challenge the student in the following two domains: (1) cognitive—the student is tested orally and then required to take a written examination and (2) psychomotor—the student must physically demonstrate the skills and techniques, with emphasis placed on his instinctive ability to apply the correct technique.

148. TRAIN THE WAY YOU WILL REACT.
Never forget that under stress, in a real fight, you will instinctively revert to the way you have been trained.

149. REMEMBER THAT EXPERIENCE IS ALWAYS THE BEST TEACHER.
There is no real substitute for actual fighting experience.

150. DON'T FORGET WHAT YOU'VE LEARNED.
Unless you have ingrained your combat skills into your psyche by imprinting your memory through repetition, you will often forget what you have learned.

151. CONTEMPLATE HYPOTHETICALS.
Analytical exercises should be a regular part of your training. During idle times, practice problem-solving skills. For example, move hypothetical criminals into different ranges of combat and select and visualize appropriate targets, weapons, and combinations. Mentally gauge openings and ranges of attack, or scrutinize the five tactical responses (comply, escape, de-escalate, assert, and fight back) as they relate to a variety of possible scenarios, such as the following: (1) being held at knife point, (2) being kidnapped, (3) being held hostage at gunpoint, and (4) being attacked by multiple assailants.

152. ACQUIRE THE THREE TRAINING DOMAINS.
There are three general training domains that must be acquired in order to master the skills and tools of combat, as follows: (1) cognitive domain—encompasses the specific knowledge related to the tool or technique; (2) psychomotor domain—includes the physical skills necessary to execute the tool or technique; and (3) affective domain—includes the attitudes, philosophies, ethics, values, discretionary use of force, and the spirit (killer instinct) required to use the tool or technique appropriately.

TRAINING PRELIMINARIES

153. SEE A DOCTOR.
Before you begin an exercise program, make certain that you have been cleared by your doctor. Since there is always some risk involved in self-defense training, and because each person is unique, it is important that before beginning any type of training program you have a complete physical examination by your physician.

154. KNOW HOW TO TAKE YOUR PULSE.
The only real way to know if you're exercising in your training zone is to take your pulse. There are two primary locations for taking your pulse: (1) The wrist—specifically the radial artery. Place both your index and middle fingers below the base of your thumb, just above the tendons. Press lightly against the inside of the wrist until you feel a steady beat. (2) The neck—specifically the carotid artery. Place both your index and middle fingers on either the right or left side of your Adam's apple in front of the muscles running down the side of the neck. Press firmly against the neck until you feel a steady pulse.

Once you find the pulse on either your neck or wrist, count the number of beats for 10 seconds, then multiply that number by six. This will give you your heart rate for one minute. *REMEMBER: If your heart rate is below 70 percent of your maximum heart rate, increase the intensity of your workout. (See secret number 155 in this chapter for the formula to calculate your training zone.)*

155. DETERMINE YOUR TRAINING ZONE.
To benefit from any aerobic workout (e.g., running, skipping rope, stationary bicycling), you must elevate your heart rate to its proper training

TRAINING AND CONDITIONING

zone. The training zone (or target heart rate) is a safe and effective level of physical activity that produces cardiorespiratory fitness. Your training zone can be anywhere between 70 and 85 percent of your maximum heart rate.

To find your training zone, use the following formula: (1) calculate your base training level by subtracting your age from 220, then multiply that number by 70 percent, or .70; (2) to calculate your upper training level, repeat the first step but multiply by .85 (85 percent) instead of .70.

For example, a man who is 30 years of age would calculate his training zone as follows: (1) 220 - 30 = 190 and 190 x .70 = 133 beats per minute (bpm); (2) 190 bpm x .85 = 162 bpm. Therefore, our 30-year-old man's training zone ranges from 133 beats per minute to 162 beats per minute. Keep in mind that exercising below 70 percent of your maximum heart rate does little for improving your cardiovascular fitness level. ***WARNING: Stop exercising immediately if you experience any of the following symptoms: (1) chest pain, (2) shortness of breath when not exercising hard, (3) nausea, (4) dizziness, and (5) irregular heartbeat.***

156. WARM UP.

Every workout should begin with a series of mild exercises, stretches, and movements designed to prepare the fighter for more intense exercise. Properly warming up before a tough workout is important for the following reasons: (1) it gradually increases your body temperature, (2) it safely increases your heart rate, (3) it helps prevent muscle and tendon strains, and (4) it provides psychological preparation for your workout.

ROUTINES AND WORKOUTS

157. EMPLOY THE HARD DAY/EASY DAY ROUTINE.

You can't train hard all the time. You must also incorporate easy days into your training schedule. This is important for the following reasons: (1) it helps significantly reduce the possibility of getting injured, (2) it helps prevent overtraining, (3) it adds a bit of variety to your training, and (4) it allows your body to properly recuperate and adapt to the demands of the hard-core training. The following is just one sample of a hard day/easy day training routine:

Monday—hard day (ground fighting, full-contact sparring, and stick fighting)
Tuesday—easy day (shadow fighting, footwork drills, and defense against locks, chokes, and holds)
Wednesday—off day (rest)
Thursday—hard day (focus-mitt training, simulated street fighting, proficiency training)
Friday—hard day (knife fighting, heavy-bag training, impact tolerance)
Saturday—easy day (firearms training, gun disarms, knife disarms, bludgeon disarms) or off day (depending on how you feel)
Sunday—hard day (striking-shield training, sparring reaction drills, street training methodology on focus mitts)

158. DEVELOP THESE COMPOUND ATTACK SEQUENCES.

The truth in offense rests in the compound attack. The following are 10 compound attack sequences you can add to your training (these can be delivered from both right and left stances and should be practiced when shadow fighting or working out on the heavy bag, double-end bag, or focus mitts): (1) finger jab/rear cross/lead hook punch/rear hook punch; (2) lead straight/rear cross/lead straight/rear cross; (3) hook kick/rear hook punch/lead hook punch/rear uppercut; (4) push kick/rear uppercut/lead uppercut/rear vertical knee strike; (5) vertical kick/rear vertical hammer fist/rear vertical knee strike; (6) rear horizontal elbow/lead horizontal elbow/rear vertical knee strike; (7) side kick/rear hook punch/lead uppercut/rear diagonal elbow/lead diagonal elbow; (8) finger jab/rear palm heel/lead palm heel/rear hook punch; (9) double thumb gouge/foot stomp/rear vertical knee; and (10) lead straight/rear cross/lead straight/rear cross/lead straight/rear cross.

159. BIG OR SMALL, FIGHT THEM ALL.

The only way to be truly prepared for the street is to train with a variety of partners, each with different somatotypes. For example, see what it is like to spar someone who is a foot taller than you, or experience what it is like to ground fight someone who is 100 pounds heavier than you. These different types of builds will help you understand your strengths and limitations in combat.

160. BE ON THE LOOKOUT.

In the course of training, you are likely to encounter a wide variety of personality types in class. When training, try to avoid the following types of students: (1) the conversationalist—this one talks too much and often disturbs others in class; (2) the challenger—this student is naturally argumentative and tries to test the instructor's knowledge and patience; (3) the ego tripper—this one will do anything in class to prove just how tough he is, and he usually enjoys full-contact drills and likes to injure others; (4) the shy one—this type of student is hesitant to participate in training; (5) the know-it-all—this type of student thinks he knows anything and everything about self-defense training; and (6) the dilettante—this type of student is training for the fun of it and fails to understand the importance of self-defense training.

161. TRAIN TO MUSIC.

Your physical performance and mental attitude can be enhanced dramatically by training to music. It is my experience that training to fast, rhythmic music works wonders for conditioning training, whereas hard-driving aggressive rock music works best for proficiency and street training methods. Also try listening to classical music when stretching out and warming up.

Here are 11 music groups that I listen to when engaged in hard-core training: (1) KISS, (2) Ministry, (3) White Zombie, (4) Nine Inch Nails, (5) The Cure, (6) Queensryche, (7) Soundgarden, (8) Motley Crüe, (9) Mega Deth, (10) Billy Idol, and (11) Guns 'n Roses.

162. KEEP ACCURATE TRAINING RECORDS.

Record keeping is one of the most important and often neglected aspects of effective training. Make it a habit to keep accurate records of your workouts in a personal journal. This type of record keeping is important for the following reasons: (1) it will help you monitor your progress, (2) it will keep you organized, (3) it will keep you motivated in your training, (4) it will help prevent potential injuries, and (5) it will help you guard against overtraining.

163. TRAIN IN ADVERSE WEATHER.

Training outdoors in adverse weather conditions will give you a substantial edge over your assailant. Here are a few suggestions: (1) practice de-escalation scenarios in the rain, (2) work out on the focus mitts in freezing winter temperatures, (3) execute compound attacks in hot, humid summer weather, (4) ground fight in the snow, (5) spar when it's foggy outside, (6) practice kicks on the striking shield in gusty wind, (7) try firing your gun in poor lighting conditions, and (8) try speed-loading your gun when your hands are wet from rain.

164. VISUALIZE REGULARLY.

Visualization is the purposeful formation of mental images to improve your combative performance. This natural and relatively simple exercise serves many purposes, including the following: (1) it improves your general reaction time, (2) it develops sharper psychomotor skills, (3) it improves your confidence, (4) it helps cultivate the killer instinct, (5) it helps you maintain motivation during tough workouts, and (6) it improves shadow fighting workouts. ***NOTE: When visualizing, it's important that your mental images are clear, strong, and consistent. There are generally three different mental speeds in which you can visualize: (1) slow, (2) moderate, and (3) fast, as well as in reverse.***

165. TRAIN WHEN YOU'RE SICK.

You must be able to fight when you least expect it. Now is the time to see if you can defend yourself when you're handicapped or ill. This is known as disability training. Here are a few suggestions that will help get you started: (1) practice compound attacks when you're plagued with a migraine headache, (2) practice close-quarter techniques when sitting in a wheelchair, (3) spar with one arm in a sling, (4) practice self-defense skills while standing on crutches, (5) practice kicks when you have the flu, (6) attempt to yell when you have a sore throat, (7) work out on the heavy bag when you have a bad cough, (8) try ground fighting when you are fatigued and exhausted, (9) fight multiple assailants when you are suffering from a hangover, and (10) practice escaping from grabs, chokes, locks, and holds while you are blindfolded.

166. PREPARE FOR MULTIPLE ASSAILANTS.

Now is the time to participate in multiple-assailant training. Here are a few suggestions to get you started: (1) try sparring three assailants at the same time, (2) experience what it is like to ground fight two assailants at the same time, (3) conduct a

TRAINING AND CONDITIONING

simulated street fight with three attackers, (4) try to knife fight two assailants simultaneously, and (5) defend against two bludgeon-wielding assailants at the same time. Whatever scenario you choose, you'll acquire a greater understanding and appreciation for the dynamics of multiple-assailant assaults.

167. PRACTICE THE SOLO BLOCKING DRILL.

The solo blocking drill is used to sharpen and refine basic blocking movements without the pressure of timing. To begin the drill, apply the following: (1) assume a proper fighting stance in front of a full-length mirror, execute a high block at moderate speed, note any flaws in the execution of the movement, alternate right and left arms, and return to the starting position; (2) next, execute a midblock at moderate speed, note any mistakes in the execution of the movement, alternate right and left arms, and return to the starting position; (3) now, execute a low block at moderate speed, note any flaws in the execution of the movement, alternate right and left arms, and return to the starting position; (4) finally, execute an elbow block at moderate speed, note any flaws in the execution of the movement, alternate right and left arms, and return to the starting position. *NOTE: The solo blocking drill can also be conducted with the eyes closed to develop a kinesthetic feel for the technique.*

168. PRACTICE THE 360-DEGREE BLOCKING DRILL.

The 360-degree blocking drill is excellent for developing defensive reaction time. To begin, apply the following: (1) have your training partner stand approximately three feet from you, (2) position yourself in a 45-degree stance with both of your arms hanging at your sides, (3) without him telegraphing his intentions, have your training partner deliver a random swing at your head or torso, (4) immediately respond with the appropriate block, (5) return your arm to the starting position, (6) have your partner immediately attack with another swing at a different angle. As you become more proficient with this drill, your training partner should deliver a sequence of random swings with greater speed and force. In addition, you can have your partner incorporate linear blows into the drill. *CAUTION: Remember to start out slowly and progressively build up the speed and force of your strikes.*

169. SHARPEN YOUR SENSES.

Your five senses (sight, smell, touch, sound, and taste) can be sharpened through a variety of exercises designed to develop both raw detection and learned identification abilities. For example, sit on a park bench for a given period of time and catalog the various objects and actions your five senses detect, then list the possible sources of the sensory data. With sufficient practice, you will make significant progress from being unable to detect a particular sound or smell to not only detecting it quickly and accurately, but also identifying its source. Remember that sensory development increases as these exercises are performed in different environmental settings.

170. TRY THE EMOTIONAL RECOGNITION DRILL.

The objective of this drill is to sharpen your ability to recognize and identify various emotional states in people, especially those that are associated with violence. To apply the drill, spend approximately 20 minutes in a busy public place (boxing match, hockey game, courtroom, shopping mall, emergency room, airport, etc.) sitting back and observing people's emotional states. Pay close attention to their posture, voice, demeanor, hand movements, and facial expressions.

171. SHADOW FIGHT REGULARLY.

Shadow fighting is the creative deployment of offensive and defensive tools and maneuvers against imaginary assailants. It requires intense mental concentration, honest self-analysis, and a deep commitment to improve. For the fighter on a tight budget, the good news is that shadow fighting is inexpensive. All you need is a full-length mirror and a place to work out. The mirror is vital. It functions as a critic, your personal instructor. If you're honest, the mirror will be too. It will point out every mistake—telegraphing, sloppy footwork, poor body mechanics, and even lack of physical conditioning.

Proper shadow fighting develops speed, power, balance, footwork, compound attack skills, sound form, and finesse. It even promotes a better understanding of the ranges of combat. As you progress, you can incorporate light dumbbells into shadow fighting workouts to enhance power and speed. Start off with one to three pounds and gradually work your way up. Weighted vests can also be worn to develop footwork, kicks, and knee strikes.

Traditional martial artists will notice that shadow fighting is much more difficult than katas because of its arbitrary nature.

172. REST.

Resting the body is just as important as training. Training intensely day after day will lead to either burnout (overtraining) or injury. The body needs time to recoup and replenish itself from grueling workouts. Remember, there is growth in rest.

173. AVOID BURNOUT.

Burnout is defined as a negative emotional state acquired by physical overtraining. Some symptoms of burnout include physical illness, boredom, anxiety, disinterest in training, and general sluggish behavior.

Whether you are a teacher or student, novice or expert, you're susceptible to burnout. Here are a few suggestions to help avoid burnout in your training: (1) make your workouts intense but enjoyable; (2) vary your training routine (i.e., hard day/easy day routine); (3) train to different types of music (i.e., hard rock, classical, techno, classic rock, and new age); (4) pace yourself during your workouts—don't try to do it all in one day; (5) listen to your body—if you don't feel up to working out, skip a day; (6) work out in different types of environments; (7) use different types of training equipment; (8) work out with different training partners; (9) keep accurate records of your training routine; and (10) vary the intensity of your training throughout your workout.

174. PRIORITIZE OFFENSE WHEN TRAINING.

When working out, make it a habit to begin your training with offensive tools and techniques. This is important because it helps reinforce the offensive mentality and guarantees that training time will be applied to the most important aspect of street survival—offense.

175. CLOSE YOUR EYES.

If you want to make your movements instinctual, practice them in a slow and controlled fashion with your eyes closed. Closing your eyes when training will help you develop a complete kinesthetic feel for the movement.

176. LOCK OUT YOUR SIDE KICK.

To develop balance when executing your side kick, lock out your kick for a prescribed period of time (anywhere from one to five minutes). This will develop balance, kinesthetic perception, skeletal alignment, and discipline.

177. PRACTICE YELLING.

A strong and powerful yell can be a very effective tool in the street, and a good place to practice yelling is in your car. The interior of the car insulates and amplifies your voice, giving you a good sense of its effectiveness. Practice prolonged yells and intermittent, explosive ones. The yell should also be used judiciously in sparring situations to test its effectiveness.

178. TRY PROFICIENCY TRAINING.

If you are looking for a surefire method of perfecting your technique, try proficiency training. This method of training is designed to sharpen one particular tool, technique, tactic, or maneuver at a time by executing it over and over again for a prescribed number of repetitions. Each time, the tool or technique is executed with form and at various speeds. Techniques can even be practiced with the eyes closed to develop a kinesthetic "feel" for the movement. Remember to take your time with each repetition. Proficiency training can be performed on all training equipment.

179. TRY CONDITIONING TRAINING.

Conditioning training sharpens a fighter's tools and conditions his entire body by developing cardiorespiratory endurance and muscular strength. It also develops rhythm, balance, speed, agility, and footwork. This method of training should be practiced in controlled environments, such as a martial arts studio, basement, or garage, to allow sufficient room for you and your training partner to really move around.

In conditioning training you execute kicks, punches, and strikes in different combinations for three- or four-minute rounds. Once the round is over, rest for 30 seconds and then go again. A good workout consists of five rounds. Remember to pace yourself through each round, because "pouring it on" in the beginning will lead to premature fatigue. It is also essential to maintain a proper breathing pattern; under no circumstances should you hold your breath.

TRAINING AND CONDITIONING

Conditioning training can be performed when sparring or when working out on focus mitts, striking shields, heavy bags, double-end bags, or against imaginary assailants in shadow fighting.

180. TRY STREET TRAINING.

Street training is the final preparation for the real thing. Since most physical confrontations last approximately 20 to 30 seconds, you must prepare for this type of scenario. Street training requires you to deliver explosive and powerful compound attacks with vicious intent for 20 to 30 seconds, rest for one minute, then repeat the process. In the street training methodology, it is essential to attack with 100-percent conviction and give it all you've got.

Street training prepares you for the stress and fatigue of a real fight. It also develops speed, power, explosiveness, target selection, timing, footwork, and even balance.

181. DO FOOTWORK DRILLS REGULARLY.

Proper footwork is one of the most neglected aspects of training. Here are five movements that should be practiced on a regular basis: (1) advance, (2) retreat, (3) sidestep right, (4) sidestep left, and (5) switch your stance.

Footwork skills should also be practiced from two different states: static and ballistic. Static footwork movements are executed from a static or stationary position. Ballistic footwork movements are executed while you are moving.

182. USE THE SIDESTEPPING DRILL.

Once a week practice sidestepping with a training partner. This drill is important for refining evasion skills and for enhancing your sense of range and timing. To practice the sidestepping drill, employ the following: (1) begin with your training partner standing approximately 10 feet from you; (2) assume a stance (i.e., fighting, de-escalation, natural, knife defense); (3) without telegraphing his intentions, your training partner should charge at you full-speed; (4) if you're standing in a right (southpaw) stance, quickly step with your right foot to the right and have your left leg follow an equal distance. Your partner should miss you and you should be balanced and ready to effectively counterattack. Practice the sidestepping drill with different stances, at various distances, in different lighting conditions, and while standing on different surfaces.

183. EMPLOY THE PUMMEL DRILL.

The pummel drill is designed to develop and refine the pummel technique, which is used when ground fighting (see Chapter 5: Grappling and Ground Fighting for specific details). To execute the pummel drill, apply the following: (1) place the heavy bag on the floor, (2) have your training partner tie a rope (approximately five feet long) to the top of the bag, (3) mount the heavy bag (the same way you would mount an assailant in a ground fight), (4) for 30 seconds employ full-speed, full-force strikes (linear blasts, hammer fists, and hook punches) on the upper portion of the heavy bag, (5) have your training partner pull vigorously (side to side, and up and down) on the rope while you deliver the blows, (6) maintain a good base and avoid losing your balance when your partner tugs the bag.

184. PRACTICE DE-ESCALATION SKILLS IN FRONT OF A MIRROR.

One of the best ways to develop and refine de-escalation skills is to practice in front of a mirror. To begin, stand in front of a full-length mirror and picture a de-escalation scenario in your mind. Envision a very angry and hostile person screaming at you. Once this scenario is crystal clear, assume the proper de-escalation stance and look into the mirror. Now, assess your stance while being cognizant of your physiology and hand positioning. Next, speak out loud and verbally defuse the situation with this imaginary hostile person. Remember to always use selective semantics (choice words) for your scenario. To evaluate your performance, you may want to tape record or videotape the exercise.

There are hundreds of possible de-escalation scenarios to practice. Here are a few to get you started: (1) angry bar patron, (2) disgruntled employee, (3) angry spouse, (4) resentful relative, (5) irate customer or client, (6) drunken friend, (7) enraged motorist, (8) unbalanced street vagrant, (9) egotistical punk, and (10) jealous or suspicious friend.

185. FEEL THE IMPACT.

Impact training is a series of physical exercises that condition your mind and body to withstand the trauma of kicks and blows. In unarmed combat, there are two types of striking impact: snapping and breaking. Snapping impact shocks the head or body but does not fully penetrate it. It's quick but lacks substantial follow-through. A snapping blow usually makes a brisk, sharp cracking sound when it connects with its target. In contrast, breaking impact shocks and moves the head or body. It can break or fracture bones easily because it follows through its target (approximately three inches). You must be physically and psychologically prepared to tolerate both types of impact.

Impact training requires both forms of impact to be administered to specific body parts, including the shoulders, back, chest, biceps, triceps, abdominals, thighs, and calves. Striking these targets will not cause serious or permanent injury. **WARNING: *Never strike the face, neck, throat, solar plexus, spine, groin, or joints during impact training. These anatomical targets are very sensitive and cannot be conditioned to withstand deliberate impact. Striking these targets can cause severe and permanent injury. It is imperative that your training partner deliver accurate blows and avoid these targets during training.***

For impact training, your training partner will need a pair of boxing gloves or focus mitts to deliver the blows. When you begin, have your partner start off slowly with light strikes to your muscle groups, alternating snapping and breaking blows. Always remember to exhale when the blow makes contact. Over time, your partner can increase the speed and force of the strikes. Be patient with each other. It will take time and some experimentation before you and your partner can properly gauge the amount of force. Impact training sessions should last approximately five minutes and should be conducted at least twice a month.

Impact training with the focus mitts.

186. BE SPONTANEOUS WHEN TRAINING.

Learning to integrate the frightening and spontaneous elements of a real fight into your training routine will take serious thought and planning. Ironically, you have to plan spontaneity in training.

187. TRAIN IN DIFFERENT ENVIRONMENTS.

A prepared fighter is an adaptable fighter. Make it a habit to work out in different types of environments. For example, experience what it is like to train in a dark and unfamiliar alley, in a telephone booth, between two parked cars, in a swimming pool, on a flight of stairs (be careful), or while sitting behind the wheel of your car. Find out what it is like to execute a compound attack while standing in your shower stall. This dynamic form of environmental training will provide you with the experience necessary to handle the unpredictable nature of street fighting.

188. PARTICIPATE IN PSYCHOEMOTIONAL TRAINING.

Train when you are experiencing different types of emotional states. For example, work out when you feel angry and frustrated. Is there a noticeable difference in your performance? Are your skills and techniques enhanced when you're happy and energetic? What is your energy level when you're sad or depressed? Does your emotional state change after a taxing training session? If so, how? Experiment and see how well you ground fight when slightly intoxicated, tired, or drowsy. ***WARNING: Always have a sober and trustworthy training***

Train in different environments. In this photo, students refine their stick fighting skills in the woods.

TRAINING AND CONDITIONING

partner with you when experimenting with alcohol. And never experiment with alcohol and firearms. They are a deadly combination.

189. EXPERIENCE DIFFERENT TERRAINS.

Now is the time to see what will work on different types of terrain and surface areas. Try sparring in tall grass. What happens to your balance when executing kicking techniques on ice or wet grass? Does the snow or sleet affect your visibility when you execute a compound attack? What happens when you ground fight in the mud or sand? Experiment and find out. The more varied the terrain you train on, the better prepared you will be for street encounters.

190. CONFRONT YOUR FEARS.

Write down 10 of your greatest fears. They can be anything from financial worries to a knife fight with a vicious psychopath. Once you have made your list, put them in an envelope, seal the envelope, and put it in a safe place where no one will find it. After one year has passed, open the envelope and see if you have conquered any of those fears.

191. SAFETY IS PARAMOUNT.

When it comes to martial arts training, safety is of paramount importance. Some martial artists will avoid using safety equipment because of big egos, laziness, ignorance, and a variety of other reasons. However, it behooves you to take the proper safety precautions. Here are a few suggestions to help minimize the possibilities of injury: (1) buy the best training equipment that you can afford, (2) know the proper way to use training equipment, (3) regularly inspect your equipment for wear and defects, (4) avoid ego-driven training partners, (5) be especially aware when training with someone of superior size, skill, or experience, (6) always warm up before training, (7) drink plenty of water during training sessions to avoid dehydration, and (8) be cautious when performing training drills for the first time.

192. BE RUTHLESSLY REALISTIC WHEN TRAINING.

Whether you are training for armed or unarmed combat, your training sessions must be completely realistic. You must methodically integrate the frightening and spontaneous elements of fighting safely into your routines. Such reality-based training is a surefire method of preparing you for the real thing. For example, conduct simulated street fights with fully padded assailants. Work out in dark, cramped, and unfamiliar environments. Train with focus mitts, mannequin heads, chalkable rubber knives, trigger-sensitive mock pistols, and foam and plastic baseball bats. Strategic histrionics should be

Safety is of paramount importance. In this photo, two students are attired in full-contact gear.

Make certain your training is realistic. In this photo, Franco (right) works on gun-disarming scenarios with a student.

developed through countless de-escalation scenarios.

Since no two attacks are ever the same, you need to incorporate a wide variety of combative scenarios into your training program. This realistic and dynamic form of training will provide you with the experience necessary to handle the unpredictable nature of combat. ***WARNING: Inadequate or unrealistic training is a complete waste of time and extremely dangerous. Always train for the reality of combat.***

193. TRY SPORTS MASSAGE.

A complete workout program includes not only excercise but also caring for the wear and tear on the body. The physiological benefits of sports massage make it a significant component of a conditioning program. A regular sports massage program benefits a fighter for the following reasons: (1) it helps your body recover more quickly from your workouts, (2) it improves blood circulation, (3) it promotes muscular relaxation, (4) it promotes faster healing from injuries, and (5) it aids in the removal of cell waste products and promotes better cell nutrition.

Here are a few suggestions to make the most out of a massage session: (1) schedule your sports massage after your workout or on your rest day, (2) tell the massage therapist about any past or present injuries that continue to cause you pain, (3) give feedback to your massage therapist regarding sore or tender areas on your body, (4) try to maintain a consistent sports massage program (at least once per month).

EQUIPMENT

194. USE A CLOCK WHEN TRAINING.

A clock is an important piece of training equipment that can significantly enhance your skills and abilities. A clock/timer can be used for the following: (1) to accurately measure your current level of fitness and conditioning, (2) to monitor your progress in your training, (3) to test the speed of your techniques (i.e., drawing and shooting speed, punching and striking speed, escaping speed, and threat-assessment speed), and (4) to add a bit of healthy competition to your training routine. ***REMEMBER: When selecting a clock for your training, make certain that the numbers are clear and visible and that the clock has a second hand.***

195. SPARE NO EXPENSE.

When purchasing training gear, spare no expense. Self-defense training is a serious matter, and your training gear should reflect it. Good equipment will provide years of reliable use and enhance your skills. Here is a brief list of the training gear that you'll need: 28-inch gym bag, leather headgear, mouthpiece and carrying case, groin cup, leather boxing gloves (12 ozs. minimum), leather bag gloves, leather skip rope, two 26-inch rattan sticks, rubber training knife, and mock training pistol.

196. USE A CAMCORDER.

If you really want to see your skills and abilities, videotape your workouts. The video will provide you with a more accurate picture of what you are doing in your training. You will be able to observe mistakes and recognize your combat strengths and weaknesses. The video recorder will also motivate you to train harder. Date each videotape; later on you will be able to compare and see marked improvements in your fighting performance.

197. VARY THE EQUIPMENT.

Equipment is a vital part of training. It will systematically develop your tools, skills, and

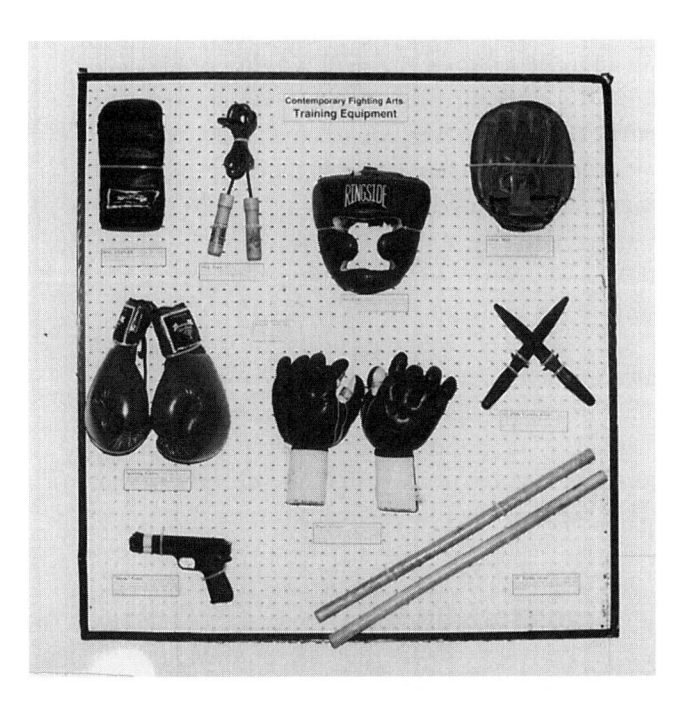

Training gear (from left to right): bag gloves, skip rope, headgear, focus mitts, boxing gloves, digit gloves, rubber training knives, mock training pistol, and rattan sticks.

attributes of both armed and unarmed combat. However, to maximize your training, you should use a wide variety of equipment. For example, mannequin heads are ideal for finger jabs, eye rakes, and thumb gouges. Kicks and knee strikes can be developed on striking shields. Leather focus mitts will sharpen all of your striking tools as well as the fundamental attributes of combat. A full-length mirror will help you critique and refine your stances, maneuvers, and de-escalation skills. Boxing gloves, durable headgear, and other protective equipment will permit effective and safe sparring. The heavy bag is excellent for developing power in all of your natural body weapons. Foam and plastic baseball bats are a must for bludgeon defenses. Chalkable rubber knives are essential for practicing edged-weapon defenses and knife-fighting skills. Trigger-sensitive (mock) pistols should also be used to practice disarming techniques, quick-draw skills, firearm stances, and firearm fundamentals. Dummy cartridges are also excellent for speed-loading drills.

198. FOLLOW THESE IMPORTANT GUIDELINES.
To maximize your training and minimize the possibility of injury, follow these important guidelines when using impact equipment (i.e., striking shields, heavy bags, focus mitts) for the first time: (1) begin with light impact and progressively build up to approximately 75 percent power and speed, (2) be cognizant of your form when delivering your blows, (3) be aware of proper skeletal alignment, (4) be especially careful when executing open-hand techniques on impact equipment.

199. HIT THE HEAVY BAG.
For unarmed combat, the heavy bag is the single most important piece of training equipment. Its primary purpose is to develop power in all of your offensive techniques. This cylindrical-shaped bag is approximately 40 inches in height and is constructed of either top-grain leather, heavy canvas, or vinyl. The interior of the bag is generally filled with some type of cotton fiber. Heavy bags can weigh anywhere from 35 to 200 pounds; however, the average bag weighs approximately 85 pounds.

Here are some important tips when working out on the bag: (1) gradually build up the force of your blows—a beginner's wrists are generally too weak to accommodate full-force punches; (2) maintain your balance—never sacrifice balance for

The heavy bag develops power, coordination, and endurance. Here, a student delivers a series of powerful vertical kicks.

power; (3) snap your blow—avoid "pushing" the bag; (4) keep your wrists straight when your fists hit the bag; (5) maintain proper form when striking the bag; (6) move around—avoid remaining stationary when striking the bag; (7) harmoniously integrate your kicks, punches, and strikes to develop devastating compound attacks; (8) pace yourself—avoid premature exhaustion; (9) wear protective bag gloves; and (10) stay relaxed—avoid unnecessary muscular tension.

200. AVOID SKINNING YOUR KNUCKLES.
If you're skinning your knuckles when throwing linear punches on the heavy bag, you are most likely dropping your fist slightly during the retraction phase of your technique. Learn to retract your fist through the same trajectory that you used in initiating the punch.

201. USE HAND WRAPS.
When engaged in all-out heavy bag sessions, it

1001 STREET FIGHTING SECRETS

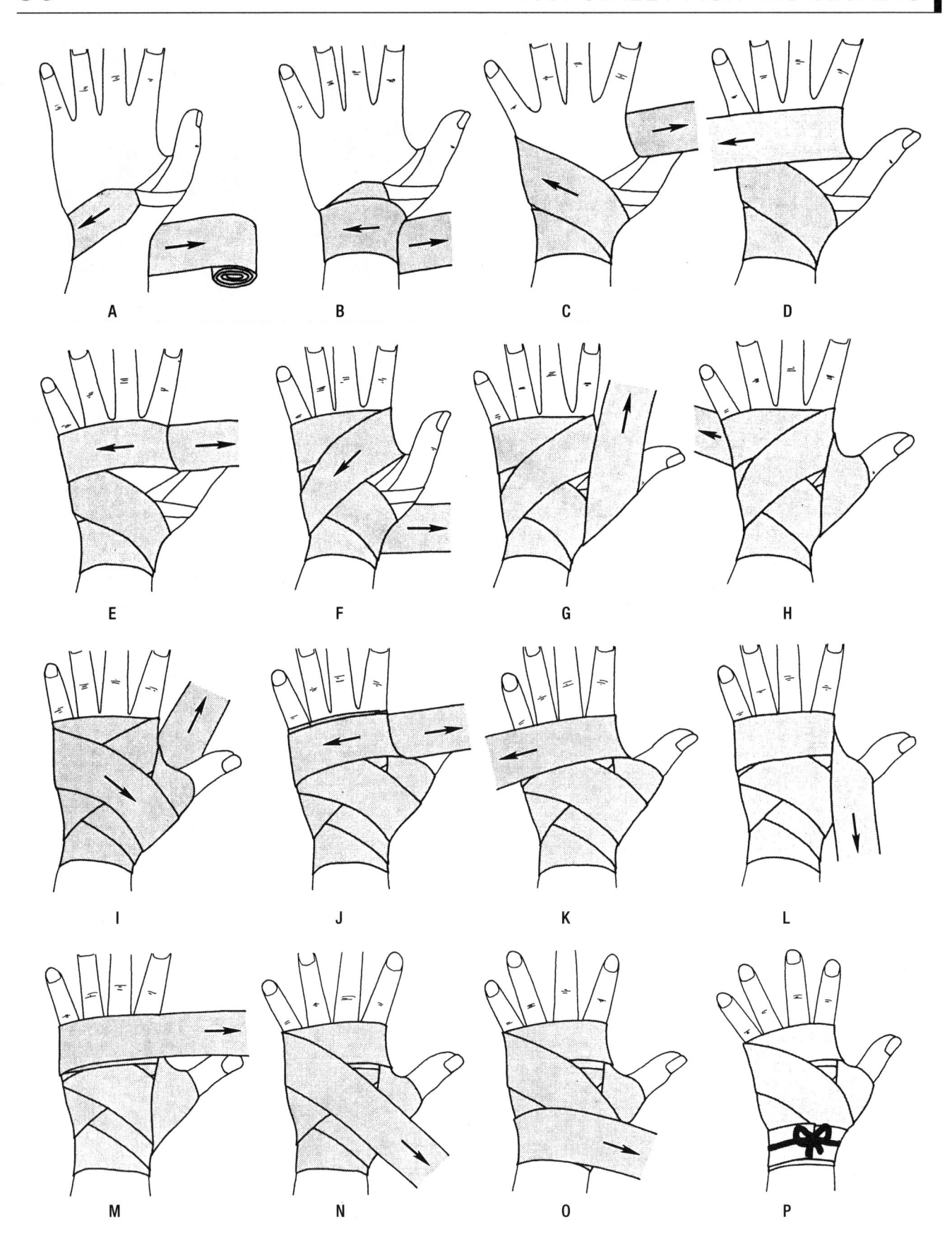

How to wrap the hands

TRAINING AND CONDITIONING

is wise to protect your hands and wrists with hand wraps. Hand wraps are sold at sporting goods stores. They are long strips of cloth measuring 2 inches wide and 9 feet long. They are washable and should be cleaned after every workout. Although there are a wide variety of hand-wrapping methods, the procedure shown on page 50 is suggested.

202. USE THE DOUBLE-END BAG.

The double-end bag is a small leather ball suspended by a bungee cord. It is a valuable piece of training equipment that develops timing, accuracy, rhythm, coordination, footwork, and speed. The double-end bag requires considerable practice and a lot of patience. In fact, it is probably one of the most difficult pieces of training equipment to master. Most beginners become very frustrated when working with the double-end bag. To properly control the movement of the bag, you must hit it directly in the center. If you don't strike it dead center, it will bounce uncontrollably to the right and left.

203. DRAW Xs.

To develop more precise targeting, draw small Xs on your heavy bags, focus mitts, and striking shields. This practice will help develop accuracy in your striking techniques.

The double-end bag is a great device for conditioning training. It helps develop footwork, timing, coordination, and speed.

Bag gloves offer excellent protection for your hands when working out on either the heavy bag or focus mitts

204. LEARN FROM FEEDBACK.

When working out on the heavy bag (or any piece of equipment for that matter), learn from the negative or painful feedback, such as strains or sprains on your joints or wrists. They are telling you something about your technique.

205. WEAR BAG GLOVES.

Bag gloves offer excellent protection to the hands when working out on either the heavy bag or focus mitts. Bag gloves are constructed of either top-grain cowhide or durable vinyl. There are many different models available. Some have a metal weight sewn into the palm grip area to aid in punching power. Sizes available are usually small, medium, large, and extra large.

206. TAKE OFF YOUR BAG GLOVES OCCASIONALLY.

Although bag gloves are important for protecting your hands when training, every once in a while you should work out without them. This will give you a much more realistic feeling for punching.

207. TRAIN WITH THE STRIKING SHIELD.

The striking shield is a versatile piece of training equipment that develops power in most of your kicks, punches, and strikes. This rectangular-shaped shield is constructed of foam and vinyl and is designed to withstand tremendous punishment. As in focus-mitt training, your partner plays a vital role in a good striking shield workout. He must hold the shield at the proper height and angle while simultaneously moving in and out of the ranges of combat. The intensity of your workout will depend on his ability to push you to your limit. More importantly, your partner must learn how to absorb a powerful kick without losing his balance or injuring himself.

208. USE MANNEQUIN HEADS.

To sharpen and refine your eye strikes, use mannequin heads. Mannequin heads can be manipulated at different heights and vantages, allowing you to sharpen the accuracy of your finger-jab strikes. They are inexpensive and can be purchased from most cosmetology schools.

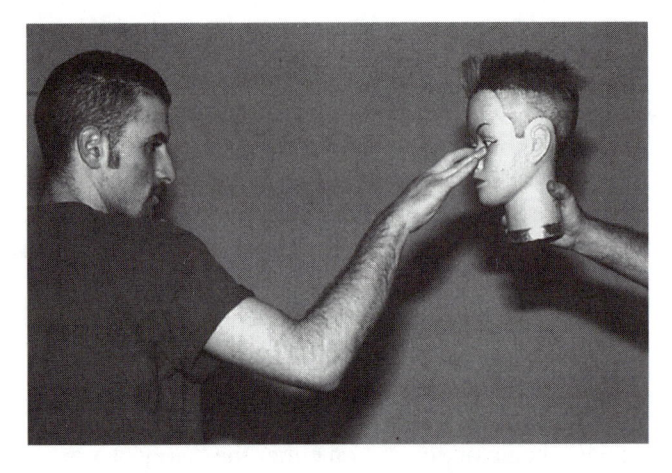

Mannequin heads are ideal for developing accurate finger-jab strikes. In this photo, a student sharpens his finger-jab strike.

209. TRAIN WITH FOCUS MITTS.

The focus mitt is an exceptional piece of training equipment that can be used by anyone. It develops accuracy, speed, target recognition, target selection, target impact, and timing in all offensive techniques. By placing the mitts at various angles and levels, you can perform every conceivable kick, punch, or strike. Properly utilized, focus mitts will refine your defensive reaction time and condition your entire body.

Focus mitts are constructed of durable leather designed to withstand tremendous punishment. Compared to other pieces of training equipment, the focus mitt is relatively inexpensive. However, an effective workout requires two mitts (one for each hand). Your training partner (called the feeder) plays a vital role in focus-mitt workouts by controlling the tools you execute and the cadence of delivery. The intensity of your workouts will depend largely upon his or her ability to manipulate the mitts and push you to your limit. ***REMEMBER: There is an old saying in CFA regarding focus-mitt feeders. A good focus-mitt feeder is one step ahead of his training partner, whereas a great focus-mitt feeder is two steps ahead of his partner.***

To truly benefit from any focus-mitt workout, you must learn to concentrate intensely throughout the entire session. Block out all distractions. Try to visualize the mitt as a living, breathing assailant, not an inanimate target. This type of visualization will make the difference between a poor workout and a great workout.

210. AVOID USING THE SPEED BAG.

The speed bag (also called the striking bag) is a popular piece of training equipment used by boxers to develop coordination, endurance, timing, and rhythm. But the speed bag is a poor training tool that can endanger a fighter by developing the following poor habits: (1) centerline exposure—to strike the speed bag effectively, you must expose your centerline completely; (2) unrealistic rhythm—the impact rhythm generated on a speed bag isn't remotely close to that generated in a street fight, because there is no real rhythm in a street fight; (3) improper fist positioning—speed striking requires you to "roll" your fists and strike the bag at an unrealistic angle; (4) poor body mechanics—to maintain a rhythm on the bag, the practitioner must abandon proper body mechanics for punching; (5) mobility inhibition—the speed bag platform restricts general mobility; and (6) lack of power—to develop a proper rhythm on the bag, the practitioner must strike the bag with light to moderate force, a habit you don't want to have when you're involved in a real fight.

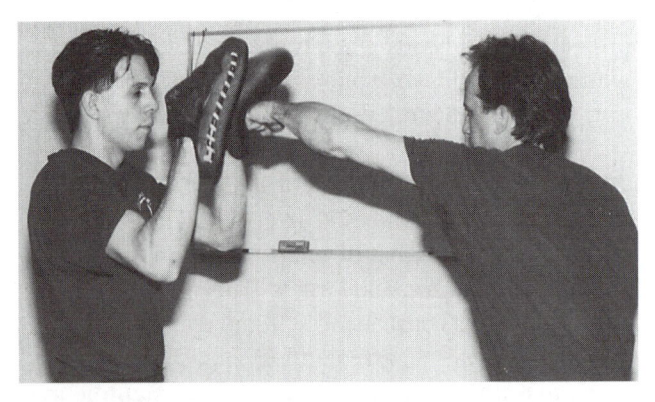

The focus mitts are essential pieces of training equipment. In this photo, a student demonstrates the rear cross.

TRAINING AND CONDITIONING

211. USE THE MEDICINE BALL.

The medicine ball is a large, heavy leather ball that is stuffed with cotton waste. It is used to strengthen and condition the abdominal wall and obliques. When used properly, the medicine ball also develops proper breathing, endurance, and the ability to withstand powerful body blows. Avoid overtraining on the ball. Practice no more than two times per week. Two of the best ways to train with the medicine ball is to have a training partner throw it into your stomach while you are standing, or to lie down on your back and have him drop it repeatedly onto your abdomen.

212. MOVE AROUND.

When working out on various pieces of training equipment (e.g., heavy bag, focus mitts, striking shield, double-end bag), try to avoid remaining stationary. Get into the habit of constantly moving around with quick, economical steps.

213. WEAR DIFFERENT CLOTHES WHEN WORKING OUT.

Make it a habit to train and work out in different types of clothes. This type of "attire training" will teach you a lot about the limitations of clothing when fighting. For example, do you notice a difference in your kicking technique when wearing shorts as compared to a suit? What is it like to fight in a robe, full-length coat, or bathing suit? What is it like to ground fight while wearing a heavy jacket? Do winter gloves affect your accuracy with a firearm? Can you fight effectively when wearing a motorcycle helmet? Do sunglasses impair your vision during a compound attack? Are your kicking techniques restricted when wearing cowboy boots or loafers? Can you kick safely when just wearing a pair of socks?

214. COMMUNICATE WITH YOUR TRAINING PARTNER.

When training with a focus-mitt feeder, you must give feedback and let your training partner know how he's doing. Remember, communication is vital during your training sessions.

215. WEAR DIFFERENT SHOES.

Practice footwork skills and kicking techniques with the following types of footwear: combat boots, hiking boots, running shoes, cross-trainers, sandals, cowboy boots, and loafers. Also practice when barefoot.

216. DRESS APPROPRIATELY.

It is important to dress appropriately for your workouts. If your body is too cold or hot, you won't perform to the best of your ability. For example, dehydration and heat stroke can occur if your body's internal temperature gets too hot, whereas an extremely cold internal temperature can lead to a variety of muscle injuries. Always wear loose-fitting clothing that will allow freedom of movement and help maintain a normal body temperature.

SPARRING

217. BUY QUALITY BOXING GLOVES.

You will not be able to benefit completely from your full-contact sparring sessions if you're not using top-quality gloves. The ideal boxing glove is one that provides comfort, protection, and durability. Depending on your training objective, the glove weight can range from 10 to 16 ounces.

Following are some other important features to be aware of when purchasing a pair of boxing gloves: (1) the glove should be composed of multilayered foam padding, (2) the glove should have a curved or attached thumb that will prevent thumb and eye injuries, (3) the glove should have a sufficient palm grip that provides comfort and fist stabilization, (4) the glove should be double-stitched to ensure durability, (5) the entire glove should be constructed of top-quality leather to increase its durability, (6) the glove's design should permit quick opening for defensive purposes, (7) the glove should be fairly easy to slip on and off, and (8) gloves should be bought from a reputable manufacturer. *WARNING: Never use karate-style gloves when sparring. These rubberized foam gloves are not designed for the impact of full-contact training.*

218. WEAR HEADGEAR.

Headgear is designed to protect your head against kicks, punches, and strikes during sparring sessions. Generally, headgear is constructed of shock-absorbing foam covered by durable leather. Headgear comes in different sizes and styles. When purchasing headgear, remember that it is important that it fit just right. If it is too tight, it can interfere with blood circulation. If it is too loose, it can twist over your face and seriously obstruct your vision. For reasons of hygiene, a fighter should not share headgear. Make certain that you purchase your own.

When purchasing headgear, you should look for the following important features: (1) offers adequate protection without losing visibility, (2) has a padded chin to protect your jawbone, (3) is of solid construction but lightweight, (4) has top-quality leather construction, (5) has an adjustable buckle or strap to facilitate proper fit, (6) has a rugged design that will provide years of use, (7) has a rear safety pad in case of accidental knockdown, and (8) has built-in cheek and nose protectors.

219. WEAR A MOUTHPIECE.

The mouthpiece is a durable rubber protector used to cover one's teeth when sparring. There are two types that can be used: single and double. The mouthpiece is a vital piece of safety equipment that can help prevent the following injuries: (1) broken jaw—the mouthpiece helps prevent a broken jaw by bracing it together when you are hit on the chin, (2) getting your teeth knocked out, and (3) biting your tongue or lips. Always wear a mouthpiece when engaging in any type of sparring drill or full-contact exercise.

220. CARRY YOUR MOUTHPIECE WITH YOU.

If your occupation requires you to regularly engage in physical altercations with the public (i.e., bouncer, city beat cop, security officer, etc.), get into the habit of carrying your mouthpiece in your pocket. This serves two purposes: (1) the mouthpiece offers excellent protection to your teeth in case your adversary lands a lucky blow and (2) the act of nonchalantly putting a mouthpiece in your mouth prior to a fight can be psychologically intimidating to your adversary.

221. AVOID PREMATURE SPARRING.

While full-contact sparring is an important component of self-defense training, it's important to integrate this training methodology at the proper time. Never introduce students to full-contact sparring drills until they have acquired the following skills: (1) a variety of offensive and defensive tools and techniques that can be applied effectively, (2) the ability to control the force of their offensive tools and techniques, (3) the fundamental attributes of unarmed combat (speed, timing, coordination, accuracy, balance, and the ability not to telegraph), and (4) a safe attitude toward training. ***CAUTION: Prematurely engaging in full-contact sparring exercises is dangerous and counterproductive.***

When introduced at the proper time, sparring is a practical and effective method of training.

222. SPAR REGULARLY.

Sparring is probably the best training exercise. It develops many combat attributes and completely conditions your body for fighting. More importantly, sparring teaches you the importance of timing and judgment of distance in relation to your offensive and defensive techniques. Sparring also conditions your body to withstand the impact of blows and kicks. However, don't be misled. Never forget that sparring does not represent the violent dynamics and real danger of a vicious street fight. Sparring is nothing more than a training methodology used to develop combat attributes. In sparring, a fighter develops rhythm. He can pace himself and create rest periods. In the streets, however, anything goes; nothing is sacred. Rhythm is destroyed. It is simply a question of survival.

Keep in mind that point-contact sparring is completely out of the question. Such training is impractical and simply stupid. Nevertheless, here are three effective sparring methods that you can incorporate into your training immediately: (1) stick and move, (2) blitz and disengage, and (3) counterfighting. Make it your mission to master the blitz and disengage methodology. It's the only one that remotely resembles a street fight.

223. TRY HANDICAPPED SPARRING.

Handicapped sparring is an excellent training methodology that teaches the importance of adaptability while sharpening and refining individual

TRAINING AND CONDITIONING

appendages. This type of sparring is conducted by having two practitioners fight one another with only one appendage (the right arm for example). Keep in mind that all techniques (offensive and defensive) can only be executed from one appendage throughout the course of a round.

224. TRY CIRCLE FIGHTING.

Circle fighting is an advanced form of training that requires a minimum of five participants. It is conducted by having all the participants form a circle (approximately 12 feet in diameter) with one person standing in the center. The instructor then randomly selects participants from the circle to attack (with sparring gear) the practitioner in the middle. The duration of the fight can last anywhere from 30 seconds to 5 minutes. It's up to the instructor. Once the attacker is finished, he returns to the circle, and the instructor immediately selects another participant to attack the person in the middle. Once the practitioners become familiar with this drill, the instructor can speed up the selection of attackers, call out multiple attackers, incorporate bludgeon and knife attacks, and even have the attackers take the fight to the ground.

225. DON'T PANIC IF YOU GET HIT.

If and when you get hit in a sparring session, stay in control of the situation and don't panic. Keep both hands up, stay mobile, and remain defensively alert. Maintain proper breathing and don't allow any negative thoughts to contaminate your mind. Stay focused on the task at hand and continue to look for openings in your training partner's defenses.

226. AVOID THESE COMMON MISTAKES WHEN SPARRING.

Here are 10 common mistakes that are made when sparring: (1) defending but failing to counterattack, (2) only fighting from one side (i.e., a right stance), (3) remaining stationary when attacking and defending, (4) random hitting or failing to select the appropriate target, (5) lack of commitment when attacking, (6) hesitating to strike, (7) turning the head or closing the eyes when a blow is delivered, (8) turning the body completely sideways from the sparring partner, (9) running away from an attack, (10) swatting at the sparring partner's glove.

227. KEEP A FIRST-AID KIT NEARBY.

If you are going to engage in any type of full-contact training, it is a good idea to have a first-aid kit readily available. A first-aid kit is intended for both minor and major injuries. The kit should be kept in a well-sealed box away from children. Don't forget to write down the emergency number for your local hospital on the box. Most first-aid kits can be purchased at your local drugstore. Each kit should contain cotton wool and hydrogen peroxide for cleaning cuts, tweezers, scissors, triangular bandages, alcohol swabs, adhesive tape, adhesive bandages, antibiotic ointment, sterile pads, gauze bandages, and elastic bandages for sprains and for elbow and knee injuries.

SUPPLEMENTAL EXERCISES

228. KNOW THE 11 REASONS TO EXERCISE.

Here are 11 reasons why you should exercise on a regular basis: (1) to be fit for combat, (2) to lose excess weight, which shortens life, (3) to improve your circulation, (4) to tone and firm muscles to acquire the physical proportions nature intended, (5) to relax from tensions causing undue fatigue and loss of sleep, (6) to stay physically fit and mentally alert, (7) to improve your metabolism, (8) to help build body resistance, (9) to acquire a more positive outlook through the feeling of good health and well-being, (10) to help maintain a youthful appearance, and (11) to get more enjoyment out of life.

229. STAY IN SHAPE.

If you're out of shape, you won't stand a chance against a good street fighter. In fact, you will never master combative techniques and skills unless you are in good shape. It's that simple.

230. BE AEROBICALLY FIT.

Since a rapid and effective response to a vicious fight imposes tremendous strain on your heart and lungs, you're going to have to do aerobic exercise, including running, biking, swimming, skipping rope, sparring, or a little of each to develop sound cardiorespiratory conditioning. Cardiorespiratory conditioning is a component of combative fitness that deals with conditioning the heart, lungs, and circulatory system for both armed and unarmed fighting.

231. RUN.

Running is one of the best ways to get into top physical condition. Running on a consistent basis improves wind capacity, endurance, circulation, and muscle tone. It strengthens the legs, burns a significant amount of calories, and stimulates the metabolism.

Running sessions should always start with a brisk jog, working up to a faster pace. Remember to start off slowly and progressively build up speed. Make it a goal to run a minimum of five times per week for a duration of approximately 50 minutes. Later on you can consider adding hills or step running to your training routine.

232. TEST YOUR SHOES.

The most important piece of equipment when running are your shoes. Before you hit the pavement in a new pair of running shoes, be certain you get the best fit. The following guidelines should help: (1) test your new shoes indoors on a carpeted surface for a minimum of one hour to make sure you have a comfortable fit, (2) your shoes should fit properly if there is a thumbnail width of space between the end of your toe and the tip of the shoe, (3) your heel and instep should feel snug, but not tight, (4) your arch should match the shoe's arch pad.

233. RUN CORRECTLY.

Running style is another important consideration. Avoid stomping on the ground. Try running lightly and rhythmically with your arms and shoulders relaxed. Let your feet glide across the floor. Running should be practically silent. In fact, if you hear your feet hit the ground you'll know that you're running incorrectly. Every running session should include the following stages: warm up, main workout, cool down, and stretches. And always buy the best running shoes you can afford. Your feet will thank you later.

234. RUN IN THE MORNING.

If possible, run in the morning. This is important for the following reasons: (1) the air is usually cleaner, (2) during the hot summer months, it's cooler, (3) there's more privacy, (4) it's quieter, (5) it accelerates your metabolism for the rest of the day, (6) your aerobic workout is taken care of so you can go about your day with peace of mind, and (7) you are mentally cleansed and energized for the rest of the day.

235. DRESS PROPERLY.

Dressing correctly for your run is also very important. Here are some important points to consider: (1) wear clothes that don't restrict your movement; (2) wear a good pair of running shoes; (3) in the summer months, dress to keep cool and comfortable; (4) in the winter months, dress warmly and in layers—sweatpants, sweatshirt, windbreaker, gloves, and hat are all important articles of clothing; and (5) wear light or bright colors for maximum visibility.

236. KNOW THE 10 REASONS WHY YOU SHOULD RUN.

Here are 10 good reasons why you should incorporate running into your training program: (1) running is one of the most efficient methods of cardiovascular conditioning, (2) running is the most easily accessible aerobic activity, (3) running is inexpensive, (4) running dramatically reduces daily stress and anxiety, (5) running is a vital component of weight management, (6) running is exhilarating, (7) running prepares you for the "escape" tactical option, (8) running is for individuals of all ages, (9) running prepares you for the tremendous physical strain of combat, and (10) running helps slow down the aging process.

237. JUMP ROPE.

If you want to be quick and light on your feet, you will need to jump rope on a regular basis. Jumping rope is also one of the most effective ways of conditioning your heart and improving coordination, endurance, balance, agility, and body composition. One of the most important factors to consider when selecting a rope is the length. A simple method to measure the rope properly is to stand on the center of the rope with one foot. The handles of the rope should reach your armpits.

Here are some other guidelines that will help you when skipping rope: (1) relax your arms and shoulders when jumping, (2) push off your toes and land gently on the balls of your feet, (3) use your wrists and forearms to turn the rope, (4) maintain good posture and bend naturally at the knees and hips, (5) jump low—approximately one inch off the ground, (6) keep your head up—avoid the tendency to look down at your feet, (7) keep both elbows close to your sides, (8) never jump rope barefoot, (9) don't get frustrated by a tangled rope, and (10) jump to different types of music.

TRAINING AND CONDITIONING

238. CYCLE.

Stationary bicycling is an excellent low-impact exercise that requires very little room. Along with conditioning the cardiorespiratory system, the exercise bike stimulates your metabolism and gives your legs a vigorous workout.

One important consideration when using an exercise bike is adjusting the seat so it fits your body properly. If the seat is too low, you'll limit your legs' range of motion and ultimately develop knee problems. If the seat is too high, your hips will rock side to side and you won't be able to pedal smoothly. The seat should be adjusted so that when you fully extend your leg, your knee is slightly bent. Also be careful when adjusting the tension of the flywheel. Too much tension will damage your knees and inhibit your workout. My best advice is to keep the tension at a level that will allow you to maintain approximately 80 revolutions per minute (RPM) for 30 to 40 minutes. Remember, if you are to benefit from the bike, you must keep your heart rate elevated for a minimum of 30 minutes.

239. WEIGHT TRAIN.

A scientific weight training program, combined with consistent stretching exercises, will significantly improve power, endurance, speed, coordination, body composition, and even pain tolerance. When training, be certain to execute all the exercises in a slow and controlled fashion. Hoisting

Weight training is an important component of any fitness program. In this photo, Franco demonstrates the incline dumbbell press.

and swinging movements will lead to serious injury and should be avoided. If you are unfamiliar with a particular exercise, ask a certified fitness instructor for assistance.

240. STRETCH EVERY DAY.

Muscular flexibility is another important component of combative fitness. You need a stretching program designed to loosen up every major muscle group. Remember that you can't kick, punch, ground fight, or otherwise execute necessary body mechanics if you are "tight" or inflexible. Stretching on a regular basis will increase the muscles' range of motion, improve circulation, reduce the possibilities of injury, and relieve tension.

Stretching should be performed in a slow and controlled manner. Always hold your stretch for a minimum of 60 seconds, and avoid all bouncing movements. Always remember to stretch before and after your training sessions. The following six stretches will help get you started.

(1) Neck stretch—from a comfortable standing position, slowly tilt your head to the right, holding it for a count of 20 seconds. Then tilt your head to the left for approximately 20 seconds. Stretch each side of the neck at least three times.

(2) Triceps stretch—from a standing position, keeping your knees slightly bent, extend your right arm overhead, bent at the elbow, then hold the elbow of your right arm with your left hand and slowly pull your right elbow to the left. Keep your hips straight as you stretch your triceps gently for 30 seconds. Repeat this stretch for the other arm.

(3) Hamstring stretch—from a seated position on the floor, extend your right leg in front of you with your toes pointing toward the ceiling. Place the sole of your left foot in the inside of your extended leg. Gently lean forward at the hips and stretch out the hamstrings of your right leg. Hold this position for a minimum of 60 seconds. Switch legs and repeat the stretch.

(4) Spinal twist—from a seated position on the floor, extend your right leg in front of you. Raise your left leg and place your left foot on the floor on the outside of your right leg. Place your right elbow on the outside of your left thigh. Stabilize your stretch with your elbow and twist your upper body and head to your left side. Breathe naturally and hold this stretch for a minimum of 30 seconds. Switch legs and repeat this stretch for the other side.

(5) Quad stretch—assume a sitting position on the floor with your legs folded underneath you. Your toes should be pointed behind you, and your insteps should be flush with the ground. Sit comfortably into the stretch and hold for a minimum of 30 seconds.

(6) Prone stretch—lie on the ground with your back to the floor. Exhale as you straighten your arms above your head. Your fingers and toes should be stretching in opposite directions. Hold this stretch for 15 seconds.

241. DO PUSH-UPS.

Push-ups are one of the best exercises to strengthen and develop the upper body (chest, shoulders, and triceps). To properly perform the push-up, lie on your stomach with your feet slightly apart. Place your hands shoulder-width apart, keep your back straight, and place your elbows close to your sides. Exhale as you push your body up from the ground. From the upward position, inhale and slowly lower your body down approximately three inches from the floor. Repeat this movement until your chest muscles become fatigued. Push-ups should always be performed in a slow and controlled manner.

242. STRENGTHEN YOUR ABDOMINALS.

Strong abdominal muscles are essential to a fighter. They protect internal organs, maintain proper posture, and support the lower back. One of the best exercises to develop the abdominal muscles is the crunch. To perform this exercise, start by lying with your back on the floor, arms folded across your chest, with your feet on a bench. Now pull your chin to your chest and contract your abdominals to move your torso (upper body) upward. Avoid lunging forward and lifting your lower back off the ground. Be certain to exhale as you approach the upward position. Remember to pause momentarily at the top. Return to the starting position in a controlled manner by inhaling and slowly lowering your shoulders to the floor. Repeat this exercise until your abdominal muscles fatigue. To develop muscular strength and endurance you'll need to perform this exercise at least four times a week.

243. STRENGTHEN YOUR HANDS.

To strengthen your fingers, hands, wrists, and forearms, try squeezing a tennis ball. Strong fingers and hands are important. They improve tearing, crushing, and gouging techniques as well as overall grappling skills. In addition, they make knife-disarming techniques safer and weapon-retention techniques more effective. Strong fingers and hands also tend to improve the structural integrity of your fists.

244. TREAT STRAINED MUSCLES.

Despite effective warm-ups and safe training, injuries can still occur. One of the most common types of training injuries is a muscle pull or strain, which is simply a partial tear in the width of the muscle fiber. It is a painful injury that can set you back significantly in your training. The best way to treat it is by applying ice to the injured area as soon as possible. Icing the injury helps control internal bleeding and swelling. Apply ice treatment until the bleeding and swelling stop. Approximately 48 hours later, apply heat to the injured muscle. This will help increase circulation and accelerate the natural healing process.

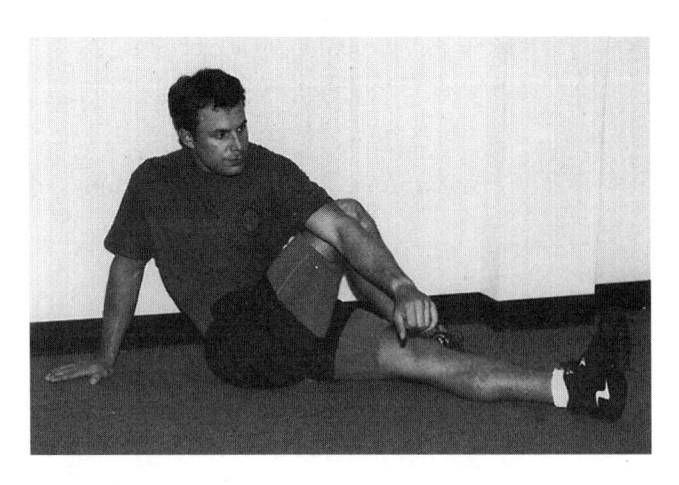

The spinal twist.

TRAINING AND CONDITIONING

245. COOL DOWN.

Cooling down from a strenuous workout is just as important as warming up. A cool-down is a series of light exercises and movements that immediately follow a workout. The purpose of the cool-down is to hasten the removal of metabolic wastes and gradually return the heart to its resting rate. A proper cool-down will also reduce the likelihood of stiffness. Simply halting your workout can cause sluggish circulation, blood pooling, and slow waste-product removal. Some experts say that it contributes to muscle soreness and cramping.

Here are a few suggestions: (1) make your cool-down last a minimum of five minutes, (2) light stretching exercises are the best way to cool down, (3) brisk walking is another effective cool-down method.

246. AVOID CRAMPING.

Muscle cramping is the result of a particular muscle contracting for too long. It is often recognizable as a sudden and painful tightening of the muscle. The three primary causes of muscle cramping are (1) salt depletion because of excessive sweating, (2) muscle fatigue, and (3) injury. The best way to avoid cramping is to hydrate properly. Drink plenty of water before and during your workout. If you do get a muscle cramp, the best method of relieving it is to relax the muscle by either stretching it or massaging it with the fingers. Keep in mind that the muscle can be worked again after the cramping subsides.

247. DRINK PLENTY OF WATER.

Dehydration can have a negative effect on your workout, and it can also be dangerous. Always hydrate before your workout by drinking at least one pint of water, and always drink plenty of water during your workout as well. Get into the habit of taking a water bottle with you to your workouts. During the summer months, drink more water than usual.

NUTRITION

248. PERFORM BETTER BY TAKING MCTS.

Medium-chain triglycerides (MCTs) are a quick-acting, highly concentrated liquid energy source that can improve your workout performance dramatically. MCTs also provide more than twice the energy power of carbohydrates. For best results, take two tablespoonfuls of MCT oil one-half hour before working out. You'll see a noticeable improvement in your workout.

249. EAT RIGHT.

A fighter's diet is one of the most neglected aspects of combat fitness. A true diet refers to a lifestyle of eating right.

Sixty percent of your daily caloric intake should consist of complex carbohydrates. Carbohydrates, the body's primary source of energy, are found in vegetables, fruits, potatoes, pasta, and all grain products.

Next we have proteins, which are essential for muscle and tissue growth. Poultry, fish, and legumes are excellent sources of low-fat proteins. Unless you are on a serious weight-gain program, you should devote no more than 30 percent of your daily caloric intake to proteins.

Finally, unsaturated fats are vital to proper metabolic function and vitamin absorption and should make up 10 percent of your calories. Don't confuse unsaturated fats with their nasty relatives, saturated fats. Saturated fats, found in ice cream, chocolate, cakes, and so on, are a big NO. Forget them. They will only make you fat and sluggish. Look for natural unsaturated fats in such foods as nuts, seeds, and various grains.

Keep in mind that nutritional supplements should also be taken to ensure that you get all the necessary vitamins and minerals.

250. TAKE YOUR VITAMINS.

A vitamin is any of various fat-soluble (stored in the body fat) or water-soluble (dissolve in water) organic substances essential for the growth and maintenance of the body. Vitamins are a necessary part of the fighter's diet. As a matter of fact, the word "vitamin" comes from the Latin word *vita*, meaning "life." A well-balanced diet will ensure that you are taking in the necessary amounts of vitamins. However, vitamin deficiencies can occur, and they can have a negative effect on your performance. *WARNING: Avoid excessive amounts of fat-soluble vitamins, because they can cause severe toxicity.*

Let's look at a brief list of important vitamins.

(1) Vitamin A—this fat-soluble vitamin is important for normal cell growth and development. A deficiency of vitamin A is also known to cause night blindness

and the degeneration of mucous membranes. Vitamin A can be found in fish-liver oils, carrots, liver, fortified dairy products, and some yellow and dark green vegetables.

(2) Vitamin D—this fat-soluble vitamin helps build healthy bones and teeth, and it can be obtained from fortified milk, fish, and eggs and by exposing your body to sunlight.

(3) Vitamin E—this fat-soluble vitamin is used to treat abnormalities of the muscles, red blood cells, liver, and brain. In fact, some people say that vitamin E actually slows down the aging process. This vitamin can be found in seed oils, especially wheat germ oil, plant leaves, and milk.

(4) Vitamin K—this fat-soluble vitamin is important for blood clotting and preventing hemorrhaging. It can be found in fish oils, liver, egg yolks, tomatoes, and green, leafy vegetables.

(5) Vitamin B_1 (thiamin)—this water-soluble vitamin functions as a coenzyme and is necessary for carbohydrate metabolism and neural activity. Thiamin can be found in meat, yeast, and the bran coat of grains.

(6) Vitamin B_2 (riboflavin)—this is the primary growth-promoting factor in the vitamin B complex. It can be found in milk, leafy vegetables, liver, nuts, brewer's yeast, meat, and egg yolks.

(7) Niacin—this is a component of the vitamin B complex used to treat and prevent pellagra (a disease that includes skin eruptions, nausea, vomiting, nervous system disturbances, and mental deterioration). Niacin can be found in meat, fish, poultry, wheat germ, dairy products, and yeast.

(8) Vitamin C (ascorbic acid)—this water-soluble vitamin prevents scurvy and a variety of dental problems. Vitamin C can be found in citrus fruits, tomatoes, turnips, sweet potatoes, potatoes, and green, leafy vegetables.

251. LIGHTEN UP.

Excessive body fat will only be a hindrance when fighting. It interferes with agility, speed, and endurance, and it continually taxes the heart. If you are overweight, here are 10 suggestions to help you lighten the load: (1) set a realistic caloric deficit level, (2) lose weight slowly (no more than one pound per week), (3) avoid foods that are high in fat, (4) eat four small meals per day, (5) drink plenty of water throughout the day, (6) avoid diet fads, (7) weigh yourself only once per week, (8) partake in at least four aerobic workouts (running, biking, rope skipping, etc.) per week and make certain each one is a least 45 minutes in duration, (9) if you slip up with your diet or workout program, don't beat yourself up; realize that you are only human and try again, and (10) limit red meat consumption to only once per week.

READING AND RESEARCH

252. READ, READ, READ!

The intellectual, or academic, aspects of combative training cannot be overstated. You must possess an insatiable desire to learn. Effective academic research involves voracious reading. The body of printed materials on combat and fighting has grown astronomically. Read anything you can get your hands on. Don't make the common mistake of passively reading material. Get into the habit of dissecting and noting literature. Strategically sound theories and concepts should be noted and remembered. Books should be read over and over again until practical concepts are intellectually solidified. Always read material with an open mind balanced with healthy skepticism.

253. NEVER LEND OUT YOUR BOOKS.

The books you own are very precious. Never lend them out. In most cases, people will not treat your books with the same respect that you would. And many times you will never see them again.

254. READ *STREET LETHAL: UNARMED URBAN COMBAT*.

This book will give you an introductory

TRAINING AND CONDITIONING

foundation to Contemporary Fighting Arts and provide you with many of the physical techniques of the system. This book is available from Paladin Press.

255. READ *KILLER INSTINCT: UNARMED COMBAT FOR STREET SURVIVAL*.
This book will provide you with deep insight into the combat mentality and the strategies of CFA. It is available from Paladin Press.

256. READ *WHEN SECONDS COUNT: EVERYONE'S GUIDE TO SELF-DEFENSE*.
This book will take you into the dark mind of the street criminal. Make notes in the margins on every page. This book is also available from Paladin Press.

257. READ *THE ART OF WAR*.
Read this book at least 10 times, and don't forget to make notes in the margins.

258. READ *GRAY'S ANATOMY*.
Anyone who is genuinely interested in neutralizing a formidable assailant must have a working knowledge of the strengths and weaknesses of the human anatomy. Begin by reading *Gray's Anatomy*. This comprehensive book will give you a strong foundation in the human anatomy.

259. READ THE NEWSPAPER.
Your local newspaper can provide you with a wealth of information about violence and crime. Get into the habit of reading it regularly. Pay close attention to what you are reading and find out the motivations, mentalities, and methods of street criminals.

260. READ THE UNIFORM CRIME REPORT.
Every year read the *Uniform Crime Report (UCR)*. By keeping yourself informed through this official source, you will gain a necessary grasp of the types and trends of violence and crime. Pay particular attention to the demographic, seasonal, and regional variations in crime.

261. BE SKEPTICAL YET OPEN-MINDED.
When reading martial arts books and magazines or watching training videos, always observe with a skeptical eye and look for the combative utility of every technique. Whenever you learn a new self-defense technique, ask yourself, "Will this really work in the unpredictable environment of a real fight?" If your answer is no, then forget it.

THE INSTRUCTOR

262. LISTEN TO YOUR INSTRUCTOR.
Your instructor is there to evaluate your performance during your workouts. Listen very carefully to what he has to say. A good combat instructor will be brutally honest and tell you what you are doing correctly and what you are doing wrong. Put your ego aside and heed what he says.

263. BE SELECTIVE.
Choose a self-defense instructor the very same way that you would choose a surgeon to perform a difficult operation. In both cases, your life is in his hands. Here are the questions to get answers to when selecting a competent instructor: (1) How long has he been studying martial sciences? (2) How long has he been teaching self-defense? (3) Exactly what aspects of combat is he qualified to teach? (4) What agency, institution, or person certified him? (5) Is he well known for his expertise? (6) Is he articulate with combative nomenclature? (7) Does he practice what he preaches? (8) Is the instructor published? (9) Does the instructor answer all of your questions? (10) Does he injure his students? (11) Does he project a professional image? (12) Does his attitude show patience and respect toward his students? (13) What is his temperament—is he friendly and serious or cynical and negative? (14) Does he seem oriented toward safety?

264. FOLLOW THESE TRAINING DOs AND DON'Ts.
Here are 10 training DOs and DON'Ts for self-defense instructors: (1) DO encourage friendly and healthy competition between your students, (2) DO try to find out what causes your students to make mistakes and take action to prevent recurrences, (3) DO admit your mistakes, (4) DO maintain a professional attitude at all times, (5) DO let every one of your students know what is expected of him, (6) DO encourage your students to overcome their weak points, (7) DON'T expect beginner students to be perfect, (8) DON'T expect your students to progress as quickly as you do, (9) DON'T allow misinformation to be disseminated in the ranks, (10) DON'T let incorrect habits go uncorrected in class.

265. TEACH OTHERS TO TEACH THEMSELVES.

If you're a self-defense instructor, teach your students to train themselves. Avoid "spoon-feeding" information. Every so often use the Socratic method of teaching. Make your students answer their own questions through mental and physical inquiry.

266. BE RESPECTFUL.

Always treat your instructor or mentor with the highest level of respect. Display a willingness to show consideration and appreciation for his teachings. Make it a habit to be polite and courteous whenever you are in his presence. Polite expressions of consideration or deferential regard are also in order. Courteously yield to his opinions, wishes, and judgments. Never violate his rules or interfere with his teaching. Remember, your life is in his hands.

267. REALIZE THAT GOOD INSTRUCTORS ARE HARD TO FIND.

A good self-defense instructor knows how to push his students. He knows how to motivate the weak and browbeat the strong.

268. TALK TO COPS.

If you ever have the opportunity, talk to law enforcement officers about their encounters with street criminals. Law enforcement people are generally very candid, and they can teach you a lot about the realities of street violence.

SCHOOL SELECTION

269. LOOK FOR AN ECLECTIC SCHOOL.

When looking for a realistic self-defense school, choose one that is strictly devoted to the art and science of combat. The school you select should also be eclectic, drawing from such fields as martial science, criminal justice, military and police science, psychology, sociology, conflict management, histrionics, kinesics, anatomy, kinesiology, firearms science, and emergency medicine. Also be sure that the tools, techniques, and tactics are all predicated on efficiency, effectiveness, and safety.

270. FIND THE ANSWERS TO THESE IMPORTANT QUESTIONS.

Here are some important questions to ask when selecting a self-defense school: (1) Is the training practical and realistic? (2) Are questions permitted in class? (3) Does the school stress the importance of range proficiency? (4) Is safety stressed during training? (5) Does the instructor discuss the legal ramifications of self-defense? (6) Are training materials available for the students? (7) Are full-contact exercises conducted? (8) Are ground fighting techniques taught? (9) What types of weapons are taught? (10) Is the information presented in a methodical and organized fashion? (11) How proficient are the advanced students of the particular system? (12) What is the general atmosphere of the school? (13) Does the instructor seem to be in control of the studio? (14) Can you afford the membership fees?

271. CHOOSE CAREFULLY— ALL SCHOOLS ARE NOT CREATED EQUAL.

You must be cautious when choosing a martial art or self-defense school. They don't all have the same objective. Here are some important points to keep in mind.

(1) If you are looking for practical self-defense training, stay clear of traditional martial art studios. A karate or kung-fu instructor is no more qualified to teach you street combat than a ballet teacher or fitness trainer. When all is said and done, the traditional martial arts have absolutely nothing to do with serious combat training.

(2) Don't select a school simply because of geographical proximity. Don't let your laziness force you to sacrifice quality self-defense training.

(3) Look for a reputable school that instructs students in both armed and unarmed self-defense tactics.

272. DON'T BELIEVE EVERYTHING YOU HEAR.

Martial artists are notorious for exaggerations and blatant lies. Don't believe what you hear in the martial arts community—especially stories about so-called ancient masters. They are nothing more than a bunch of cheap magicians who exploit the dreams and aspirations of weak people.

273. BOYCOTT MARTIAL ART TOURNAMENTS.

Martial art tournaments are for egotistical

TRAINING AND CONDITIONING

martial artists who are too afraid to really fight. They parade around in unusual clothing and win the admiration of ignorant spectators who have absolutely no idea of what real combat is. It's a million-dollar business that perpetuates the myth of martial arts. Life is short. Don't waste your time and pollute your mind at the same time. If you must watch a spectator sport, try attending boxing, wrestling, or kickboxing matches. And don't be impressed by martial art demonstrations. They prove nothing.

CHAPTER THREE

Attributes of Combatants

"A kick, punch, block, or any other technique is useless unless accompanied by specific combative attributes."

COGNITIVE ATTRIBUTES

274. **BE WELL-ROUNDED IN THE QUALITIES OF COMBAT.**
A kick, block, submission hold, or any self-defense technique, for that matter, is useless unless accompanied by specific combat attributes. Attributes are qualities that enhance your particular tool, technique, or weapon. For example, speed, power, finesse, range specificity, target orientation, and balance are just a few combat attributes that must be present if any technique or maneuver is to be effective.

275. **BE DECISIVE.**
Combat demands that you be decisive about your decisions and actions. Decisiveness is your ability to be unwavering and focused when following a tactical course of action. Remember that indecisiveness in combat can lead to dangerous vulnerabilities.

276. **BE PERCEPTIVE.**
Perception is the interpretation of information acquired from one's senses when faced with a dangerous or hostile situation. You gather information through your five senses. Your eyes, ears, nose, and senses of touch and taste will provide a wealth of vital information about a threatening assailant and the environment. With adequate training, your senses can be sharpened and your powers of observation enhanced.

The ability to process information varies from person to person. In fact, two people who witness the same event are likely to report it differently. This is referred to as "individual perception." In part, previous experiences can determine the manner in which a person will interpret stimuli. When it comes to effective self-defense, you must attempt to remove preconceived notions, assumptions, and biases that may lead to dangerously incorrect conclusions or oversights. These false reactions form barriers to your ability to grasp reality.

277. **MASTER DISTANCING.**
Distancing is your ability to understand spatial relationships. A fighter must understand the strategic extent of space. During both armed and unarmed combat, a fighter must instinctively know the opportunities and limitations of the range he is engaged in.

278. **BE INSENSITIVE.**
Tactile sensitivity is an attribute promulgated by misguided theoreticians who have obviously never experienced a vicious fight. How much sensitivity does a nuclear explosion, plane crash, or tornado exhibit? Such catastrophes are similar in nature to a combat situation.

279. **BE VICIOUS.**
If you want to prevail in a fight, you must be more vicious and ruthless than your assailant. At the same time, you must calculate your tools and tactics strategically to maximize efficiency and effectiveness. Viciousness is the propensity to be extremely violent and destructive. It is characterized by intense savagery.

Viciousness is also a vital component of the

killer instinct that can be instilled mentally by pseudospeciating your adversary. Pseudospeciating means assigning inferior qualities to your adversary. Viciousness should not be misinterpreted as wrong, evil, immoral, or depraved. Some of you may wonder how I can reconcile viciousness with virtue. The concept of viciousness conjures up images of helpless victims being preyed upon by cruel aggressors. But it is this erroneous perception that must be reversed. The bottom line is that there are times when viciousness must be met with greater viciousness. Viciousness is a necessary means to achieve and sustain safety, justice, and peace. This may sound paradoxical and extreme, and you may challenge the compatibility of virtue and the capacity for brutal destructiveness. But there is, in fact, no inherent incompatibility. The advanced fighter must be virtuous and yet altogether capable of unleashing a controlled explosion of viciousness and brutality.

280. BE INTUITIVE.

Learn to rely on your innate ability to know or sense something without the use of rational thought. In many circumstances, immediate cognition will provide you with the necessary time to respond to a threatening situation. In some situations, going with your "gut" reaction can be just what is called for. Remember, when something doesn't seem right or the objective data doesn't add up, then chances are something is wrong.

281. BE WILLING TO EMPLOY YOUR KILLER INSTINCT.

During the dynamics of a real fight, you must utilize a combat mentality to channel a destructiveness exceeding that of your adversary. This is the killer instinct, that cold, primal mentality and spirit that surges to your consciousness and turns you into a vicious combatant. A reservoir of energy and strength, the killer instinct can channel your destructiveness by producing a mental source of cold, destructive energy. If necessary, it fuels the determination to fight to the death.

282. BE TELEGRAPHICALLY COGNIZANT.

A superior fighter is aware of everything, including his assailant's intentions to attack. Telegraphic cognizance is the ability to recognize both verbal and nonverbal signs of impending aggression or assault.

(1) Verbal signs (assault is imminent): abnormal stuttering, rapid speech, incoherent speech, extreme sarcasm, threats, challenging statements, screaming and yelling, and swearing.

(2) Nonverbal signs (assault is possible): increased breathing and pulse rate, excessive sweating, pulled shoulders, clenched teeth, direct and uninterrupted eye contact, acting as if he is ignoring you, drunken behavior, immediately changing from uncooperative to cooperative.

(3) Nonverbal signs (assault is imminent): clenched fists, quivering hands, cessation of all movements, reddened face (from blood surge), protruding veins (from face, neck, or forearms), extreme body tension, shoulder telegraph, target stare (looking at groin, jaw, etc.), finger pointing, pacing, quick turning, fist threats with arm bent, hands on hips, 1,000-yard stare (looking through you), hand concealment, rocking back and forth, and a change in stance.

283. BE ADAPTABLE.

In combat, factors change like the wind. A poor fighter will expect his environment to adapt to him, whereas a smart fighter adapts to his environment. Adaptability allows one to adjust to new or different conditions or circumstances both physically and psychologically. In the heat of combat, a fighter should not question change, and he should not scrutinize a particular situation excessively. A fighter must simply conform to the necessary demands of his predicament.

284. BE KNOWLEDGEABLE ABOUT THE LAW.

Developing a deadly capability to protect yourself carries tremendous moral and social responsibility, as well as the risk of civil liability and criminal jeopardy. There is an interesting irony facing most martial artists and self-defense experts: the more highly trained, knowledgeable, and skilled you are in firearms, knives, unarmed combat tactics, martial arts, and other self-defense skills, the higher the standards you must follow when protecting

ATTRIBUTES OF COMBATANTS

yourself and others. Remember, if you act too quickly or use what others might consider "excessive force" in neutralizing an assailant, you may end up being a defendant in a legal process. If you are involved in a vicious street fight, where do you stand in the eyes of the law? If it becomes necessary to fight, you must know the answers to the following two important questions: (1) Exactly when can I use force? (2) How much physical force is legally justified?

285. BE SELF-AWARE.

Self-awareness is a critical attribute of combat. This means knowing and understanding aspects of yourself that may provoke criminal violence, and which, if any, would promote a proper response in a self-defense situation. The following questions are designed to get you started on the important process of developing self-awareness. Use them to form a profile of yourself.

(1) Physical attributes. What are your physical strengths and weaknesses? Do you possess the physical skills and attributes necessary for effective self-defense? Are you a natural athlete or a klutz? Are you overweight or underweight? Are your body language and the manner in which you carry yourself more likely to provoke or deter a violent attack? Are you in good shape? Do you smoke or drink excessively?

(2) Mental attributes. What are your mental strengths and weaknesses? Do you possess the specific concepts, principles, and knowledge related to self-defense and combat? Are you quick and intelligent? Can you think on your feet in a dangerous situation? How do you handle stress and anxiety? Do you panic or frighten easily? Can you make proper "use-of-force" decisions?

(3) Affective attributes. What are your emotional strengths and weaknesses? Are your attitudes, philosophies, ethics, and values congruent to the realities and rigors of combat? Do you know how to tap the proper fighting spirit for combat (killer instinct)?

(4) Communication attributes. What are your strengths and weaknesses in communicating with others? Do you possess the ability to effectively defuse a hostile situation? Can you communicate effectively under stressful and dangerous situations, or do you become nonplused?

(5) Occupation. Does the nature of your occupation make you or your family vulnerable to different forms of criminal violence? Are you involved with the military or law enforcement? Are you a celebrity? Do you have diplomatic or political connections? Do you control large sums of money or valuable drugs? Does your political affiliation make you a likely target for kidnapping or terrorism?

(6) Personality traits. What type of person are you? Are you passive or aggressive? Are you opinionated and argumentative or open-minded and deliberative? Are you fiery, loud, and boisterous or quiet, subdued, and calm? Are you quick to anger? Do you harbor grudges? Are there sensitive issues, remarks, or statements that may cause you to lose control?

(7) Gender and age. What are the different types of violent crimes that may be directed toward you because of your sex? For example, women are much more likely than men to be raped or abused by their spouses. On the other hand, males are more likely than females to be victims of homicide. Is your age an open invitation for an attack on the street? For example, children and teens are more likely to be molested and kidnapped than adults, and senior citizens are slower, weaker, and more vulnerable to attack than young adults.

(8) Income level. What types of crime may be directed toward you because of your income level? Are you wealthy, comfortable, or dirt-poor? Does your income level make you or your family

vulnerable to kidnapping for ransom? Or does your financial situation force you to live in poor neighborhoods that breed violent crime? Are you wealthy and flashy, displaying outward evidence of your wealth?

286. BE SITUATIONALLY AWARE.

Situational awareness is total alertness, presence, and focus on virtually everything in your immediate surroundings. Situational awareness requires you to detect and assess the people, places, objects, and actions that can pose a danger to you.

Do not think of situational awareness simply in terms of the customary five senses of sight, sound, smell, taste, and touch. In addition to these, the very real powers of instinct and intuition must also be developed and sharpened. Situational awareness, in terms of threats posed by human attackers, begins with an understanding of criminal psychology. It is a common misconception that all street criminals are stupid and incompetent. On the contrary, they can be shrewd, methodical, bold, and psychologically dominant. The especially dangerous ones are often expert observers of human behavior, capable of accurately assessing your body language, walk, talk, state of mind, and a variety of other indicators. Street criminals know what to look for and how to exploit it. They are selective predators who employ carefully designed measures to evaluate fear, apprehension, and awareness. Seasoned street criminals are always looking for easy targets. Chronic barroom brawlers, street punks, bullies, and muggers operate in the same basic manner. They look for weak, timid, and unaware people.

As you develop situational awareness, you transmit a different kind of signal to the enemy's radar. Weakness and uncertainty are replaced by confidence and strength. Your carriage and movements change dramatically. You will be seen as assertive and purposeful. You will be less likely to be perceived as an easy mark, and your chances of being attacked will diminish significantly.

Situational awareness also reduces the potency of the street criminal's favorite weapon—the element of surprise. Your ability to foresee and detect danger will diminish the assailant's ability to stalk you or lie in wait in ambush zones. In addition to enhancing your ability to detect, avoid, and strategically neutralize ambush zones, situational awareness allows you to detect and avoid threats or dangers not necessarily predicated on the element of surprise. Some situations will actually afford you the luxury of seeing trouble coming. Nevertheless, it's remarkable how many people fail to heed obvious signs of danger because of poor awareness skills.

Very few people take the time to utilize their situational awareness skills for a variety of reasons. Some are in denial about the prevalence of street violence, whereas others are too distracted by life's everyday problems and pressures to pay attention to the hidden dangers that lurk around them. Whatever the reasons, poor situational awareness skills can get you into serious trouble and could cost you your life.

287. BE CRIMINALLY AWARE.

Open your eyes and ears to the many lessons of criminal awareness. Criminal awareness is a passive combative attribute that involves a general understanding and knowledge of the nature and dynamics of a criminal's motivations, mentalities, methods, and capabilities to perpetrate violence. By keeping yourself informed of local and global incidents through the media, official crime reports, and other credible sources, you will gain a necessary grasp of the types and trends of violent acts and the reasons behind them.

When analyzing a violent act you have read about, ask yourself the following six questions: (1) Who? Who was attacked, and who was the attacker? (2) What? What happened? What were the circumstances? (3) Where? Where did the attacker develop the means to carry out the act, and where did the act actually take place? (4) When? When was the act committed? (5) Why? Why did the act take place? Why that perpetrator, why that victim, why that particular act? (6) How? How was the act committed?

The answers to these questions will obviously differ with every violent incident, but through this type of analysis, your ignorance and naiveté will be replaced by an enhanced awareness of potentially violent acts and how they occur. You will become familiar with the personality types of various street aggressors, including information about their age, sex, education, values, cultural eccentricities, and combat mannerisms.

288. BE CONFIDENT.

Self-confidence means having trust and faith in yourself. Self-assurance is vital when you are

ATTRIBUTES OF COMBATANTS

staring into the face of danger. You must be certain of your skills and abilities. When all is said and done, you cannot afford to doubt yourself.

289. BE PHILOSOPHICALLY RESOLUTE.

To be adequately prepared to fight, you must philosophically resolve issues of combat before you encounter an assailant. Philosophical resolution is essential to a fighter's mental confidence and clarity. In learning the art of war, you must find the ultimate answers to questions concerning the use of violence in defense of yourself or others. To advance to the highest levels of combative awareness, you must find clear answers to such provocative questions as (1) Could you take the life of another in defense of yourself or a loved one? (2) What are your fears? (3) Who are you? (4) Why are you reading this book? (5) What justifies the use of violence? (6) What is good and what is evil? If you haven't begun the quest to formulate the answers to these important questions, then take a break. It's time to figure out just why you want to know the laws and rules of destruction.

290. BE PREPARED.

A superior combatant is always ready. He's taken the time to prepare himself for the brutal realities of combat. There are three components of combative preparedness: (1) cognitive preparedness—you are mentally and psychologically prepared for the horrors of combat and equipped with the necessary concepts, principles, and knowledge critical for combat; (2) psychomotor preparedness—you are physically prepared for the rigors of combat and possess all of the physical skills and attributes necessary to fight effectively; and (3) affective preparedness—you are emotionally and spiritually prepared for the demands and strains of combat, you have philosophically resolved issues related to combat, and your attitudes, ethics, and values are congruent with the task of fighting.

291. BE TARGET-ORIENTED.

Knowing where to attack your assailant is just as important as knowing how and when to attack him. Target orientation means having a workable knowledge of the various anatomical targets presented in both armed and unarmed encounters.

Target orientation is divided into the following six categories: (1) impact targets—anatomical targets that can be struck with your natural body weapons; (2) nonimpact targets—anatomical targets that can be strangled, twisted, torn, crushed, clawed, gouged, or strategically manipulated; (3) edged-weapon targets—anatomical targets that can be punctured or slashed with a knife or edged weapon; (4) bludgeon targets—anatomical targets that can be struck with a stick or bludgeon; (5) ballistic targets—anatomical targets that can be shot with a firearm; and (6) chemical irritant targets—anatomical targets that can be exposed to chemical irritants.

292. BE EMOTIONLESS.

Emotions are extremely powerful feelings that have tremendous influence over our actions. A fighter must not experience emotions while engaged in combat with an adversary. A fighter must learn to eliminate fear, anger, remorse, and ego from his consciousness temporarily. Emotion serves no purpose in combat. In fact, emotions are dangerous because they create indecisiveness, apprehension, and dangerous vulnerabilities.

293. BE FAST IN YOUR DEFENSIVE REACTION TIME.

Defensive reaction time is the elapsed time between your assailant's attack and your defensive response to that attack. In combat, your goal is to always try to increase the elapsed time by increasing the distance between you and your assailant. Generally, in unarmed combat situations, the neutral zone will provide adequate defensive reaction time for the fighter. Defensive reaction time can also be enhanced by recognizing telegraphic movement before the assailant launches his strike effectively.

294. BE STREET-SMART.

Street smarts can be defined as the knowledge, skills, and attitude necessary to avoid, defuse, confront, and neutralize both armed and unarmed assailants. When a self-defense technician strategically integrates the attributes of awareness, assessment, and combat preparedness, he will have acquired street smarts.

295. BE PATIENT.

Patience is the ability to endure and calmly await the outcome of a situation. This combat attribute is particularly important when you are "locked up" with your assailant in a ground fight, or when you are held down by suppression fire in a gunfight.

296. BE COURAGEOUS.
Courage is both a mental and spiritual attribute that will enable a fighter to face danger or vicissitudes with confidence, resolution, and bravery. A coward dies many deaths!

297. BE SUSPICIOUS.
In the streets you need to have a suspicious nature. A suspicious nature consists of (1) being distrustful of strangers, (2) always mentally questioning the presence of strangers, and (3) never taking your eyes off strangers.

PHYSICAL ATTRIBUTES

298. SPEED IT UP.
If you want to increase the speed of your natural body weapon, try some of the following: (1) focus on retraction speed—concentrate on speeding up the retracting motion of strikes when training, (2) minimize target follow-through—don't allow your strike to completely "settle" in the selected target, (3) step with the strike—step in the direction of the blow to accelerate its velocity, (4) practice psychomotor repetition—repeat the desired movement thousands of times to sharpen and crystallize the physical movement, (5) visualize regularly—envision the strike being delivered at great speed, (6) relax—avoid unnecessarily tensing your body and relax your muscles prior to executing your technique, (7) breathe properly—exhale during the execution of your movement, (8) acquire kinesthetic perception—acquire a keen sense of body mechanics through movement, and, finally, (9) think fast.

299. BE REALISTIC ABOUT RHYTHM.
Rhythm is defined as combat movements characterized by the natural ebb and flow of related elements. Although rhythm is considered by many martial art instructors to be a combat attribute, it is really seldom used. Real combat usually does not allow you the opportunity to dance around your assailant and execute a rhythmic combination of strikes. Combat is similar to a car wreck. It's spontaneous, explosive, and unmerciful. When your assailant explodes through the ranges of unarmed combat in an attempt to rip you apart, it is very difficult to maintain a rhythmic flow of strikes.

Furthermore, the concept of "breaking" your assailant's rhythm is absolutely ridiculous. In a vicious street fight, you won't have the time or opportunity to study and analyze your assailant's movements. You don't have time to learn your assailant's pattern of blows prior to breaking them. Such sparring concepts have no place in the world of actual fighting.

300. BE AGILE.
Agility is an important attribute that will be called upon in both armed and unarmed encounters. Agility is defined as the ability to move one's body quickly and gracefully. In unarmed combat, you need to move your body through the ranges quickly and easily. Agility is important because it minimizes your target exposure, economizes your offensive and defensive movements, and accelerates the velocity and power of your strikes.

301. BE FLEXIBLE.
Flexibility is important to a fighter because it ensures muscle suppleness and the ability to move through the maximum range of motion. This is particularly important when ground fighting with an assailant. Muscular flexibility will also allow you to deploy your striking techniques with greater speed and ease.

302. BE TOLERANT OF PAIN.
Pain tolerance is the ability to withstand pain both physically and psychologically. A practitioner who is not prepared to tolerate pain is in grave danger. In unarmed combat, when a fighter is struck with a powerful blow and his mind goes into shock, his concentration breaks, his spirit weakens, and he begins to panic, he will almost always be defeated.

303. BE FAST.
Speed is a vital attribute of both armed and unarmed combat. There are two types of speed that you need to be concerned with: (1) mental speed—the rate at which you can employ your cognitive skills (i.e., assessment, awareness, tactical option response, and discretionary use of force) in a self-defense situation and (2) psychomotor speed—the rate at which you can move your body (e.g., to punch, block, evade, draw, and shoot a firearm) in a self-defense situation.

304. STAY BALANCED.
Balance is a critical attribute of both armed and unarmed combat. Balance is simply defined as a

ATTRIBUTES OF COMBATANTS

fighter's ability to maintain equilibrium while stationary or moving. The bottom line is this—never lose your balance in a fight. In many emergency situations, if you lose your balance, you will lose your life.

Balance is critical for the following reasons: (1) you can change your direction of movement quickly and efficiently, (2) it enhances your general reaction time, (3) it enhances your mobility, (4) it permits quick recovery from a committed movement, (5) it prevents the assailant from exploiting you in a ground fight, and (6) it prevents unnecessary target exposure to your assailant.

Balance is often lost because of (1) poor body mechanics, (2) poor kinesthetic perception, (3) improper weight shift, (4) excessive follow-through, and (5) improper skeletal alignment.

305. BE AMBIDEXTROUS.

You must be able to fight your adversary with equal ability on both the right and left sides of your body. Here are three important reasons why ambidexterity is essential: (1) your strong hand or leg might be injured or wounded in combat, (2) you might be assaulted on the weak side of your body, and (3) your strong hand or leg might be occupied at the time of the assault.

Ambidexterity must also be mastered in the following components of combat: (1) stances—both armed and unarmed combat stances; (2) submission holds—in both vertical and horizontal grappling planes; (3) natural offensive body weapons—kicks, punches, and various other striking techniques; (4) natural defensive body weapons—blocks, parries, and various other body evasion skills; (5) knives and edged weapon skills; (6) makeshift weapon skills; (7) stick and bludgeon skills; (8) chemical irritants; and (9) firearm skills.

306. BE COORDINATED.

Coordination is simply the harmonious functioning of muscles (or groups of muscles) in the execution of any tool, technique, or maneuver. Coordination is vital because it ensures that your tool, technique, or maneuver is (1) delivered with maximum accuracy, (2) performed with complete efficiency, (3) performed with balance and control, and (4) delivered with proper timing.

307. BE A MASTER OF THE HIERARCHY OF WEAPONS.

If you want to be a superior combatant, then you must possess the knowledge, skills, and attitude necessary to master the complete hierarchy of weapons. The hierarchy of weapons includes (1) natural body weapons (offense and defense), (2) chemical irritants (OC), (3) sticks and bludgeons, (4) makeshift weapons, (5) knives and edged weapons, and (6) firearms.

308. BE HARD IN APPEARANCE.

The way you appear to others can play a big role on the streets. A formidable fighter is one who possesses a "hard look" that tells everyone, including potential attackers, that he's not to be bothered with. A hard look has the following two components: (1) facial—when your facial expression appears situationally aware, dead serious, and confident; and (2) physical—when your body and physique appear solid, strong, and powerful. Remember, if you're fat, underweight, or visibly out of shape, no one will ever take you seriously.

309. BE DISTRACTIVE.

Distraction is a critical component of combat; you must possess distractive tactics. Distractive tactics can be divided into the following two categories: (1) verbal—utilizing your voice to distract your assailant, including selective semantics (choice words) and voice (tone, pitch, tempo, and volume); (2) physical—utilizing physical movements or gestures to distract your assailant, including eye movements, body shifts, head turns, and appendage movements.

310. BE RANGE PROFICIENT.

Combat is unpredictable: it can occur anytime and anywhere. If you want to be prepared to handle any type of situation, you'd better be range proficient. This means that you can fight your adversary in all possible situations. Unarmed range proficiency is the ability to fight and defend from all three distances of unarmed combat.

(1) Kicking range. At this distance, you are usually too far away to strike with your hands, so you would use your legs to strike your adversary. For real-life combat, you should only employ low-line kicks, which are directed to targets below the assailant's waist, such as the groin, thigh, knee joint, and shinbone. Effective low-line kicks include side

kicks, push kicks, hook kicks, and vertical kicks.

(2) Punching range. This is the midrange of unarmed combat. At this distance, you are close enough your assailant to strike him with your hands. Hand strikes do not require as much room as kicking strikes, and the surface that you are standing on is not as much of a concern. Punching range tools include finger jabs, palm-heel strikes, lead straights, rear crosses, knife-hand strikes, horizontal hooks, shovel hooks, uppercuts, and hammer-fist strikes.

(3) Grappling range. The third and closest range of unarmed combat is the grappling range. At this distance, you are too close to your adversary to kick or execute most hand strikes, so you would use close-quarter tools and techniques to neutralize your assailant. As we learned in Chapter 1, the grappling range is divided into two planes: (1) vertical—you and your assailant are standing and (2) horizontal—you are ground fighting with your assailant. Grappling range tools and techniques include head butts; biting, tearing, clawing, crushing, and gouging tactics; foot stomps; horizontal, vertical, and diagonal elbow strikes; vertical and diagonal knee strikes; chokes; strangles; joint locks; holds; reversals; and escapes.

313. BE EVASIVE.

Evasiveness is the ability to avoid threat or danger. There are generally two types of evasion—contact evasion and confrontation evasion. Contact evasion is when you physically move or manipulate your body targets to avoid being struck (i.e., slipping your head to the side or sidestepping away from a charging assailant). The key to a successful contact evasion is proper timing: you should always wait until the very last moment. Move too soon and your assailant will track you. Move too late and he will maul you. Confrontation evasion is when you strategically manipulate the distance or environment to avoid a possible confrontation with an assailant (i.e., crossing the street long before a shoulder-to-shoulder encounter with a pack of street punks moving up the sidewalk). Effective confrontation evasion requires keen situational awareness skills.

312. BE INSTINCTIVE ABOUT STANCE SELECTION.

Stance selection is the ability to select a stance appropriate for a particular combat situation instinctively. Effective stance selection requires you to understand and master the following stances and postures: (1) natural stance—a strategic stance one assumes when approached by a suspicious person who appears nonthreatening, (2) fighting stance—a strategic posture one assumes when face-to-face with an unarmed assailant, (3) knife defense stance—a strategic stance one assumes when confronted by an edged weapon attacker, (4) knife fighting stance—a strategic stance one assumes when armed with a knife or edged weapon, (5) de-escalation stance (kicking, punching, and grappling ranges)—a strategic and nonaggressive stance one assumes when de-escalating a hostile individual, (6) standing firearms stance—a strategic stance one assumes when standing with a handgun, (7) kneeling firearms stance—a strategic stance one assumes when kneeling down with a handgun, and (8) prone firearms stance—a strategic stance one assumes when lying down with a handgun.

313. BE QUICK IN YOUR OFFENSIVE REACTION TIME.

Offensive reaction time is the elapsed time between your target selection and target impaction. In both armed and unarmed combat, your objective is to always try to reduce the elapsed time.

314. BE ACCURATE IN YOUR TIMING.

Timing is your ability to execute a technique or movement at the optimum moment to achieve the most desirable effect. Accurate timing is enhanced through (1) accurate and rapid assessment skills, (2) accurate and proper distancing from your selected target, (3) accurate and rapid mental speed, and (4) psychomotor speed and overall proficiency.

315. BE ABLE TO RECOGNIZE TARGETS.

Target recognition is the ability to recognize specific anatomical targets immediately during a self-defense situation. This will vary depending on the type of weapon or tool you would use in a self-defense situation. The following are just a few examples.

(1) Natural body weapon targets. When you are going to strike your assailant with your natural body weapons, targets include the eyes, temple, nose, chin, back of neck, front of neck, solar plexus, ribs, groin, thighs, knees, shins, and, in some cases, the fingers.

(2) Submission hold targets. When you are employing submission holds on your assailant, some targets include the neck and throat, elbow joint, shoulder joint, waistline, wrists, legs, ankles, and fingers.

(3) Edged-weapon targets. When you are utilizing a knife or edged weapon in a self-defense situation, some targets will include the ear cavities, eye sockets, temples, base of skull, cervical vertebrae, jugular vein, underside of the chin, carotid artery, subclavian artery, heart, lungs, wrists, back of knees, Achilles tendons, brachial arteries, radial arteries, third and fourth rib regions, solar plexus, groin, and femoral arteries.

(4) Bludgeon targets. When utilizing a bludgeon in a self-defense situation, some of your targets will include the head, throat, back of neck, clavicle, lower back, elbows, hands and forearms, ribs, thighs, and knees.

(5) Ballistic targets. When you are utilizing a firearm in a self-defense situation, some of your targets will include the head, torso (center of mass), pelvic region, and, in some cases, the thighs.

(6) Makeshift weapon targets. When utilizing a makeshift weapon in a self-defense situation, some targets will include a) striking weapons—head, throat, back of neck, clavicle, lower back, elbows, hands and forearms, ribs, thighs, and knees; b) distracting weapons—face and eyes, groin, and legs; c) cutting weapons—ear cavities, eye sockets, temples, base of skull, cervical vertebrae, jugular vein, underside of the chin, carotid artery, subclavian artery, heart, lungs, wrists, back of knees, Achilles tendons, brachial arteries, radial arteries, third and fourth rib regions, solar plexus, groin, and femoral arteries.

(7) Chemical irritant targets. When utilizing chemical irritants (OC) in a self-defense situation, targets will include the mucus membranes (i.e., eyes, nose, and mouth).

316. BE RELAXED WHEN FIGHTING.

You must be able to relax your body during a threatening situation. Your body must be free of muscular tension from the psychological pressure of combat. There are four effective ways to reduce nervous tension and enhance physical relaxation during a fight.

(1) Preparation. Be prepared to handle numerous combat situations by possessing the three components of combative preparation: a) cognitive preparedness—you're mentally and psychologically prepared for the horrors of combat, b) psychomotor preparedness—you're physically prepared for the rigors of combat, and c) affective preparedness—you're emotionally and spiritually prepared for the demands and strains of combat.

(2) Proper breathing. Control and pace your breathing during the threatening encounter.

(3) Fight-or-flight response. Control your fight-or-flight response by unleashing your killer instinct at the proper time.

(4) Proper attitude. Always maintain a positive attitude during a threatening situation.

(5) Kinesthetic perception. Kinesthetic perception is important because it allows you to effectively regulate or monitor the muscular tension in your body.

317. BE UNIFORM IN COMBAT.
One of the most important and often neglected attributes of combat is uniformity, meaning that you properly perform a specific task or action the same way every time. Uniformity is important in some of the following aspects of combat: (1) weapon uniformity—you grip or draw your hand-held weapon the same way every time (the grip or draw will depend largely on the weapon of choice), (2) natural body weapon uniformity—you deliver your natural body weapons the same way every time, (3) stance uniformity—the different stances are employed the same way every time, (4) technique uniformity—your technique or maneuvers are performed the same way every time, and (5) attribute uniformity—your attributes (i.e., speed, power, accuracy, balance, etc.) are consistent.

318. BE SKILLED IN ESCAPE TECHNIQUES.
You must possess the skill and ability to escape from a variety of grabs, chokes, locks, and holds. Here are a few that you need to be aware of: (1) single-hand wrist grab (both cross grab and mirror image grab), (2) two-hand wrist grab (with hands held both high and low), (3) one-hand shoulder grab (mirror image and cross grab), (4) single- and two-hand throat choke (both from the front and rear), (4) single-arm throat choke (both right and left sides), (5) front and rear bear hugs (arms both free and pinned to your sides), and (6) finger poke (both right and left arms). ***REMEMBER: Escaping from various chokes and holds requires intuitive reaction. It must be second nature the instant you feel contact.***

319. BE POWERFUL.
There are numerous forms of power necessary for combat, including (1) impact power—delivered with natural body weapons, bludgeons, and some makeshift weapons; (2) crushing and squeezing power—strength or force exerted primarily in the grappling planes of unarmed combat; (3) muscular power—the state or quality of being physically strong; (4) stopping power—a firearm's ability to stop the assailant from continuing any further action; (5) leadership power—the ability or official capacity to exercise command or great influence over others; and (6) combat power—the ability or capacity to perform or act effectively in combat.

320. BE DECEPTIVE.
A clever tactician is a deceptive tactician. Deceptiveness is an important attribute for combat. Make your techniques as deceptive as your thoughts. Your objective is to delude your assailant into an error in judgment. Deception can be subtle or simply inflammatory. It depends on the self-defense situation.

321. BE SKILLED IN KINESICS.
You must master the science of body language. This means that you must understand the behavioral pattern of nonverbal communication. Nonverbal communication includes your stance and posture, walk, carriage, eye and mouth movements, and arm, hand, and leg movements.

322. BE AWARE OF NOMENCLATURE.
You should be able to understand names that fall into the various classifications of combat systems, including (1) natural body weapon nomenclature—the names of various natural body weapons, (2) submission hold nomenclature—the names of various submission hold techniques, (3) edged-weapon nomenclature—the names of component parts of a knife or edged weapon, (4) bludgeon nomenclature—the names of component parts of a stick or bludgeon, (4) firearm nomenclature—the names of component parts of a firearm (long and short guns), (5) ammunition nomenclature—the names of component parts of a firearm cartridge, (6) makeshift weapon nomenclature—the names of component parts of various makeshift weapons, and (7) chemical irritant nomenclature—the names of component parts of a chemical irritant (OC) canister.

323. BE FRACTALLY COGNIZANT.
Fractal cognizance is an important combat attribute reserved only for the most advanced fighter. Fractal cognizance is the awareness and strategic utilization of subcombat ranges (armed and unarmed). This combative attribute is important for the following reasons: (1) it bridges the gap between the ranges of armed and unarmed combat, (2) it maximizes the effectiveness of a compound attack by maintaining the offensive flow, and (3) it introduces a completely new dimension to combat.

324. BE ANATOMICALLY AWARE.
The serious fighter must be knowledgeable of

ATTRIBUTES OF COMBATANTS

the various weaknesses of the human anatomy. This is important for (1) target orientation—you must know what the vulnerable anatomical targets on the assailant's body are in order to become a more efficient fighter and (2) target protection—you must understand the vulnerable targets on your body that must be protected from the assailant.

325. BE COMPOSED.

If you lose your mental composure in a self-defense situation, you probably won't survive. Composure is defined as a quiet and focused mindset that enables you to acquire your combat agenda. Mental composure can only be acquired by controlling your fear and anxiety.

326. BE IN CONTROL OF YOUR FEAR.

Fear is a strong, unpleasant emotional reaction to a real or perceived threat. If uncontrolled, fear quickly leads to panic, and then it's too late to protect yourself effectively. Here are a few suggestions to help you control the deleterious effects of fear: (1) learn effective combat skills and tactics, (2) be confident and competent with your combat skills, (3) regularly practice crisis rehearsal (visualization) scenarios, (4) understand and accept the physiological responses of the fight-or-flight syndrome, (5) learn to tap into and control your killer instinct, (6) listen to and trust your instincts, (7) stay in good physical shape, (8) always maintain a positive and analytical attitude in combat, (9) maintain a high degree of awareness (criminal-, situational-, and self-awareness), and (10) evaluate your past reactions to dangerous or threatening situations.

327. BE SKILLED IN TARGET SELECTION.

Target selection is the cognitive process of selecting the appropriate anatomical target to attack. Selecting the appropriate target is predicated on three important factors: (1) proximity—how far the assailant is from your tool, technique, or weapon; (2) positioning—exactly where the assailant is positioned and at what angle and height; and (3) use of force—the amount of force (nondeadly or deadly) that is legally warranted for the particular situation.

328. BE ADROIT.

This means have finesse, which is usually the by-product of the complete harmonious interplay of combative attributes. It is the ability to execute a movement or a series of movements skillfully and with grace and refinement. This attribute is especially important when applying submission holds in the grappling range of unarmed combat.

329. BE KINESTHETICALLY PERCEPTIVE.

Kinesthetic perception is the ability to feel one's body accurately during the execution of a particular movement. This movement can be a punch, kick, block, or slash of the knife. Kinesthetic perception is important for both armed and unarmed combat for the following reasons: (1) it allows you to effectively regulate or monitor the tension in your body, (2) it enhances speed and minimizes telegraphic movements in combat, (3) it bridges a strong mind and body link for the practitioner, and (4) it informs you of psychomotor disturbances (i.e., balance disruption, equilibrium breakdown, and skeletal misalignment).

330. BE ACCURATE.

Accuracy is the ability to execute a movement with precision and exactness in combat. There are different forms of combat accuracy. Here are a few examples: (1) striking accuracy—the ability to strike your assailant with precision and exactness (this includes natural body weapons, bludgeons, and some makeshift weapons), (2) cutting accuracy—the ability to cut your assailant with precision and exactness, (3) shooting accuracy—the ability to shoot your assailant with precision and exactness, and (4) manipulation accuracy—the ability to manipulate your assailant's limbs and joints with precision and exactness.

331. BE UNIFIED MENTALLY.

A unified mind is one that is free and clear of distractions and fully focused on the combat at hand. Distractions can be internal, when the fighter's mind either wanders off or panics prior to or during combat, or external, when an outside source distracts the fighter (e.g., the assailant "psyches you out" or such environmental conditions as poor weather, lighting, terrain, or noise exist). ***NOTE: Always remember that in combat, a clouded mind sees nothing.***

332. BE SKILLED AT TRAVERSING.

Traversing skills are essential attributes in both armed and unarmed combat. Traversing is

particularly important when under limited environmental conditions or when confronted with multiple assailants who try to outflank you. Traversing skills can be employed when unarmed and fighting multiple assailants or when bludgeon fighting and knife fighting. Also keep in mind that when you are engaged in a gunfight, you can employ traversing skills while standing or kneeling.
REMEMBER: The two primary components of effective traversing (while standing) are to keep your knees bent and flexible while twisting freely at your waist to either your right or left side.

333. BE SKILLED AT RANGE MANIPULATION.

Range manipulation is the ability to strategically manipulate the ranges of combat (both armed and unarmed). The following are the two forms of range manipulation that you must master: (1) offensive range manipulation (ORM)—the skillful and strategic exploitation of the ranges of combat for offensive purposes and (2) defensive range manipulation (DRM)—the strategic manipulation of ranges for defensive purposes. Effective range manipulation requires keen awareness skills accompanied by superb timing.

334. BE EXPLOITATIVE OF TARGETS.

Once you have acquired awareness of reaction dynamics, you can implement target exploitation. Target exploitation is a combative attribute that allows you to strategically maximize your assailant's reaction dynamics during the fight. Target exploitation skills can be applied in both armed and unarmed encounters.

335. BE SKILLED AT TROUBLESHOOTING.

Sometimes things don't work out as planned. No matter how much you prepare and train, there is always the possibility that there will be a problem or setback in combat. And a prepared fighter is one who anticipates such problems and is equipped to handle them.

Troubleshooting skills can be defined as your ability to diagnose and solve problems immediately when engaged with your assailant. They can be used in the following situations: (1) ground fighting—when a particular submission hold is not working effectively; (2) combat shooting—when you cannot hit your target effectively or when faced with firearm malfunctions; (3) striking techniques—when a particular strike (natural body weapon or bludgeon) is not neutralizing your assailant.

336. BE TERRAIN-ORIENTED.

The terrain you're fighting on is a critical environmental factor. Every good fighter should know the strategic implications of the terrain he is standing on. One of the best ways to prepare yourself is through terrain orientation. This means developing a working knowledge of the various types of environmental terrains and their advantages, dangers, and strategic limitations.

Terrains fall into one of the following two categories: (1) stable terrain—principally characterized as stationary, compact, dense, hard, flat, dry, or solid ground; and (2) unstable terrain—principally characterized as mobile, uneven, flexible, slippery, wet, or rocky ground. You must be particularly familiar with unstable terrains, including ice, snow, wet grass, wet concrete, wet leaves, wet metal, wet wood, sand, gravel, mulch, muddy areas, rocky areas, and escalators.

337. BE STRONG AND HAVE STAMINA.

Muscular strength and endurance are important attributes of both armed and unarmed combat. The most effective method of developing your muscular strength is by systematically and progressively overloading your muscles through weight training. Muscular strength and endurance are important for combat for the following reasons: (1) they will enhance the power of your natural body weapon strikes and bludgeon strikes, (2) they will give you a clear advantage in a ground fighting situation, (3) they improve your overall fighting performance by synergizing with your combative attributes, and (4) they function aesthetically as a deterrent to a potential attacker.

338. BE TACTILELY VISUAL.

Tactile sight is the ability to "see" through physical contact with your assailant, and it is used predominantly in close-quarter confrontations (i.e., ground fighting with your assailant).

339. BE RANGE SPECIALIZED.

Although range proficiency is a critical component of combat, it is also important to specialize in a particular range of unarmed combat. This is known as range specialization. Range

ATTRIBUTES OF COMBATANTS

specialization is important for the following reasons: (1) it gives you a combat advantage over your adversary, and (2) it provides a combat "comfort zone." NOTE: For unarmed combat, specialize in the punching range.

340. BE MOBILE.

Never remain still in a fight. Always keep mobile. Mobility is the ability to move your body quickly and freely while maintaining your balance. There are several strategic reasons for mobility, including the following: (1) your entire body becomes an elusive target, (2) your offensive movements are less telegraphic, (3) you overcome inertia, (4) you enhance the striking power of your blows, (5) you keep the pressure on during a compound attack, and (6) you throw your assailant's timing off.

341. BE CONSISTENT WITH FOLLOW-THROUGH.

Follow-through is an important attribute for both armed and unarmed combat. It's important because it maximizes the effectiveness of your weapons.

In unarmed combat, there are different forms of follow-through, as follows: (1) impact follow-through—when striking the assailant (with a natural body weapon), always drive your blows approximately three inches through your selected target and (2) submission follow-through—when applying a submission hold, you follow through the complete range of motion to maximize the damage to the selected target.

There are different forms of follow-through in armed combat as well, including the following: (1) bludgeon follow-through—when striking your assailant with a bludgeon or makeshift weapon, you allow the weapon to follow through and penetrate its target; (2) edged weapon follow-through—when slashing or stabbing with a knife or edged weapon, you allow the blade to penetrate the assailant; and (3) firearm follow-through—when firing a firearm, you continue to apply all the proper shooting fundamentals throughout the execution of the shot.

CHAPTER FOUR

Tactics and Strategy

"In street fighting, strategic preparedness can make the difference between life and death."

GENERAL TACTICS

342. BE AWARE AT ALL TIMES.
When walking the streets, get into the habit of constantly scanning your environment, thoroughly and quickly noting potential problems.

343. MAINTAIN DIRECT EYE CONTACT WITH PEOPLE.
When conversing with friends, always maintain direct eye contact. Eye contact in noncombative situations shows confidence, internal strength, and, most important, respect for the other person.

344. CROSS THE STREET.
If you think you are being followed when walking down a street, cross the street at a 90-degree angle immediately and observe the behavior of everyone around you. Remember, you can be surveyed or trailed from directions other than behind you.

345. TURN WIDE CORNERS.
When walking on the streets, always turn wide corners. Do not go around corners within five feet of a wall, building, or shrubbery. This tactic will enhance your defensive reaction time if you are ambushed.

346. PREPARE YOURSELF FOR A KIDNAPPING.
If you are kidnapped or taken hostage, remain as calm as possible. Don't argue, question, or lecture your captors. Prepare yourself for possible verbal and physical abuse, as well as lack of food, water, and sanitation. Wait for a solid opportunity to escape and take it. Don't hesitate, but don't attempt escape prematurely.

347. KNOW HOW TO HANDLE A TROUBLEMAKER.
The next time a troublemaker asks you a question you really don't want to answer, look sharply into his eyes and ask, "Why do you want to know?"

348. LOOK STRONG AND CONFIDENT.
Street punks and chronic brawlers are expert observers of human behavior. When walking in public places, always keep your head up and walk with confidence and purpose. Also, avoid looking lost, fatigued, uncertain, or preoccupied.

349. BE LEERY OF SPECTATORS.
During a fight, always be cognizant and suspicious of all spectators. Onlooker intervention is a common occurrence during a street fight. Ironically enough, Americans are inveterate supporters of the underdog. They hate to see anyone lose a fight. ***REMEMBER: Never trust anyone in a fight.***

350. SHORTCUTS ARE DANGEROUS.
Be especially careful when taking shortcuts. This includes alleys, parking lots, tunnels, construction sites, or abandoned buildings.

351. USE WINDOWS TO YOUR ADVANTAGE.
When walking the streets, use store windows or any other reflective sources to identify whether you are being followed by someone.

Always have at least one hand free at all times. Do not make this tactical mistake.

352. KEEP AT LEAST ONE HAND UNOCCUPIED.

When walking the streets, always have at least one hand free and unoccupied.

353. AVOID CERTAIN ACTIONS.

If you want to increase your safety in the streets, then avoid the following: (1) counting your money in public; (2) openly displaying jewelry; (3) sleeping on public transportation; (4) having contact with strangers on the street; (5) getting into staring contests on the street; (6) losing your temper; (7) picking up hitchhikers; (8) laughing at strangers; (9) daydreaming in public; (10) using boxing techniques in a street fight—you will lose; (11) asking strangers for directions; (12) leaving your valuables in your car; (13) tailgating other motorists; (14) getting into shoving matches with an assailant; (15) fighting over a woman—it's not worth it; (16) overeating when dining out—eat light and you'll move more quickly if a fight occurs; (17) threatening anyone—if something needs to be done, just do it; and, finally, (18) getting drunk—you'll make a fool out of yourself, and you won't be able to protect yourself effectively.

354. BE APPROPRIATELY ARMED IN THE WILDERNESS.

When camping or hiking in the woods, always carry a sharp hunting knife with you. Rather than providing refuge from the violence of the city streets, backcountry areas, by virtue of their being so remote, can leave you particularly vulnerable to assault if you're unprepared for potential trouble.

355. AVOID AMBUSH ZONES.

Ambush zones are strategic locations (in everyday environments) from which an assailant can launch a surprise attack. Ambush zones can be found and exploited in both unfamiliar and familiar environments, even in your home, and in both unpopulated and populated areas. An ambush zone can be set in a dark or poorly lit area as well as in a well-lit location. Ambush zones can be established in a variety of common places, such as under, behind, or around trees, utility boxes, and shrubs, beds, corners, Dumpsters, doorways, walls, tables, automobiles, trash cans, rooftops, bridges, ramps, and mailboxes. Now is the time to familiarize yourself with these various types of ambush zones and avoid them whenever possible.

356. AVOID CROWDS OR LARGE EVENTS.

Avoid crowds, especially during political demonstrations, sporting events, and strikes. If panic breaks out, you could find yourself in a riot situation and possibly be trampled in the crowd.

Ambush zones are everywhere.

TACTICS AND STRATEGY

357. MOVE CAUTIOUSLY IN DARK ENVIRONMENTS.

When fighting in dark or poorly lit environments, move cautiously. A twisted ankle or a broken leg will take you out of the fight.

358. PARK STRATEGICALLY.

Park your vehicle next to the end curb in a parking lot. It will have half the chance of getting scratched, and this fact will reduce the possibility of a fight.

359. DON'T RETALIATE.

If another motorist drives aggressively, cuts you off, tails you too closely, gives you a gesture of contempt, or screams at you, don't retaliate. It's just not worth the risk.

360. CHECK YOUR MIRRORS.

When driving in your car, check your side and rearview mirrors to see if you are being followed. If you are unsure, take a diversionary route to make sure you're not.

361. DON'T GET TOO CLOSE TO THE CAR IN FRONT OF YOU.

When stopped in traffic, stay far enough behind the car in front of you to safely pull around it and drive away. This extra distance will permit you to escape quickly if it becomes necessary.

362. KEEP YOUR CAR IN GEAR.

When approaching intersections or stoplights, always keep your car in gear and be prepared to drive away immediately.

363. DUCK AND FLOOR IT.

If an assailant is shooting at you while you're driving your car, duck down low, sound the horn, and floor it.

364. ACQUIRE BARROOM ETIQUETTE.

Apply these strategies when visiting a bar, saloon, or nightclub: (1) be aware—be aware of your environment, especially makeshift weapons (glasses, bottles, and dining implements); (2) stand up—when trouble approaches the bar, get out of your seat immediately, because it is very difficult to defend yourself when seated in a chair or on a barstool; (3) expect no space—you will have to employ close-quarter tools and techniques in a bar fight; (4) expect obstacles—people, barstools, pool tables, etc., will get in your way when fighting; (5) appear strong—always look strong, calm, and confident when you enter a drinking establishment; (6) position yourself strategically—try to keep your back to the bar; (7) assess your environment—take a minute and look around at various possible escape routes; (8) limit your conversation—avoid letting someone lure you into a conversation about a heated subject; (9) keep your hands free—try to keep your hands unoccupied as much as possible; (10) hit hard—since alcohol has a tendency to increase your assailant's pain threshold, strike him harder and longer than usual.

365. BEFRIEND THE BOUNCERS.

If you frequent a particular bar or night spot, always befriend the bouncers and know each of them by name.

366. KNOW YOUR WAY OUT.

Whenever you enter a bar, always have an emergency escape route in mind in case you need to exit immediately.

367. LEAVE IMMEDIATELY.

If a brawl breaks out in a bar or any other drinking establishment, leave immediately. The entertainment value of a fight is not worth its potential danger.

368. BE CAUTIOUS IN HIGH-RISK SETTINGS.

Be exceptionally alert and cautious in the following environments: (1) 24-hour convenience stores, (2) liquor stores, (3) bars, saloons, and night clubs, (3) motorist rest stops, (4) ATMs, (5) banks, (6) public rest rooms, and (7) parking garages.

369. DON'T CALL ATTENTION TO YOURSELF.

When visiting recreational facilities (beaches, parks, movie theaters, bars, etc.), avoid calling attention to yourself with loud or boisterous behavior.

370. ALWAYS EMPLOY THE FOLLOWING.

Here are a few tips and suggestions that you should follow: (1) always keep a low profile when entering a bar or nightclub; (2) always expect the unexpected in a bar fight; (3) always be leery of an assailant who offers peace too soon in a conflict; (4) when sitting in a movie theater, always position yourself close to an exit or in an aisle seat to allow a quick avenue of escape; and (5) always try to keep your back to the wall when sitting in a bar or restaurant.

CLOTHING AND GROOMING

371. WEAR COMFORTABLE CLOTHING.

Avoid wearing restrictive clothing in public places. For example, tight pants restrict kicking techniques and the ability to run from danger, dress ties can be used to strangle, manipulate, or throw you off balance, and bulky winter coats can inhibit striking and grappling techniques. Light running shoes offer poor ankle support during lateral or otherwise evasive footwork. Earrings can be torn from the earlobes during a ground fight. Always try to wear clothes and shoes that facilitate quick and free movement. Leather jackets are good protection to the arms and extremities during a knife fight. Heavy athletic shoes (i.e., cross-trainers, court shoes) can enhance your footwork and kicking techniques.

372. KEEP YOUR HAIR SHORT.

Try to keep your hair short, especially at the back of your head. Long hair or trendy ponytails can be dangerous and risky for the following reasons: (1) vision—they can temporarily impair your vision during the course of a compound attack or during a ground fight, (2) manipulation—in a ground fight your assailant can pull your hair and manipulate your balance as well as easily control you and throw you by the hair, and (3) immobilization—your assailant can immobilize you by grabbing your hair.

ASSESSMENT

373. ASSESSMENT IS CRITICAL.

Tactical assessment is the process of rapidly gathering and analyzing information and then accurately evaluating it in terms of threat and danger. In general, you can assess people, places, actions, and objects.

Accurate assessment of a self-defense situation is critical for the following reasons: (1) it enhances your overall safety; (2) it helps in determining the appropriate level of force; (3) it helps in choosing the appropriate tactical option (i.e., comply, escape, de-escalate, assert, or fight back); and (4) it will help you to defend yourself if you have to go to court. Accurate assessment skills help promote a "reasonable force" response.

374. CHOOSE THE APPROPRIATE FORCE RESPONSE.

Properly assessing a threatening situation will also allow you to select the appropriate level of force for a self-defense situation. Following are the different levels of force that you must be able to choose and execute correctly.

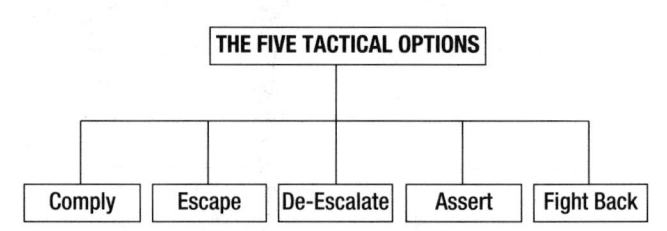

```
                THE FIVE TACTICAL OPTIONS
    ┌───────────┬──────────┬────────────┬──────────┬────────────┐
  Comply      Escape    De-Escalate   Assert     Fight Back
```

The five tactical options to any self-defense situation.

(1) Presence response—the first level of interaction with your assailant. At this level, your presence is known (i.e., you are standing in front of your adversary).

(2) Verbal response—the second level of interaction with your assailant. At this level, you verbally communicate with your assailant (e.g., de-escalation scenario or assertion scenario).

(3) Restraint response—the third level of interaction with your assailant. At this level, you physically control or restrain your adversary by either utilizing chemical irritants or a variety of submission holds.

(4) Impact response—the fourth level of interaction with your assailant. At this level, you physically strike your assailant to incapacitate him temporarily (i.e., with natural body weapons, bludgeons, or makeshift weapons).

(5) Deadly force response—the fifth and final level of interaction with your assailant. At this level, you employ deadly weapons (e.g., firearms, edged weapons, makeshift weapons, and, in some cases, natural body weapons) to stop your assailant's threat of death or great bodily harm.

TACTICS AND STRATEGY

375. CHOOSE THE APPROPRIATE TACTICAL OPTION.

Accurate assessment skills will also permit you to choose the appropriate tactical option. There are five tactical options to any self-defense situation. They are listed here in order of increasing level of resistance: (1) comply—to obey the assailant's commands, (2) escape—to safely and rapidly flee from the threat or danger, (3) de-escalate—to defuse the situation strategically, (4) assert—to stand up for your rights verbally, and (5) fight back—to use various physical and psychological tactics and techniques to stun, incapacitate, cripple, or kill your attacker.

376. ASSESS THE ENVIRONMENT.

A fight can occur anywhere. In any combative situation you must quickly evaluate the strategic implications of your environment. It can be a bar, street, alley, bedroom, movie theater, airport, grocery store, gas station, elevator, your office, inside your car, or on the beach. There are six essential factors to consider when assessing your environment. They are as follows: escape routes, barriers, makeshift weapons, terrain, positions of cover, and positions of concealment.

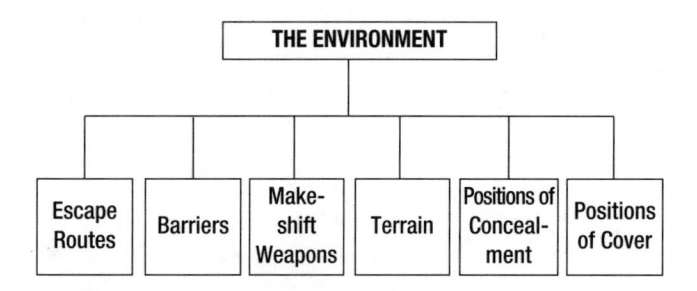

```
                    THE ENVIRONMENT
    ┌─────────┬─────────┬─────────┬─────────┬─────────┐
  Escape    Barriers   Make-    Terrain  Positions of  Positions
  Routes              shift              Conceal-     of Cover
                      Weapons            ment
```

The positions of concealment.

(1) Escape routes. These are the various avenues or exits that allow you to flee from the threatening situation safely. Examples of escape routes are windows, fire escapes, doors, gates, escalators, fences, walls, bridges, and staircases. ***WARNING: Be careful that your version of a safe escape route doesn't lead you into a worse situation.***

(2) Barriers. A barrier is any object that obstructs the assailant's path of attack. At the very least, barriers give you some distance and some time, and they may give you some safety—at least temporarily. A barrier, however, must have the structural integrity to perform the particular function that you have assigned it. Barriers are everywhere and include such things as large desks, doors, automobiles, Dumpsters, large trees, fences, walls, heavy machinery, and large vending machines. ***CAUTION: Barriers should not be confused with positions of cover or concealment.***

(3) Makeshift weapons. These are common, everyday objects that can be converted into offensive and defensive weapons. Like a barrier, a makeshift weapon must be appropriate to the function you have assigned to it. You won't be able to knock your assailant out with a car antenna, but you could whip it across his eyes and temporarily blind him. Although you could knock your assailant unconscious with a good, heavy flashlight, you could not use it to shield yourself from a knife attack. Makeshift weapons can be broken down into the following four types: a) striking, b) distracting, c) shielding, and d) cutting.

(4) Terrain. This is a critical environmental factor. What are the strategic implications of the terrain you are standing on? Will the surface interfere with your ability to fight your adversary?

(5) Positions of cover. A position of cover is any object or location that temporarily protects you from the assailant's gunfire. Some examples include large concrete utility poles, large rocks, thick trees, an engine block, the corner of a building, concrete steps, and so on. Positions of cover are important not only because they protect you from gunfire but because they buy you some time and allow you to assess the situation from a position of safety. When choosing a position of cover, avoid selecting the

following objects because bullets can penetrate them: a) internal doors, b) small trees, c) car doors, d) all glass windows, e) drywall, f) tall grass, g) the trunk of a car, h) overturned tables, i) trash cans, j) shrubbery, and k) fences.

(6) Positions of concealment. These are various locations or objects that allow you to hide from your adversary temporarily. Positions of concealment are most commonly used to evade engagement with your assailant, and they permit you to attack with the element of surprise. Positions of concealment include trees, shrubbery, doors, dark areas, walls, stairwells, cars, and other large and tall objects. ***WARNING: Don't forget that positions of concealment do not protect you from an assailant's gunfire.***

377. ASSESS THE INDIVIDUAL.

In a potentially dangerous situation, you must assess the source of danger. Who is posing the possible threat? Is it someone you know, or is he a complete stranger? Is it one guy or two or more? What are his intentions in confronting you? Pay very close attention to all available clues, especially nonverbal indicators. Your answers to these important questions will shape your overall tactical response. Let all of your five senses go to work to extract the necessary information. And don't forget to listen to what your instincts are telling you about the threatening person. The following are five essential factors to consider when assessing a threatening individual: demeanor, intent, range, positioning, and weapon capability.

THE INDIVIDUAL

Demeanor | Intent | Range | Positioning | Weapon Capability

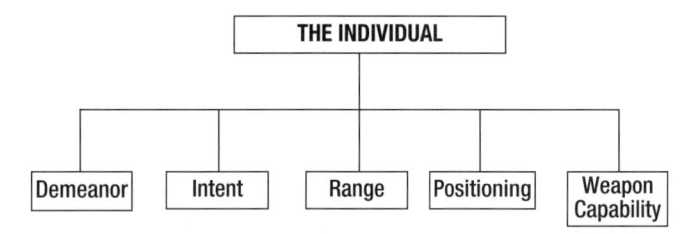

Factors to consider when assessing an individual.

(1) Demeanor. If time permits, assess the assailant's outward behavior. Be on the lookout for both verbal and nonverbal clues. For example, is he shaking or is he calm and collected? Are his shoulders hunched or relaxed? Are his hands clenched? Is his neck taut? Is he clenching his teeth? Is he breathing hard? Does he seem angry, frustrated, or confused? Does he seem high on drugs? Is he mentally ill or simply intoxicated? What is he saying? How is he saying it? Is he making sense? Is his speech slurred? What is his tone of voice? Is he talking rapidly or methodically? Is he cursing and angry? All of these verbal and nonverbal cues are essential in accurately assessing the assailant's overall demeanor and adjusting your tactical response accordingly.

(2) Intent. Once you have assessed the assailant's demeanor, you'll be better equipped to assess his intent. In other words, why is this person confronting you? Does he intend to rob or kill you? Is he trying to harass you? Is he seeking vengeance for something you have done? Or is he a troublemaker looking to pick a fight with you? The assailant's intent is perhaps the most important assessment factor, but it also can be the most difficult to determine. Furthermore, in the world of self-defense, things can change very quickly. For example, an intent to rob can quickly turn into an intent to murder. In any event, the appropriate tactical response is highly dependent upon a correct assessment of your assailant's intent.

(3) Range. Range is simply the spatial relationship between you and your assailant in terms of distance. In unarmed combat, for example, there are three possible ranges from which your adversary can launch his attack—kicking, punching, and grappling ranges. When assessing your assailant, you'll need to recognize the strategic implications and advantages of his range immediately. For example, is he close enough to land a punch effectively? Is he

TACTICS AND STRATEGY

at a distance from which he could kick you? Is he in a range that would allow him to grab hold of you and take you down to the ground? Is he within range to slash you with a knife or strike you with a bludgeon? Is the assailant moving closer to you? If so, how quickly? Does the assailant continue to move forward when you step back?

(4) Positioning. Positioning is the spatial relationship between you and the assailant in terms of threat, tactical escape, and target selection. In combat, it's important to understand the strategic implications of the assailant's positioning prior to and during the fight. For example, is the assailant standing squarely or sideways? Is he mounted on top of you in a ground fight? Or is he inside your leg guard? What anatomical targets does the assailant present you with? Is he blocking a door or any other escape route? Is his back to a light source? Is he close to your only possible makeshift weapon? Are multiple assailants closing in on you? Is your assailant firing his gun from a position of cover or concealment? You must answer these questions before choosing a tactical strategy appropriate to the situation.

(5) Weapon capability. Always try to determine whether your assailant is armed or unarmed. If he is carrying a weapon, what type is it? Does he have an effective delivery method for the particular weapon? Is he armed with more than one weapon? If so, what are they and where are they? There are four general points of concern when assessing the assailant's weapon capability, including hands/fingers, general behavior, clothing, and location.

(a) Hands/fingers. When strategically scanning your assailant for weapons, quickly glance at his hands and all his fingertips. Can you see them? Is one hand behind

How would you rate this assailant's weapon capability?

him or in his pocket? If you cannot see his fingers, he could be palming a knife or some other edged weapon. Be extremely cautious when the assailant's arms are crossed in front of his body or when he keeps his hands in his pockets.

(b) General behavior. How is the assailant behaving? For example, does he pat his chest frequently (as a weapon security check)? Does he act apprehensive, nervous, or uneasy? Or does he seem to be reaching for something? Is your assailant's body language incongruous with his verbal statements.

(c) Clothing. What the assailant is wearing can also clue you in on what he may be concealing. For example, is the assailant wearing a knife sheath on his belt? Could there be a knife concealed in one of his boots? At other times you may have to be a bit more analytical. For example, is your assailant wearing a jacket when it is too hot for one? Could it be to conceal a gun at his waist or shoulder?

(d) Location. Does the assailant seem suspiciously rooted to a particular spot? Or is he running back to his car, possibly to get his gun? Is he close enough to grab that beer bottle on top of the bar? How far is the assailant from a makeshift weapon?

378. REMEMBER WHAT YOUR ASSAILANT LOOKS LIKE.

Accurate assessment skills will allow you to describe your assailant to the authorities. If you do decide to report a criminal assault, notify the police while your recollections are still fresh. Jotting down a few notes immediately after the altercation is also a good idea.

When filing your report with the authorities, try to include the following: (1) number of assailants, (2) sex of assailant(s), (3) somatotype, (4) approximate height and weight, (5) hair color/style, (6) deformations, (7) speech/accent, (8) race/ethnicity, (9) descriptions of eyes/nose/mouth/teeth, (10) facial hair, (11) type of clothing worn, (12) type of weapon used, (13) tattoos, (14) automobile model/color, (15) jewelry, and (16) whether he was right- or left-handed.

379. KNOW WHEN NOT TO ASSESS.

Although assessment skills are a vital component of self-defense, there are times when you must forget about assessment. For example, a street punk lunges from behind a car, grabs you, and throws you to the ground. It's obviously too late for assessment skills. In such a situation, you must act intuitively and immediately to neutralize him, or you're going to be hurt. Time is of the essence, and your instinctive reaction and reflex must take the place of assessment.

DE-ESCALATION TACTICS

380. DE-ESCALATE THE SITUATION IF POSSIBLE.

De-escalation is the strategic process of defusing a potentially violent confrontation. Its goal is to eliminate the possibility of an agitated individual resorting to physical violence. Effective de-escalation is a delicate mixture of science and art, psychology and warfare. You must use both verbal and nonverbal techniques to calm the hostile person, while

In this self-defense situation, it's obviously too late for assessment skills. You must act intuitively and immediately to neutralize your attacker, or you're going to be hurt.

employing tactically deceptive physical safeguards to create the appearance that you are completely nonaggressive. You must be in total control of yourself, both physically and emotionally, in order to deal effectively with someone on the verge of losing complete control.

You should always try to de-escalate a hostile situation for the following five reasons: (1) violence can often be avoided, (2) you have a moral imperative to prevent violence, (3) de-escalation polices or controls your destructive abilities, (4) it enhances courtroom defensibility, and (5) it helps reduce the possibility of spectator intervention.

381. EMPLOY THE SEVEN DE-ESCALATION PRINCIPLES.

There are seven de-escalation principles that you need to master. Let's start with nonverbal principles. They include: (1) emotional control—the ability to remain calm when faced with a hostile person, (2) proximity—the ability to maintain a safe

TACTICS AND STRATEGY

Effective de-escalation is a delicate mixture of science and art, psychology, and warfare. Here, a student (right) attempts to de-escalate the situation.

distance from a hostile person, (3) strategic positioning—the ability to tactically position oneself to either escape, move behind a barrier, or utilize a makeshift weapon, (4) nonaggressive physiology—strategic body language used to defuse a potentially violent person, and (5) perception—the ability to accurately interpret vital information acquired from one's senses when confronted with a hostile person. Verbal principles of de-escalation include: (1) voice control—the ability to control and manipulate your voice when faced with a hostile person, and (2) selective semantics—the ability to select and utilize choice words when faced with a hostile person.

382. KNOW THE DIFFERENT STATES OF MIND.

De-escalation skills are best applied with the following states of mind: (1) egomaniac—a hostile person who simply has a big ego, (2) drunkard—a hostile person who is intoxicated and fueled with "liquid courage," (3) frustrated—a hostile person who is frustrated or irritated, (4) frightened—a hostile person who is afraid, (5) angry—a hostile person who is generally angry by nature.

383. BE SKILLED IN THE USE OF SELECTIVE SEMANTICS.

Words are powerful. In fact, great nations have gone to war over mere words. Likewise, in individual combat, a poorly chosen word can provoke an immediate attack by a hostile individual. It behooves you to employ selective semantics. For our purposes, selective semantics can be defined as the strategic manipulation of choice words to de-escalate a hostile situation effectively. Your objective is to convince a hostile person that you are willing to compromise. Avoid commands like "relax, " "calm down," "shut up," "stay back," "keep your distance," or "chill out." Such statements will likely provoke hostility and anger. Instead, get into the habit of saying, "Hey, I'm really sorry," "Please, let's talk this out," or "I can understand your anger." Also use phrases like "Pardon me," "OOPS—my fault," or "Excuse me" when someone accidentally bumps into you.

384. BE POKER-FACED.

When faced with a hostile individual, you must be capable of masking your emotions with a poker face. The poker face is a neutral and attentive facial expression that is used when de-escalating a hostile situation. It is critical because it prevents the hostile person from reading your true intentions and feelings. Most importantly, the poker face personifies control and clarity and instills emotional control.

385. BE VOCALLY CONTROLLED.

The quality of your voice is naturally linked to your demeanor and psychological state. You can easily hear anger, fatigue, and many other emotions in the emanations of the voice. This is why it is essential that you remain calm and in complete control of a potentially hostile situation, or your voice will give you away. Voice control requires you to have complete control over the four components (tone, pitch, volume, tempo) of your voice during a threatening situation.

(1) Tone is the overall quality and character of your voice. The tone of your voice projects your emotions and feelings. When confronted with a hostile person, you must remove all threatening aspects from your voice. Always maintain a tone of voice that is serious and nonthreatening.

(2) Pitch is the relative highness or lowness of your voice. We all have a natural range or average pitch for our voices. However, when we become anxious, frustrated, or excited, our pitch usually goes up. When talking to a potential adversary, try to maintain a moderate voice pitch.

(3) Volume is the amplitude, or loudness, of your voice. Loud voices are often associated with anger, hostility, and aggression, whereas soft voices could be associated with fear, apprehension, or weakness. When confronted with a threatening individual, always try to maintain a moderate voice volume. Speak loudly enough to be heard clearly under the immediate circumstances, but avoid yelling. If you're in a situation where you'd have to yell to be heard—like on a busy street or in a nightclub—you would be better off to attempt nonverbal communication techniques.

(4) Tempo is the speed or rate at which one speaks. Rapid speech usually indicates excitement, high energy, fear, nervousness, or anger. A slow tempo can be interpreted as being condescending, unsure, depressed, or ambivalent. When de-escalating a hostile person, speak at a moderate tempo to convey calmness, confidence, and control.

386. NEVER DROP YOUR HANDS TO YOUR SIDES.

When facing a hostile person and attempting to de-escalate the situation, never drop your hands to your sides; put your hands in your pockets or cross your arms. Keeping your hands down at your sides won't provide you with the necessary reaction time to defend against your assailant's attack effectively. You've got to have your hands up to protect your anatomical targets and, if necessary, to strike your assailant with your natural body weapons. Don't point your finger or clench your fists. Keep your hands open loosely, both facing the hostile person.

387. BE CONGRUENT.

Effective de-escalation can only be achieved when you harmoniously orchestrate your verbal and nonverbal skills. This is known as "congruency." Significantly neglecting any one of the de-escalation principles will result in incongruence, which can lead to disaster. For example, if you're pointing your finger in someone's face, your selective semantics really won't matter. If your body language is perfect and your voice exact, but your choice of words is poor, you won't be congruent. Remember, for effective de-escalation, your entire body, mind, voice, choice of words, and emotions must be unified into a congruent whole.

388. BE A GOOD ACTOR; APPLY DECEPTIVE HISTRIONICS.

In some self-defense situations, you may need to act or modify your behavior until you reach your desired objective. For example, you might have to play a diplomatic and concerned role when de-escalating an angry and threatening individual. Or you may have to act out compliance to achieve a strategic position over your firearm-wielding assailant before you attempt to disarm him. Mastering histrionics will allow you to act successfully in a threatening encounter. Histrionics and combat deception go together.

Deceptive acting during a potentially dangerous encounter is no simple task. Effective histrionics will require you to control both your verbal and nonverbal behavior. Your emotions, physiology, and voice tone, pitch, volume, and tempo must all be congruent to the role that you have chosen.

389. DON'T TOUCH HIM.

When de-escalating, never attempt to console a hostile person by putting a comforting hand on his shoulder or offering a peaceful handshake. This act will reduce your tactical advantage and may, contrary to your intentions, be interpreted as an invasion of the other person's space.

390. KEEP IN MIND THAT DE-ESCALATION DOESN'T ALWAYS WORK.

There is no real guarantee that de-escalation skills will work on every person. There are people who are going to attack you no matter how skillful and sincere you are in your efforts to avoid violence. Always keep in mind that when you're dealing with human behavior, anything can happen. So be alert and be prepared for the worst possible scenario.

YOUR ADVERSARY

391. DON'T DISHONOR YOUR ADVERSARY.

Never make your adversary feel cowardly in front of people he loves or respects. Do not appear dominating, threatening, abrasive, condescending, or challenging. Remember, people will go to great lengths to protect their egos.

TACTICS AND STRATEGY

392. DON'T UNDERESTIMATE YOUR ADVERSARY.
Never assume that your adversary is stupid or incompetent. Always treat him as if he is an expert in both armed and unarmed combat.

393. GIVE YOUR ADVERSARY AN AVENUE OF ESCAPE.
Always allow your assailant the opportunity to escape with his ego and pride intact. In many cases, violence is symptomatic of someone who feels powerless or backed into a corner.

394. BE AWARE WHEN YOUR ADVERSARY TURNS HIS BACK TO YOU.
He may be setting you up for a "sucker punch."

395. LET YOUR ADVERSARY BE THE FOOL.
The next time your adversary invites you outside to fight, agree with him and let him walk out first. Once he turns his back to you, knock him out. Remember, nothing is sacred in a street fight.

396. BE AWARE OF THE THREE UNPREDICTABLE Ds.
The three most unpredictable types of assailant that you will come across are as follows: (1) drunk, (2) drugged, and (3) deranged.

397. WATCH WHAT YOUR ASSAILANT IS DOING.
What your assailant is doing is much more important than what he is saying.

398. PREPARE FOR THE BEST AND THE WORST.
Always prepare for the best and the worst type of assailant. It's a big mistake to prepare yourself only for a refined fighter. There are many poor fighters out there who have a unique and unpredictable style of fighting that can cause you severe bodily injury. For example, a fighter with erratic movements can throw off the most seasoned fighter.

399. KNOW THE THREE BODY POSITIONS.
There are three general body positions that your assailant can assume when standing in front of you. They include: (1) zero-degree position—this is when his entire body is facing you, including the majority of his anatomical impact targets. (2) 45-degree position—this is when his body is bladed 45

Do you have the knowledge, skills, and attitude necessary to handle this deranged assailant?

degrees to you. He can effectively attack and defend from this position. (3) 90-degree position—this is when his body is sideways to you. His rear appendages (arm and leg) are severely limited, but he can strike effectively from his lead side.

RANGES OF COMBAT

400. KNOW WHAT YOU'RE DOING.
One of the highest levels of combative mastery requires a precise understanding of how specific striking tools relate to ranges of unarmed combat. The chart below will help you with this critical association.

KICKING RANGE	PUNCHING RANGE	GRAPPLING RANGE
Vertical Kick	Finger Jab	Head Butt
Side Kick	Palm Heel	Biting Tactics
Push Kick	Knife Hands	Thumb Gouge
Hook Kick	Lead Straight	Foot Stomp
	Rear Cross	Horizontal Elbow
	Hook	Vertical Elbow
	Uppercut	Diagonal Elbow
	Shovel Hook	Vertical Knee
	Hammerfist	Diagonal Knee
		Tearing Tactics
		Clawing
		Crushing Tactics
		Linear Blasts

401. SPECIALIZE IN PUNCHING RANGE.

Although range proficiency is a critical component of fighting, it's also important to specialize in a particular range of combat. This is known as range specialization. For all intents and purposes, you should specialize in the punching range for the following strategic reasons: (1) the assailant's defensive reaction time is reduced in the punching range; (2) unlike with the kicking range, you can efficiently neutralize your adversary in punching range; (3) punching-range tools are more efficient than those for the other ranges of unarmed combat; (4) punching-range tools are less telegraphic than kicking-range tools; (5) compared to grappling range (vertical and horizontal planes), punching range only requires moderate bodily commitment; (6) there is less of a "space requirement" necessary to deploy most of your punching-range tools; (7) terrain is not so critical a factor in the punching range; (8) since there is no bodily entanglement, multiple assailants can be fought in the punching range; (9) punching-range tools can be executed while moving, and (10) punching-range tools require moderate weight transfer and shifting and are therefore faster than kicking techniques.

402. KNOW THE PROS AND CONS OF COMBAT RANGES.

The ability to master the ranges of unarmed combat requires that you acquire a foundational understanding of each range. The following chart will give you strategic insight into the pros and cons of each range of unarmed combat.

For example, the grappling range of unarmed combat: (1) requires a very high degree of commitment to the assailant, (2) offers a reduced amount of defensive reaction time, (3) provides enhanced offensive reaction time, (4) has a very low potential for telegraphing an attack, (5) has a very high potential for neutralizing an assailant, (6) has a very high risk of danger for the practitioner, (7) requires a very high degree of energy expenditure, (8) has a very high likelihood of engagement, (9) has a very high potential for maintaining its range during the course of the fight, (10) the average layperson has a very low level of awareness and ability in this combat range, (11) it has a moderate terrain stability requirement, and (12) it has a very low preference for engagement.

RANGE CHARACTERISTICS	KICKING RANGE	PUNCHING RANGE	GRAPPLING RANGE
1. Commitment level	very low	moderate	very high
2. Defensive reaction time	enhanced	reduced	reduced
3. Offensive reaction time	reduced	enhanced	enhanced
4. Telegraphic potential	very high	moderate	very low
5. Neutralizing potential	very low	very high	very high
6. Risk of danger	low	moderate	very high
7. Energy expenditure	moderate	moderate	very high
8. Likelihood of engagement	low	high	very high
9. Maintainability	very low	moderate	very high
10. Layman awareness/ability	low	very high	very low
11. Terrain stability requirement	high	low	moderate
12. Preference for engagement	moderate	very high	very low

403. USE OFFENSIVE RANGE MANIPULATION.

This is the skillful and strategic exploitation of the ranges of combat for offensive purposes. Since punching range is the most advantageous range of unarmed combat, your objective is to maintain this distance while delivering an overwhelming compound attack.

Here is an example: if the fight commences from the neutral zone, take the initiative and close the distance between you and your assailant with a quick, nontelegraphic low-line kick. When your kick hits its target, explode into the punching range. Proceed with a flurry of full-force, full-speed blows. Be absolutely certain your blows are appropriate to the assailant's targets and reaction dynamics. If your assailant freezes in his tracks, stay in punching range and keep the pressure on. However, stay defensively alert because some fighters may decide to counterpunch or charge forward in an attempt to take you to the ground. If your adversary decides to move into grappling range (vertical), immediately employ a flurry of elbow strikes, knee strikes, and head butts with the same overwhelming speed of your punching tools. Don't allow your adversary to break your offensive flow. If the assailant retreats into the kicking range, immediately respond with a quick low-line kick and explode into the punching range. Continue your blitzkrieg until your adversary is out of commission.

TACTICS AND STRATEGY

404. UTILIZE DEFENSIVE RANGE MANIPULATION.

If you're confronted with a vicious compound attack, defensive range manipulation is your only hope for survival. A well-executed compound attack is simply too fast, unpredictable, and powerful to block, parry, or slip. Attempting to coordinate a defensive response for each one of the assailant's blows is absurd and impossible. If you want to protect yourself effectively, you must disengage the range of assault. Defensive range manipulation will allow you to strategically disengage the assailant's compound attack quickly and safely so that you can counter the assault.

Here is an example of defensive range manipulation: if your assailant's attack begins from the punching range, immediately retreat to the kicking range. Once you are balanced, counter with a quick low-line kick. This will disrupt your assailant's balance and impede his offensive flow. However, be certain your kick is accurate, powerful, and properly timed. Once your kick impacts with its target, seize the opportunity to commence with your own flurry of full-speed, full-force blows. Keep the pressure on until the adversary is neutralized.

405. STAY AWAY FROM YOUR ADVERSARY.

Proximity is a vital consideration in both armed and unarmed combat. The farther away you are from an assailant, the greater your defensive reaction time, and the greater the visual picture you will have of your assailant. The closer you are to your assailant, the fewer options you have. For example, in grappling range, any strike delivered by your assailant will most likely land, no matter how fast you can react. You simply cannot defeat the laws of nature.

406. USE THE NEUTRAL ZONE TO YOUR ADVANTAGE.

Contrary to what some people might think, the neutral zone is not a range of unarmed combat. It is simply the distance at which neither you nor your assailant can strike or kick each other. The strategic implication of the neutral zone is that it creates distance between you and the assailant. This, in turn, will provide you with enhanced reaction time so that you can protect yourself adequately. However, don't become complacent; not all situations or environments will afford you the luxury of maintaining a neutral zone.

The neutral zone should be used primarily (1) to safely assess a potential threat, (2) to de-escalate a hostile situation, and (3) to assert yourself to someone.

VISUAL CONSIDERATIONS

407. BE AWARE OF THE VISUAL MONITORING POINTS.

Most fighters don't know where to look when fighting an adversary. Monitoring points are specific locations on your assailant's body that you should be focused on, including the throat triangle, shoulder region, hands, torso, and knees.

The monitoring point that you choose in a fight will ultimately depend on the following three important factors: (1) range of combat, (2) type of confrontation, and (3) type of combat (i.e., armed or unarmed).

408. AVOID DIRECT EYE CONTACT WITH YOUR ADVERSARY.

When engaged with an assailant, avoid direct and steady eye contact. A quick glance is fine, but avoid becoming transfixed. Looking into the assailant's eyes is dangerous for several reasons, including the following: (1) it provides no vital data about your assailant's attack, (2) it draws your attention away from the immediate threat, (3) you can easily be "psyched out," (4) you can fall victim to a variety of visual feints, (5) you cannot assess the assailant's weapon capability effectively, (6) it limits your target recognition, and (7) it inhibits accurate assessment of the combat environment.

The farther away you are from an assailant, the greater your defensive reaction time. In this photo, a student (left) takes advantage of the neutral zone.

OFFENSIVE TACTICS

409. EMPLOY THE ELEMENT OF SURPRISE.
A surprise attack will automatically give you a 50 percent advantage in a street fight.

410. DON'T FORGET THAT YOU WILL LOSE YOUR ENERGY QUICKLY.
If you are in above-average shape, your ability to exert 100 percent effort during the course of an offensive attack will last approximately 90 seconds. Even with a maximum adrenaline surge, your energy level will drop significantly after one and a half minutes of all-out fighting.

411. KNOW REACTION DYNAMICS.
Knowledge of your assailant's reaction dynamics is vital in combat. In fact, you must know every possible reaction dynamic to every tool, technique, and weapon in your arsenal. Reaction dynamics can be defined simply as the assailant's physical responses to a particular tool, technique, or weapon after initial contact is made.

Different reaction dynamics come into play in each of the following situations: (1) when your assailant is struck with a natural body weapon, (2) when a submission hold is applied on your assailant, (3) when your assailant is cut by a knife or an edged weapon, (4) when your assailant is struck with a stick or bludgeon, (5) when your assailant is struck by a bullet, (6) when your assailant is either struck, distracted, or cut by a makeshift weapon, and (7) when your assailant is exposed to a chemical irritant.

412. KNOW THE DEATH FORMULA.
There are many combat situations that do justify and warrant the use of deadly force. It's imperative that you know the two factors that determine the lethality of a natural body weapon. They are: (1) target selection—the anatomical target that you select and (2) amount of force—the amount of force that is delivered to the selected target.

413. PSEUDOSPECIATE YOUR ADVERSARY.
Pseudospeciation is the ability to assign inferior and subhuman qualities to another person immediately in a threatening encounter. This psychological stance is important in combat because it blinds the fighter from the limitations of combat etiquette. It allows the fighter to fight his assailant with vicious intent and determination. It permits you to unleash your killer instinct immediately, while freeing you from the inherent dangers of apprehension. Simply put, pseudospeciation allows you to get the job done.

414. BE COOL AND COLLECTED.
If you are going to prevail in a fight, then you must learn to be in control of the situation and keep your cool. In extremely hostile situations, losing control, showing fear, or expressing frustration or anger will only exacerbate matters greatly. In many ways, it's like pouring gasoline on a fire. You must learn not to take it personally if someone says something offensive or makes an insulting gesture toward you. The bottom line is, if you have a high degree of self-esteem and confidence, you'll be far less inclined to lose control.

415. STRIKE BEFORE YOU CONTROL.
Always strike your assailant before you even attempt a control and restraint technique. This is critical for the following reasons: (1) striking temporarily stuns your assailant, (2) striking buys you some time to apply the control technique effectively, (3) striking disrupts the assailant's balance, (4) striking will temporarily distract the assailant, (5) striking disorients the assailant, (6) striking causes extreme pain for the assailant, (7) striking creates motor dysfunction, (8) striking creates a reflex response that you can exploit, and (9) striking often will loosen the assailant's limbs, permitting easier manipulation.

416. KNOW THE FOUR ELEMENTS OF ATTACK.
The following four elements must exist if your assailant is to commit an attack: (1) intent—the assailant must have the state of mind to execute the action, (2) opportunity—the assailant must have the time and necessary circumstances to attack effectively, (3) weapon—the assailant must have a weapon to attack (e.g., natural body weapon, knife, bludgeon, gun, or makeshift weapon), and (4) delivery method—the assailant must have an effective vehicle or method of delivering his weapon.

417. KNOW HOW TO KICK YOUR ASSAILANT WHEN HE'S DOWN.
There are situations that legally warrant kicking a man when he's down. However, such a

TACTICS AND STRATEGY

method of attack is not as easy as it seems. It requires a considerable amount of skill and technique. Here are some important targets to look for: (1) posterior impact targets, including the temple, back of the neck, spine, fingers, elbow joint, ribs, back of the knee, and ankle and (2) anterior impact targets, including the face, throat, solar plexus, front of the ribs, groin, and the front and side of the knee.
WARNING: Be careful! A skillful ground fighter can pull you down to the ground during the course of your assault.

418. STRIKE FIRST.

Whenever you are squared off with your assailant and there is no way to escape safely, you must strike first, fast, and with authority and keep the pressure on. This offensive strategy is called the first strike principle (FSP), and it is essential to the process of neutralizing a formidable adversary. Allowing the assailant the opportunity to deliver the first strike is tactical suicide. It's like allowing a gunslinger to draw his weapon first. In unarmed combat, if you allow the assailant to strike you first, he might injure or possibly kill you, and he will most certainly force you into an irreversible defensive flow that will inhibit you from issuing a counterattack.
WARNING: When employing the FSP, you must also be certain that your initial strike is warranted and justified in the eyes of the law.

419. BE EXPLOSIVE.

When attacking your assailant, explosiveness is the vehicle for a compound attack. The offensive tools that barrage your assailant should possess a sudden and immediate outburst of violent energy. A compound attack should never be progressive in nature; it does not build in speed and power. It begins and ends explosively. Explosiveness is not just limited to the natural body weapons of unarmed combat. The fuel of explosiveness should also be used with footwork, firearms, knives, and bludgeons.

420. EMPLOY THE COMPOUND ATTACK.

To neutralize a vicious assailant effectively, you will almost always have to do more than execute a single punch or strike. Most unarmed combat situations will demand that you initiate a compound attack against your adversary. A compound attack is the logical sequence of two or more tools strategically thrown in succession. The objective is to take the fight out of the assailant and the assailant out of the fight by overwhelming his defenses with a flurry of full-speed, full-force strikes.

Kick your assailant when he's down! In this photo, Franco delivers a vertical kick into his assailant's ribs.

Based on speed, power, target selection, and target exploitation, the compound attack also requires calculation, control, and clarity. To maximize your offensive attack, you must have a thorough knowledge and understanding of the anatomical targets presented by your adversary. Unless your assailant is in full body armor, there are always targets. It simply is a question of your recognizing them and striking quickly with the appropriate body weapons.

421. MAINTAIN THE OFFENSIVE FLOW.

When you proceed with a compound attack, always maintain the offensive flow. The offensive flow is defined as a progression of continuous offensive movements designed to neutralize or terminate your adversary. When attacking your adversary, keep the pressure on and don't stop until he is completely neutralized. ***WARNING: Stagnating your offensive flow will open you up to numerous dangers and risks. Avoid it at all costs!***

422. DELIVER YOUR CLOSEST WEAPON TO THE ASSAILANT'S CLOSEST TARGET.

In most self-defense situations, the "closest weapon/closest target principle" should be applied. This principle states that when physical danger is imminent, you should launch your closest weapon to the assailant's closest target. This is strategically viable for the following reasons: (1) it creates the most direct and efficient route of travel, (2) it accelerates your offensive reaction time, (3) it reduces telegraphing, (4) it reduces your assailant's defensive reaction time, (5) it improves the overall accuracy of your strike, and (6) it is safer for you.

423. END THE CONFRONTATION AS QUICKLY AS POSSIBLE.

Every physical confrontation should end quickly. Remember, the longer a fight lasts, the greater your chances of serious injury. A fight should be over as quickly as it begins. Your tools, techniques, and tactics must be quick and decisive. There is no time to design a battle plan or test the assailant's ability with probing techniques.

Here is a brief list of things that can occur during the course of your fight: (1) spectators can intervene, (2) you can make a tactical error that can cost you your life, (3) your immediate physical condition may worsen, and (4) the level of force between you and the assailant will escalate progressively.

424. NEVER DRAW AN ATTACK.

Attack by drawing is a method of attack where the fighter offers his opponent an intentional opening designed to lure an attack. Two common drawing techniques are a wide hand positioning and a low hand guard, as if to say, "Come on, take your best shot!" Once the opponent takes the bait, the martial artist swiftly defends and counters.

This method of attack is ineffective for the following reasons.

(1) Who is to say you can stop and counter the assailant's first strike? For example, would you try this technique against a professional boxer who has lightning-fast hands?

(2) By allowing the assailant to act and forcing yourself to react, you automatically put yourself at a disadvantage.

(3) Who is to say that the assailant will go for the bait? He may attack a completely different target zone.

(4) What happens if the assailant attacks with a flurry of vicious blows? You will find yourself in an irreversible defensive flow that could get you killed. Deception is an important combat skill; however, the drawing method is a gamble that might get you killed.

425. FORGET SINGLE-STRIKE VICTORIES.

The "single attack" is a method of fighting where the martial artist delivers a solitary offensive tool to either terminate the fight or "probe" the assailant. Advocates of this method of attack argue that is the safest method of attack because it does not require full commitment to the adversary. Others profess it to be the highest form of combat when one quick, powerful blow ends the fight. Both theories are dead wrong. First, you cannot neutralize an assailant by lingering at the perimeter of the encounter. In real fights, you must always commit yourself 100 percent with the most effective flow of offensive tools appropriate to the range, angle, force level, and targets the assailant presents. Second, never assume one kick, punch, or strike will end a fight. Subscribing to this type of faulty logic could get you killed in a vicious fight. The bottom line is that single-strike victories are few and far between.

426. AVOID THE IMMOBILIZATION ATTACK.

Don't attempt immobilization attack (trapping) techniques when standing face-to-face with your adversary. The immobilization attack is a highly complex system of moves and countermoves that allows you to control and manipulate the assailant's limbs (usually his arms and hands) temporarily in order to create an opening to attack. Vertical trapping techniques require lightning-quick reflexes and highly developed touch sensitivity.

Vertical trapping techniques are ineffective for a variety of reasons, including the following:

(1) The ability to use effective trapping techniques is based on the assailant

TACTICS AND STRATEGY

presenting a proper structure in response. His hands must accept your feed in just the right way. The trapping feed or "attachment" may be either a linear or circular tool to engage the assailant's counter or guard. Once the initial lockup takes place, the trapper can go to work with parries, blocks, energy reversals, and other techniques aimed at neutralizing the assailant and creating openings. All of this may sound impressive; however, you simply cannot rely on your assailant's presentation of the predefined structure necessary for various trapping techniques to succeed.

(2) If your attachments are not adequately engaged by the assailant, you can't build a trapping structure.

(3) If your adversary disengages, which is extremely likely in a real fighting situation, your trap disintegrates immediately.

(4) Your assailant can easily counter with a series of head butts, elbows, knees, and other close-quarter tools.

(5) Vertical trapping techniques can lead to a ground fight, which is the last thing you want in a street fight. *NOTE: Don't confuse the ineffective (vertical) trapping techniques with the functional (prone) trapping movement that can be applied in a ground fight. For more information on prone trapping, see Chapter 5.*

427. DON'T USE THE INDIRECT ATTACK.

The indirect attack is a progressive method of attack. It always involves more than one technique. Do not, however, confuse the indirect attack with its superior cousin, the compound attack.

The indirect attack builds through stages. The initial technique is not the coup de grace, i.e., the knockout weapon. In fact, in many indirect attacks, the initiating technique is not even a weapon, but one of any number of feints or other deceptions designed to open the assailant up for the follow-up blow. Even when the initiating tool is an actual kick, punch, or strike, it serves merely as a setup for the finishing blow.

In competition or sparring, the initiating technique sets up or accumulates valuable points, wears down the assailant, and opens him up to more devastating blows. In real combat, however, where points are of no consequence and setups are not safe, the progressive indirect attack should never be employed.

In the explosive and dangerous situation of a fight, you cannot afford the risk of a setup technique. Any initiating tool or technique delivered with less than maximum speed and power will likely be ignored and will certainly be countered with viciousness.

As stated earlier, assumptions and experimentation in the face of danger are invitations to disaster. The indirect attack involves far too much risk and uncertainty. It lacks the all-out explosiveness, power, and commitment required to face an assailant hell-bent on your destruction. Remember, in real combat, no rules apply. You are subject to an attack from anywhere and anything. You cannot allow your assailant even the slightest opportunity to gain the upper hand. You've got to go full force all the way to ensure victory. By definition, the indirect attack is inconsistent with this approach and should not, therefore, be used in a real fight.

428. HEAD-HUNT.

Be a headhunter in the streets. Head-hunting means strategically pursuing and selecting the assailant's head as your primary impact target.

In this photo, Franco (right) demonstrates the attachment, assuming his assailant will respond as anticipated.

Remember, if you have the option of attacking your assailant's head or torso, go for his head. The incapacitation potential in much greater.

429. CALL THE SHOTS.

Contrary to what many theoreticians may say, you must call the shots in a fight. Your decision to launch a particular tool or technique (in stand-up combat) should not be influenced by your assailant's technique, method of fighting, or form of defense. Your adversary's technique does not decide your technique. Rather, it is the angle of attack, range of combat, and use-of-force justification that sets the standard for weapon selection in a fight.

430. YOU WON'T KNOW TILL IT'S OVER.

The concept of avoiding your assailant's strengths and exploiting his weaknesses is a competition-oriented strategy (often used in sparring) that can't be effectively employed in a vicious street fight. Since a street fight is so dynamic and explosive, you will not have the time or luxury to assess your adversary's fighting method. There simply isn't enough time. By the time you recognize his strengths and weaknesses, the fight will be over.

431. NEVER EMPLOY A MINOR BLOW IN A STREET FIGHT.

A minor blow is defined as a strike or kick (i.e., boxer's jab, hand slap, backfist punch, roundhouse snap kick, etc.) that is not used as a knockout or finishing blow. Minor blows are generally used for the following reasons: (1) to irritate your assailant, (2) to throw your assailant off balance, (3) to set your assailant up for a finishing blow, (4) to offset or prevent a possible counterattack, and (5) to test or probe your assailant's fighting abilities. *WARNING: Minor blows are combatively deficient and have no business in a real fight. Completely eliminate them from your arsenal of striking tools.*

432. YELL.

The voice is a very powerful tool. When fighting, the yell is a natural manifestation of the voice. Yelling actually serves several strategic purposes in combat. Yelling while fighting can distract, startle, and temporarily paralyze your assailant. It can cause the adversary to freeze in his tracks, allowing you a split-second advantage to

Yelling serves many strategic purposes in fighting.

deliver the first debilitating strike and thus gain offensive control. Yelling can also be used to psyche out the assailant and synchronize your state of mind with the physical process taking place. It is the catalyst that sets off the killer instinct and the primal expression that harbors the killer instinct. In addition, yelling actually may draw attention to your fight.

433. ATTACK PRESSURE POINT AREAS.

A pressure point is a specific area on the human body where a nerve lies close to the surface and is supported by bone or a muscle mass. Direct pressure can be applied to a pressure point area by striking it with a natural body weapon. Some effective pressure point areas include the common peroneal nerve, the femoral nerve, and the infra orbital.

A powerful strike to a pressure point area will cause the following physiological responses: (1) extreme pain, (2) a stunning effect, (3) motor dysfunction, (4) balance disruption, and (5) reflex response.

434. KNOW WHEN TO ESCALATE.

Know how and when to escalate your level of force quickly and accurately in a fight.

POSITIONING TACTICS

435. UTILIZE STRATEGIC POSITIONING.

In combat, always try to position yourself strategically from your adversary. For example, when faced with a threatening assailant, try to subtly

TACTICS AND STRATEGY

maneuver yourself into a position that will allow you to escape safely. Or, if the ability to escape is not in the cards, then quickly check for any physical barriers and try to position yourself behind one.

There are other important considerations of strategic positioning, such as keeping a keen eye out for possible makeshift weapons and positioning yourself accordingly. Or, when faced with multiple assailants, avoiding backing yourself into a wall and letting them surround you. Lighting is another important component of strategic positioning. Try to position yourself so that the immediate light source (sun, auto headlights, street lamp, etc.) glares into your adversary's eyes and not yours. Terrain is also important. Try to force your assailant to stand on unstable terrain.

436. MOVE TO YOUR ASSAILANT'S DEAD SIDE.
When squared off with your assailant, try to move strategically to your assailant's dead side. The dead side is the lead side of the assailant's body. It is the safest direction to move toward because it is farthest away from the assailant's rear appendages.

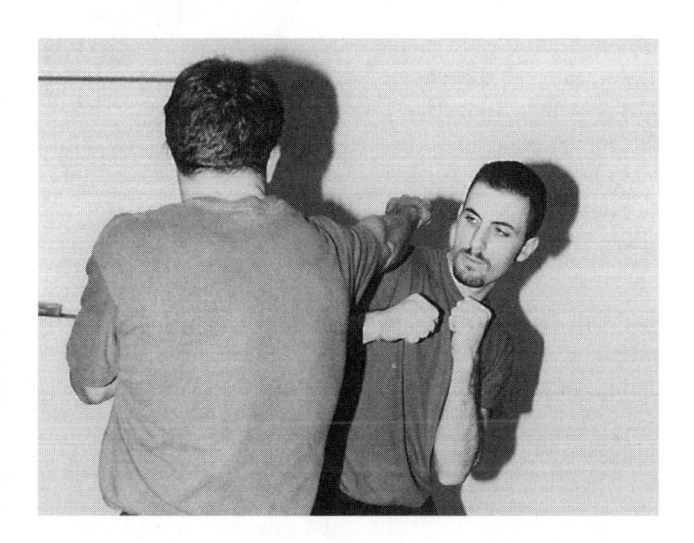

In this photo, a student slips and moves to his assailant's dead side.

437. STEP FORWARD.
When someone aggressively taps you on the shoulder, be certain to step forward and then turn around with both of your hands up and be ready to defend or attack.

438. KEEP THE LIGHT BEHIND YOU.
Always have a powerful light source (e.g., sun, moon, street lamp, auto headlights, reflection source, etc.) behind you and facing your adversary. This is important for two reasons: (1) it helps illuminate your target, and (2) it inhibits your adversary's vision.

439. FACE YOUR ADVERSARY WITH YOUR STRONGER SIDE FORWARD.
If you have the option and luxury of assuming a stance (i.e., fighting stance, natural stance, de-escalation stance, knife-defense stance, knife fighting stance, bludgeon fighting stance), always try to face your assailant with your stronger and more coordinated side. This will position your more powerful and coordinated limbs closer to the assailant. If you are right-handed, generally your right side is stronger and more coordinated. *NOTE: This combat axiom excludes firearm stances.*

440. MANEUVER YOURSELF TO AN ESCAPE ROUTE.
When squared off with an assailant, always try to subtly maneuver yourself into a position to safely escape, or close to avenues of escape (windows, gates, open doors, stairs, etc.).

441. BE CAUTIOUS OF YOUR ASSAILANT'S INSIDE POSITION.
One of the most dangerous areas is your assailant's inside position. The inside position is the area between both of his arms where he has the greatest amount of control.

442. GET BEHIND YOUR ADVERSARY.
If you want the greatest and safest position in a fight, attack your assailant from behind. A rear assault is generally effective for the

The assailant's inside position.

If ever you have the luxury of assuming a fighting stance, try to face your assailant with your strongest and most coordinated side. In this photo, Franco (right) squares off in a right-lead stance.

following two reasons: (1) the assailant cannot see what you are doing, and (2) the assailant has the least amount of control when assaulted from the rear.

443. DON'T TURN YOUR BACK.

Avoid turning your back on a potential assailant unless he is so far away he can't grab, punch, kick, slash, or club you. Turning your back to someone is a sign of trust; remember, trust no one in the streets.

ANATOMICAL CONSIDERATIONS

444. ATTACK THE ASSAILANT'S EYES.

Eyes are ideal targets for street combat because they are one of the most important organs your assailant needs to fight effectively, not to mention that they are extremely sensitive and difficult to protect. Also, striking them requires very little force. The eyes can be poked, scratched, and gouged from a variety of angles and vantages. Depending on the force of your strike, it can cause numerous injuries, including watering of the eyes, hemorrhaging, blurred vision, temporary or permanent blindness, severe pain, rupture, shock, and even unconsciousness.

445. ATTACK THE ASSAILANT'S THROAT.

In a life-and-death situation, attacking your assailant's throat can save your life. The throat is considered a lethal target because it is only protected by a thin layer of skin. This region consists of the thyroid, hyaline cartilage, cricoid cartilage, trachea, and larynx. The trachea, or windpipe, is a cartilaginous cylindrical tube that measures four and a half inches in length and approximately one inch in diameter. A direct and powerful strike to this target may result in unconsciousness, blood drowning, massive hemorrhaging, strangulation, and death. If the thyroid cartilage is crushed, hemorrhaging will occur, the windpipe will quickly swell shut, and the assailant will die of suffocation. You can effectively strike the assailant's throat with knives, hands, and elbow strikes.

The eyes can be poked, scratched, and gouged from a variety of angles and vantages. Here, a student demonstrates a devastating eye rake.

The throat is considered a lethal target. In this photo, Franco crushes his assailant's windpipe.

446. STRIKE THE ASSAILANT'S TEMPLE.

The temple or sphenoid bone is a thin, weak bone located on either side of the skull approximately one inch from the eye. Because of its inherently weak structure and close proximity to the brain, a very powerful strike to this anatomical target can be deadly. Other possible injuries include unconsciousness, hemorrhaging, concussion, shock, and coma. You can use the following body weapons

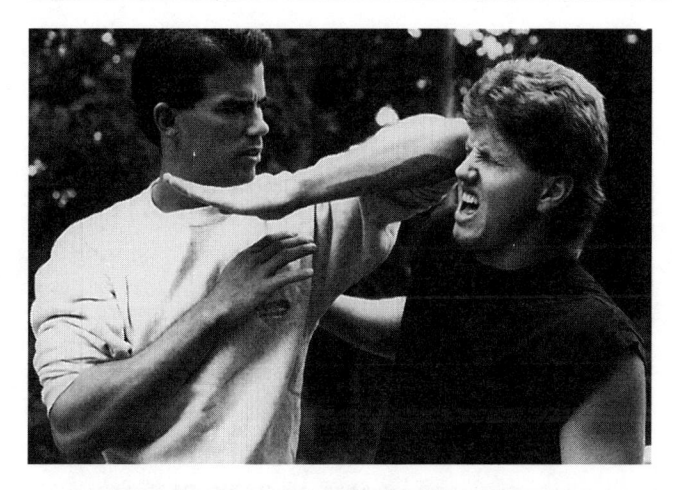

TACTICS AND STRATEGY

In this photo, a student delivers a lead horizontal elbow strike to his assailant's temple.

to strike the assailant's temple: elbow strikes, hook punches, and, in some cases, the knee strike.

447. STRIKE THE ASSAILANT'S NOSE.

The nose is made up of a thin bone, cartilage, numerous blood vessels, and many nerves. It is a particularly good impact target because it stands out from the assailant's face and can be struck in three different directions (up, straight, and down). A moderate blow can cause stunning pain, eye-watering, temporary blindness, and hemorrhaging. A powerful strike can result in shock and unconsciousness. Lead straights, rear crosses, palm heels, uppercuts, hammer fists, elbow strikes, and knee strikes can be delivered effectively to the assailant's nose.

448. HAMMER-FIST THE ASSAILANT'S NOSE.

The vertical hammer fist can also be delivered to the bridge of the assailant's nose. To deliver this deceptive and painful strike, apply the following steps: (1) assume a de-escalation stance with both hands open and facing your assailant; (2) while conversing and distracting your adversary, quickly whip your rear hammer fist down the bridge of his nose. Be certain not to retract or chamber your strike prior to its execution. Follow up with either a vertical knee strike or uppercut to the assailant's face.

449. HIT THE ASSAILANT'S CHIN.

In Western boxing, the chin is considered a "knockout button," responsible for retiring hundreds

In this photo, a student delivers a rear vertical hammer fist to his assailant's nose.

In this photo, a student delivers a rear uppercut to his assailant's chin.

of boxers. The chin is also a good target for unarmed combat. When the chin is struck at a 45-degree angle, shock waves are transmitted to the cerebellum and cerebral hemispheres of the brain, resulting in paralysis and immediate unconsciousness. Depending on the force of your blow, other possible injuries include broken jaw, concussion, and whiplash to the assailant's neck. Some of the best body weapons to strike the chin are uppercuts, elbow strikes, knee strikes, palm heels, and even head butts.

450. STRIKE THE ASSAILANT'S CERVICAL VERTEBRAE.

The back of the assailant's neck consists of the first seven vertebrae of the spinal column. They function as a circuit board for nerve impulses from the brain to the body. The back of the neck is a lethal target because the vertebrae are poorly protected.

A very powerful strike to the back of the assailant's neck can cause shock, unconsciousness, a broken neck, complete paralysis, coma, and death. Two of the best body weapons with which to strike the cervical vertebrae are hammer fists and elbow strikes.

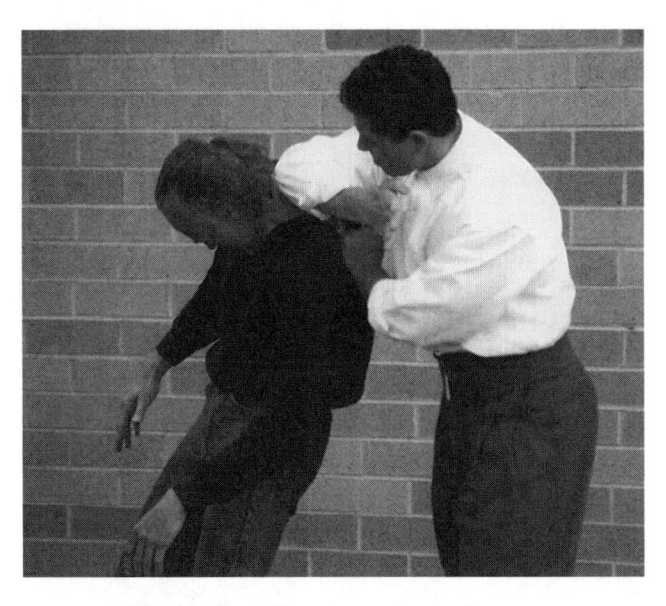

In this photo, Franco (right) delivers a horizontal elbow strike to his assailant's cervical vertebrae.

451. ATTACK THE ASSAILANT'S RIBS.

There are 12 pairs of ribs in the human body. Excluding the 11th and 12th ribs, they are long and slender bones that are joined by the vertebral column in the back and the sternum and costal cartilage in the front. Since there are no 11th and 12th ribs (floating ribs) in the front, you should direct your strikes to the 9th and 10th ribs.

A moderate strike to the anterior region of the ribs may cause severe pain and shortness of breath. An extremely powerful 45-degree blow could break the assailant's rib and force it into a lung, resulting in the lung's collapse, internal hemorrhaging, air starvation, unconsciousness, excruciating pain, and possible death. Some of the best offensive tools to deliver to the ribs are shovel hooks, uppercuts, elbow strikes, and knee strikes.

452. HIT THE ASSAILANT'S SOLAR PLEXUS.

The solar plexus is a large collection of nerves situated below the sternum in the upper abdomen. A moderate blow to this area can cause nausea, pain, and shock, making it difficult for the adversary to breathe properly. A powerful strike to the solar plexus can result in severe abdominal pain and cramping, air starvation, and shock.

In this photo, a student delivers a rear uppercut to his assailant's solar plexus.

453. STRIKE THE ASSAILANT'S GROIN.

Just about every person will agree that the groin is an extremely sensitive target. The testes can be kicked, punched, or crushed. A moderate kick or strike to an assailant's groin can cause a variety of possible reactions, including severe pain, nausea, vomiting, shortness of breath, and possible sterility. A powerful strike to the groin may crush the scrotum and the testes against the pubic bones, causing shock and unconsciousness.

TACTICS AND STRATEGY

454. STRIKE THE ASSAILANT'S THIGHS.

Many good fighters overlook the thighs as an impact target. As a matter of fact, because the thighs are large and difficult to protect, they make excellent striking targets in a fight. Although you can kick the thighs at a variety of different angles, the ideal location is the assailant's common peroneal nerve located on the side of the thigh, approximately four inches above the knee. Striking this area can result in extreme pain and immediate immobility of the afflicted leg. An extremely hard kick to the thigh may result in a fracture of the femur, internal bleeding, severe pain, intense cramping, and long-term immobility.

The thigh is an excellent target. In this photo, Franco (right) delivers a powerful hook kick to his assailant's common peroneal nerve.

A powerful and accurate kick to your assailant's knee can produce devastating results. Here, Franco (left) delivers a side kick to his assailant's knee.

455. ATTACK THE ASSAILANT'S KNEES.

The knees are relatively weak joints that are held together by a number of supporting ligaments. When the assailant's leg is locked or fixed in position and a forceful strike is delivered to the front of the joint, the crucial ligaments will tear, resulting in excruciating pain, swelling, and immobility. Located on the front of the knee joint is the kneecap, or patella, which is made of a small, loose piece of bone. The patella is also vulnerable to possible dislocation by a direct, forceful kick. Severe pain, swelling, and immobility may also result.

456. KICK THE ASSAILANT'S SHINS.

Like the thighs, the shins are excellent striking targets because they are very difficult to protect. The shins are also very sensitive because they are only protected by a thin layer of skin. A powerful kick delivered to this target may fracture it easily, resulting in extreme pain, hemorrhaging, and immobility of the afflicted leg.

457. BREAK THE ASSAILANT'S FINGERS.

The fingers are exceptionally weak and vulnerable. They can easily be jammed, sprained, broken, torn, and bitten. While a broken finger might not stop a determined fighter, it will certainly force him to release his hold. A broken finger will also make it very difficult for the assailant to clench his fist or hold a knife or bludgeon. When attempting to break the fingers, it's best to grab the finger securely and then forcefully tear backward against the knuckle.

The fingers are exceptionally weak and vulnerable. They can easily be jammed, sprained, broken, torn, and bitten. Here, the author breaks his assailant's finger to escape a hold.

458. STOMP THE ASSAILANT'S TOES.

In grappling range, a powerful stomp of your heel can break the small bones of the assailant's toes, causing severe pain and immediate immobility. Stomping on the assailant's toes is also one of the best ways for escaping many holds. Keep in mind that you should avoid attacking the toes if the attacker is wearing hard leather boots (e.g., combat, hiking, or motorcycle boots).

FIGHTING MULTIPLE ATTACKERS

459. STRIKE AND MOVE SIMULTANEOUSLY.

Learn how to strike and move simultaneously. This is important for the following reasons: (1) it will enhance the power of your strike, (2) it helps maintain the offensive flow, (3) it makes you more elusive to a counterattack, (3) it can place you in a more advantageous position, (4) it helps you exploit your assailant's reaction dynamics, and (5) it will give you a fighting chance against multiple attackers.

460. USE PROPER TACTICS AGAINST MULTIPLE ATTACKERS.

Since most street punks characteristically attack in groups, it's important to learn how to defend against multiple attackers. Since power lies in numbers, the odds are heavily against you. Nevertheless, you can survive a confrontation with multiple attackers by applying knowledge, skill, and raw courage.

In summary, you must apply the following seven strategic principles when you are unarmed and defending against multiple assailants: (1) try to escape, (2) utilize makeshift weapons, (3) keep mobile, (4) avoid being surrounded, (5) determine who is the immediate threat, (6) attack the immediate threat and make an example of him, and (7) escape once the threat is neutralized.

461. DIVIDE AND CONQUER.

When unarmed and faced with multiple attackers, you must divide them and attack the assailant who presents the most immediate threat. This is accomplished by quickly moving to his right or left flank and commencing with a barrage of swift blows. Your tactical objective is to injure him as quickly and as efficiently as possible. Remember to strike first, strike fast, strike with authority, and keep the pressure on.

Time is critical at this point, so keep your movement as economical as possible. While delivering your blows, try to keep your adversary between you and his partners. Keep the pressure on and stay mobile. Because of the extreme threat and danger posed by multiple attackers, it is imperative that you make an example of your first assailant. Attack him with extreme prejudice. For example, if the other assailants see their partner violently choking from repeated throat strikes, it will kill their spirit, and they will be less inclined to continue their assault on you.

462. NEVER LET YOURSELF BE SURROUNDED.

Never let yourself be surrounded by multiple assailants. It is simply impossible to defend yourself in every direction all at once. Mobility can help prevent you from being trapped. Constantly angle your body so there is always one assailant between you and the rest of them. Take advantage of your environment by trying to maneuver yourself in strategic positions, such as between parked cars or doorways. This prevents your assailants from utilizing their full strength and can permit you to fight them one at a time.

463. ESCAPE FROM MULTIPLE ATTACKERS.

When faced with multiple attackers, quickly scan your environment and look for any possible escape routes. Look for windows, doors, fire escapes, gates, bridges, staircases, fences, escalators, or any other avenue that will allow you to flee quickly and safely from this dangerous altercation. If the opportunity presents itself for you to run and escape safely, take it. Don't let your ego get in the way. *WARNING: Make sure that your version of an escape route doesn't lead you into a worse situation.*

464. KEEP MOVING.

Whenever faced with multiple attackers, always keep moving. Mobility makes you a difficult target to hit and prevents your assailants from surrounding you. Mobility also enhances the power of your blows and makes your attackers misjudge your range. Most importantly, mobility may help you locate an open area in which to safely escape.

465. NEVER BACK YOURSELF INTO A WALL.

When confronted by one or more assailants, never back yourself into a wall. This is dangerous for

TACTICS AND STRATEGY

the following five reasons: (1) it inhibits your tactical mobility, (2) it eliminates the escape option, (3) it inhibits the body mechanics of certain kicking techniques, (4) it provides a possible striking surface for your assailant to smash your head or body, and (5) it usually prohibits makeshift weapon acquisition.

Never back yourself into a wall.

466. APPLY THE HUMAN SHIELD PRINCIPLE.

In a multiple-assailant situation, it is also important to apply the human shield principle. Use one of your assailants as an obstacle (natural barrier) by pushing or swinging him into the other attackers. This will slow down the other assailants and give you a few seconds to either escape or attack again.

In this photo, the author (left) utilizes the human shield principle.

467. DETERMINE WHO IS THE IMMEDIATE THREAT.

When confronted with multiple attackers, you must determine which assailant poses the most immediate threat to you. Usually, an armed assailant is your most immediate threat. If none of the attackers is armed, then go for the man who is closest to you. If more than one assailant is of equal distance to you, then the assailant who is blocking your escape route is the most immediate threat. Finally, if more than one assailant is blocking your escape route, go for the leader of the group. It is usually the one with the biggest mouth.

When faced with multiple assailants, it's important to determine which one is the immediate threat.

468. REMEMBER, YOU CAN'T STOP FIGHTING.

Whenever you defend yourself against a group of assailants, you cannot stop fighting until one of the following occurs: (1) every assailant is neutralized, (2) the assailants decide to cease their attack, or (3) the opportunity to safely escape presents itself.

MAKESHIFT WEAPONS

469. AVOID USING FLEXIBLE WEAPONS.

Chains, belts, and other flexible weapons are ineffective in a street fight for the following reasons: (1) they are generally difficult to control, (2) they lack neutralizing force, (3) they lack quick retraction, (4) they must follow through the complete range of motion to be re-executed, (5) they open up your body targets to a variety of possible counters, and (6) they can get snagged on your assailant's body or limbs.

470. USE MAKESHIFT WEAPONS.

A well-seasoned fighter should have the

knowledge and skills necessary to effectively use makeshift weapons. Makeshift weapons are common, everyday objects that can be converted into either offensive or defensive weapons. There are four makeshift weapon classifications: (1) cutting weapons—objects or implements used to stab or slash your assailant; (2) shielding weapons—objects used to shield yourself from attack; (3) distracting weapons—objects that can be thrown into your assailant's face, torso, or legs to temporarily distract him; and (4) striking weapons—objects used to strike the assailant.

A wide variety of makeshift weapons.

471. USE "DISTRACTING" MAKESHIFT WEAPONS.

Distracting makeshift weapons are various items and objects that can be thrown at your assailant to distract him temporarily. Distracting makeshift weapons offer the following strategic advantages in a fight: (1) surprise—you can catch the assailant off guard and launch the rest of your offensive attack, (2) visual impairments—certain objects can impair the assailant's vision temporarily or permanently, (3) time—distracting makeshift weapons will also buy you a little time from the adversary, (4) windows of opportunity—throwing objects into the assailant's face almost always causes a reaction dynamic that permits you to exploit his targets, and (5) defensive flow—distracting makeshift weapons put the assailant into a defensive flow.

Generally, distracting makeshift weapons are thrown into your assailant's face. Some examples include sunglasses, magazines, car keys, wallets, ashtrays, books, salt shakers, alarm clocks, coins, bottles, bars of soap, shoes, dirt, sand, gravel, rocks, videotapes, small figurines, cassette tapes, hot liquids, paperweights, pesticide sprays, and oven cleaner spray.

472. USE ITEMS IN YOUR AUTOMOBILE AS WEAPONS.

Many motorists don't realize just how many different makeshift weapons are available in their cars. Here is a brief list. Screwdrivers can be used for stabbing your assailant. Tire-changing equipment can be used as a striking makeshift weapon. Briefcases are excellent shielding and distracting makeshift weapons. Ice scrapers can be used as cutting makeshift weapons. Liquid de-icer can be sprayed into your attacker's face. Your car door can be slammed into your assailant's legs, and your actual car can be used to run over your adversary.

473. CARRY A PEN WITH YOU.

Pens and pencils are ubiquitous. They are also very effective stabbing makeshift weapons that can puncture and seriously wound your assailant. A pen or pencil can be thrust into the following anatomical targets: (1) eye socket, (2) ear cavity, (3) under the chin, (4) the base of the skull, (5) throat, (6) groin, (7) top of the hands, and (8) solar plexus. As the saying goes, "The pen is mightier than the sword."

474. USE "STRIKING" MAKESHIFT WEAPONS.

Striking makeshift weapons are common, everyday objects that you can use to strike an assailant. When selecting a striking makeshift weapon, make certain that it is appropriate to the tactical function you have assigned it.

Examples of striking makeshift weapons include sticks, bricks, crowbars, baseball bats, shovels, golf clubs, lamps, books, light chairs, pool cues, pipes, heavy flashlights, hammers, binoculars, glass bottles, beer mugs, telephones, tool boxes, briefcases, car doors, canes, walking sticks, an automobile, light dumbbells, 2 x 4s, etc.

475. USE "SHIELDING" MAKESHIFT WEAPONS.

In some self-defense situations, a shielding makeshift weapon may be the only thing that stands

TACTICS AND STRATEGY

A heavy flashlight is an excellent striking makeshift weapon.

between you and death. Shielding makeshift weapons are ubiquitous items that can shield you effectively and temporarily from the assailant's punch, kick, or strike. However, in most cases, shielding makeshift weapons are used to protect against knife and bludgeon attacks.

Examples of shielding makeshift weapons include briefcases, trash-can lids, bicycles, thick sofa cushions, backpacks, barstools, lawn chairs, drawers, cafeteria trays, suitcases, thick pillows, leather jackets/coats, sleeping bags, motorcycle helmets, small end tables, hubcaps, etc. Once again, be certain that your makeshift weapon has the structural integrity to get the job done effectively.

476. AVOID DEPENDENCY.

Far too many people assume that the mere possession of a weapon (e.g., firearm, knife, bludgeon, OC spray, makeshift weapon) will save them from peril. This faulty logic forms the delusion of "dependency." Dependency is the sole reliance on a particular tool or weapon for self-defense. Although a .45 semiautomatic can stop just about anyone, no single weapon, tool, or technique is the absolute answer. Every weapon has its combat limitations. Guns can jam, knives can be dropped accidentally, sticks can break, and OC canisters can clog. Further, not all street fights justify the use of a weapon. Consider, for example, that a hostile scuffle with your unarmed brother-in-law won't justify self-defense with a weapon.

477. LEARN WEAPON-RETENTION SKILLS.

Learn retention skills for the following hand-held weapons: (1) handguns, (2) rifles, (3) shotguns, (4) knives and edged weapons, (5) sticks and bludgeons, (6) makeshift weapons, and (7) chemical irritant canisters.

OLEORESIN CAPSICUM

478. USE OLEORESIN CAPSICUM.

If you must select a self-defense spray, consider using OC, or oleoresin capsicum. OC (also known as "pepper spray") is a resin extracted from finely ground, dried chili peppers of the botanical group capsicum, which is then converted into an oil. Pepper spray is an inflammatory agent that affects the assailant's mucus membranes (eyes, nose, throat, and lungs). When OC is sprayed in the assailant's face, it causes the eyes to swell shut immediately, restricts breathing, and severely burns the entire face. The assailant's vision is impaired for approximately 10 minutes, and breathing is inhibited for about 30 minutes.

OC is considered the best spray for self-defense because it is potent and works almost immediately on your assailant. Unlike Mace or CS (Orthochlorbenzalmalonontrile, or choking gas), pepper spray will incapacitate an adversary regardless of his tolerance to pain. When used properly, OC spray can neutralize large and powerful assailants, psychotics, drug users, and violent drunks. Depending on the model you purchase, spraying distances will vary from 8 to 10 feet. Some models will even shoot up to 40 feet. *WARNING: If you intend to use OC spray for self-defense, get training from a qualified instructor. You must learn several essential tactics before using this tool on the streets. Before you purchase or carry OC, check with your local and state laws regarding its possession and use. Also remember that it is a federal offense to carry an OC aerosol spray unit aboard an aircraft.*

479. KNOW HOW TO USE OC.

If you are going to use OC or cayenne pepper, remember the following guidelines: (1) in order to ensure that the aerosol unit is functioning properly, make sure it is shaken and tested before initial use; (2) spray from an upright position; (3) spray from a 4- to 6-foot distance or as recommended by the manufacturer; (4) spray directly into the assailant's face with a 1- or 2-second burst depending on his distance, speed of movement, and wind conditions; (5) if the assailant is holding his breath, use multiple short bursts; and (6) use lateral movement when spraying.

Oleoresin capsicum, or OC, comes in a variety of different canisters.

480. KNOW WHICH DIRECTION THE WIND IS BLOWING.

Don't be the victim of your own OC. When using OC it is critical that you know which way the wind is blowing so that you can position yourself accordingly. Be especially careful of breezeways, hallways, and dead-end alleys since the air flow in these environments tends to be unpredictable.

481. ASSUME THE PROPER STANCE WHEN USING OC.

Your stance is very important when you are using pepper spray. A proper stance will put you in a position of tactical advantage. Remember to apply the following: (1) position your body at a 45-degree angle to your adversary, (2) keep your weak side to the front of your adversary and your strong side to the rear, (3) hold the OC unit in your strong hand between the weak hand and the center of your body, (4) keep your feet shoulder-width apart with your weight evenly distributed, and (5) keep your weak hand open and slightly bent.

482. KNOW THE REACTION DYNAMICS OF OC.

If you are going to use OC or cayenne pepper as a self-defense tool, make certain you are aware of the assailant's possible reaction dynamics, including the following: (1) his hands will go directly to his face, (2) he will drop whatever is in his hands, (3) his upper body will bend forward, (4) he will shake uncontrollably, (5) he will grope around for the floor, (6) he will drop to his knees for stability, and (7) his body will become rigid and he will not respond to your voice commands.

483. DON'T USE MACE.

When considering self-defense sprays, avoid using Mace. CN, or Mace, is a chemical tear gas that causes tearing, burning of the eyes, and minor difficulty in breathing. Mace, however, won't work on crazed assailants who have high tolerances to pain, such as psychotics, drug abusers, and violent drunks. In many cases, Mace makes these aggressors angrier and more violent.

484. DON'T RELY ON SELF-DEFENSE SPRAYS.

Never forget that all self-defense sprays have their limitations. First, you must always have the unit in your hand and ready to fire. It won't do you any good if the canister is in your car when you are suddenly jumped by an attacker. Second, if there is a strong or unpredictable wind, the spray can be useless. Aerosol canisters can also jam, and you cannot spray someone in a confined area like a car or phone booth.

DEALING WITH THE POLICE

485. KNOW HOW TO DEAL WITH THE POLICE.

After a street fight, there is always the possibility that you will have to talk to the police. Here are a few important suggestions: (1) be polite and respectful—don't ever talk back to police officers, and always address them as either "sir" or "ma'am"; (2) watch what you say—speak slowly and clearly, avoid using profanity, sarcasm, and racial or derogatory remarks, and realize that what you say can be used against you; (3) identify yourself—identify yourself as the victim and be prepared to show identification, but carefully avoid quick or sudden movements when reaching for your wallet, and always try to keep your hands in plain view; (4) explain what happened—clearly describe the sequence of events that led to the fight, and if the assailant used a weapon in the fight or said anything to you, report it; (5) follow orders—if the officer orders you to wait at a particular spot while he sorts out the matter, obey him; and finally, (6) don't get angry—if you get angry or hostile with the police officers, you will land in jail for the night.

TACTICS AND STRATEGY

486. USE "REST GESTE" STATEMENTS.

After a street fight, be very careful about what you say to a police officer. If you must speak, consider using rest geste statements. Rest geste statements are defined as statements that you couldn't control something. Such statements will help you establish a legal defense if you have to go to court. They include the following: (1) "I didn't mean to"—this establishes that you did not mean to hurt your adversary, (2) "He wouldn't stop"—this establishes that your adversary was the predator and you were the victim, (3) "I was just trying to defend myself"—this establishes that you possessed a self-defense mind-set, (4) "I thought he was going to kill me"—this establishes that you were in fear for your life. *NOTE: Keep in mind that all rest geste statements should be repeated several times in a distraught and remorseful manner.*

487. KNOW YOUR RIGHTS.

Whenever you are involved in a self-defense situation, there is always the possibility that you will be arrested by the police. If you are taken into police custody, you have the right to remain silent, obtain a lawyer, be informed of the charges against you, and have a judge decide whether you should be released on bail until your trial.

488. REMEMBER THAT COPS CAN APPROACH YOU.

Police officers are permitted to approach you in a public place and request information. If a police officer reasonably suspects that you are committing, have committed, or are about to commit a crime, he or she may detain you briefly for questioning.

If a police officer reasonably suspects that you are armed and dangerous, he or she is permitted to frisk you without making an arrest. If while frisking you for weapons or evidence the officer finds anything illegal, he can confiscate it and arrest you.

THE AFTERMATH OF A STREET FIGHT

489. CHECK YOURSELF OUT.

Once the fight is over and you have fled the scene safely, conduct a quick inventory of your body. Quickly scan your torso, hands, arms, legs, and feet for any possible signs of injury. Run both hands down your face and over your head and neck to check for blood. This is important because many times fighters are seriously injured after a fight and don't even know it because the adrenaline rush from the fight-or-flight response shuts off the pain.

490. KNOW HOW TO TREAT BATTLE WOUNDS.

It is important that you know how to treat some of the most common injuries that occur in a fight. Here are five injuries that you should be aware of:

(1) Sprained thumb—this is caused by connecting improperly with your target. A sprained thumb is usually accompanied by swelling and aching pain due to ruptured cappilaries and torn ligaments. First, apply a large bandage, then apply ice to the area and keep your thumb immobilized. See your family physician as soon as possible.

(2) Split lip—this is caused by a blow that forces the soft tissue of your lip against your teeth. Place a gauze bandage against the cut. Keep pressure on the cut until the bleeding stops.

(3) Abrasions—these are caused by blows that remove the top layer of the skin. Apply antiseptic to the area and cover with a sterile pad.

(4) Nosebleed—this is caused by a blow that ruptures the small capillaries in the septum. To stop the bleeding, compress the nostrils together for a few minutes until the bleeding stops.

(5) Black eye—this is caused by a blow that ruptures the small capillaries around the eye. Apply ice directly to the injured area and then use heat packs once the swelling has stopped.

491. GET MEDICAL TREATMENT IMMEDIATELY.

If you find that you are seriously injured after a fight, seek medical assistance immediately. Have a good friend drive you to the hospital or dial 911 and request an ambulance. Try to stay calm, breathe slowly, and tell the emergency dispatcher your exact location. If you are bleeding heavily, apply direct pressure to the wound site. If the wound is on a limb, elevate the extremity above the level of the heart. This will slow down the loss of blood. If you get cut or shot in the leg, do not try to stand up or walk. This will worsen the injury and increase the loss of blood.

492. PREPARE FOR REVENGE.

No one likes to lose. In fact, whenever you defeat an assailant in a fight, there's always the possibility that he will seek revenge. Some assailants are direct. They'll wait a few days and launch a surprise attack. I know of one street fighter who sought revenge by hiding behind a tree with a baseball bat. When his victim walked by, he turned him into a bloody pulp. Other assailants are more twisted and indirect. Some get tremendous satisfaction by attacking or terrorizing your family, blowing up your car, harassing you at work, breaking into your home, or mutilating your pet. The best advice to avoid revenge or retaliation is to avoid disclosing any information about yourself or your family. If the fight occurs next to your car, avoid letting your assailant see your license plate. Once the assailant is out of the fight, leave the scene immediately. You don't want him to remember what you look like. If the fight was newsworthy, stay clear of the press. You don't want your name or face on the 11 o'clock news or in the morning paper.

493. PREPARE FOR A LEGAL BATTLE.

You should prepare yourself for a possible legal battle. Not all combat situations end in a desolate alley. Many are dragged into the courtroom. In America, anybody can sue anybody for anything. Maybe your assailant can find a legal basis for a lawsuit. Martial artists, self-defense experts, and firearms instructors should be particularly careful when fighting. If you're not careful, you can be ruined financially or thrown into jail. Now is a good time to find an attorney who can represent you if a situation arises. Make certain that your attorney specializes in criminal law. Find out his or her exact credentials and record. More importantly, you want an attorney who can be reached when you may need him or her the most.

CHAPTER FIVE

Grappling and Ground Fighting

"Approximately 90 percent of all street fights go to the ground. Need I say more?"

THE BASICS

494. KNOW YOUR ODDS.
Regardless of how proficient your striking arsenal may be, there is still a very strong possibility that the fight will go to the ground. As a matter of fact, nine out of ten fights go to the ground. Make certain that you are equipped with the knowledge and skills necessary to handle a ground fight.

495. MASTER BOTH GRAPPLING PLANES.
If you want to be truly prepared for the street, make certain that you can fight in both the vertical and horizontal grappling planes. Many fighters assume that grappling can only take place on the ground. To the contrary, grappling often occurs while two fighters are standing toe-to-toe with one another.

496. MASTER THE GROUND.
Though there are many strategic reasons to master ground fighting, range proficiency is one of the most important. Ground fighting mastery means possessing the knowledge, skills, and attitude necessary to fight your adversary efficiently and effectively on the ground.

To master the ground fight, you must study and ultimately possess a wide variety of skills and tactics. Here is a brief list: (1) using anatomical handles; (2) establishing and maintaining the mounted position; (3) applying submission holds from the mounted position; (4) striking from the mounted position; (5) defending against the mounted assailant; (6) establishing and maintaining the leg guard position; (7) applying submission holds from the leg guard position; (8) striking from the leg guard position; (9) defending against the leg guard position; (10) escaping various submission holds from a variety of angles and vantages; (11) possessing a variety of conventional ground fighting tactics that can be employed in nonlethal situations; and (12) possessing a variety of nuclear ground fighting tactics that can be used in lethal force situations.

497. BE PREPARED FOR THE GROUND FIGHT.
If you're not prepared for a potential ground fight, you may be subjected to (1) premature exhaustion (to the untrained, ground fighting is the most exhausting form of fighting), (2) panic, (3) injury or possible death, (4) humiliation, (5) defeat, and (6) suffocation.

498. ACCEPT THE FACT.
Accept the fact that if your assailant is determined to take you to the ground, he will most likely succeed.

499. KNOW THE TACTICAL LIMITATIONS OF GROUND FIGHTING.
Never forget the following tactical limitations of ground fighting: (1) multiple assailants—since ground fighting requires maximal body entanglement, it is virtually impossible to fight multiple attackers; (2) edged weapons—it is often difficult to defend against knives and other edged weapons when locked up with your assailant; (3) spectator intervention—spectator intervention can

occur when you are locked up in a ground fight; (4) positional asphyxia—when ground fighting a heavier assailant, a position that interrupts breathing, causing unconsciousness or death, can occur if you're not careful; (5) terrain—the type of terrain you're ground fighting on can be dangerous (e.g., broken glass, sharp metal, broken wood, etc.); (6) environmental dangers—your environment and immediate surroundings can harm you (i.e., heavy traffic, a cliff, a street curb, etc.); (7) limited vision—ground fighting can significantly inhibit your peripheral vision; and (8) limited mobility—you cannot move quickly when you are locked in a ground fight.

Don't forget the tactical limitations of ground fighting. Remember, it's virtually impossible to fight multiple attackers.

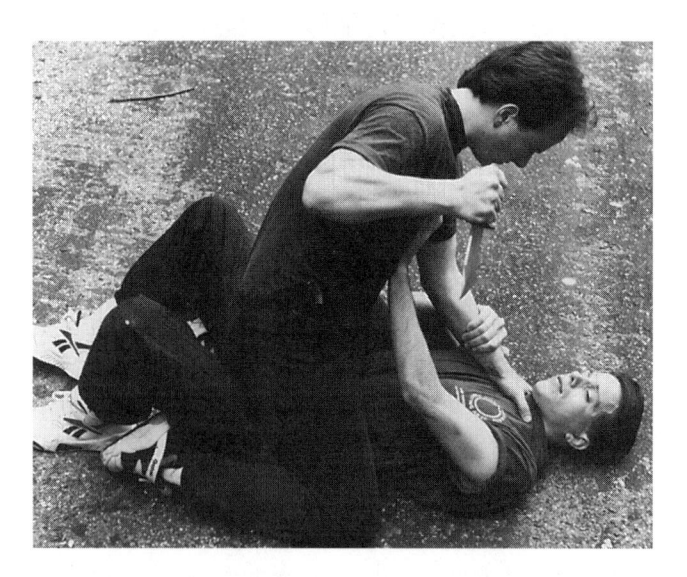

It's extremely difficult to defend against knives and other edged weapons when locked up with your assailant on the ground.

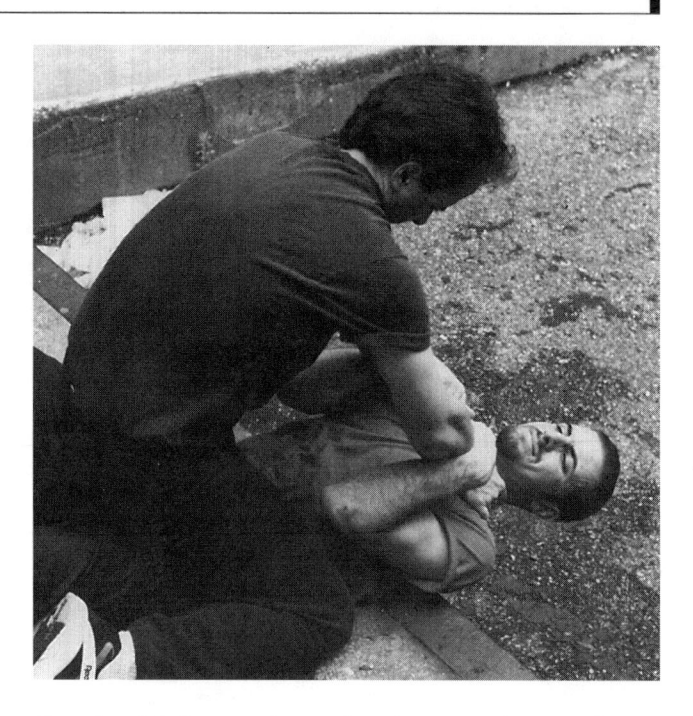

Never forget that your environment can harm you when ground fighting. In this photo, the man on the bottom has a lot more to worry about than just a choke.

500. **KNOW THE INHERENT DANGERS OF SUBMISSION HOLDS.**
Although control and restraint techniques (submission holds) are a necessary component of your combat cache, never forget their inherent risks and limitations, some of which are based on the following factors: (1) somatotypes—many ground fighting maneuvers and techniques will not work effectively against large and anatomically flexible assailants; (2) assailant's size and strength—these factors can often negate the effectiveness of certain submission holds; (3) psychoactive drugs—their effects will often nullify your control and restraint techniques; (4) exact anatomical positioning—this is crucial to any submission technique's working effectively; (5) frenetic movements—it is often difficult to apply precise submission holds because of your assailant's frenetic movements; and (6) clothing—you can't employ certain submission holds effectively when wearing thick or cumbersome clothing (i.e., rain slickers, goose-down jackets, snow suits, etc.).

501. **KNOW THE FOUR SUBMISSION CLASSIFICATIONS.**
There are four submission hold classifications

GRAPPLING AND GROUND FIGHTING

that you must be aware of. They include (1) pain-compliance submission holds; (2) asphyxiation submission holds involving a) air—the air supply is temporarily cut off and b) blood—oxygenated blood is cut off temporarily; (3) joint-manipulation submission holds involving a) counter-joint movement—pressure is applied against the motion of the joint and b) hyperextension—the joint is forced beyond its natural range of motion; and (4) immobilization submission holds.

502. KNOW THE FIVE GROUND FIGHTING POSITIONS.

Although ground fighting is a very dynamic form of unarmed combat, these are the five general positions that you will find yourself in: (1) mounted position—this is when you are sitting on top of your assailant's torso or chest; (2) perpendicular mount—this is when both of your legs are on one side of your assailant's body, and your body runs perpendicular to your assailant's body; (3) guard position—this is

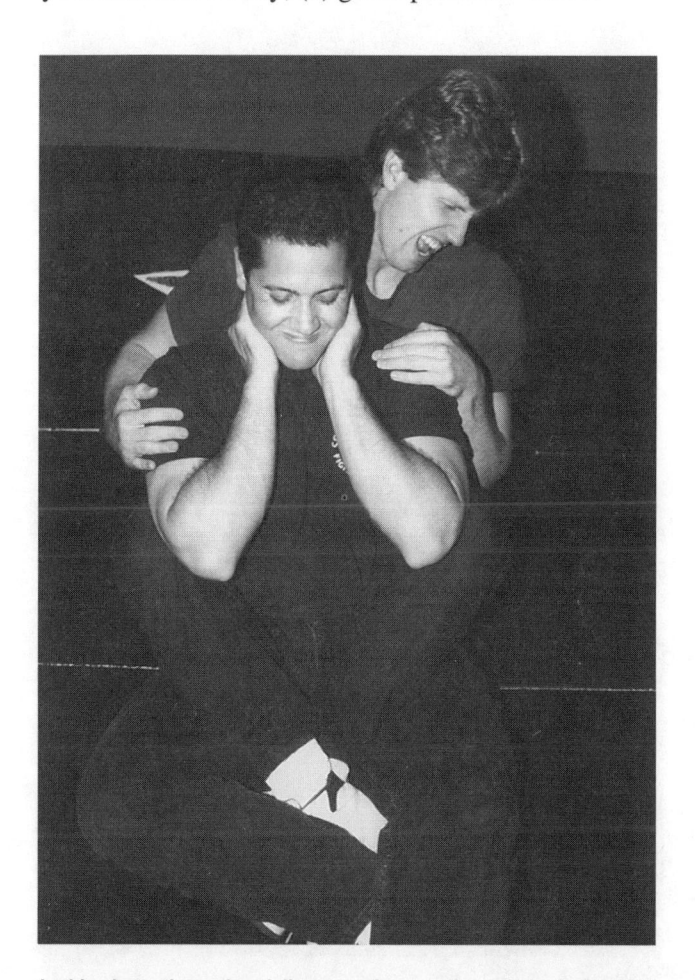

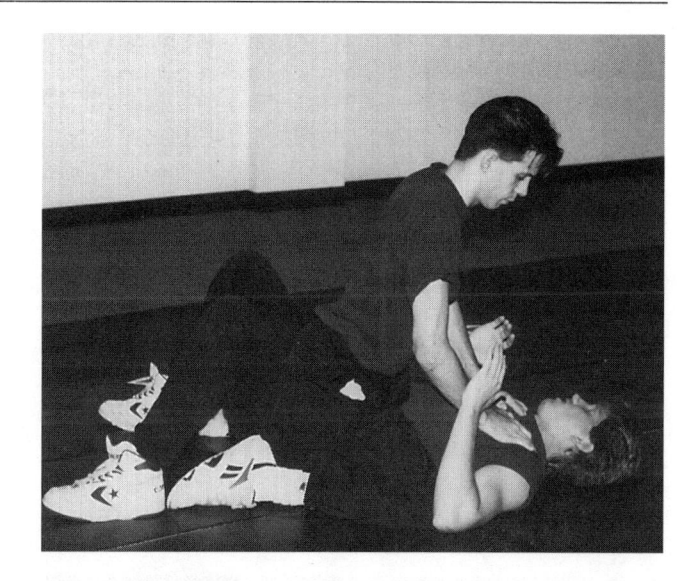

The mounted position.

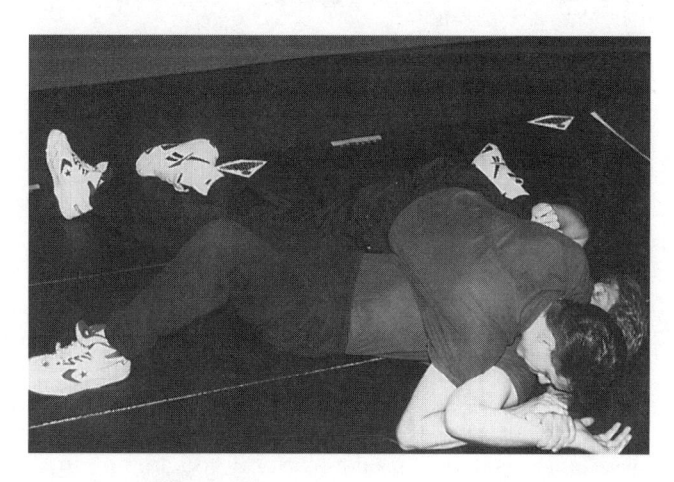

The perpendicular mount.

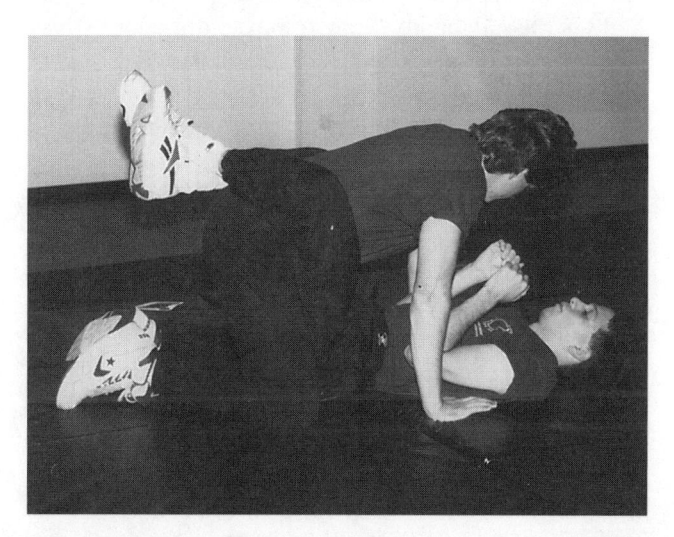

In this photo, the author delivers a pain-compliance submission hold.

The guard position.

The back position.

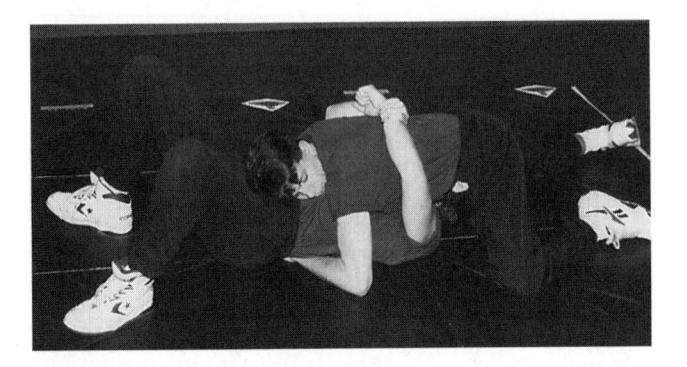

The opposite pole position.

when your assailant's torso is held between your legs; (4) back position—this is when your chest is on the assailant's back (it does not matter if you are on top of him, he is on top of you, or you are both on your sides); and (5) opposite poles—this is when both you and your assailant are facing opposite directions (this often occurs when sprawling against your adversary).

503. KNOW THE STANDING, KNEELING, AND PRONE VARIATIONS.

In grappling range, there's a variety of postures from which you can engage your assailant. They include the following: (1) both you and your assailant are prone, (2) you are kneeling and your assailant is prone, (3) your assailant is kneeling and you are prone, (4) both you and your assailant are kneeling, (5) you are standing and your assailant is prone, (6) your assailant is standing and you are prone, (7) you are standing and your assailant is kneeling, (8) your assailant is standing and you are kneeling, and (9) both you and your assailant are standing.

GRIPS

504. KNOW THE DIFFERENT HAND GRIPS.

The foundations of many submission holds are predicated on your hand grip. There are many different types of hand grips. Here are three that you should know: (1) three-finger grip—join your hands together and place your thumb between the index and middle finger of your other hand, then clasp your hands together; (2) knife-hand grip—join your hands together by grasping the knife edge of your other hand; and (3) wrist grip—join your hands together by grasping the wrist of your other hand. ***NOTE: Make certain you can apply them with both your right and left hands.***

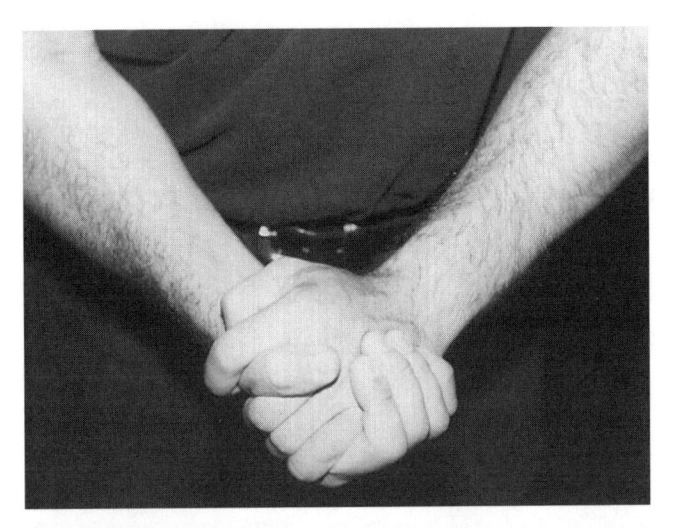

The three-finger grip.

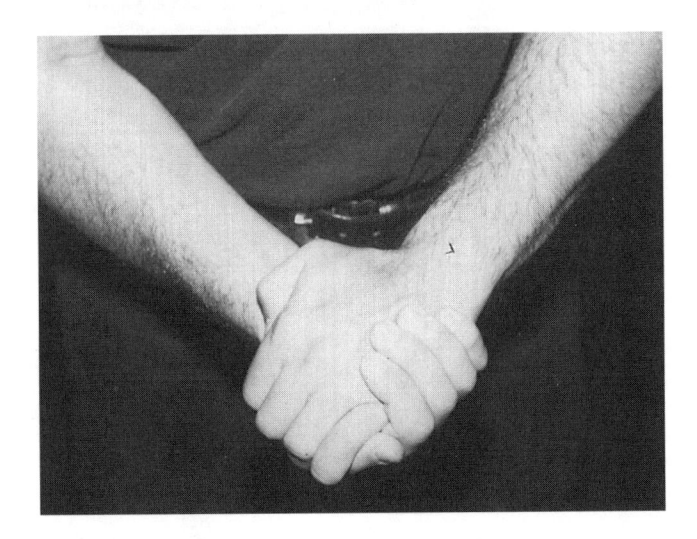

The knife-hand grip.

GRAPPLING AND GROUND FIGHTING

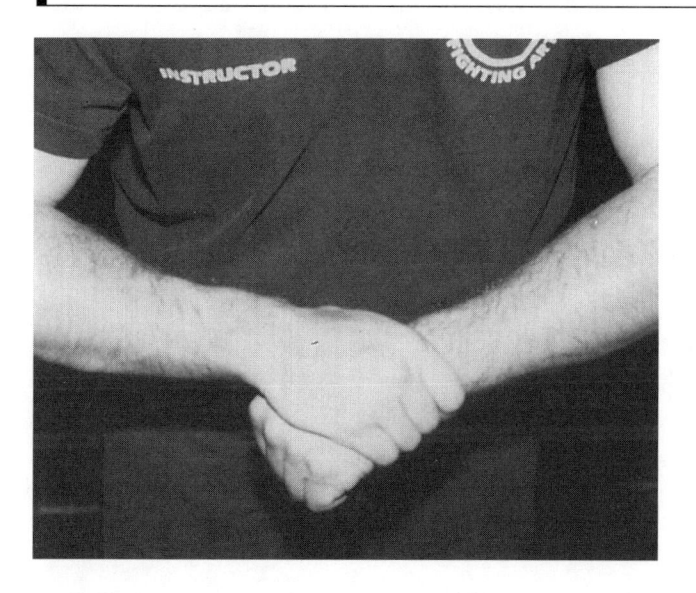

The wrist grip.

The Indian grip.

505. NEVER INTERLACE YOUR FINGERS.
The finger interlace grip is one of the most common and ineffective hand grips. Under no circumstances should you ever interlace your fingers to establish a grip. The finger interlace grip is dangerous for the following reasons: (1) it dramatically inhibits your ability to switch to another grip or hold, (2) it provides poor structural integrity, and (3) if your assailant can reach your fingers, he can squeeze them together, causing extreme pain and a possible finger dislocation.

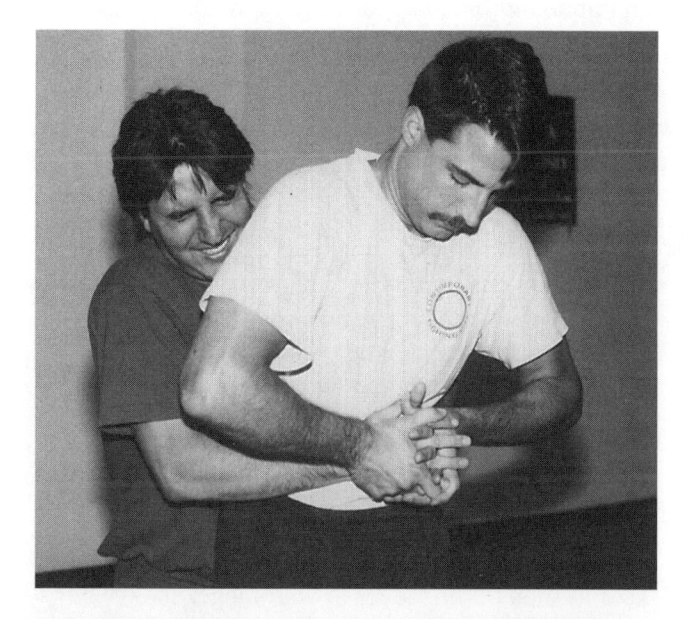

Look what can happen to you if you use the finger interlace grip.

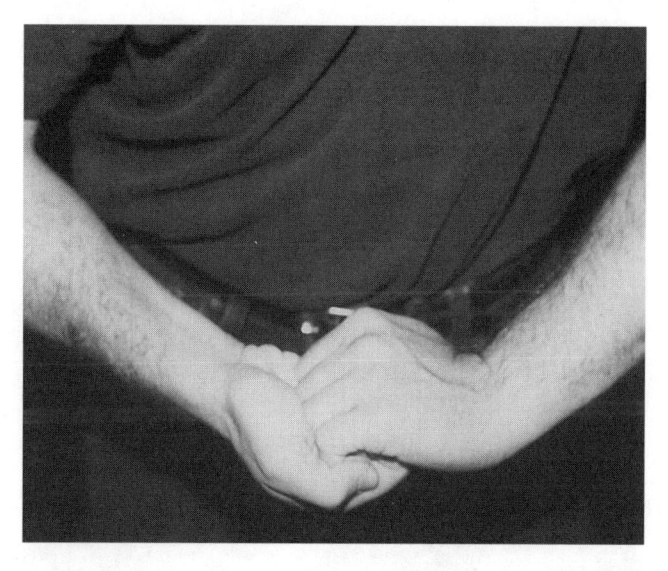

506. NEVER USE A FULL-HAND GRIP.
When ground fighting with your adversary, never use a full-hand grip. This feckless grip is combatively deficient because it separates your thumb too much from your other four fingers. This weakens the structural integrity of your grip, thus allowing your assailant to escape your hold. Consider using the Indian grip instead.

CONVENTIONAL SUBMISSION TECHNIQUES

507. POSSESS CONVENTIONAL GROUND FIGHTING TOOLS AND TECHNIQUES.
In fighting situations where lethal force is unwarranted (i.e., schoolyard fight, feud between relatives, unarmed scuffle with drunk friend, etc.), conventional ground fighting tactics are in order. Conventional ground fighting techniques are not designed to maim or terminate your assailant. However, when applied properly, they will put him out of commission. Some conventional tactics include (1) all submission holds and locks, (2) certain choking techniques, and (3) certain striking techniques.

508. LEARN BY FEELING.
The only real way to learn ground fighting skills is to experience them. "Feeling" every movement is your first step to grappling mastery.

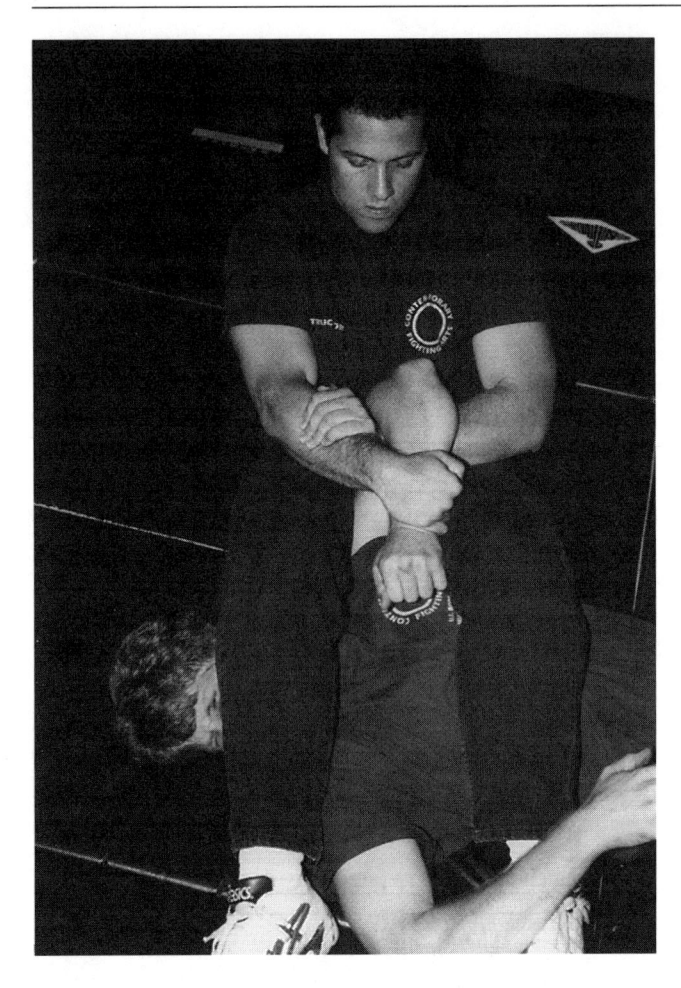

The figure four modification is a common conventional ground fighting technique.

The chicken wing is another conventional ground fighting technique.

In this photo, a student (bottom) immobilizes his assailant with the scissors hold.

509. MASTER THE SCISSORS HOLD.

When you're on your back, one of the best methods of preventing the assailant from establishing the mounted position is to employ the scissors hold (leg guard). To apply the scissors hold, wrap both of your legs around the assailant's waist and hook your ankles together. Be certain to keep both of your legs tightly secured around his waist. You inflict pain on the assailant by straightening your legs and simultaneously squeezing them together. Keep in mind that strong adductor (inner thigh) muscles play an important role in solidifying the hold.

510. TAILSPIN.

In a street fight, there is always the possibility that you may slip and fall to the ground. While your assailant does have the tactical advantage, you can use the tailspin technique to get yourself out of trouble. The tailspin technique is executed by first chambering one of your legs back (to launch a kick) and then pivoting and rotating your body in the direction of your assailant. Quick pivoting can be accomplished by spinning on your butt while your elbows maintain your balance.

The tailspin technique will allow you to accomplish the following objectives: (1) temporarily prevent your assailant from either rushing, jumping, or kicking you; (2) keep your assailant back; (3) injure your assailant if he moves in your range; and (4) buy you a little time to further assess your situation.

GRAPPLING AND GROUND FIGHTING

511. USE THE CHEST COMPRESSION.

The chest compression is one of the most effective methods of throwing your assailant into a state of panic. To execute this submission hold, apply the following steps: (1) from the mounted position, drop down and pull your assailant's face deep into your chest cavity; (2) let your body weight sink into your assailant's nose and mouth; (3) stabilize your assailant's head by grasping the nape of his neck with both hands; (4) make certain to keep both of your elbows in, close to your body; (5) keep your head down and your entire body low to the ground; and (6) spread both of your legs wide apart or maintain a tight grapevine on both of your assailant's legs. (The grapevine is so named because the body mechanics of the technique are similar to a grapevine entwined around a post.)

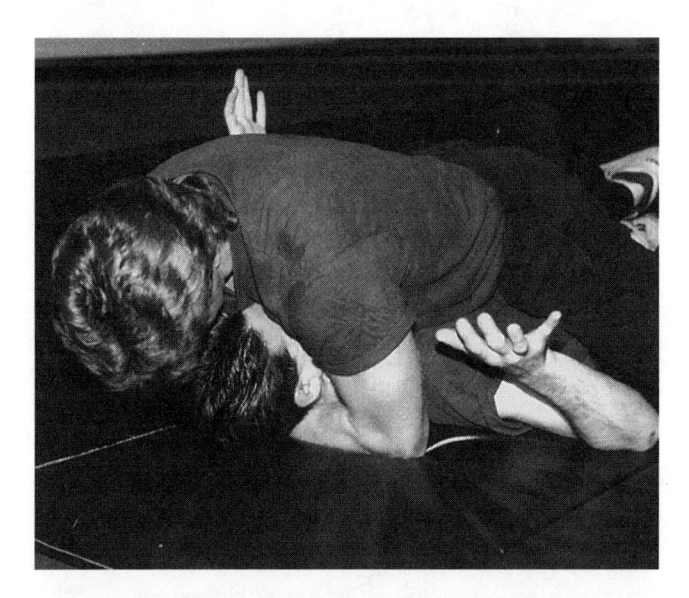

The chest compression can throw the most seasoned grappler into a state of panic.

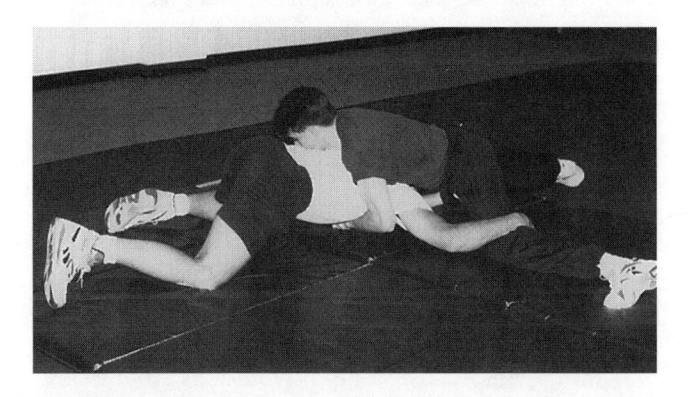

Here, a student (top) demonstrates the sprawl technique against a charging aggressor.

512. SPRAWL.

Sprawling is one of the best methods of countering an assailant who attempts an appendage takedown (e.g., double-leg takedown). The sprawl is accomplished by lowering your hips to the ground while simultaneously shooting both of your legs back. The primary objective of sprawling is to get your legs back and force your body weight onto your assailant's shoulders and head.

513. GRAPEVINE YOUR ADVERSARY.

A grapevine is a stabilizing technique used when your assailant is on his back. The grapevine is applied when you have either one (single-leg grapevine) or both (double-leg grapevine) of your feet hooked around the assailant's legs.

The grapevine serves several strategic purposes, including the following: (1) it can stabilize or immobilize your assailant's movement, (2) it causes your assailant to panic, (3) it causes pain for your assailant, and (4) it prevents your assailant from bumping you from the mounted position.

514. CHOKE YOUR ASSAILANT OUT.

There are several chokes that can be applied in the grappling range. However, one of the most effective chokes you can employ is the naked choke. The naked choke is known for putting an assailant to sleep in a matter of seconds.

To apply the naked choke effectively, follow these important steps: (1) be certain to apply the choke from behind your assailant, (2) begin the naked choke by positioning your right arm around your assailant's neck with your palm facing down, (3) make certain the assailant's windpipe is positioned in the crook of your right elbow, (4) put your right hand

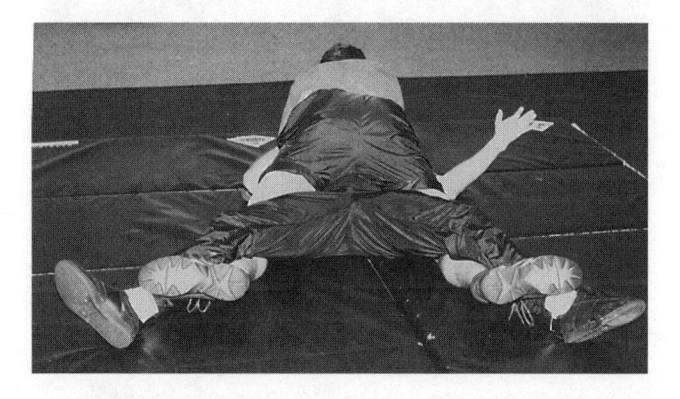

The double-leg grapevine.

The naked choke. Begin the technique by positioning your right arm around your assailant's neck with your right palm facing down. Be certain the assailant's windpipe is positioned in the crook of your right elbow.

Place the blade side of your left forearm on the back of the assailant's neck. With your right arm, slowly squeeze the sides of the assailant's neck.

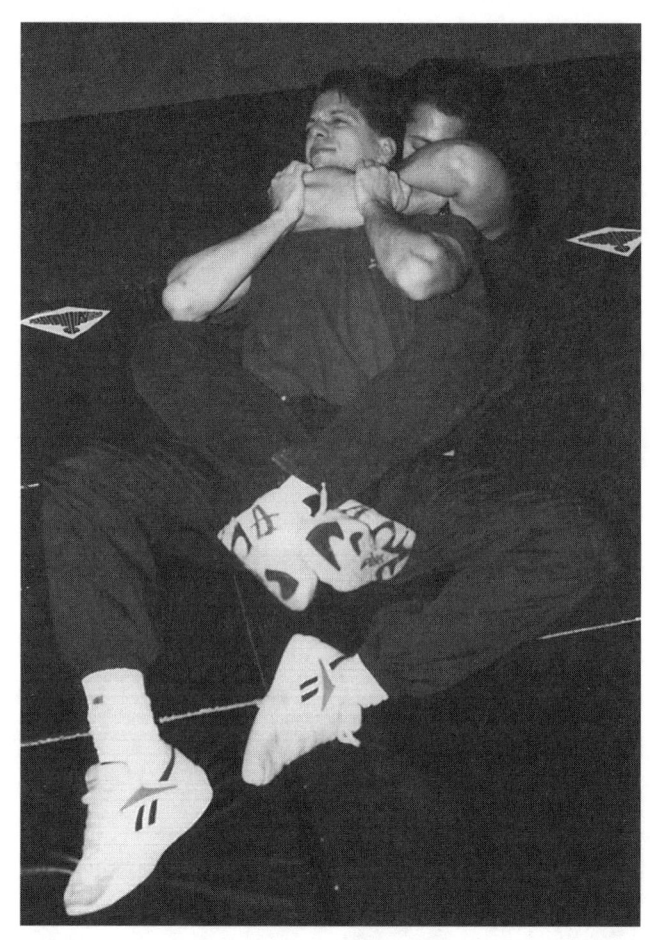

Wrap your legs around his waist and fall back.

on your left shoulder, (5) place the blade side of your left forearm on the back of the assailant's neck, and (6) with your right arm, slowly squeeze the lateral sides of the assailant's neck.

515. CRANK YOUR ASSAILANT'S SHOULDER.

The shoulder crank is an effective technique that is applied when your assailant is held inside your scissors hold. To apply the shoulder crank, do the following: (1) with your assailant lying on top of you, uncross your scissors hold and grab the assailant's right wrist with your left hand; (2) quickly reach over his right arm (triceps region) with your right arm and grab your left wrist; (3) elevate the assailant's elbow and crank his right arm backward as he falls onto the floor; and (4) shuffle and turn your body sideways so the assailant's face and chest are flat against the floor; (5) once again, scissors both of your legs around the assailant's waist; and (6) maintain pressure on his shoulder joint.

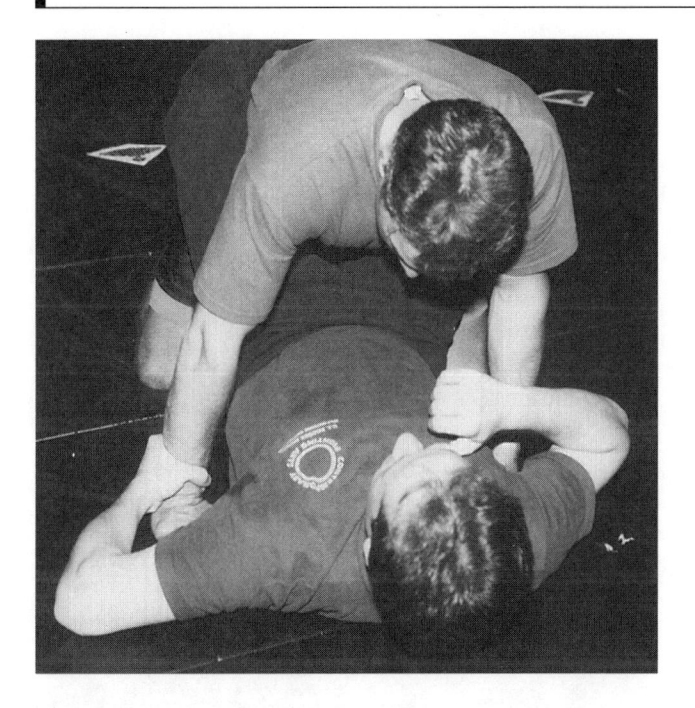

GRAPPLING AND GROUND FIGHTING

The shoulder crank. First, with your assailant lying inside your leg guard, uncross your scissors hold and grab the assailant's right wrist with your left hand.

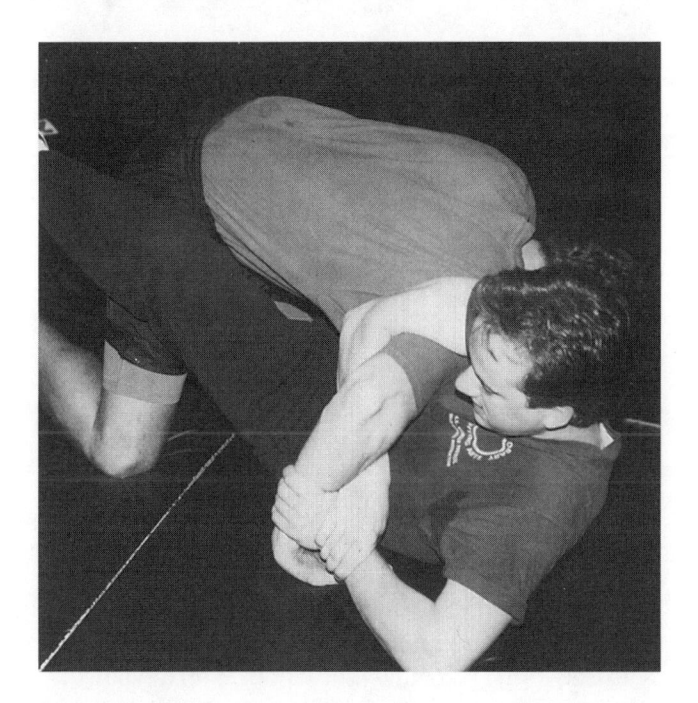

Now quickly reach over his right arm (triceps region) with your right arm and grab your left wrist. This is known as a figure four hold.

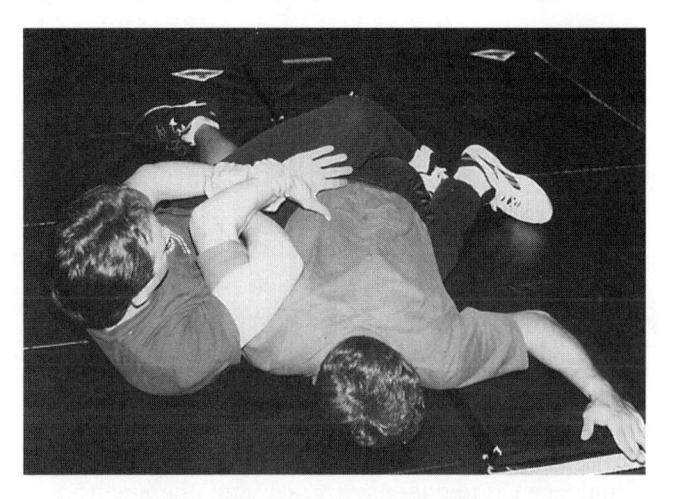

Finally, elevate the assailant's elbow and crank his right arm backward as he falls onto the floor. Shuffle and turn your body to the side so the assailant's face and chest are flat against the floor. Once again, scissors both of your legs around the assailant's waist and maintain pressure on the shoulder joint.

516. KNOW THE LEG GUARD STRATEGY.

There is much more to the leg guard (scissors hold) than simply wrapping your legs around your assailant's waist and holding him in place. The leg guard is an excellent grappling hold that will permit you to execute a variety of techniques and maneuvers. Some include the following: (1) reverse and turn your assailant onto his back, (2) apply joint locks, (3) squeeze your assailant into submission, and (4) choke your assailant out.

Here are a few more reasons why the leg guard should be employed in a ground fight: (1) it prevents your assailant from mounting you, (2) it causes extreme pain for your assailant, (3) it restricts your assailant's breathing, (4) it bruises and injures your assailant's internal organs, (5) it restricts your assailant's mobility, and (6) it controls your assailant for submission manipulation. **WARNING: Be careful when placing your assailant in a leg guard. If you don't embrace the range and tie up his hands and arms, he might be able to strike you.**

517. MASTER THE JAPANESE ARM BAR.

The Japanese arm bar is a versatile submission hold that can be used in a variety of different positions. One of the best positions is when you have mounted your assailant and he unknowingly offers you an outstretched arm.

To execute the Japanese arm bar from this position, follow these important steps: (1) place both of your palms on the assailant's chest (make certain that the assailant's right arm is between both of your arms); (2) without telegraphing your movements, push off the assailant's chest and lift your entire body up and around the assailant's torso; (3) simultaneously grab hold of the assailant's right wrist with both of your hands, stretching it out as you fall onto your buttocks; (4) once you're on the floor, your body should lie perpendicular to the assailant's body, and his right arm should be between your legs (try to keep your groin region close to the assailant's right shoulder); (5) to guarantee proper arm alignment, make certain your assailant's right thumb is pointing upward and your inner thighs are close together; and (6) to inflict pain on the assailant's elbow, simultaneously arch your back and pull his right wrist toward your chest.

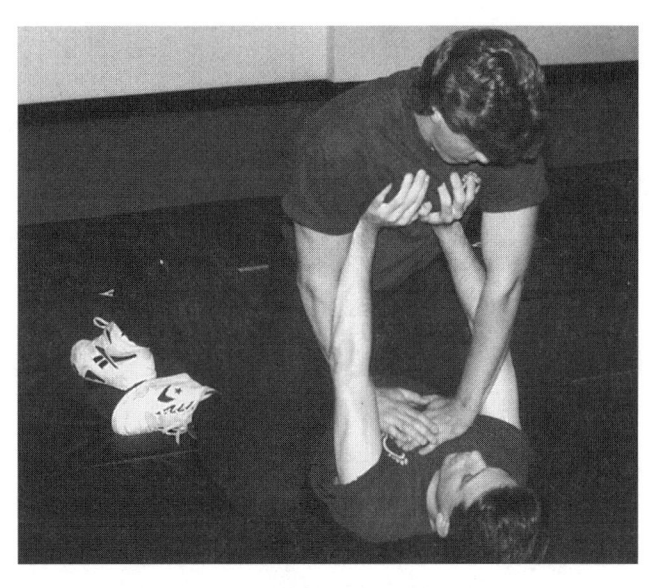

The beginning stage of the Japanese arm bar.

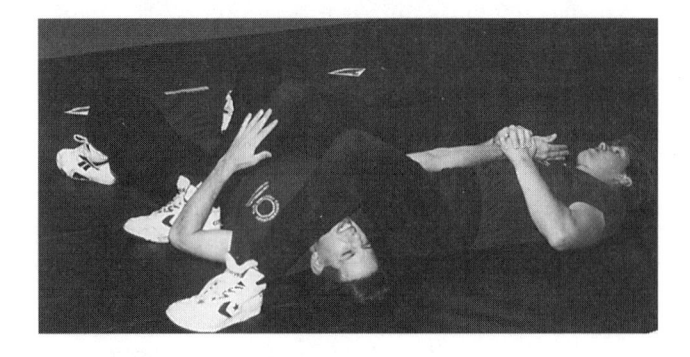

The completion phase of the Japanese arm bar.

518. APPLY THE BOX.

The box technique is a painful submission hold that can be applied when you have perpendicularly or vertically mounted the assailant. To apply this hold, follow these important steps: (1) with your assailant lying on his back, let the weight of your body rest on his chest; (2) quickly grab the assailant's left wrist with your left hand (make certain your left hand is held in the thumb-over position); (3) insert your right hand underneath the assailant's left arm and on top of your left wrist and hold it securely (also make certain your right hand is held in the thumb-over position); and (4) once the hold is positioned, raise the assailant's left elbow slightly and drag his hand down toward his legs (be certain to keep the assailant's wrist on the floor as you drag his arm downward).

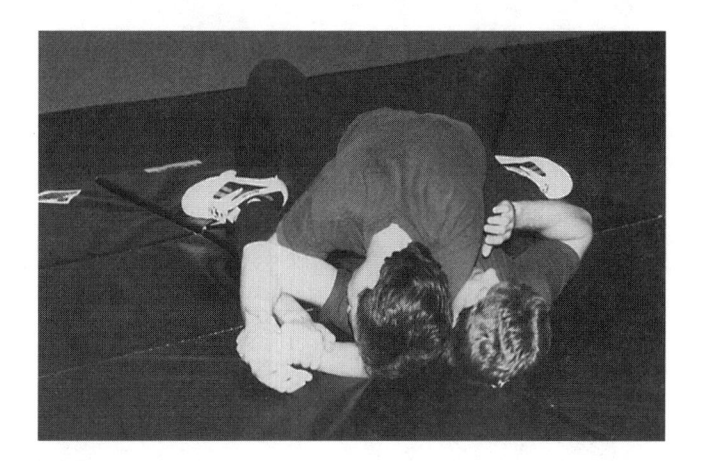

The box technique.

519. KNOW HOW TO COME TO A BASE.

One of the fundamental elements of ground fighting is learning how to correctly "come to a base." Coming to a base means getting up to your hands and knees from the prone position. This is important for the following reasons: (1) it conserves energy, (2) it provides quick defensive capability, (3) it minimizes appendage exposure, and (4) it provides powerful body lift. The proper method of coming to a base consists of first bringing your left knee up to your side and then simultaneously bringing your left elbow into your knee and pushing yourself over that knee.

520. GET OUT OF YOUR ASSAILANT'S LEG GUARD.

Getting out of an assailant's leg guard (scissors hold) is not an easy task. Many well-known grappling

GRAPPLING AND GROUND FIGHTING

arts have attempted to address this issue, yet failed. Basically, there are two effective methods: (1) striking method—attacking the assailant with a flurry of hammer fists to the groin region until the scissors hold is released and (2) submission hold method—strategically twisting and torquing the assailant's ankle and knee.

521. LEAN BACK.

Once you have successfully bumped your assailant out of the mounted position and he has placed you into his leg guard, be certain to lean back. Leaning back is important for the following reasons: (1) it prevents your assailant from embracing you, (2) it offers you the range and angle to strike his groin repeatedly, (3) it will allow you to strike his face effectively if he decides to reach and grab you, and (4) it puts you in a position to escape from his leg guard.

522. MASTER THE BICEPS CHOKE.

The biceps choke is another effective method of controlling your assailant. To apply the biceps choke, take the following steps: (1) with your assailant lying on his back, place your left arm around his neck; (2) with your right hand, push the assailant's left arm across his own neck; (3) use your head to press his left arm against his neck; (4) grab your left arm with your right hand to secure the choke; and (5) drag your right elbow down toward your waist (this will tighten the choke on your assailant).

523. MAINTAIN A LOW BASE.

Whenever you are mounted on your assailant, it is equally important to maintain this position. Maintaining the mounted position is not always an

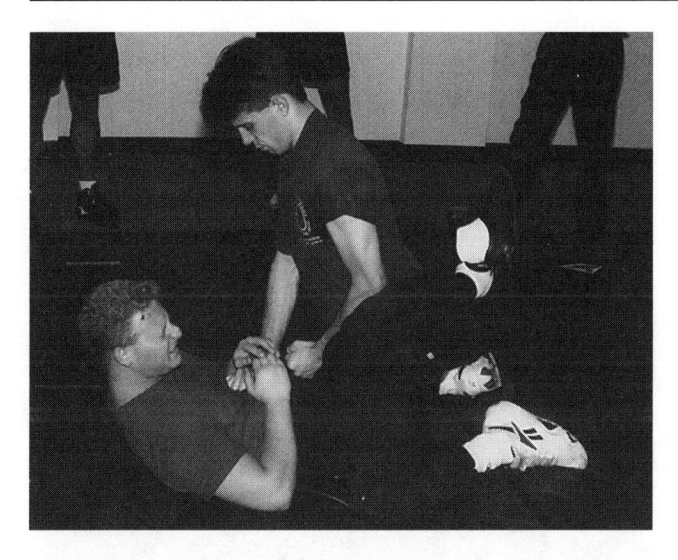

The striking method is one of the most efficient ways of escaping from your assailant's leg guard. Here, a student delivers a series of powerful hammer fist strikes to his assailant's groin.

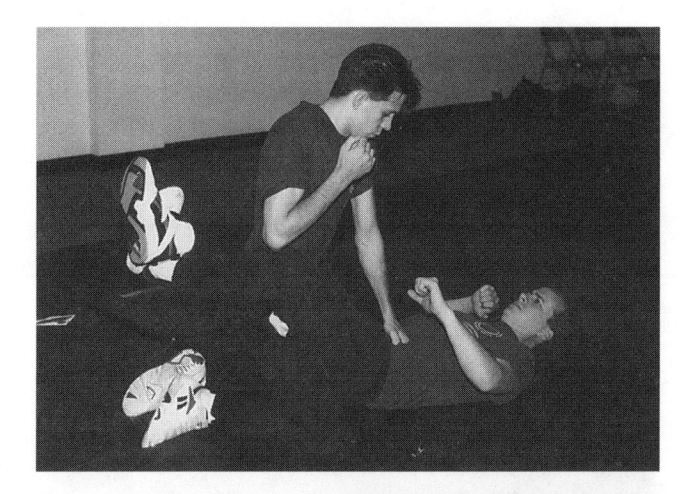

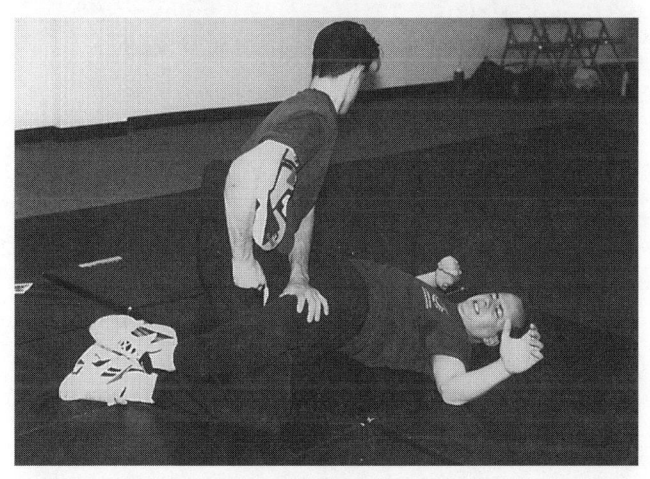

The submission hold method is another way of escaping from your assailant's leg guard. Here, a student applies the escape movement.

The biceps choke.

easy task. Here are some important points to remember: (1) relax your body—a tense or rigid torso makes it easier for the assailant to throw you off; (2) keep your center of gravity low and close to the assailant—when applying submission holds from the mounted position, always keep your chest married against the assailant's chest; (3) be cognizant of where you place your arms—they can be grabbed by the assailant and used as levers to bump you; (4) if possible, keep your feet tucked under his thighs—this creates a "crazy glue" effect between you and the assailant; and (5) be patient—wait for your assailant to make the move that will lead to his demise.

524. MASTER THE WRIST LEVER.

To apply the wrist lever, follow these important steps: (1) from the mounted position, drop your body weight onto the assailant and grab the back of his left hand (his palm facing upward) with your right hand; (2) to stabilize your base, place your left elbow and forearm against the left side of the assailant's head; (3) place the left side of your head on the outside of the assailant's left elbow; and (4) smoothly pull the assailant's left wrist away from the left side of his head.

525. MASTER THE FOREARM CHOKE.

You can choke your assailant from the mounted position by using the forearm choke. To apply this technique, follow these important steps: (1)

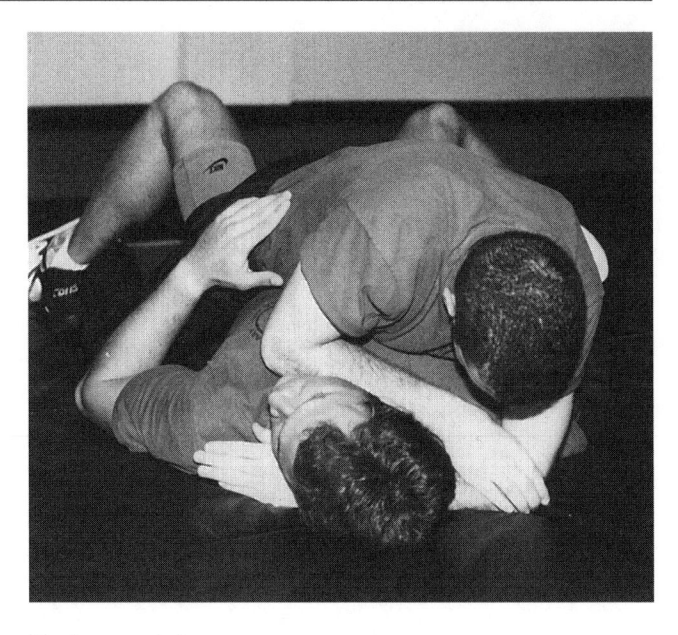

The forearm choke.

from the mounted position, place your left forearm behind the assailant's neck; (2) insert the web of your right hand into the crook of your left forearm and place the blade side of your right forearm into the assailant's windpipe; (3) compress and scissors both of your forearms into one another; and (4) keep your base as low as possible and tuck your face away from the assailant (be sure to employ the double-leg grapevine when applying the forearm choke, because this will prevent your adversary from bumping you out of the mounted position). ***WARNING: The forearm choke can easily crush the assailant's windpipe, causing death. This ground fighting technique should be used only in life-and-death situations when lethal force is warranted.***

526. USE THE ANKLE HOLD.

Contrary to what some fighters might think, there is a time and place for ankle holds. To apply the ankle hold, execute the following: (1) with the assailant on his back, wrap your left arm around his left ankle (make certain the blade of your left forearm is against his left Achilles tendon); (2) with the assailant's left instep tucked in your left armpit, grab your left wrist with your right hand; (3) place your left leg over his left thigh; (4) place your right leg over your left instep and scissor your legs together; and (5) slowly arch your body back while stretching your legs out (pressure is on the assailant's left Achilles tendon).

The wrist lever.

GRAPPLING AND GROUND FIGHTING

In this photo, a student (right) applies the ankle hold.

527. MASTER THE PARTY FLEX.
The party flex is a submission hold that has a wide variety of applications and can be applied while standing or ground fighting. To apply the party flex from the mounted position, apply the following steps: (1) stabilize the assailant's elbow by grabbing his left elbow with your left hand, with your left elbow placed against the left side of his head and (2) use your right hand to flex the assailant's left wrist toward the ground.

The party flex applied from the mounted position.

528. MASTER THE STRAIGHT ARM BAR.
The straight arm bar is another versatile submission hold that can be applied in a variety of different positions. To apply the straight arm bar from a perpendicular mounted position, apply the following: (1) with the assailant on his back and his right arm extended straight out, grab the assailant's right wrist with your left hand; (2) insert your right

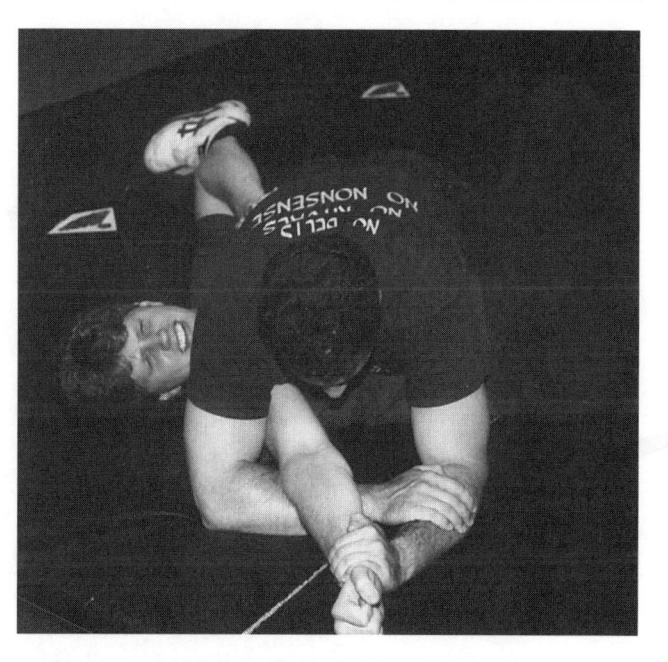

In this photo, Franco applies the straight arm bar from the perpendicular mounted position.

forearm under the assailant's right elbow and grab hold of your left forearm; and (3) while making certain the assailant's right thumb is pointing up, force his right wrist down while forcing his right elbow up with your right forearm (pressure is on his right elbow).

529. PULL YOUR ASSAILANT IN AND CONTROL HIS ARMS.
When applying the leg guard position (scissors hold) on your assailant, be certain to pull him close to your body (embrace the range) and try to control his arms. This is important for the following reasons: (1) it prevents your adversary from effectively striking your groin, (2) it restricts your assailant's ability to strike your face and stomach accurately, (3) it negates the necessary leverage for your assailant to apply locks and chokes, and (4) it allows you the opportunity to apply a variety of submission holds and maneuvers.

530. COUNTER BEAR HUGS.
The bear hug is an ineffective and energy-consuming hold that can expose you to a variety of openings and counters. Bear hugs are used primarily to immobilize your body and throw you to the ground. Nevertheless, the bear hug is a feckless hold that can be countered readily. There are four effective counters to various types of bear hugs.

(1) If you're attacked from the rear and your arms are free, immediately lower your weight and simultaneously widen your feet; thrust your hips and buttocks backward, throwing your attacker backward; then counter with powerful knuckle raps to your assailant's hand. Once his grip is loosened, finger peel your way out of the hug and neutralize him.

(2) If you're attacked from the rear and your arms are pinned to your sides, immediately lower your weight and simultaneously widen your feet, then thrust your hips and buttocks backward, throwing your attacker backward. Counter with multiple hammer fists to the assailant's groin, followed by elbow strikes to his solar plexus.

(3) If you're attacked from the front and your arms are free, you should counter with either hammer fists to the attacker's nose or attack with eye rakes or thumb gouges to his eyes until he releases his hold.

(4) If you're attacked from the front and your arms are pinned to your sides, immediately head butt your attacker's nose and bite if possible, or try to crush his testicles until he releases his hold.

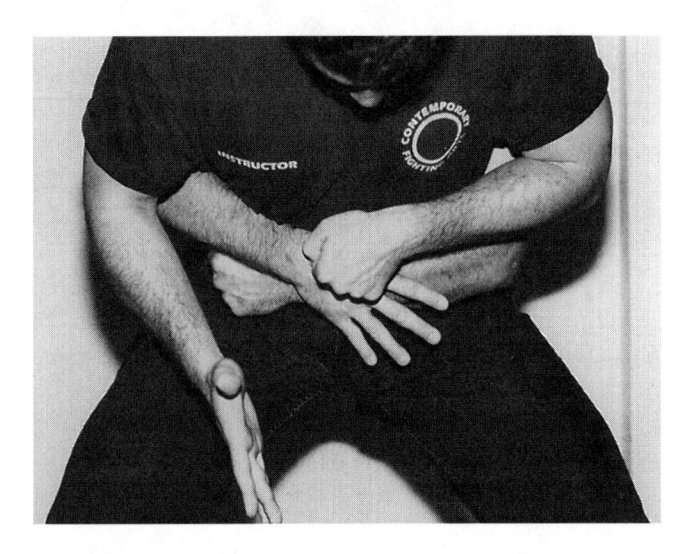

Then counter with a series of quick and powerful knuckle raps to your assailant's hand.

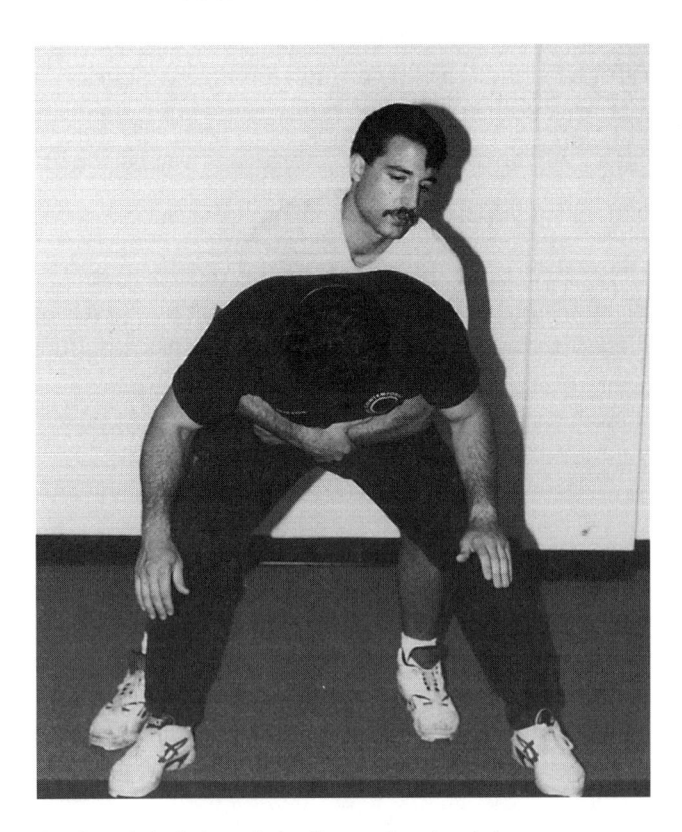

Another method of countering the rear bear hug (when your arms are free) is the knuckle-rap technique. Begin by immediately dropping your weight and simultaneously widening your feet.

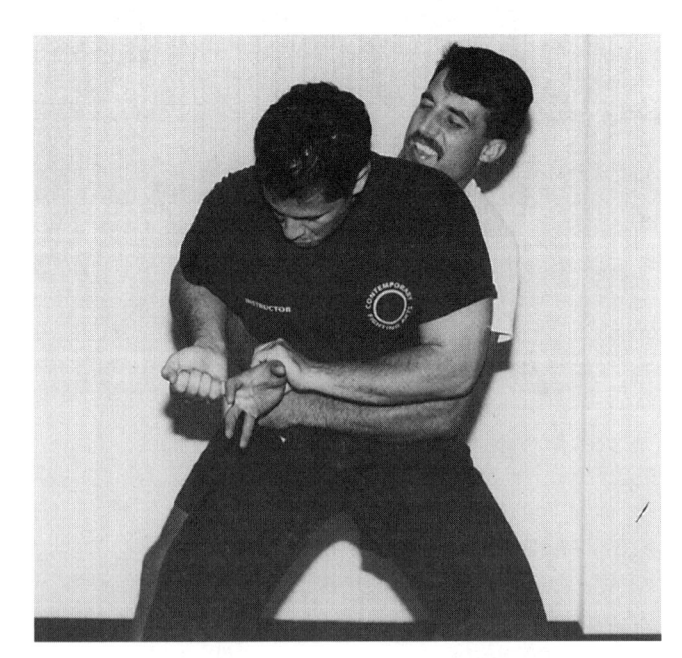

Once the assailant's grip is loosened, you can either finger peel your way out of the hug or break his finger. In this photo, Franco chooses the latter option.

GRAPPLING AND GROUND FIGHTING

STRATEGIES

531. DON'T LET YOUR ASSAILANT BREAK YOUR BALANCE.

If your assailant is to take you down to the ground, he must first disrupt or "break" your balance. Here are the four primary ways he can accomplish this: (1) redirection of force—when your adversary exploits your energy or dynamic pressure; (2) strength manipulation—when your adversary uses his raw power and strength to disrupt your balance; (3) striking—when your assailant hits you and then throws you off balance; and (4) feinting/faking—when your assailant feints and draws a defensive reaction from you and takes you down to the ground.

532. BEWARE OF POSITIONAL ASPHYXIA.

Positional asphyxia is a position that causes a lack of oxygen or excess of carbon dioxide in the body that is usually caused by interruption of breathing and that causes unconsciousness or death. Make it your mission to avoid the dangers of "positional asphyxia."

533. SIT ABOVE YOUR ASSAILANT'S HIPS.

When mounting your assailant, always try to sit above his hips and as close to his chest as possible. This is important for the following reasons: (1) it prevents the assailant from bumping you; (2) it places you closer to the assailant's facial targets so you can effectively strike them; (3) it brings you closer to the assailant's arms and throat for instantaneous submission holds and chokes; and (4) it helps marry his back to the floor.

534. MOVE ON THE GROUND.

One of the foundational elements of effective ground fighting is being able to move well on the floor. Ground fighting mobility is just as important as standing mobility.

535. KNOW YOUR GROUND FIGHTING WEAPONS.

When ground fighting, you have a wide variety of weapons at your disposal. Your ground fighting arsenal is divided into the following five categories: (1) immobilization techniques—various techniques designed to immobilize your adversary; (2) locks—various submission holds designed to manipulate and injure your assailant's limbs; (3) chokes—various techniques designed to restrict your assailant's air or blood supply; (4) natural body weapons—various natural body weapons designed to inflict severe damage (i.e., tight punches, hammer fists, biting, gouging, tearing, etc.); and (5) pain-compliance holds—various techniques that create extreme pain for your adversary.

536. SEIZE THE OPPORTUNITY.

In any grappling situation, you must know how to take advantage of an opportunity. To accomplish this, three elements must be present: (1) you must recognize the opportunity immediately, (2) you must know the proper technique or maneuver that should be applied, and (3) you must be capable of applying the appropriate technique with precision, finesse, and proper timing.

537. MASTER THE THREE GROUND FIGHTING OBJECTIVES.

When engaged in a ground fight, there are three primary objectives that must be acquired. They include (1) controlling or maintaining your position, (2) changing your position (if necessary), (3) acquiring submission (either through striking, joint locks, or chokes).

538. USE ALL THREE ELEMENTS TO CONTROL YOUR ASSAILANT.

There are three primary elements that can be used to control or trap your adversary during a ground fight: (1) your body, (2) your asssailant's body, and (3) the ground.

539. NEVER, EVER ROLL ONTO YOUR STOMACH.

One of the cardinal rules for ground fighting is that under no circumstances should you ever roll over onto your stomach. This is dangerous for the following reasons: (1) the assailant can easily choke you out; (2) your assailant can deliver a barrage of blows to your head, neck, and back; (3) it's virtually impossible to defend against your assailant from this position; and (4) you cannot effectively counterstrike from this position.

540. UTILIZE YOUR DEAD WEIGHT.

When in the mounted position or in a perpendicular mount, always relax your body and rest your dead weight on the assailant's chest, ribs, and diaphragm. This makes your adversary work for every breath.

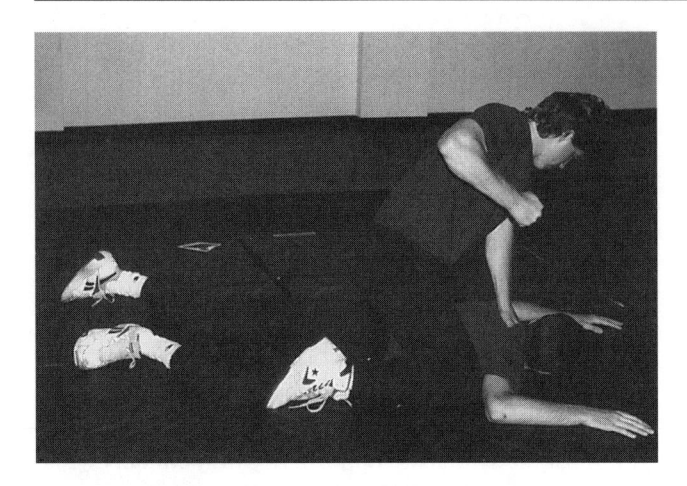

One of the cardinal rules for ground fighting is that under no circumstances should you ever roll over onto your stomach. The dangers should be obvious.

541. EMPLOY ANTI-GRAPPLER STRATEGIES.

When standing toe-to-toe with a grappler, apply the following strategies: (1) stay mobile by moving on the balls of your feet; (2) strike first and try to inflict as much damage on him as you can before he locks up with you; (3) never kick at a charging attacker, as this will throw you off balance, allowing your assailant to control the takedown; (4) when your assailant locks up with you, embrace him and attack with a variety of close-quarter tools; (5) when the fight goes to the ground, immediately go for the mounted position and try to maintain it; and (6) once the mounted position is established, attack the assailant with a barrage of vicious strikes to his facial targets until he is neutralized.

542. DON'T BE DUPED BY A SUCKER PUNCHER.

Since conventional ground fighting tactics are used in non–life threatening situations involving two consenting individuals (squabble with a brother-in-law, drunk friend, or in a schoolyard fight, etc.), you must be aware of the sucker puncher. The sucker puncher is a deceptive assailant who usually feigns submission or compliance in order to be released. Once he is free he will coldcock you. *CAUTION: Be exceptionally careful when releasing your adversary from a submission hold.*

543. MASTER TRANSITIONAL HOLDS.

To minimize your chances of being sucker-punched when releasing a submission hold, you will have to employ a transitional hold. A transitional hold is a sequence of moves that allows you to progressively abort your submission hold in order to safely disengage your assailant.

544. AVOID THROWING YOUR ASSAILANT.

Avoid utilizing throwing techniques in a street fight. Throwing techniques are generally used for one of two reasons.

(1) To use an impact surface to injure your assailant. (This violates the economy of motion principle. Instead, use a natural body weapon as your impact surface.)

(2) To take the fight to the ground. (Remember, the ground is the last place you want to be in a street fight.)

Throwing techniques are risky and inherently dangerous. For example, they require you to place one or both hands on the assailant to lift or lever him into the desired throwing position. This can open you up to a variety of counterstrikes.

545. RELY ON FEEL, NOT SIGHT.

A good ground fighter can control and dominate his assailant by tactile feeling. Tactile "sight" is a critical attribute that will permit you to excel in the ground fight.

546. GRAB YOUR ASSAILANT'S ANATOMICAL HANDLES.

Effective grappling requires a thorough understanding of the assailant's anatomical handles. Anatomical handles are various body parts (i.e., appendages, joints, and, in some cases, organs) that can be grabbed, held, pulled, or otherwise manipulated during a ground fight.

Anatomical handles should be utilized for the following strategic reasons: (1) to temporarily control or immobilize your adversary; (2) for leverage; (3) to injure your assailant; (4) to maintain your balance; (5) to throw, lift, or direct your adversary in a particular direction; and (6) to throw your adversary off balance.

There are numerous anatomical handles, including hair, eye sockets, nose, chin, jaw, ears, throat, neck, elbows, wrists, arms, back of knees, ankles, and hip region.

GRAPPLING AND GROUND FIGHTING

547. DON'T OFFER YOUR ARMS TO YOUR ASSAILANT.

If your assailant has established the mounted position during the ground fight, be certain NOT to offer him an extended arm. This can be dangerous for the following reasons: (1) your elbows will lose strategic placement on his thighs, thus allowing him the opportunity to ride higher in the mounted position, which will give him the ability to force you over and onto your stomach; (2) your assailant can perform a variety of holds and chokes, including the biceps choke and the Japanese arm bar.

548. WORK QUICKLY AND PRUDENTLY.

The longer a fight lasts, the greater your chances of injury or death. This is especially true in a ground fight. When grappling with an assailant, it's essential that you don't rush a movement or technique.

If you work too quickly, you will be subjecting yourself to the following potential risks and dangers: (1) you can lose your positional advantage, (2) you can lose your balance, (3) you can lose your leverage and expose yourself to a variety of counterholds by the assailant, and (4) the strategic timing to the application of a technique will be compromised, and the technique will not work.

549. SHOOT YOUR LEGS BACK.

When riding on top of your assailant's back, it is important to get him flat on his stomach as quickly as possible. The best method of accomplishing this task is by leg shooting. Leg shooting is applied as follows: (1) maintain your position by grabbing hold of your assailant's neck; (2) when the assailant attempts to stand up, let the weight of your entire body drop onto his back and then insert both of your legs inside his legs; (3) quickly drive both of your legs down and into his inner thighs while simultaneously thrusting your hips and upper body forward, forcing your legs to stretch out; (4) this will force the assailant to drop flat on the ground where you can proceed with a variety of techniques.

550. FORGET EMPLOYING TAKEDOWNS.

Takedowns are various maneuvers designed to take your assailant down to the ground. Takedown techniques can be applied to either the assailant's upper or lower body, and they can be initiated from a variety of positions.

Although takedowns may sound effective, they present significant dangers and should be eliminated from your repertoire of techniques. Here are the reasons why: (1) they provoke a ground fight, (2) they require significant energy expenditure, (3) they bring your facial targets within knee- and elbow-strike range, (4) they can be negated with effective sprawling maneuvers, and (5) they present the risk of your being suffocated.

551. EXPLOIT YOUR ENVIRONMENT.

Once you've established the mounted position, you can take advantage of your environment and use it to your advantage. Here are a few examples: (1) drive or smash the assailant's head or face into the pavement or street curb; (2) force your assailant's head under water, sand, snow, thick mud, or a pile of wet leaves for a prolonged period of time; (3) shove your adversary's head or eyes into broken glass; (4) thrust your assailant's eyes or head into barbed or razor wire; and (5) maneuver your assailant's entire head into the pathway of moving machinery.

WARNING: This type of environmental exploitation should only be used in life-and-death encounters where lethal force is warranted and justified in the eyes of the law.

552. KICK YOUR ADVERSARY FROM THE GROUND.

There are some instances during a ground fight when you'll have the opportunity to launch a quick kick at your adversary. For example, if the assailant attempts an ankle hold, a quick kick to his face or throat may be in order. Depending on his angle and vantage, some anatomical targets may include the

If your assailant attempts an ankle hold, a quick kick to his chin or throat may be in order.

assailant's thighs, shins, knees, groin, face, or throat. **WARNING: Be prudent when delivering kicking techniques during a ground fight. Avoid full chambering positions prior to delivering your kick. Not only will this telegraph your movements, but it will also allow the assailant to trap and control your lower body.**

553. KEEP YOUR KNEES UP.

Whenever your assailant mounts you, it's important to instinctively keep your knees raised up. This is important for the following reasons: (1) it brings your foot closer to the trapping foot position necessary to bump the assailant off you; (2) it offers greater leverage and thrusting power than straight legs; (3) raised knees also facilitate mobility on the ground; and (4) a raised knee (chambered position) is a prerequisite for an effective kick from the ground.

Whenever your assailant mounts you, it's important to instinctively keep your knees raised. In this photo, a student raises his right knee and traps his assailant's mounting leg.

554. EMBRACE THE RANGE.

Embracing the range is a ground fighting strategy that is often used when your assailant has mounted you and you cannot escape immediately. Embracing the range means pulling or embracing your assailant. This is often accomplished by securing his neck with a hooked arm.

Embracing the range is important for the following reasons: (1) it negates the assailant's reach and angle to deliver accurate blows; (2) it negates the assailant's gravitational advantage to deliver powerful blows; (3) it brings your assailant closer to you so you can execute an escape technique effectively; and (4) it temporarily prevents your assailant from applying various locks and chokes. The best hand grip for embracing the range is the Indian grip. *NOTE: Embracing the range can also be applied when your assailant is inside your leg guard.*

555. KEEP YOUR HEAD.

As in all forms of combat, it is essential that you keep your head during the course of a ground fight. Losing your temper or panicking can cost you your life. The following are various reasons why you must keep your cool during the course of a ground fight: (1) it conserves your energy, (2) it keeps your mind focused on the task at hand, (3) it keeps your psychomotor skills sharp, (4) it enhances your combat perceptions, (5) it enhances your killer instinct, (6) it aids in accurate assessment skills, (7) it significantly reduces your target exposure, and (8) it psyches out your adversary.

556. MOUNT YOUR ADVERSARY IMMEDIATELY.

When a street fight goes down to the ground, it behooves you to acquire the mounted position immediately. The fighter who establishes the mounted position has a tremendous tactical advantage in the ground fight. In many ways, the mounted position is the "cockpit" from which to ground fight effectively. The most important aspect of the mounted position is that it facilitates your delivering of a variety of blows and submission holds while making it very difficult for your assailant to counter or escape effectively.

557. HIDE YOUR FACE.

When applying various submission holds and chokes from the mounted position (i.e., box, party flex, wrist levers, forearm or biceps chokes), make it a habit to keep your face and head tucked away. Tucking your face into your shoulders will lower your base and also reduce the possibility of your assailant striking you.

558. CHOOSE THE APPROPRIATE BLOW.

Depending on the "use-of-force" justification, you must choose the appropriate blow when sitting in the mounted position. Generally, linear punches (e.g., lead straights, rear crosses) are much more destructive than circular blows, because the

GRAPPLING AND GROUND FIGHTING

When applying various submission holds and chokes, make it a habit to keep your face and head tucked away.

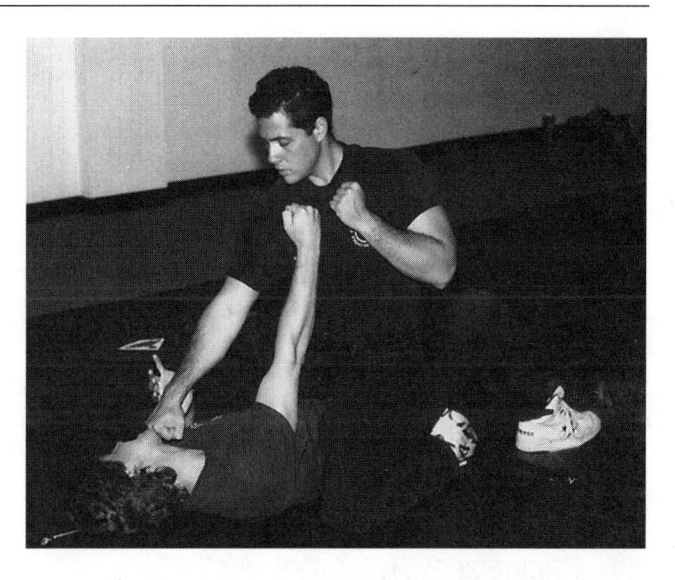

Generally, linear punches are much more destructive than circular blows, because the assailant's head is married to the floor and he is forced to absorb the force of your blow completely. In this photo, the author demonstrates this advantage of the mounted position.

assailant's head is married to the floor and he is forced to absorb the force of your blow completely.

559. MOVE CORRECTLY IN THE GRAPPLING RANGE.

When grappling in the vertical plane, it's important to move correctly. Improper footwork can subject you to a wide variety of dangers and risks. Here are a few key points that apply: (1) keep your weight equally distributed on both legs, (2) stay flat-footed and avoid moving on the balls of your feet, (3) always take short, deliberate steps, (4) don't cross-step, and (5) apply the step-and-drag footwork.

560. STAND UP CORRECTLY.

Strategic standing from the ground is essential for the following reasons: (1) it will minimize your target exposure, (2) it facilitates your balance, (3) your counterstrike ability is established quickly, and (4) mobility can be employed immediately. It is also important to be able to stand up correctly and efficiently from both the right and left sides.

561. RECOGNIZE AN OPPORTUNITY.

In a ground fight, there are many opportunities that can be exploited to your advantage. Here are just a few examples: (1) the assailant turns over onto his stomach, (2) the assailant loses his balance on the ground, (3) the assailant loses his leverage during the application of a technique, (4) the assailant becomes exhausted during the course of the ground fight, (5) the assailant begins to panic during the course of the struggle, and (6) the assailant unknowingly offers you a limb for manipulation.

562. NEVER FORCE A SUBMISSION HOLD.

When ground fighting with your adversary, avoid forcing a lock, choke, or hold. If you have to "force" the technique, chances are it's tactically inappropriate. The correct application of a submission technique can only be found within a window of opportunity.

Generally, six elements must be present for a submission technique to be applied effectively: (1) the assailant's appendage is exposed and free from obstruction, (2) you are in the proper range to apply the technique, (3) you are in the correct position to apply the technique, (4) you have the most efficient angle of application, (5) your submission technique does not place you in harm's way, and (6) you have the necessary leverage to apply the technique effectively.

563. KNOW THE SIX WAYS TO GO TO THE GROUND.

There are six ways that your adversary can take you down to the ground. They include (1) throwing techniques—your assailant arcs your body through the air before it impacts with the floor (i.e., hip throws or fireman's carry); (2) tripping techniques—your adversary strategically plants his leg and pushes you over it; (3) sweeping techniques—your assailant sweeps your foot, or feet, off the ground through a dynamic motion of his leg; (4) appendage takedowns—your assailant applies pressure or dynamic force to your appendage to take you down (i.e., double-leg takedown); (5) locking throws—your assailant locks your joint so he can take you down or throw you; and (6) striking takedowns—your assailant strikes you and causes you to fall to the ground (this is the most indirect form of a grappling takedown).

564. REMEMBER, IT'S DIFFICULT TO RECOVER FROM A THROW.

Since one of the primary objectives of a grappler is to take you off your feet and slam you onto the ground, you'd better know how to break your fall. Keep in mind that it's often difficult to recover from a violent throw onto the concrete or asphalt. There are no mats in a vicious ground fight.

565. LEARN HOW TO FALL SAFELY.

The importance of learning how to fall safely cannot be overstated. It is an invaluable skill that can greatly reduce the possibility of injury. Here are some important principles to employ when falling: (1) keep your body relaxed, (2) roll with the force, (3) protect your head and neck as you fall, (4) at impact, a forceful exhalation should be made to reduce shock and help control your breathing, (5) slap the ground with your palms to lessen the shock and then return your arms back to a defensive position, (6) do not fall "flat" on the ground, and (7) do not break your fall with your arms or wrists.

There are many types of falls that you can practice. Here is one that you can start with: (1) standing rear fall—from a standing position, bend your knees to a full squatting position. Roll back while maintaining a tucked position, and as your diaphragm area (middle of back, lower edge of shoulder blades) makes contact, extend your arm (slightly bent at the elbow), slap the ground and exhale, and automatically return your arms to a defensive position. Keep in mind that when learning how to fall for the first time, begin from the ground (in a squatting position) and gradually work your way up to a standing position.

NUCLEAR TACTICS

566. POSSESS NUCLEAR GROUND FIGHTING TOOLS.

When faced with a life-and-death encounter where lethal force is warranted and justified (i.e., criminal assault with intent to kill), prudence demands the use of nuclear ground fighting tactics. Nuclear ground fighting tools are specific techniques designed to inflict immediate and irreversible damage, rendering the criminal assailant helpless. Some nuclear tools and tactics include the following: (1) biting, (2) tearing, (3) crushing, (4) long-term choking, (5) gouging, (6) raking, and (7) all striking techniques.

567. CRUSH IT.

When faced with a deadly force situation, you must employ nuclear ground fighting tactics to ensure your survival. These techniques are the quickest and most efficient method of terminating your adversary. One brutal technique is crushing, which can be employed when standing in grappling range or lying in the prone position. The two primary crushing targets are the assailant's throat and testicles, although crushing the assailant's throat is not an easy task. It requires quick and exact digit placement and sufficient leverage accompanied by the vicious determination to destroy your assailant.

568. TEAR IT.

Another nuclear ground fighting tactic is tearing. Tearing tactics are quick, efficient, and can be employed while standing, kneeling, and lying in the prone position. They are applied primarily with your fingers. Viable anatomical targets include the assailant's eyelids, ears, and fingers. Like crushing techniques, tearing requires a vicious determination to destroy your adversary.

569. PUMMEL YOUR ASSAILANT.

Know how to pummel your assailant into submission. The pummel tactic is generally applied when you have mounted your assailant and your hands are free to strike. Once your balance is established in the mounted position, proceed with a vicious flurry of offensive strikes designed to take your assailant out of the fight. The power of your blows is not such a critical concern because you have the gravitational advantage and your assailant's head

GRAPPLING AND GROUND FIGHTING

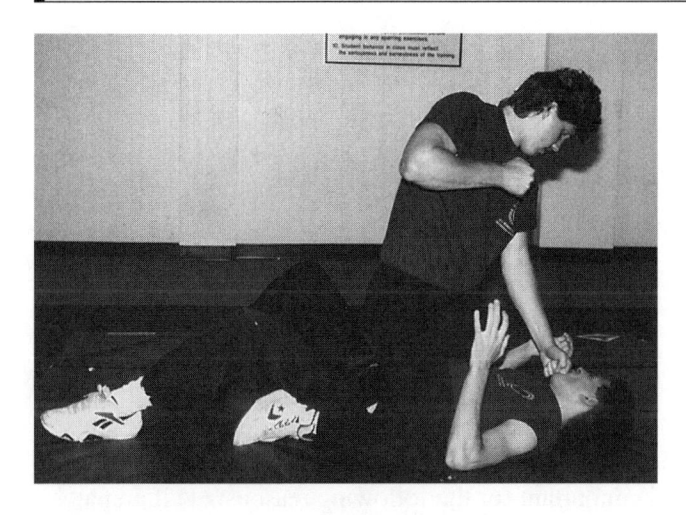

Here, a student (top) executes the pummel assault.

is flush against the floor (the ground functions as a stabilizer that concentrates your impact). The best blows for the pummel assault are tight linear punches, tight hooks, hammer fists, and, in some cases, elbow strikes. *WARNING: Because of the primitive and vicious characteristics of the pummel tactic, spectator intervention is a strong possibility. Be aware of your surroundings!*

570. MANIPULATE HIS HAND GUARD.

When sitting in the mounted position and employing the pummel technique, you can manipulate your assailant's hand guard in one of two different ways: (1) narrowing the hand guard—by employing linear blows directly into his face you will draw his hand guard inward (narrowing) and create openings for circular or hooking blows and (2) widening the hand guard—by employing circular blows to the assailant's face, you will draw his hand guard outward (widening) and create openings for linear blows.

571. USE THE FLUID SHOCK STRIKE.

If you want to maximize the damage during your pummel assault, employ the fluid shock strike. The fluid shock strike is performed by allowing your fist to remain on and pressed into the target area for a brief but definite period of time. This action prevents the target tissue from immediately bouncing back (due to its elastic nature), therefore causing the force of the strike to penetrate deeply. By penetrating the muscle and affecting the nerves within, the effect on your adversary will be greatly multiplied in comparison to a jabbing strike, which only affects the surface of the target. *WARNING: This technique can cause permanent brain damage and even death. Be absolutely certain your actions are legally justified.*

TRAINING

572. PRACTICE GROUND FIGHTING REGULARLY.

To be truly prepared for a violent street fight, you must engage in rigorous and frequent ground fighting with a competent instructor. Strive to train at least three times a week for a minimum of one hour per session. Take your time and work slowly through the various techniques.

Here are some important techniques to work on: (1) maintaining ground fighting mobility, (2) maintaining the mounted position, (3) escaping the assailant's guard, (4) escaping the assailant's mounted position, (5) defending against the pummel, (6) escaping from the side headlock, (6) escaping from various submission holds and chokes, (7) establishing the mounted position, (8) executing the pummel assault from the mounted position, (9) establishing the perpendicular mount, (10) maintaining the perpendicular mount, (11) switching from the guard position back to the mounted position, (12) grapevining techniques, (13) utilizing anatomical handles, and (14) body shielding.

573. PRACTICE GROUND FIGHTING TWO PEOPLE AT ONCE.

The unfortunate fact about grappling is that you may be faced with more than one adversary. Therefore, it's imperative that you experience what it's like to ground fight two assailants at the same time. This type of training can be conducted while you and your training partners are either standing, kneeling, or lying in the prone position. *REMEMBER: It's important that your training partners work slowly with you through the training session.*

574. GROUND FIGHT WITH DIFFERENT WEAPONS.

Experience what it is like to ground fight with different types of weapons. Experiment and see what it's like to grapple with edged weapons (use rubber training knives only), sticks and bludgeons, and various types of makeshift weapons.

575. FOLLOW SAFETY GUIDELINES WHEN PRACTICING GROUND FIGHTING.

Considerable attention must be given to safety when ground fighting. Here are a few rules and guidelines you should follow: (1) always warm up prior to ground fighting sessions; (2) keep your fingernails well trimmed; (3) don't wear jewelry, including rings, earrings, necklaces, and bracelets, during training sessions; (4) avoid ground fighting next to walls, mirrors, windows, or doors; (5) practice with a training partner who is trustworthy and can control his techniques; (6) keep your training mats clean and disinfected; and (7) avoid training with someone who is sick or has an infection.

576. DON'T INJURE YOUR PARTNER.

When conducted properly, ground fighting training can be an injury-free activity. Nevertheless, because of its dynamic nature, there is always the possibility of injuries. Here are some common injuries that can occur if you're not careful in your training sessions: (1) cauliflower ear—a deformity caused by repeated injury to the ear, which results in the irregular buildup of scar tissue; (2) impetigo, boils, herpes, or ringworm—caused by unsanitary mats or by a training partner who has a virus or infection; (3) torn cartilage, bone fracture, or dislocations—primarily caused by submission holds; and (4) general sprains—caused by improper falling or by forcing a joint beyond its normal range of movement.

577. EXPERIENCE OLEORESIN CAPSICUM AND GROUND FIGHTING.

Experience what it's like to ground fight when you've been exposed to a chemical irritant such as OC.

578. PRACTICE HEADLOCK COUNTERS.

Although the side headlock is a feckless submission hold that exposes a fighter to a variety of openings, it's also one of the most common locks. Therefore, it's important for you to know its various counters and escapes.

Following are the two different types of side headlocks that you must know how to escape from: (1) standing position—your assailant applies the side headlock when you're both standing in the grappling range and (2) prone position—your assailant applies the side headlock when you are lying on the floor ground fighting.

579. GROUND FIGHT WITH ONLY ONE ARM.

If you want to be exceptionally prepared for the ground fight, you'll need to experience what it's like to fight with only one arm. Find a trustworthy partner with whom you can work (he can use both arms but you can only use one). This type of training is important for the following reasons: (1) it prepares you both physically and psychologically to fight while handicapped, (2) it enhances your awareness of your arm when ground fighting, (3) it reinforces good tactics, and (4) it builds ground fighting confidence.

Experience what it's like to ground fight two assailants at the same time.

580. GROUND FIGHT WHILE BLINDFOLDED.

In the course of your training, you should regularly experience what it's like to ground fight while blindfolded. This is important for the following reasons: (1) it helps you develop a keen sense of kinesthetic awareness, (2) it helps prepare you to ground fight while visually handicapped, (3) it develops anatomical orientation, (4) it reinforces proper body mechanic skills, and (5) it cultivates your tactile "sight."

CHAPTER SIX

Bludgeons and Stick Fighting

"Sticks and bludgeons are ubiquitous. Make certain you know how to use them."

THE BASICS

581. MASTER STICK FIGHTING.
A great fighter must master the entire hierarchy of weapons, including sticks and bludgeons. Stick-fighting skills are important for several reasons, including the following: (1) in order to defeat a stick-wielding assailant, you must know and understand his weapon's strengths and limitations; (2) you may be required to use a stick or bludgeon in a self-defense situation; and (3) sticks and bludgeons are ubiquitous.

582. GRIP YOUR STICK CORRECTLY.
When holding your stick or bludgeon, allow enough room (one fist length) on the bottom portion of your weapon. When you hold your stick in this fashion, it offers you the following advantages: (1) one stick becomes two weapons—the end portion can be used for butting techniques at close-quarter range, (2) it offers greater leverage for striking, and (3) it promotes enhanced weapon retention.

583. DON'T HOLD YOUR STICK TOO TIGHTLY.
You should apply a moderate amount of pressure when gripping your stick. Grasping your stick too tightly can be problematic for the following reasons: (1) it will tire your hands and cause unnecessary cramping, (2) it may telegraph your striking movements, (3) it will significantly reduce the speed of your strikes, (4) it will reduce the power of your strikes, and (5) it will throw off your offensive and defensive timing.

The proper method of gripping a stick.

584. MASTER THE DIFFERENT STICK/BLUDGEON GRIPS.
There are several stick/bludgeon grips that you should be aware of, including (1) hammer grip, (2) ice-pick grip, (3) modified ice-pick grip, (4) baseball-bat grip, (5) saber grip, and (6) quarter-staff grip. Make certain that you are proficient with all six.

585. STICK FIGHT FROM DIFFERENT POSITIONS.
There are nine general positions in which you and your adversary can stick fight. They include the

The hammer grip.

The baseball-bat grip.

The ice-pick grip.

The saber grip.

The modified ice-pick grip.

The quarter-staff grip.

BLUDGEONS AND STICK FIGHTING

following: (1) both you and your assailant are prone; (2) you are kneeling and your assailant is prone; (3) your assailant is kneeling and you are prone; (4) both you and your assailant are kneeling; (5) you are standing and your assailant is prone; (6) your assailant is standing and you are prone; (7) you are standing and your assailant is kneeling; (8) your assailant is standing and you are kneeling; and (9) both you and your assailant are standing.

TECHNIQUES AND ANGLES

586. MASTER THE AMERICAN STICK STRANGLE.

The American stick strangle is a brutal strangle hold that should only be used in life-or-death self-defense situations. To apply the strangle, perform the following steps: (1) with your right hand, hold the stick in front of your assailant, parallel to the floor and against his throat; (2) place your left arm (triceps area) over your adversary's left shoulder while making certain that the end of your stick rests in the crook of your left elbow; (3) place the palm of your left hand against the back of your assailant's neck, and (4) in one fluid motion, apply pressure with your left hand against the back of your adversary's neck while simultaneously pulling your stick toward yourself with your right hand. ***WARNING: Prolonged lack of oxygen to the brain may cause permanent injury or death. Stick strangles can be lethal and should only be used in situations that legally warrant their use.***

The American stick strangle (rear view).

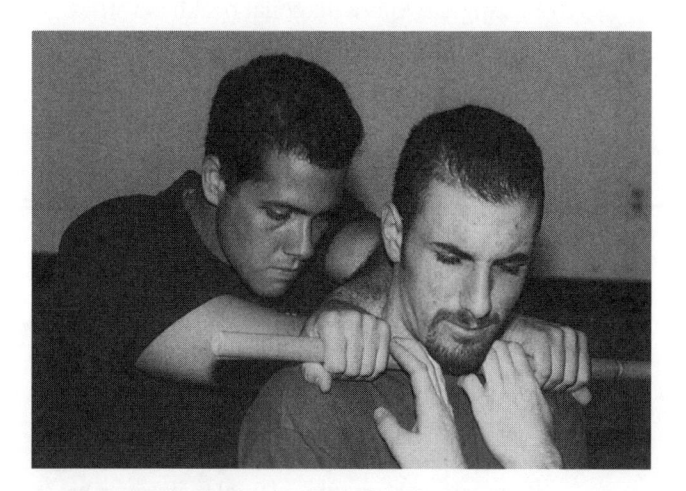

The ice-pick strangle.

587. MASTER THE ICE-PICK STRANGLE.

The ice-pick strangle is another vicious strangle hold that can be applied with minimal effort. To apply the ice-pick strangle, follow these important steps: (1) standing behind your assailant with your stick in your right hand and in the ice-pick grip, insert the bottom portion of your stick around the front of your assailant's neck from your left side; (2) make certain that your stick rests against the front of your assailant's throat and is parallel to the floor; (3) cross your left arm over your right forearm and grasp the stick on the right side of your assailant's neck; and

In this photo, Franco demonstrates the American stick strangle (front view).

(4) while making certain that both of your hands are close to the assailant's neck, apply immediate pressure by pulling both of your hands backward.

588. MASTER THE FOLLOW-THROUGH STRIKE.

When striking at your adversary with a stick or bludgeon, always use a follow-through strike. The follow-through strike is the most effective strike for stick combat because it creates the necessary amount of force to incapacitate your adversary.

589. MASTER THE NINE ANGLES OF ATTACK.

Knowledge of the basic striking angles is essential for effective stick fighting. Make certain that you can deliver the following nine angles:

(1) Angle one is a diagonal forehand strike traveling from right to left. Anatomical targets include your assailant's temple, clavicle, elbow, ribs, thigh, and knee joint.

(2) Angle two is a diagonal backhand strike traveling from left to right. Anatomical targets include your assailant's temple, clavicle, elbow, ribs, thigh, and knee joint.

(3) Angle three is a horizontal forehand strike traveling from right to left. Anatomical targets include your assailant's temple, clavicle, elbow, ribs, thigh, and knee joint.

(4) Angle four is a horizontal backhand strike traveling from left to right. Anatomical targets include your assailant's temple, clavicle, elbow, ribs, thigh, and knee joint.

(5) Angle five is an upward diagonal forehand moving from right to left. Anatomical targets include your assailant's temple, clavicle, elbow, ribs, thigh, and knee joint.

(6) Angle six is an upward diagonal backhand strike moving from left to right. Anatomical targets include your assailant's temple, clavicle, elbow, ribs, thigh, and knee joint.

(7) Angle seven is a linear thrust delivered anywhere on the assailant's centerline. Anatomical targets include your assailant's face, throat, torso, back, and groin. *CAUTION: Don't forget that thrusting movements with a bludgeon or stick are inherently dangerous and should only be employed in certain circumstances.*

(8) Angle eight is a downward vertical strike. Anatomical targets include your assailant's head, clavicle, elbow, ribs, thigh, and knee joint.

(9) Angle nine is an upward vertical strike. Anatomical targets include your assailant's head, elbow, ribs, groin, thigh, and knee joint.

590. BEND YOUR ELBOW AND USE A SHORT-ARC STRIKE.

When delivering a blow with your stick, keep your elbow bent and attack with a short-arc strike. This is important for the following reasons: (1) it prevents hyperextension of your elbow, (2) it enhances the speed of your strike, (3) it enhances the power of your blow, (4) it reduces telegraphic

The short-arc strike is safest for combat.

BLUDGEONS AND STICK FIGHTING

movement, (5) it promotes a short-arc strike, (6) it makes it difficult for your assailant to defend against your strike, and (6) it minimizes your target exposure.

591. KNOW THE LONG ARC DEFICIENCIES.

Avoid executing the long-arc strike in combat. The long-arc strike is ineffective for the following reasons: (1) it's easier for your assailant to defend against, (2) it is a relatively slow strike, (3) you can possibly hyperextend your elbow when you impact with your target, (4) it lacks sufficient neutralizing power, (5) it promotes telegraphic movement, (6) your adversary can zone your strike, and (7) it maximizes your target exposure.

The long-arc strike is combatively deficient and should not be used in real combat.

592. AVOID THRUSTING YOUR STICK.

Avoid executing thrusting motions when stick fighting. Thrusting your stick or bludgeon can be risky for the following reasons: (1) your assailant can avoid your weapon easily, (2) thrusting motions place tremendous strain on the side of your wrist, (3) you can lose your weapon when impacting with a strong surface area, and (4) thrusting motions lack neutralizing power. *NOTE: Thrusting motions with a stick or bludgeon should be used sparingly and only under certain combat circumstances. Generally, thrusting motions should be used with knives and other pointed weapons.*

593. APPLY DYNAMIC AND EXPLOSIVE FOOTWORK.

Effective stick fighting requires you to be dynamic and explosive with your footwork. A static or rigid stance will almost certainly get you injured in combat. Good footwork means quick, economical steps performed on the balls of the feet while you are relaxed, alert, and balanced. When moving, remember to keep your arms up, your legs shoulder-width apart, and your weight evenly distributed.

Footwork for stick combat is structured around four general movements described in secret 673.

WARNING: Avoid cross-stepping when stick fighting. Remember to apply the standard footwork rule of thumb—first move the foot closest to the direction that you want to go and the other leg should follow an equal distance. This applies to both linear (advance and retreat) and lateral (right and left) movement.

594. BE COGNIZANT OF YOUR CENTERLINE.

When stick fighting, avoid exposing your centerline unnecessarily. Not only does this expose your vital targets, it also diminishes your balance and inhibits efficient footwork. During stick combat, try to maintain a 45-degree stance in relation to your adversary.

595. DON'T DROP YOUR WEAPON.

When engaged in stick fighting, avoid dropping your weapon. Here are some important reasons why: (1) if your assailant is armed with a weapon he will now have the tactical advantage; (2) if your assailant is unarmed, he can pick up your weapon and use it against you; (3) spectators can attack you with it; (3) you can possibly trip over it and lose your balance. *NOTE: There are some combat situations that will require you to drop your weapon to defeat your adversary.*

596. MAKE IT FAST.

There are several ways to increase the speed of your stick strike, including the following: (1) minimize target follow-through—don't allow your strike to completely "settle" in the selected target; (2) step with the strike—step in the direction of your blow; (3) use repetition—practice various angles of attack thousands of times to sharpen and crystallize the movement; (4) visualize regularly—visualize the strike being delivered at great speed; (5) relax—avoid unnecessarily tensing your body and relax your muscles prior to the execution of your strike; (6) breathe—exhale during the execution of your strike;

(7) act—learn to act rather than react to a self-defense situation; (8) kinesthetic perception—develop and refine your kinesthetic perception; (9) moderate grip—try to maintain a moderate stick grip; (10) wrist snap—snap your wrist prior to impact with your target.

597. USE YOUR SECONDARY HAND IN CLOSE-QUARTER RANGE.

The secondary hand is a close-quarter technique that permits you to move from defense back to offense. The primary function of your secondary hand is to hold your assailant's weapon hand in place after you have employed a defensive maneuver. In this way, you can prevent him from returning with another strike. When you are fighting with a single stick, your secondary hand is the one not holding the weapon. ***NOTE: When engaged in either the mid- or long range, your secondary hand is kept close to your face and body.***

598. KEEP YOUR STICK MOVING.

When squared off with your assailant, always keep your stick moving. This is important for the following reasons: (1) it prevents inertia from setting in, (2) it enhances the overall velocity of your strikes, (3) it minimizes telegraphing prior to striking, (4) it enhances your defensive reaction time, (5) it minimizes your hand and digit exposure, (6) it significantly enhances your offensive flow, and (7) it causes your assailant to misjudge your weapon's range.

In this photo, the author (right) uses his secondary hand to control his assailant's weapon.

599. MASTER ALL STICK-FIGHTING RANGES.

The following are three separate distances of stick fighting that you must master: (1) long-range combat—the farthest distance at which you can strike only your assailant's hand with your stick; (2) midrange combat—the distance at which you can strike your assailant's head, arms, and body with your stick; (3) close-quarter-range combat—the third and final distance at which you can strike your assailant with the butt of your weapon and employ a variety of elbow, knee, and head butt strikes.

The farthest range of stick fighting is called long range.

The second range of stick fighting is called midrange.

BLUDGEONS AND STICK FIGHTING

The third and closest range of stick fighting is called close-quarter range.

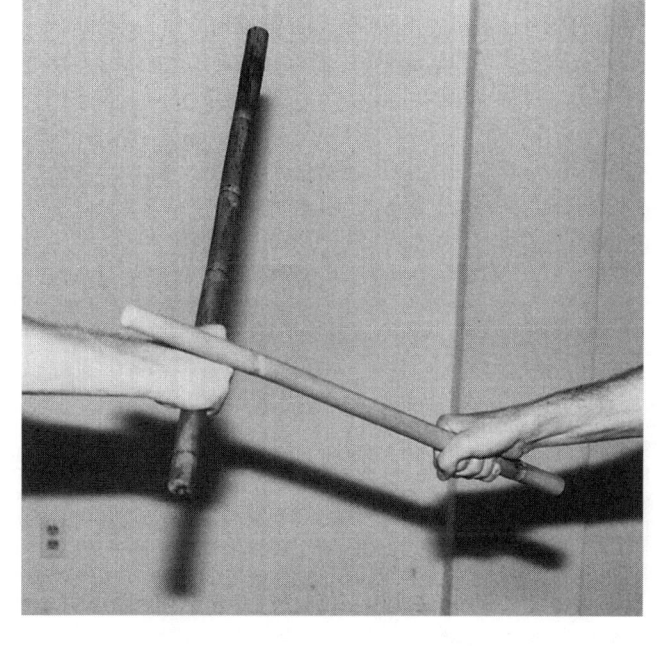

When using a stick to protect yourself against an armed assailant (i.e., bludgeon, knife, or any other nonballistic weapon), try to strike your assailant's weapon hand.

600. FORGET THE SNAP-BACK STRIKE.
The snap-back strike, also called the "witik," is a popular method of striking. The snap-back strike is delivered the same way as a follow-through strike. However, when the stick impacts with its target, it is retracted immediately. Nevertheless, in a real fight, the snap-back strike is inherently dangerous because it lacks the necessary power to injure or incapacitate your assailant. Always remember to strike your assailant with authority.

601. ATTACK YOUR ASSAILANT'S WEAPON HAND.
When using a bludgeon to protect yourself against an armed assailant (i.e., bludgeon, knife, or any other nonballistic weapon), try to strike your assailant's weapon hand. In most combat situations, if your assailant loses his weapon, he will lose the fight.

602. HIDE BEHIND YOUR WEAPON.
When stick fighting, keep your stick in front of your face and torso. Learn to "hide behind your weapon."

603. KNOW YOUR FOUR OPTIONS.
When a stick attack comes your way, you only have four options: (1) evasion—you can move out of the angle of attack, (2) deflection—you can deflect the attack, (3) block—you can block the oncoming attack, and (4) striking—you can strike the assailant's weapon hand. Make certain you can execute all four of these options with ease and efficiency.

604. DON'T FAN YOUR STRIKES.
Some fighters advocate fanning strikes during combat. The fanning strike or abaniko is simply a snap-back strike that rapidly changes the angle of attack. Fanning techniques can be executed vertically, horizontally, and diagonally, and they are often used to fake out or set up an assailant.

Nevertheless, fanning strikes are risky and ineffective for real combat. Here are some important reasons why they should not be employed: (1) they lack the significant follow-through necessary to incapacitate a powerful and formidable assailant, (2) they unnecessarily prolong a combat encounter, and (3) in most cases, they will simply agitate your assailant.

605. KNOW HOW TO DEFLECT IT.
You must be proficient with stick deflections. Unlike the stick block, a stick deflection is used to redirect your assailant's stick strike. Generally, deflections will flow into a counterstrike, and they

In this photo, Franco performs a stick block.

are used most commonly when you're attacked with a light stick.

606. KNOW HOW TO BLOCK IT.

Know the difference between a deflection and a block. A stick block is performed by meeting your assailant's stick with direct force. Blocks generally do not flow naturally into a counterstrike. Generally, the weight of your assailant's stick will determine whether you need to block or deflect it. If your assailant's stick is heavier than yours, you will most likely have to block his attack.

607. KNOW THE LIMITATIONS OF ZONING.

Zoning is a defensive maneuver designed to evade or block your assailant's strike through strategic movement and precise timing. Zoning can be accomplished by either moving in the direction of your assailant's strike (before it generates significant force) or by moving completely out of the stick's arc. While this may sound prudent and effective from a theoretical perspective, zoning does not always work.

Zoning prior to or after your assailant's swing will only work against an unskilled assailant who is wielding a heavy bludgeon (e.g., baseball bat). However, it won't work against a formidable stick fighter who's wielding a light bludgeon. Light bludgeons move with minimal telegraphing and can travel at speeds in excess of 100 miles per hour. The bottom line is that you can't zone against a light bludgeon, even if you have the luxury of knowing where it's coming from.

608. POSSESS STICK-RETENTION SKILLS.

A well-trained stick fighter is trained adequately in stick- and bludgeon-retention skills. He knows effective counters to various types of grabs. Don't engage in a stick fight unless you're certain you can maintain complete control over your weapon. And remember to practice stick- and bludgeon-retention skills on a frequent basis.

609. THE ANGLE OF ATTACK IS CRITICAL.

When defending against a bludgeon attack, your primary tactical concern should be your assailant's angle of attack.

610. DON'T UNDERESTIMATE THE SPEED OF A STICK.

When defending against a stick or bludgeon, don't underestimate its blistering speed. Many strikes can travel in excess of 100 miles per hour and be delivered in two-tenths of a second.

611. KNOW WHEN TO MOVE IN.

When you are unarmed and defending against a bludgeon attack, it's critical that you know when to move in on your adversary. Ideally, the best time to "choke" your assailant's weapon is either during the initiation or completion phase of his bludgeon swing.

612. KNOW THE CHARACTERISTICS OF A BLUDGEON.

Like all weapons of combat, there are unique characteristics to different types of bludgeons. For example, a light bludgeon will usually have the following attributes: (1) fast moving, (2) less telegraphic, (3) faster on recoil, (4) difficult for your adversary to zone against, (5) conducive to snapping impact, (6) less deadly, (7) conducive to a short arc, (8) easier to manipulate in close-quarter range, (9) less intimidating looking, and (10) superior with regard to weapon retention.

A heavy bludgeon will usually have the following characteristics: (1) slower moving, (2) more telegraphic, (3) slower on recoil, (4) easier to zone against, (5) conducive to breaking impact, (6) more deadly, (7) conducive to a longer arc, (8) more difficult to manipulate in close-quarter range, (9) more intimidating looking, and (10) weaker with regard to weapon retention.

613. STICK DISARMS ARE DIFFICULT TO APPLY.

Because a light stick can travel in excess of 100 miles per hour, it's very difficult to counter by attempting a lock or disarming technique. However, disarming techniques can be effective when defending against a slow and heavy bludgeon.

614. BLUDGEON DISARMS DO WORK.

Since a heavy bludgeon usually cannot generate a high retraction speed, disarm techniques can be applied. There are three primary principles that must be employed to disarm a heavy bludgeon successfully: (1) move out of the weapon's line of attack, (2) control the assailant's weapon, and (3) neutralize your assailant.

615. MASTER BLUDGEON DEFENSE SKILLS.

When you are unarmed and faced with a potential bludgeon attack, you should adhere to the following 14 principles: (1) become familiar with different types of bludgeons and sticks; (2) always respect the bludgeon; (3) try to determine your assailant's intent; (4) keep your cool; (5) try to escape safely or run if possible; (6) create distance between you and the bludgeon; (7) stay balanced and mobile; (8) try to utilize makeshift weapons; (9) maintain a strategic stance; (10) assess the bludgeon grip; (11) determine the bludgeon's range of impact; (12) determine the bludgeon's angle of attack; (13) attack your adversary first, engage, and control the bludgeon; and (14) neutralize your assailant.

616. BEWARE OF THE REVERBERATION PATH.

When blocking or deflecting your assailant's blow, stay clear of your stick's reverberation path. Stick reverberation occurs when your weapon (usually a light bludgeon) absorbs the assailant's force, causing it to bounce back at you.

617. BECOME FAMILIAR WITH ALL TYPES OF BLUDGEONS.

One of the fundamental principles of bludgeon disarms is familiarity. Take the time to familiarize yourself with as many types of bludgeons as possible. Learn the different types of grips, stances, chamber positions, weights, and materials. Try to find a knowledgeable instructor who can teach you about bludgeons, stick fighting concepts, and effective defenses. Familiarity is critical because it will help eliminate some of the fear associated with this weapon and will better prepare you to protect yourself if faced with a bludgeon attack.

618. DETERMINE THE ASSAILANT'S INTENT.

It's critical to make an accurate threat assessment when confronted by a bludgeon-wielding assailant. Use split-second judgment to determine exactly what your adversary wants to accomplish. Some assailants might not want to harm you if they can avoid it. Others may be dead set on smashing your skull to pieces. If you have determined that your assailant plans to harm you, you must resort to aggressive disarming tactics immediately.

619. MASTER THE CENTER, LEFT, AND RIGHT HIGH BLOCK.

The center high block is used to defend against a powerful bludgeon strike directed toward the top section of your head and shoulders. The left high block is used to defend against a powerful bludgeon strike directed toward the left side of your head and shoulders. The right high block is used to defend against a powerful bludgeon strike directed toward the right side of your head and shoulders. Each block is performed by raising your stick up to meet the assailant's descending strike while your free hand grips the other end of your stick.

620. MASTER THE LEFT AND RIGHT MID BLOCK.

The left mid block is used to defend against a powerful bludgeon strike directed toward the left side of your chest and torso. The right mid block is used to defend against a powerful bludgeon strike directed toward the right side of your chest and torso. Each block is performed by moving your stick across your body to meet the assailant's strike while your free hand grips the other end of your stick.

621. MASTER THE LEFT AND RIGHT LOW BLOCK.

The left low block is used to defend against a powerful bludgeon strike directed toward the lower left section of your torso. The right low block is used to defend against a powerful bludgeon strike directed toward the lower right section of your torso. Each block is performed by lowering your stick to meet your assailant's swing while your free hand grips the other end of your stick.

622. MASTER THE CENTER LOW BLOCK.
The center low block is used to defend against a powerful bludgeon strike directed toward the lower section of your torso and groin. The block is performed by lowering your stick to meet your assailant's upward swing while your free hand grips the other end of your stick.

623. KNOW THE THREE STAGES OF A STICK SWING.
There are three stages or phases to a stick or bludgeon strike. They include (1) initiation phase, (2) mid phase—the contact or impact point of your swing, and (3) completion phase.

TRAINING

624. TRAIN WITH RATTAN STICKS.
For a good portion of your training, use rattan sticks. These training sticks are preferred over others because rattan is generally inexpensive and safe to work with.

625. CHOOSE THE PROPER LENGTH.
Though rattan sticks come in a variety of lengths (anywhere from 21 to 26 inches), the most preferred length for training is approximately 26 inches. If your stick is too short, it will negate your weapon's range capability; if it is too long, it will be difficult to manipulate in close-quarter combat.

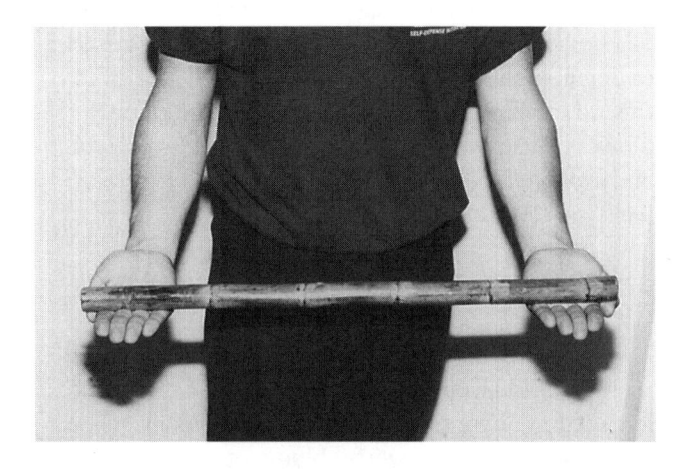

The rattan stick.

626. OCCASIONALLY TRAIN WITH AX HANDLES.
To strengthen your wrists, hands, arms, and shoulders, occasionally train with oak ax handles. Ax handles can be purchased at your local hardware store.

627. WARM UP YOUR WRISTS.
To develop a flexible and strong wrist, hold your stick in its center and rapidly twist it back and forth. This warm-up movement should be performed before and after your training routine.

628. TWIRL YOUR STICK.
The stick twirl is an excellent dexterity exercise that should be performed on a regular basis. To perform the forward stick twirl, hold your stick tightly between your thumb and index finger and then forcefully twirl the entire weapon forward at your side, allowing your other three fingers to move freely. To perform the backward stick twirl, hold your stick tightly between your thumb and index finger, then forcefully twirl the entire weapon backward at your side, allowing your other three fingers to move freely. You can also twirl two sticks at the same time.

629. USE THE REST POSITION.
To minimize the chances of injury in class, know how to assume the rest position. The rest position is used during idle periods in class (e.g., talking to other students, receiving instructions). To assume this position, stand with both legs approximately shoulder-distance apart. With your stick in your right hand, place it under your left armpit and grab your right forearm with your left hand.

630. PRACTICE WITH DIFFERENT TYPES OF BLUDGEONS.
When preparing to defend against bludgeon attacks, it's important to have your training partner attack you with a wide variety of sticks, including the following: (1) long, (2) short, (3) light, (4) heavy, (5) balanced, (6) unbalanced, (7) makeshift, (8) wooden, and (9) metal.

631. PREPARE FOR ALL THE ANGLES OF ATTACK.
If you want to be completely prepared for a bludgeon attack, make certain that you are trained to defend against the following angles of attack (in both long and short arcs): (1) vertical plane, (2) horizontal plane, (3) diagonal plane, and (4) longitudinal plane.

BLUDGEONS AND STICK FIGHTING

632. OCCASIONALLY SHUT YOUR EYES.

When performing stick fighting drills with your partner, occasionally close your eyes and feel the movements. This type of training will enhance your kinesthetic perception.

633. PERFORM PENALTY PUSH-UPS.

To show respect for your stick (or any weapon, for that matter), if you ever drop it accidentally during training, immediately drop to the ground and perform 25 penalty push-ups.

634. UTILIZE FIGURE-EIGHT DRILLS.

Utilize figure-eight drills to develop speed, coordination, and fluidity with your stick strikes. Figure-eight movements will also sharpen and refine overhand strikes, backhand strikes, and upward strikes. Remember when executing figure-eight movements to keep your arcs short and tight.

635. PRACTICE STICK FIGHTING EVERYWHERE.

Practice your stick fighting techniques in a variety of different environments, terrains, locations, and positions, including in doorways, in hallways, on the stairs, ascending a hill, descending a hill, on top of a car, in a ditch, in an elevator, on an escalator, on a bridge, under a bridge, standing in the water, in the snow, in the mud, in the sand, in tall grass, in between shrubbery, between trees and branches, in the kneeling position, and in the prone position.

636. PRACTICE SINGLE- AND DOUBLE-STICK DRILLS.

The only real way to be prepared for stick fighting is to engage in a variety of different drills regularly. Stick fighting drills can be performed with either one or two weapons and will provide the following benefits: (1) improved confidence, (2) increased speed, (3) more powerful blows, (4) minimized telegraphic movements, (5) improved eye-hand coordination, (6) improved ability to adapt to unpredictable angles of attack, (7) reinforced good habits, (8) refined and enhanced mobility, (9) sharpened sense of timing, (10) learned range specificity, and (11) reinforced target recognition.

CHAPTER SEVEN

Knife Defense and Knife Fighting

"The knife is an awesome weapon. Depending on who wields it, it can be your best friend—or your worst enemy."

FACTS

637. REMEMBER—KNIVES ARE UBIQUITOUS.

Look out! Street criminals can hide knives or edged weapons anywhere. Here are just a few possible locations: in newspapers, magazines, books, shopping bags, briefcases, pockets, tote bags, wallets, purses, hats, sleeves, shoes, socks, belts, automobiles, and motorcycles; under their arms; and behind their forearms.

638. KNOW WHY CRIMINALS PREFER KNIVES.

Street criminals prefer knives to commit crimes for the following reasons: (1) they are silent, (2) they don't misfire or jam, (3) they do not require reloading, (4) they are easy to conceal, (5) they are easy to dispose of, (6) they are symbolic to psychopaths, (7) they leave no ballistic clues, (8) the courts tend to be more lenient with knives than guns, (9) they are ubiquitous, (10) they are inexpensive, and (11) makeshift knives are easy to create.

639. KNOW WHY SOME CRIMINALS HOLD A KNIFE IN THEIR REAR HAND.

The following are four general reasons why criminal assailants will hold a knife in the rear hand: (1) protection—their front hand is free to block or deflect any strikes launched against them; (2) grabbing—their front hand is free to grab and pull victims off balance, thereby exposing vital targets; (3) distracting—their front hand is free to cause feints or other distractions; and (4) striking—their front hand is used as a secondary weapon that can punch or strike at will.

640. KNOW THAT KNIVES ARE GREAT EQUALIZERS.

Armed with a knife, a small person can easily dispatch a vicious 200-pound killer, provided that the knife wielder has the proper mental and physical

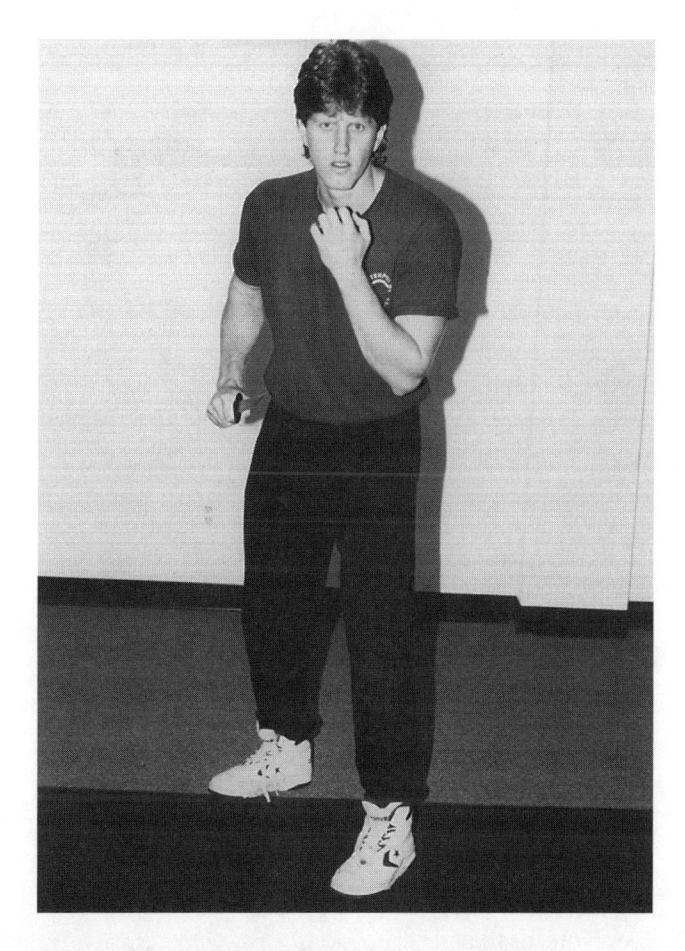

Beware of the assailant who holds a knife in his rear hand.

training and a razor-sharp blade. Unlike in unarmed combat, when you are armed with an edged weapon, physical strength is no longer a necessary consideration. It takes little real strength to stab into one of the assailant's vital organs or slash a major artery.

KNIFE DEFENSE

641. MASTER KNIFE-DEFENSE SKILLS.

When you are unarmed and faced with an edged-weapon attack, here are 12 principles that you should follow: (1) become familiar with all types of knives and edged weapons, (2) always respect the knife, (3) try to determine your assailant's intent, (4) keep your cool, (5) try to escape safely or run if possible, (6) create distance between you and the blade, (7) stay balanced and mobile, (8) utilize makeshift weapons, (9) maintain a strategic stance (i.e., knife-defense stance), (10) focus on the knife, (11) attack your adversary first and control the knife, and (12) terminate your assailant with extreme prejudice.

642. MASTER THE KNIFE-DEFENSE STANCE.

Surviving an edged-weapon attack requires mastery of the knife-defense stance. This stance will ensure maximal mobility and minimal target exposure, and it will facilitate immediate counterstrike ability.

To assume the knife-defense stance, apply the following steps: (1) angle your body (internal organs) approximately 45 degrees to your assailant; (2) slightly hunch your shoulders forward and let your stomach sink in; (3) keep your head and face back and away from random slashes or stabs; (4) keep your hands, forearms, and elbows close to your body to diminish target opportunities for your assailant; (5) cup your hands with your palms facing you, which will turn soft tissue, veins, and arteries in the arms away from the blade; (6) keep your knees slightly bent and flexible, your feet shoulder-width apart, and your weight equally distributed on each leg; and (7) do not tense up—always stay relaxed and alert.

The knife-defense stance.

643. DON'T CLENCH YOUR HANDS TOO TIGHTLY.

When assuming a knife-defense stance, make certain that your fingers are semiclenched. Also, avoid clenching your fists too tightly. This may cause your veins to protrude from your arms.

644. MASTER THE "V" GRIP.

When defending against an edged-weapon attack, the only effective method of controlling the assailant's knife hand is to use the V grip. The V grip is applied by grabbing the assailant's wrist with both of your hands (make certain that the webs of your hands completely envelope your assailant's wrist). Once you have made contact, squeeze hard and hold on with all your might. When applied correctly, the V grip will allow you to forcefully redirect the knife away from your body targets.

645. MOBILITY AND BALANCE ARE PARAMOUNT.

Two of the most important aspects of knife defense are mobility and balance. Mobility is important for the following reasons: (1) it allows you to quickly move in

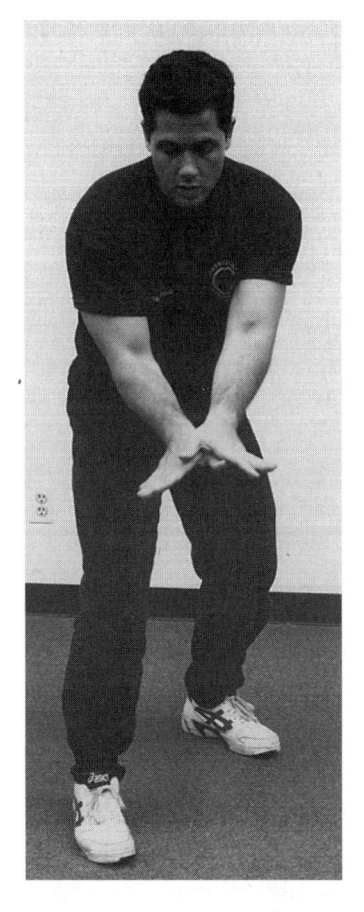

The author demonstrates the "V" grip.

KNIFE DEFENSE AND KNIFE FIGHTING

and out of the range (range manipulation) from various slashes and stabs, (2) it makes you a more evasive target, and (3) in some cases it helps minimize your assailant's complete blade penetration. Balance is critical for these reasons: (1) it permits you to change your direction of movement quickly and efficiently, (2) it enhances your general reaction time, (3) it aids your ability to be mobile, and (4) it allows you to recover quickly from a committed movement.

646. ATTACK A KNIFE ATTACKER.

If you're unarmed and faced with a knife-wielding assailant, attack him first. This is important for the following reasons: (1) it psyches him out—nothing is more shocking than an unarmed person attacking first, even though the assailant holds all of the cards; (2) it prevents the defensive flow—since you're initiating the offensive flow, it doesn't give your assailant sufficient time to force you into the defensive flow; and (3) it's conclusive—regardless of the outcome, such an act quickly formulates a conclusion to your emergency situation; you have no time to be tormented by despair and fear.

647. DON'T GO FOR THE ASSAILANT'S KNIFE.

If a knife fighter ever throws his weapon to the floor and challenges you to get it, don't! Chances are that he has another one and he is going to use it when you bend down to the ground.

648. WEAR LOOSE-FITTING CLOTHES.

The clothing that you wear on the street can play an important role when defending against a knife attack. Clothing that hugs your body will allow your assailant's slashing movement to pass through the material easily. Loose-fitting shirts and jeans will not only make your assailant misjudge the exact target distance, but they will also make it more difficult for his knife to penetrate your flesh.

649. PROTECT YOUR FLEXORS AND BLOOD VESSELS.

When unarmed and faced with a knife attack, avoid exposing the belly of your forearms. To accomplish this, keep both of your hands, forearms, and elbows close to your body to diminish target opportunities. Cup both of your hands with your palms facing you to protect your flexors and blood vessels from your assailant's blade.

650. CREATE DISTANCE BETWEEN YOU AND THE KNIFE.

When unarmed and defending against an edged-weapon attack, try to create as much distance as you can between you and the knife. Distance is critical because it enhances your defensive reaction time and allows you to control your options.

Obviously, running away is a great way to put distance between you and the blade, but you can also use different types of objects in the environment to create barriers between you and your adversary. Cars, trucks, couches, large chairs, tall fences, park benches, and large tables are only a few examples. Remember, though, that these objects are only buying you a little precious time; they don't negate the threat. The bottom line is to stay as far away from the knife as possible. Keep in mind that the only time you want to be close to a knife is for disarming purposes, and then only if the situation is absolutely unavoidable.

651. DON'T PANIC.

When unarmed and faced with an edged weapon attack, do not panic and lose your cool. This may seem difficult, but with proper training and crisis rehearsal, it can be done. People naturally freeze up when they are faced with a knife attack. This only makes it easier for your assailant to accomplish his nefarious mission. You must rise to the occasion and summon all of your spirit and courage to ward off the deleterious effects of fear, anxiety, and stress. You must be determined to fight your adversary to the death if necessary.

652. RESPECT THE KNIFE.

One often overlooked aspect of knife defense is respect of the knife or any other edged weapon. Too few people realize how deadly knives are. Even a child becomes dangerous with a knife in hand. The entertainment industry has done us a great disservice by making everyone believe that a knife-wielding assailant can be neutralized easily with one swift kick, shoulder throw, or punch. It is not like that in the real world. In fact, the odds are strongly stacked against your survival if you are unarmed and attacked by an assailant with a knife. Never underestimate the danger of a knife; it could cost you your life.

653. KNOW HOW TO DEFEND AGAINST THE OVERHEAD STAB.

When unarmed and defending against the

classical overhead stab, you have the following three options: (1) you can attempt to engage and control the assailant's knife hand with the V grip and proceed with disarming techniques, (2) you can temporarily evade the assailant's attack with strategic lateral footwork, or (3) you can temporarily redirect the assailant's knife with power parries.

654. EXPECT TO GET CUT.

Whether you're unarmed and defending against a knife attack or knife fighting with your adversary, expect to get cut. This frame of mind is critical for the following reasons: (1) it prepares you for the cold reality of edged-weapon combat, (2) it helps prevent you from going into mental shock if you do get cut, and (3) it frees you from the mental concern of your well-being.

655. NEVER KICK AT THE ASSAILANT'S KNIFE HAND.

When unarmed and defending against a knife-wielding assailant, never attempt to kick the knife out of his hand. This is asinine and hazardous for the following reasons: (1) the speed of your kick is no match for the speed of a knife; (2) to successfully hit your assailant's knife hand, you will be required to execute a high-line kick, which is suicide in any type of physical confrontation; (3) you run the risk of losing your balance and falling on the ground; (4) it unnecessarily exposes your vital targets to the knife-wielding assailant; (5) it temporarily inhibits your ability to execute quick and evasive footwork; and (6) your assailant can cut your ankle, foot, or calf when you deliver the kick.

656. TERMINATE YOUR ADVERSARY WITH EXTREME PREJUDICE.

Once you have gained solid control over your knife attacker's knife hand (via V grip), it is critical that you attack him as viciously as possible. Drive your knee repeatedly into his groin, stomp on his instep, head-butt his nose, and bite into his jugular if necessary. Attack him repeatedly with cold determination. Your goal is to kill him. As you start to gain the advantage, you can consider releasing one of your hands to gouge or rake his eyes, crush his windpipe, or strike the front of his throat with the edge of your hand. Don't stop until your adversary is permanently out of commission. Remember, he attacked you with a knife, and that's deadly force—as deadly as it gets!

657. USE MAKESHIFT WEAPONS.

When unarmed and confronted by a knife-wielding assailant, scan your environment for any makeshift weapons, especially ones that can shield against stabs and slashes. A strong briefcase is a great shield. So are metal trash can lids, sofa and chair cushions, and even small chairs and tables. Also look for makeshift weapons with which you can strike your assailant. If you can get hold of a striking weapon, use it to strike quickly at your adversary's hand—the one holding the knife. Effective striking weapons are hardwood limbs, metal pipes, and long sticks.

658. ALL DEFENSIVE MOVEMENTS MUST BE TIMED PROPERLY.

Defensive combat movements are safest when used during the initial and completion stages of your assailant's knife arc.

659. FAMILIARIZE YOURSELF WITH DIFFERENT TYPES OF EDGED WEAPONS.

There are seven different classifications of

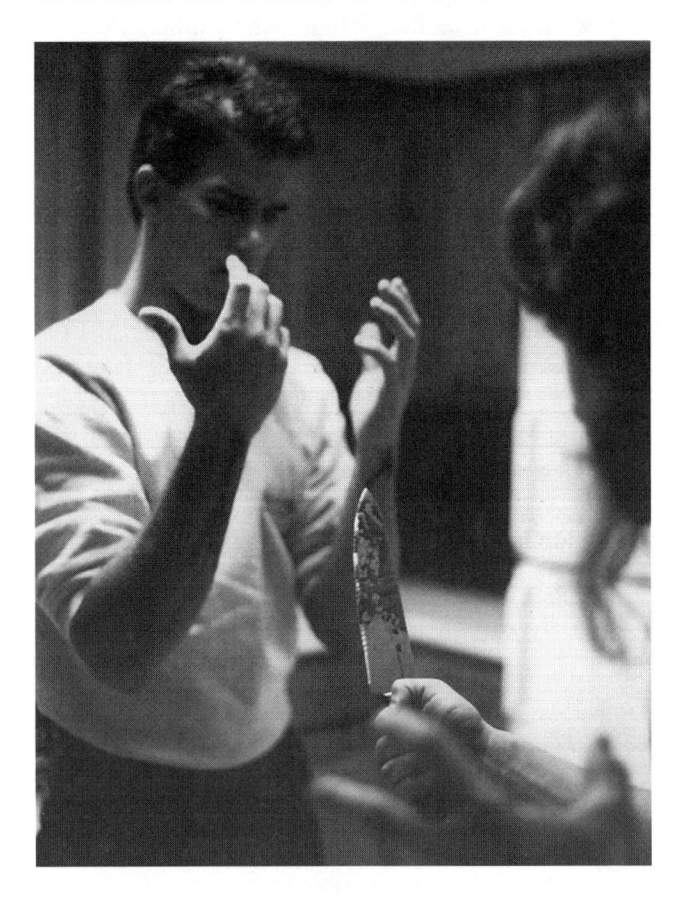

When faced with a knife-wielding assailant, expect to get cut.

KNIFE DEFENSE AND KNIFE FIGHTING

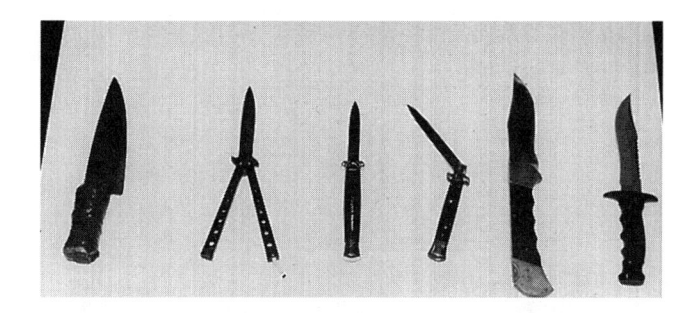

From left to right: improvised knife, gravity blade, spring blade, spring blade, lock blade, and fixed blade.

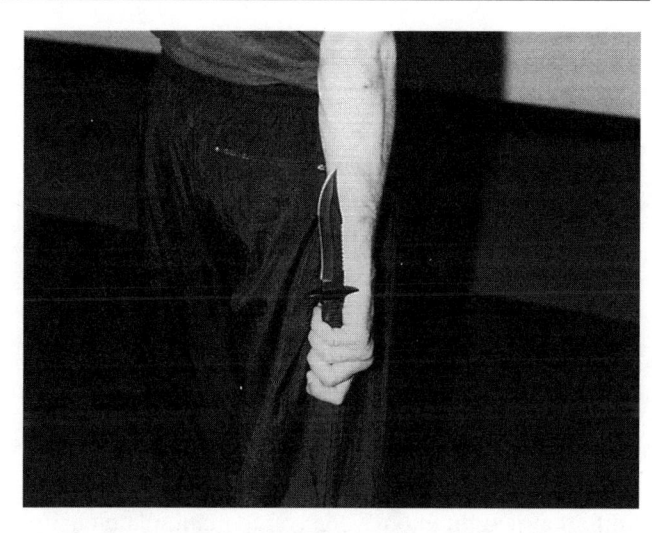

In this photo, a student demonstrates knife palming.

knives: (1) gravity blades, (2) spring blades, (3) lock blades, (4) folding blades, (5) fixed blades, (6) ballistic blades, and (7) makeshift/improvised blades.

660. DETERMINE THE ASSAILANT'S INTENT.

It's critical to make an accurate threat assessment when confronted by a knife-wielding assailant. Use split-second judgment to determine exactly what your adversary wants to accomplish. Some might not want to harm you if they can avoid it. Others may be dead-set on cutting you from limb to limb. If you have determined that your assailant plans to harm you, you must resort to aggressive disarming tactics immediately.

661. DON'T RECOVER THE KNIFE.

Once you have disarmed your assailant, don't become obsessed with recovering the blade. This will distract you from neutralizing your immediate threat (your assailant) and possibly lead to a renewed attack.

662. RECOGNIZE KNIFE PALMING.

Don't be caught off guard! Learn to recognize knife palming. Knife palming is a strategic method of concealing a knife or other edged weapon behind one's forearm. It is probably one of the most deceptive forms of knife concealment and can surprise even the most seasoned street fighter. Therefore, when confronted by a potential adversary, always be aware of his hands. If you can't see his fingertips, beware—he could be palming an edged weapon.

663. DON'T JUDGE HIS SKILL LEVEL.

When unarmed and confronted by a knife-wielding assailant, don't assume you can judge his proficiency with a knife by the way he holds one. Always assume that anyone holding a knife (or any weapon for that matter) knows how to use it and will do just that. Besides, even if your assailant is unskilled as a knife fighter, he can still kill you.

KNIFE FIGHTING SKILLS

664. MASTER THE THREE KNIFE FIGHTING STRATEGIES.

Here are the three knife fighting strategies that must be followed: (1) attack your immediate threat, (2) disarm your assailant, and (3) terminate your assailant.

665. MASTER KNIFE FIGHTING SKILLS.

It is important to develop and master knife fighting skills for the following reasons: (1) you must understand the nature of the beast—the best way to defeat a knife attacker is to first become a knife fighter, (2) knowledge conquers fear—the more you know about knives and other edged weapons, the less you will fear them, (3) knives are a component of the hierarchy of weapons, and (4) knife fighting skills complement unarmed combat skills.

666. BUY A GOOD BLADE.

Here a few important points to consider when purchasing a knife for self-defense: (1) make certain the knife fits comfortably in both your right and left hands; (2) choose a knife that is designed for slashing as well as stabbing; (3) avoid all knives with finger grooves, because they will limit your grip; (4) choose a blade that is sharp and large enough to penetrate the

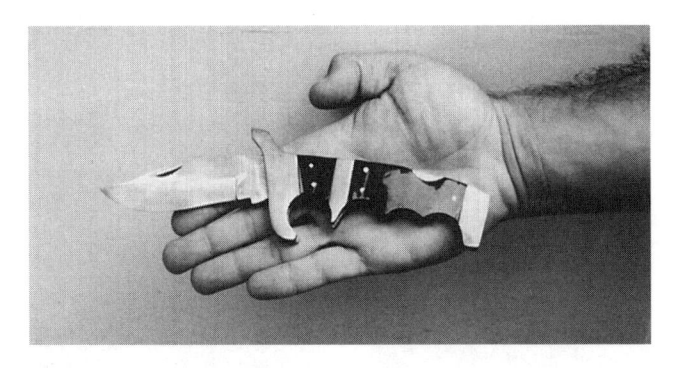

Avoid using knives with finger grooves.

assailant's vital arteries and organs; (5) choose a knife that is light enough for you to manipulate easily and quickly; (6) use either a lock blade or fixed blade made of high-carbon stainless steel; and (7) try to purchase a knife that has a hand guard, which will prevent your hand from slipping onto the blade when you thrust it (the hand guard will also offer some protection from the assailant's blade).

667. CHOOSE RUBBER GRIPS FOR KNIFE COMBAT.
Avoid using a knife that has a wood or metal grip. Wood and metal grips provide poor gripping, especially when your hands are wet. Rubberized "sure grips" are essential for edged-weapon combat. Remember, puncture wounds will make your blade and grip bloody and slippery.

668. AVOID USING SPRING BLADES.
Avoid using spring blades (i.e., switchblades, stilettos) in a knife fight. They are inherently dangerous for the following reasons: (1) the internal spring can malfunction, (2) the structural integrity of the knife is usually poor, (3) the hand grips are usually too thin and often slippery, and (4) they look menacing and have a criminal stigma attached to them. Remember, if you are later taken to court, the jury will look unfavorably at you, even though you may have been justified in killing your adversary.

669. AVOID USING FOLDING BLADES.
Avoid using folding blades (e.g., Swiss Army pocket knives, Old Timer pocket knives, etc.) in a knife fight. Folding blades are not designed for real combat, which requires aggressive cutting and slashing movements. In most cases, when you are using a folding knife in a self-defense situation, the blade will fold and close on your fingers when you make contact with your target.

670. MASTER THE TWO PRIMARY KNIFE GRIPS.
One of the foundational elements of effective knife fighting is the grip. In combat, the two primary knife grips that you must master are as follows: (1) hammer grip (2) ice-pick grip.

671. SELECT THE APPROPRIATE KNIFE GRIP FOR YOUR RANGE OF ENGAGEMENT.
When knife fighting, select the grip appropriate for your range of engagement. To accomplish this there are three knife fighting ranges you must be aware of: (1) long-range combat—the hammer grip is ideal for this range and can be used to apply both slashing and linear thrusting movements, (2) midrange combat—the hammer grip is also the most preferred grip for this distance of engagement, and (3) close-quarter-range combat—the ice-pick grip or modified-ice-pick grip is preferred in this particular range and can be used to apply tight slashing and angular stabbing movements.

The ice-pick grip is ideal for close-quarter-range combat.

672. KEEP BOTH YOUR KNEES BENT WHEN KNIFE FIGHTING.
When knife fighting, always keep both of your knees bent and have your body weight equally distributed over both legs. This will permit quick footwork, which is vital for effective knife fighting. ***WARNING: Never assume a deep or rigid stance in a knife fight. You will die!***

KNIFE DEFENSE AND KNIFE FIGHTING

673. REALIZE THAT PROPER FOOTWORK IS CRITICAL.

Footwork constitutes 90 percent of your defense in a knife fight. Remember to move the foot closer to the direction that you want to go first, and the other leg should follow an equal distance. This footwork rule applies to both linear (advance and retreat) and lateral (right and left) movement. Avoid cross-stepping in knife combat (or any form of combat for that matter); it could cost you your life!

674. NEVER THROW A KNIFE.

Contrary to what you may have seen in the movies, throwing your knife at your assailant is a dangerous idea for the following reasons: (1) few knives are specifically designed and balanced for throwing movements, (2) it is extremely difficult to hit a moving target when throwing any type of knife, and (3) if your knife misses its target, it will automatically arm your adversary.

675. IGNORE YOUR WOUND.

If you're ever cut in a knife fight, do not look at your wound. This can be dangerous for the following four reasons: (1) it takes your eyes off of your assailant and his knife, (2) it can psyche you out, (3) it may cause you to go into shock, and (4) it empowers your assailant.

The knife fighting stance.

676. DON'T FORGET YOUR SECONDARY WEAPONS.

When engaged in a knife fight, never forget that you have numerous secondary weapons at your immediate disposal. Some include the following: (1) head—used for butting your adversary in close quarters, (2) teeth—used for biting your assailant in close quarters, (3) elbows—used for striking your assailant in close quarters, (4) knees—also used for striking your adversary in close-quarters, (5) legs—used for kicking your assailant at the midrange of knife combat, and (6) hands—used for striking your assailant at the midrange of knife fighting.

677. MEET THE THREE ESSENTIAL REQUIREMENTS.

Never carry a knife unless you meet the three essential requirements to facilitate effective deployment: (1) knowledge—this means knowing and understanding the elements, nature, and characteristics of edged-weapon combat and how to apply them to any combat situation; (2) skills—this means possessing the proficiency, aptitude, and dexterity to knife fight, developed through training and experience and perfected through consistent practice; and (3) attitude—refers to your immediate state of mind or disposition toward edged-weapon combat (you must always possess a high level of awareness of edged-weapon combat).

678. NEVER THREATEN YOUR ADVERSARY.

A knife is a tool of destruction that is intended to injure or kill, not intimidate. Never pull a knife unless you're legally and morally justified to use it. A knife should only be displayed when you have no other choice but to cut your adversary to pieces.

679. MASTER KNIFE-RETENTION SKILLS.

A well-trained knife fighter is adequately trained in knife-retention skills. He knows effective counters to various types of grabs. Never pick up a knife unless you are absolutely confident that you can maintain complete control over it. Remember, if you drop your knife, you'll lose your life.

680. HOLD YOUR KNIFE IN FRONT OF YOU.

When knife fighting, hold your knife in your front hand. This knife-forward stance is critical for the following reasons: (1) it brings your closest weapon (your knife) to the assailant's closest targets, and (2) the unprotected (or unarmed) side of your body is kept back and away from your assailant's stabs and slashes. Generally, a lead-hand knife fighter will have a tactical advantage over a rear-hand knife fighter.

681. KNOW THE EXCEPTION TO SECRET #680.

There is an exception to secret #680; it's what I refer to as the "sword and shield principle." If you have the luxury of acquiring a shielding makeshift weapon, place it in your lead hand so that it may protect you from various cuts and slashes. Your rear hand should then be holding your knife.

682. LEAD WITH YOUR STRONG SIDE FORWARD.

If you ever have the option or luxury of assuming a knife fighting stance, try to position your stronger and more coordinated side forward. For example, if you are right-handed, your right side is generally your stronger and more coordinated side. This strong-side stance is important for knife combat because it maximizes the speed, power, dexterity, and accuracy of your blade movement.

683. ALLOW YOUR ASSAILANT AN AVENUE OF ESCAPE.

During a knife fight, always allow your assailant an avenue of escape. Many people will choose to run once they catch the sight of their own blood. Avoid making the tragic mistake of forcing your assailant into a corner.

684. DRIVE IT TO THE HILT.

When going for a quick-kill move, drive your weapon deep into your assailant until the surface of his body makes contact with the hilt of the knife. Once you have acquired deep penetration, twist and pump the blade repeatedly to maximize organ and tissue damage and accelerate blood loss.

685. OBEY THE LAW.

If you are going to carry a knife for self-defense, you must assume the legal and social responsibilities that go along with it. Before you purchase a knife, check your state and local laws. In some states, certain knives are prohibited altogether. If you are going to carry a knife, make certain that you do so in a manner consistent with applicable laws.

686. KEEP YOUR KNIFE CLOSE TO YOUR BODY.

When knife fighting, avoid overextending your knife hand. This is dangerous for the following reasons: (1) it inhibits your balance, (2) it leaves you vulnerable to attack, and (3) it significantly reduces your ability to attack your assailant. When holding a knife, keep it in your front hand and hold it close to your body. Keep your rear hand in with your elbow close to your body while keeping the belly of your forearm and palm facing your chest. This will keep the flexors and blood vessels of your "secondary hand" away from random slashes from your assailant. The only time your knife should be away from your body is when you are executing an attack.

687. FOCUS ON THE ASSAILANT'S KNIFE.

During a knife fight, your assailant's blade is your most immediate threat. Therefore, it's important to keep your eyes wide open and focused on the blade. Avoid unnecessary blinking. If possible, keep all light sources (sun, street lights, car headlights, etc.) to your back and in the assailant's eyes. This will assist you in creating subtle visual distractions that will impair your adversary's accuracy and reaction time.

688. STAB, DON'T JAB.

Don't jab at your assailant with an edged weapon. If you are going to commit yourself to a linear attack, deliver a quick, forceful thrust. Stabbing should always be used as a fully committed killing move.

689. MASTER DRAWING SKILLS.

Spend just as much time learning to draw your knife quickly as you would practicing your offensive and defensive skills. Also avoid using the cross-draw technique, which allows your adversary the opportunity to immobilize your drawing arm temporarily.

690. CUT YOUR ADVERSARY AT A 45-DEGREE ANGLE.

When cutting your assailant, try to direct your blade at a 45-degree angle. This cutting angle is important for the following reasons: (1) it's an efficient cutting angle, (2) it creates a larger arterial wound, and (3) it's more difficult for arteries to clot when severed at 45 degrees.

KNIFE DEFENSE AND KNIFE FIGHTING

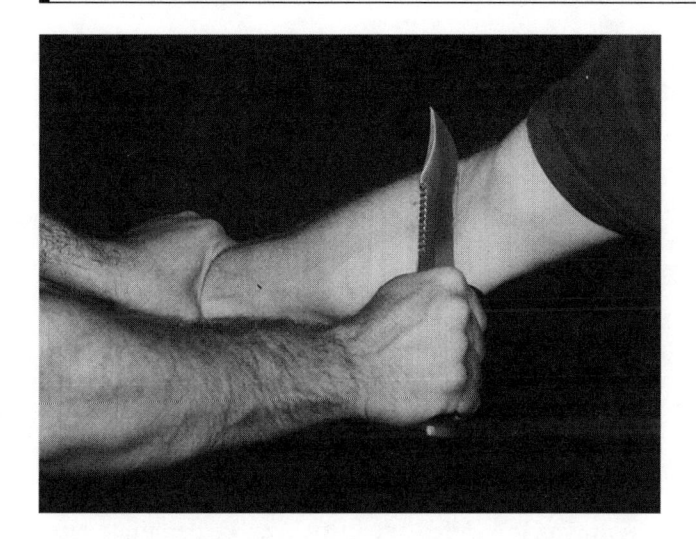

When cutting your assailant, try to direct your blade at a 45-degree angle.

691. KNOW THE CUT CHOICES.
Blood vessels, nerves, tendons, muscles, and organs are your primary targets.

692. KNOW THE DIFFERENCE BETWEEN THE TWO WAYS OF GETTING CUT.
Sound knife fighting training requires that you acquire a basic understanding of how you get wounded by a knife. There are two ways in which to get cut.

(1) Stabbing—there is a stabbing motion that punctures tissue and is more likely to be fatal. Stab wounds produce internal damage and bleeding.

(2) Slashing—unless the slash severs a major artery, it is not as immediately threatening as a stab wound. Keep in mind that both stabbing and slashing motions can be executed from a variety of grips and postures.

693. KEEP YOUR GLOVES ON.
If you can, keep your gloves on when engaged in a knife fight to protect you from cuts and slashes.

694. WEAR A LEATHER JACKET.
Leather is a knife fighter's armor because it is surprisingly resistant to cuts. When on the town, wear a thick and loose-fitting leather jacket.

695. UNDERSTAND ANATOMY.
Since knife fighting is dynamic and unpredictable, you must have a thorough understanding of the anatomical targets presented on your assailant's posterior. Some targets include the base of the skull, elbows, kidneys, the back of the knees, and the Achilles tendons.

696. EMPLOY THE FOOTWORK RULE OF THUMB DURING A KNIFE FIGHT.
The footwork rule of thumb for unarmed combat also applies to knife fighting. Remember, always move the foot closest to the direction that you want to go first, and the other leg should follow an equal distance. This rule of thumb applies to both linear and lateral movement.

697. UNDERSTAND THAT SPEED IS MORE IMPORTANT THAN POWER.
In edged-weapon combat, speed is much more important than power. Remember, a razor-sharp blade does not require a lot of power to cut effectively.

698. DON'T SHIFT YOUR WEIGHT TO YOUR REAR LEG.
When advancing in a knife fight, never shift your weight to the rear leg prior to moving forward at your assailant. Shifting your weight back prior to moving forward will telegraph your movement, waste time, and propel you upward rather than forward.

699. PULL IT THROUGH.
When slashing with your knife, always pull the blade of your knife through the target. This will maximize the penetration depth of your cut. When slashing, allow the base of the knife edge to make contact with the target first and then pull (draw) the rest of the blade through.

700. MASTER ANGULAR THRUSTS.
Master angular thrusts with your knife. Angular thrusts can be delivered using either the ice-pick or hammer grip.

701. EMPLOY THE SAFETY CHECK AFTER THE MEET.
The meet is a defensive technique applied in both the mid- and close-quarter knife ranges. Its primary function is to intercept your assailant's line of attack with a slash to his wrist. Since you are still

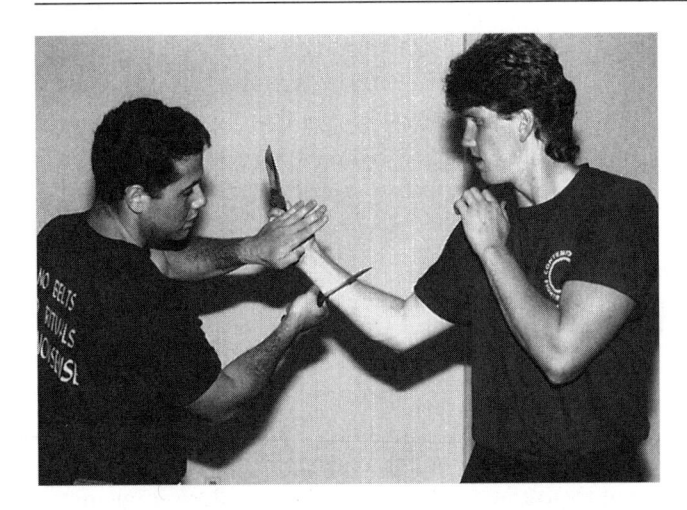

When applying the meet, be certain to use a safety check to prevent the assailant's knife from following through.

positioned in your assailant's line of attack, be certain to use a safety check to prevent the assailant's knife from following through.

702. TRY TO ESCAPE IF POSSIBLE.

If you have the chance to run and escape during the course of a knife fight, do it immediately! Quickly try to scan your environment for possible escape routes. Look for doors, windows, stairwells, or other avenues of safe escape. Under no circumstances should you engage in a knife fight unless it is absolutely necessary. Don't let your ego or pride trap you into believing that it's cowardly to run. ***WARNING: If you attempt to outrun your adversary, be certain that you have the athletic ability to really move—and don't offer him target opportunities in your flight.***

703. MASTER THE MODIFIED ICE-PICK GRIP.

If your knife is not designed with a protective hilt, then the modified ice-pick grip should be the preferred grip when violently stabbing into your assailant. The thumb positioning on the modified ice-pick grip helps prevent your hand from accidentally slipping onto your blade.

704. NEVER FORGET WHAT A KNIFE FIGHT REALLY IS.

There are many words that accurately describe the nature and characteristics of a knife fight. Here are a few to keep in mind: brutal, vicious, unpredictable, unfair, touch-and-go, hazardous, menacing, precarious, treacherous, uncertain, unsafe, quick, swift, nonstop, variable, cruel, deadly, fierce, barbarous, exhausting, difficult, ugly, graceless, grisly, and gruesome.

705. THROW YOUR ASSAILANT OFF BALANCE.

One of the other strategic benefits behind the "secondary hand" is that it can throw your assailant off balance.

706. MASTER THE PASS.

The pass is a defensive technique that can be executed in the mid- and long-knife range. Like the meet, the function of the pass is to intercept your assailant's line of attack with a cut to his wrist. When employing this defensive maneuver, be certain to lean back and angle your torso away from your assailant's strike. Generally, when employing the pass (at long-knife range), there is no need for a safety check.

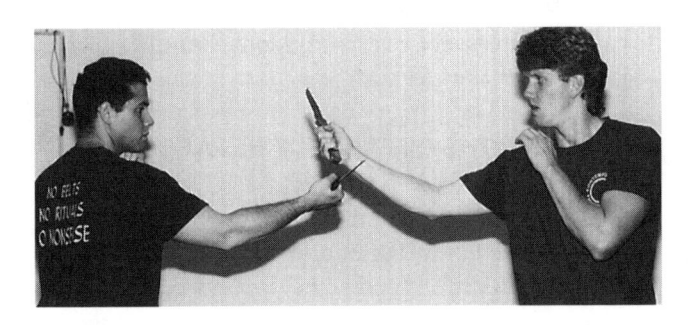

The pass.

707. MASTER THE FOLLOW.

Another defensive technique used in the mid- to long-range of knife combat is the follow. Like the pass, the follow requires you to lean back and angle your torso away from your assailant's strike. However, instead of cutting your adversary's wrist, you execute a backhand cut to his hand. In a sense, you are following your assailant's line of attack.

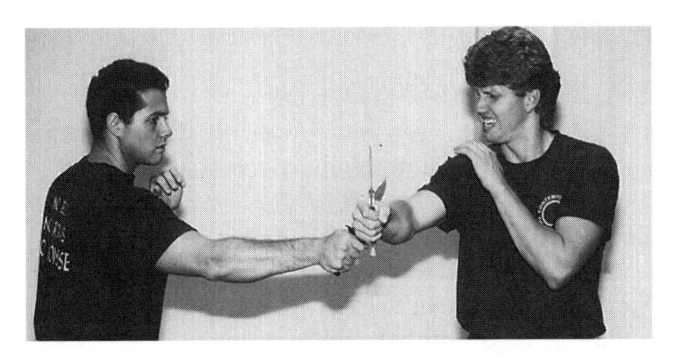

The follow.

KNIFE DEFENSE AND KNIFE FIGHTING

708. CUT AND MOVE.
As in unarmed combat, you must be able to cut your adversary and move at the same time without any preliminary movements.

709. UNDERSTAND THAT KNIFE FIGHTING IS A SCIENCE.
There is much more to knife fighting than simply slashing and stabbing. There are correct and incorrect methods of cutting an assailant.

710. CUT TIGHT AND FAST.
When executing an inward slash with your knife, avoid wide and long arcing movements. Always keep your arc tight and make your movements quick.

711. MASTER THE FIVE KNIFE FIGHTING PRINCIPLES.
To minimize your chances of injury and maximize your chances of survival, here are five knife fighting principles that you should follow: (1) maintain a 45-degree stance to minimize target exposure; (2) remain mobile, agile, and hostile; (3) keep your knife or edged weapon in your front hand; (4) keep your knife close to your body; (5) when your adversary attacks, try to angle yourself away from his line of attack and simultaneously cut his weapon hand.

712. DON'T LOCK YOUR ELBOW.
Never lock your elbow when delivering any type of slashing motion. This is critical for the following reasons: (1) it makes your elbow susceptible to a dislocation, (2) the arc of your slash will be longer and thus slower, (3) the arc of your slash will be telegraphic, (4) the arc of your slash will lack power and economy of motion, and (5) it offers your assailant the opportunity to counter effectively.

713. DON'T SLASH AT YOUR ASSAILANT'S TORSO.
Slashing movements are best delivered to the assailant's arms, eyes, neck, and knee region. Avoid slashing your assailant's torso, which is best suited for thrusts and stabs.

714. MASTER THE INWARD SLASH.
The inward slash can be delivered at various heights and planes. It can also be employed vertically, horizontally, and diagonally.

The assailant's torso is best suited for thrusts and stabs.

715. JABBING AND THRUSTING: THERE'S A DIFFERENCE.
There is a clear difference between jabbing and thrusting a knife. While both movements can puncture your assailant's body, jabbing with a knife is a quick "darting" motion that lacks the necessary force to penetrate the assailant's vital organs.

Although the thrust requires a 100-percent follow-through and deep penetration into the target, it is generally the coup de grace. When attempting to thrust your knife, be exceptionally quick about it. And don't forget that thrusting movements can be delivered at various angles to the assailant's body.

716. BE CAREFUL WHEN WITHDRAWING YOUR KNIFE.
Although thrusting motions are an essential part of a knife fighter's arsenal, beware of the following potential problems when withdrawing your knife: (1) your knife can become extremely slippery from the assailant's blood, (2) suction generates

around the wound area, which can make it difficult to withdraw the blade from the assailant's body, (3) your knife can get lodged between the assailant's bones or joints, and (4) your knife can get tangled in the assailant's clothes.

To remedy many of these inherent problems, use the push-off technique—simply push your assailant away with your free hand as you pull out your blade. This permits a quick withdrawal and throws the assailant off balance, making a counterattack difficult. For maximum power and leverage, apply the push off with your palm up.

717. TWIST YOUR BLADE CORRECTLY.

The direction that you twist your blade upon withdrawal is dependent upon the type of thrust that you deliver. For example, when delivering direct thrusts with your palm up, turn the knife counterclockwise. When delivering an inward thrust with your palm down, turn your knife clockwise. This will help increase the size of the wound channel, which will result in faster blood loss and greater structural damage to your assailant.

718. BE CAREFUL WHEN ATTACKING HIS RIBS.

Be especially careful when thrusting your knife into your assailant's ribs. There is a distinct possibility that your blade may get lodged.

719. REMEMBER THAT MULTIPLE SLASHES ARE UNLIKELY.

Although defeating your adversary with multiple slashes sounds great, it is highly improbable that this can be accomplished. Most assailants will not stand there and let you carve them up.

720. MASTER STRATEGIC LEANING.

Strategic leaning is a maneuver that permits you to evade your assailant's knife while allowing you to remain in range to counter his attack. This is particularly important when your environment won't permit you to be mobile. When performed at the proper time, strategic leaning can also increase the power of your countercut. *WARNING: When performing the strategic lean maneuver, be especially careful not to "over lean," which will cause you to lose your balance.*

721. KNOW THE INSERTION POINTS.

There are specific insertion points on your

Here, the author (left) demonstrates the strategic lean.

assailant's anatomy that can be used for slashing and stabbing attacks. Here are a few to remember: (1) ear cavities, (2) eye sockets, (3) temples, (4) base of skull, (5) cervical vertebrae, (6) jugular vein, (7) underside of the chin, (8) carotid artery, (9) subclavian artery, (10) heart, (11) lungs, (12) brachial arteries, (13) radial arteries, (14) third- and fourth-rib regions, (15) solar plexus, (16) groin, and (17) femoral arteries.

722. GRIP YOUR KNIFE PROPERLY.

A powerful and secure grip is essential for knife fighting. When gripping your knife, always make certain that the cutting edge faces your assailant. Also, be very careful not to wrap your fingers too tightly around the handle. This can be dangerous for the following reasons: (1) it restricts wrist mobility, (2) it reduces your slashing speed, (3) it weakens your forearm muscles, and (3) it creates greater target exposure by forcing your veins to protrude from your hands and forearms.

723. AVOID A KNIFE FIGHT AT ALL COSTS.

A knife fight should always be avoided at all costs. It is a desperate situation that should only be undertaken when all other means of avoiding the situation have been thoroughly exhausted. Always attempt to escape or run from a knife fight.

KNIFE DEFENSE AND KNIFE FIGHTING

724. DEVELOP THESE IMPORTANT SKILLS.

There is a lot more to knife fighting than just the knife itself. The best combat knife in the world is no substitute for skill and training. A well-trained knife fighter can stab and gouge you to death with a sharp pencil.

Here is just a brief list of some important skills that must be practiced with a qualified instructor: (1) concealment strategies, (2) grips and stance, (3) target orientation, (4) target selection, (5) drawing techniques, (6) target exploitation, (7) safe handling procedures, (8) footwork, (9) weapon control and retention, (10) range manipulation, (11) withdrawing skills, (12) secondary weapon training, (13) insertion points, and (14) strategic leaning.

TRAINING

725. PRACTICE WITH REALISTIC TRAINING KNIVES.

The only effective method of developing knife fighting skills is to practice safely with a training partner. There are numerous training knives on the market. One of the best is the Al Mar Knives (AMK) Training Knife. When looking to purchase training knives, avoid buying those rubber knives that "wiggle" when you move them. These knives are cheap and very unrealistic. ***CAUTION: Be exceptionally careful when slashing at your partner's face. To prevent eye injuries, wear some form of eye protection.***

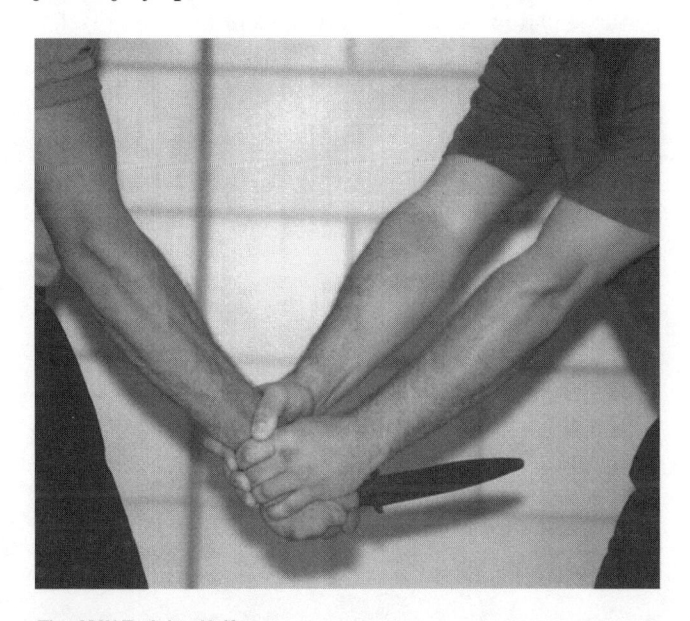

726. PRACTICE KNIFE FIGHTING WITH YOUR WEAK HAND.

When practicing knife fighting skills, always devote sufficient time to your weak hand. As in unarmed combat, ambidexterity is an invaluable skill. Here are just a few reasons why it should be developed: (1) there is a possibility that your strong hand might be injured in a knife fight, (2) it enhances your overall combat confidence, (3) it reinforces good combat skills, and (4) your strong hand might be occupied during the fight.

727. PRACTICE IN FRONT OF A MIRROR.

In front of a mirror, practice linear and lateral footwork movements with a training knife in your hand. This should be performed in both your right and left stances. Be aware of your stance as you move, keep your weight evenly distributed, keep your balance, and stay relaxed. This should be practiced on all different types of terrain (wet grass, mud, ice, wet pavement, snow, gravel, and sand).

728. PRACTICE KNIFE FIGHTING ON THE GROUND.

Practice knife fighting skills while ground fighting with your training partner. Practice from a variety of postures and positions.

729. MAKE YOUR KNIFE FIGHTING STANCE INSTINCTUAL.

You must practice the knife fighting stance

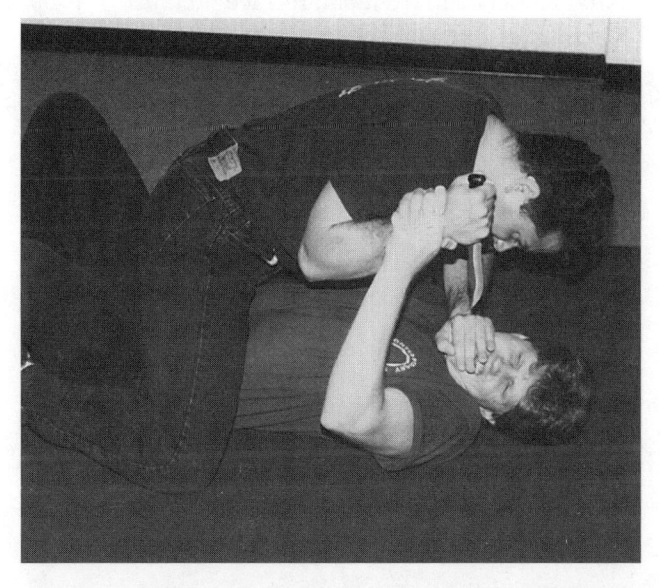

The AMK Training Knife.

Defending against a knife attack while on the ground is extremely treacherous.

In this photo, Franco (left) uses his secondary hand to control his assailant's weapon hand.

until it becomes instinctual. This means that you will have to practice in front of a full-length mirror. When you assume your stance, scrutinize yourself and pick out the strategic deficiencies. For example, what targets are exposed? Is your balance sacrificed? Are your knees bent?

730. DEVELOP SECONDARY HAND SKILLS.

You must learn to practice quick slashing movements with your secondary hand closely trailing your blade. This can be practiced and refined in front of a full-length mirror.

731. TIME YOURSELF.

Occasionally use a stopwatch to see how quickly you can open a lock blade. Time yourself with both your right and left hands.

732. PRACTICE KNIFE FIGHTING IN CLOSE QUARTERS.

Learn how to use your knife in close-quarter environments. Here are just a few examples: (1) in your car, (2) in a phone booth, (3) in an elevator, (4) on a bridge, (5) in a narrow hallway, (6) in a doorway, (7) in a bathroom stall, (8) in a crowd, (9) in a cluttered garage, (10) on a narrow stairwell, and (11) between tall shrubbery.

733. KNOW HOW TO TAKE CARE OF YOUR KNIFE.

Like any tool used for combat, your knife will require a bit of care and maintenance. Proper maintenance of your knife will ensure that it will work effectively when needed. Here are four important guidelines: (1) keep your blade clean at all times, (2) don't use your knife as a pry bar or chisel, (3) keep your knife lubricated if it's a lock blade, and (4) always keep your knife razor sharp.

CHAPTER EIGHT

Firearms and Combat Shooting

"A firearm places you in the position of judge, jury, and executioner, all in a matter of seconds."

OWNERSHIP

734. SUPPORT THE SECOND AMENDMENT.
The Second Amendment reads, "A well regulated militia, being necessary to the security of a free state, the right of the people to keep and bear arms, shall not be infringed." Each and every American citizen has a responsibility to protect and defend the Constitution of the United States, especially the Second Amendment right of the individual to keep and bear arms.

735. THINK SERIOUSLY ABOUT OWNING A FIREARM.
The decision to own a firearm warrants considerable thought and honest reflection. Here are some important questions to ask yourself: (1) Do you abuse alcohol or use drugs? (2) Are you hot tempered? (3) Could you take the life of another person? (4) Do you experience long periods of depression? (5) Do you live alone? (6) Do children live in your household? (7) Why do you want to own a firearm? (8) Have you ever shot a gun? (9) Are you a disorganized person? (10) Are you clumsy or accident-prone? (11) Are you willing to take the time to obtain the knowledge, skills, and attitude needed to handle firearms safely?

736. DO YOUR HOMEWORK.
Before you purchase a firearm, it's important that you do your homework. With so many firearms on the market, it is difficult to make a choice. Nevertheless, there are some questions that you should ask yourself that will help you with your selection. What purpose will the gun serve? Will it be used for hunting, collecting, target practice, or self-defense? Are you interested in purchasing a shotgun, autoloader, or revolver? How much money are you willing to spend? Will you be carrying the firearm, and how will you carry it?

Also consider the following helpful tips before purchasing a gun for self-defense: (1) get advice from firearm experts, knowledgeable police officers, and reputable dealers; (2) familiarize yourself with the various models on the market; (3) read various gun magazines, books, and articles and find out which guns have the greatest practicality for your use; (4) read the warranty or guarantee that comes with the firearm; (5) look for high-quality brand-name firearms; (6) be aware of the gun's recoil before you buy it; (7) buy the firearm from a reputable dealer; (8) be absolutely certain the gun fits comfortably in your hand; (9) look for a gun that is easy to clean and operate; and (10) be certain the caliber of the weapon has sufficient stopping power.

Please remember that no matter what kind of gun you purchase—if you get one—it isn't going to help you unless you know how to use it. Get trained by a qualified instructor in firearms self-defense.

737. KNOW THE FIREARM LAWS.
Before you purchase a firearm, it is your responsibility to understand and obey the various laws governing its use, possession, and transportation. Such laws vary from state to state and city to city, so learn the ones that apply to you and your community. Your local police or sheriff's department can help you.

738. **CHOOSE YOUR RESIDENCE CAREFULLY.**
If at all possible, try to avoid living in a country, state, or city that prohibits firearm ownership. Move if you can.

SAFETY

739. **DON'T BE CARELESS—GUNS DON'T DISCHARGE BY THEMSELVES.**
Never forget that the two major causes of firearm accidents are ignorance and carelessness. Ignorance means that you are unaware of the firearm safety rules, and carelessness means that you are knowledgeable of firearm safety rules but fail to apply them.

740. **TAKE A FIREARM SAFETY COURSE.**
Don't even think about owning a gun unless you have successfully completed a firearm safety course, been extensively trained in its use, and have developed the necessary confidence and proficiency.

741. **KNOW THE FIREARM SAFETY RULES.**
Safe gun handling is your responsibility, and safety must always be your concern. To ensure the safe use of any firearm, always follow these four primary safety rules: (1) take a firearm safety course before you acquire a firearm, (2) always assume that a firearm is loaded, (3) always point a firearm in a safe direction, (4) always be certain of your target, and (5) never put your finger on the trigger until you are ready to shoot.

Other gun safety rules include the following:

- Always read the owner's manual that comes with your firearm.
- Always be sure the barrel of your gun is clear of obstructions.
- Always use clean, dry, factory-made ammunition of the proper caliber.
- Always wear ear protection and safety glasses when practicing at the firing range.
- Do not leave a loaded gun unattended.
- Never allow your firearm to be used by anyone who is not knowledgeable of the safety rules.
- Never trust a safety.
- Before cleaning your firearm, make sure that the chamber is empty and be absolutely certain it is unloaded.
- Always make sure that all ammunition is stored away from the cleaning area.
- Never use alcohol or drugs before or while shooting.
- Always store guns so they are not accessible to untrained or unauthorized persons.
- Always be certain your firearm is safe to operate.
- Never fire at surfaces that can cause your bullet to ricochet.
- Always comply with the safety regulations of your firing range.

742. **NEVER FORGET THE MOST IMPORTANT SAFETY RULE.**
Although all of the firearm safety rules are important, never forget the most important rule: *Always point a firearm in a safe direction*. This way, if the firearm is discharged unintentionally, it will not cause injury or death.

743. **UNDERSTAND AND OBEY THE FIRING RANGE SAFETY COMMANDS.**
A properly supervised firing range is essential. Every shooter is personally responsible for understanding and obeying all of the range commands. The standard range commands include the following: (1) load—when the shooter is on the firing line, he may load his weapon; (2) commence fire—the shooter may begin firing the weapon when he is ready; (3) cease fire—the shooter must stop firing the firearm immediately.

744. **DON'T MAKE GUNS A TABOO SUBJECT WITH CHILDREN.**
If you own a gun and have kids, then it's your responsibility to be a positive role model for your children. You should talk openly about guns with your children. Making guns a taboo subject can elicit children's curiosity and possibly lead them to investigate guns on their own. Even if you're not a gun owner, your son or daughter may one day come in contact with a firearm at a relative or friend's house.

The best time to talk about firearms is when your child begins to show interest, e.g., when your child begins to act out gun scenes or ask questions. The amount of information and training that you give your child will depend upon the following factors: (1) the child's age, (2) the child's level of maturity, and

FIREARMS AND COMBAT SHOOTING

(3) the child's ability to reason. When discussing guns with your child, be certain to answer all questions. If you don't know the answers to particular questions, speak with a qualified firearms instructor.

745. KEEP YOUR FIREARM CLEAN.

Always keep your weapon clean. Cleaning your firearm is important for the following reasons: (1) it will ensure that your weapon will operate properly and safely when fired, (2) it will help maintain the weapon's value, (3) it will help extend the life of the weapon, and (4) it will allow you the opportunity to inspect your gun for proper functioning.

You will need the following materials to clean your gun properly: cleaning rod, cleaning rod attachment, bore brush, cleaning patch, bore cleaner solvent, gun oil, cleaning cloth, old toothbrush, and Q-tips. *WARNING: Before cleaning your firearm, be certain that it is unloaded, the action is open, and there is no ammunition present. After cleaning the firearm, always check to make sure that no cleaning patch or other obstruction is in the bore or chamber.*

FACTS

746. DON'T FORGET—IF IT'S UNLOADED IT'S USELESS.

When it comes to personal protection, never forget that an unloaded firearm is a useless firearm.

747. DON'T BLAME GUNS.

Guns are not people. They are neither good nor evil. They are simply neutral tools that can either be abused or used to protect property and lives.

748. REMEMBER THAT ABILITY OVERRIDES THE WEAPON.

Most people don't understand that it is really not the firearm that is important but the skill and ability of the person operating the weapon. *Remember, a firearm is only as effective as the person who uses it.*

749. BE ON THE LOOKOUT FOR CONCEALED WEAPON CARRY.

Criminals do not usually carry their guns in holsters. Train yourself to immediately spot unusual bulges and people who seem to be performing security body pats.

750. DON'T FORGET—THEY SHOOT BACK.

Combat is often very disjointed, hard to understand, and confusing. A gunfight is nothing like what you see on TV or in the movies. It is not romantic or antiseptic. It is horrifying, brutal, confusing, rapid, bloody, and final. And although practice is essential, never forget that training at a firing range has little to do with the explosive dynamics of a lethal gunfight. And, most important, in a real encounter, the targets move and shoot back.

751. REMEMBER—HANDGUNS ARE SUPERIOR.

In most armed self-defense situations, the handgun (autoloader and revolver) is superior to a long gun. Here are just a few reasons why: (1) unlike rifles and shotguns, handguns can be drawn and fired more quickly with practice and training; (2) handguns can be transported more easily; (3) handguns are smaller and can be concealed better; (4) in a close-quarter struggle, long guns can be disarmed more easily than handguns; (5) handguns can, if necessary, be shot with just one hand; and (6) handguns can be holstered, allowing you to utilize other "use-of-force" options and tactics on your adversary.

NOMENCLATURE AND MECHANICS

752. KNOW WHAT YOU'RE TALKING ABOUT.

Understand the nomenclature of your firearm. The following are some basic terms that you should understand clearly: (1) for the revolver—muzzle, barrel, front and rear sights, ejector rod, cylinder, trigger and trigger guard, frame, grip, cylinder release latch, hammer spur, hammer, firing pin, and chambers; (2) for the autoloader—magazine, cartridge ejection port, slide, grip, frame, front and rear sights, hammer, trigger, trigger guard, recoil spring, slide catch lever, and magazine floorplate.

753. KNOW THE DIFFERENCE BETWEEN A SEMIAUTOMATIC AND A REVOLVER.

A true combatant must understand the mechanical difference between a revolver and a semiautomatic pistol. The semiautomatic, or autoloader, differs from the revolver in many ways. They are called "semiautomatics" because when fired, they automatically feed a fresh round and eject the spent casing. All you have to do is keep squeezing the trigger. With the autoloader, rounds of ammunition are loaded vertically in a metal container called the magazine. The magazine is then inserted into the grip of the gun. Generally, autoloaders are slightly more complicated to operate than their revolver cousins.

Although the revolver is not the most efficient handgun for an armed encounter with a criminal assailant, it still has its place in the world of self-defense. This type of handgun is called a revolver because its cylinder revolves when the trigger is pulled. Revolvers can hold anywhere from five to nine cartridges, depending on the type of cylinder. They also come in single-action (you have to cock the hammer before it can be fired) or double-action (you just squeeze the trigger). Loading a revolver is generally safe and simple, and you can easily tell when it is loaded. They almost never jam, and they can be trusted to fire effectively.

754. CHOOSE THE SEMIAUTOMATIC OVER THE REVOLVER.

When compared to the revolver, the semiautomatic pistol is the superior weapon for armed combat for several reasons: (1) it has a larger ammunition capacity, (2) it is faster firing (because of the single-action trigger pull), (3) it is faster reloading, (4) it has greater hit potential, (5) it is more accurate, (6) it has greater control, (7) it has lighter trigger pull, (8) it has less kick or recoil than revolvers of equal stopping power, (9) it is more comfortable—the hand grip designs on most semiautomatic pistols tend to fit more comfortably in the hand, and (10) clearing malfunctions are quicker to remedy than with revolvers.

755. AVOID USING A SINGLE-ACTION REVOLVER.

The single-action revolver is an obsolete weapon that should not be used for combat. Here are just a few reasons why: (1) fluid and rapid firing capability is limited because the trigger must be thumb-cocked before each shot; (2) since the hammer is usually cocked by your thumb, it disturbs your grip and may affect your accuracy; and (3) reloading a single-action revolver is slow and cumbersome.

756. LEARN THE COMPONENTS OF A PISTOL CARTRIDGE.

The more you know about firearms, the better. For example, know the component parts of a pistol cartridge. A pistol cartridge consists of the following

The .45 semiautomatic.

The revolver.

When compared to the revolver, the semiautomatic pistol, such as the 9mm SIG-Sauer P226 combat pistol shown here, is the superior weapon for armed combat.

FIREARMS AND COMBAT SHOOTING

four general components: (1) case—a metal cylinder that is closed at one end, (2) primer—an impact-sensitive chemical compound, (3) powder charge—a quick-burning chemical compound used as a propellant, and (4) bullet—a projectile that travels at great velocity.

757. UNDERSTAND FIREARM MECHANICS.

Understanding the various mechanics of a firearm can go a long way. For example, is there a safety on the assailant's weapon? Is his weapon cocked to single-action, or is it in the double-action mode? Are cartridges visible in the cylinder of his revolver? Is the slide of his autoloader locked back to the rear? What do the different types of autoloader malfunctions look like? How many rounds did he fire versus the number of rounds that are available? How can you induce a malfunction in his weapon (e.g., by pushing back on the slide and stopping the cylinder from turning, etc.)?

758. DON'T TRUST YOUR SAFETY.

Never trust the safety on your gun. Like any mechanical device, a safety can fail.

759. ROTATE SPARE MAGAZINES.

Long-term compression of the magazine spring in your autoloader can prevent proper cartridge feeding. This is otherwise known as "spring set." Here are two suggestions that will help prevent unnecessary magazine spring stress in your semiautomatic pistol: (1) get into the habit of rotating your spare magazines every three months and (2) don't load your magazine to full capacity; leave at least one round out.

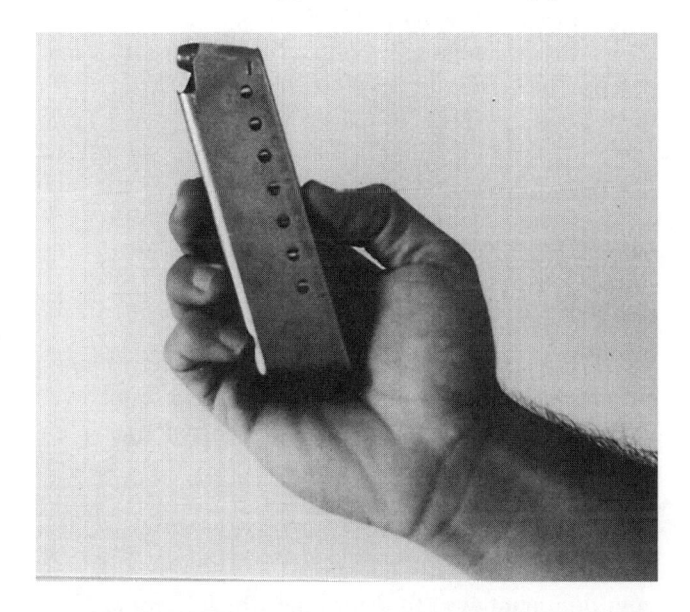

AMMUNITION

760. REMEMBER AMMUNITION CRITERIA.

When selecting a self-defense cartridge for your weapon, make certain that your ammunition fulfills these five requirements: (1) stopping power—it must be able to stop your assailant immediately from any further action; (2) controlled recoil—it should allow you to recover quickly from the recoil of your shot; (3) limited ricochet—it should significantly reduce the bullet's ability to ricochet off hard surfaces; (4) maximum penetration—it must be able to go through objects (e.g., car doors, furniture, etc.); (5) reliability—it must be free from various cartridge malfunctions (e.g., hang fire, misfire, or squib loads.)

761. STORE AMMUNITION SAFELY.

When storing ammunition, please take the following factors into consideration: (1) to ensure that your ammunition will function properly, always store your cartridges in a cool, dry place that is free from extremely high temperatures; (2) never submerge your cartridges in water or expose them to ammonia, bore cleaner, acids, salts, or petroleum products (including gun oil)—all solvents that can deteriorate the primer or power in your cartridge; and (3) for safety reasons, store ammunition so that it is inaccessible to unauthorized persons, especially children.

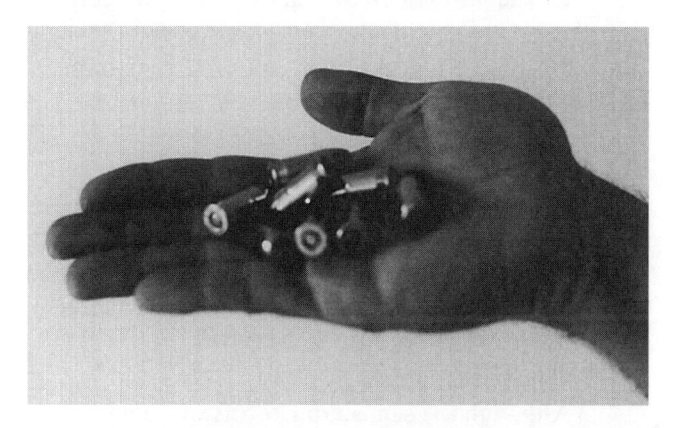

To prevent spring stress in your autoloader, rotate your spare magazines every three months.

Does your ammo fulfill the five ammunition requirements?

762. CHOOSE YOUR CALIBER CAREFULLY.
Don't make a .38- or .22-caliber pistol your first choice for personal protection. Its stopping power is somewhat questionable. Generally, when selecting a handgun for self-defense, choose a 9mm or higher caliber.

763. KNOW THE CARTRIDGE FIRING SEQUENCE.
Although it is critical to know how a firearm operates, it's also important to understand the cartridge firing sequence, which is as follows: (1) the firing pin strikes the cartridge primer, (2) the cartridge primer ignites, (3) the primer flame ignites the powder charge, (4) the powder charge burns quickly and produces a large volume of gas, and (5) the expanding gases push the bullet out of the cartridge case and sends it out of the barrel at a high rate of speed.

MALFUNCTIONS

764. KNOW THE THREE TYPES OF CARTRIDGE MALFUNCTIONS.
There are three different types of cartridge malfunctions that you need to be aware of. They include (1) misfire—the cartridge fails to fire after the primer has been struck by the firing pin; (2) hang fire—there is a delay in the ignition of the cartridge when the primer is struck; (3) squib load—there is less than normal pressure/velocity after the ignition of the cartridge.

765. USE THE TAP-RACK-BANG.
There may come a time when you will be faced with a malfunction caused by either a defective cartridge or a magazine that isn't inserted completely. When this problem occurs, you can solve it with the following tap-rack-bang technique: (1) tap—with your weak hand, tap the floorplate of the magazine back into the grip; (2) rack—with your weak hand, rack or cycle the slide, ejecting the defective cartridge and reloading a fresh one; (3) bang—resume firing your weapon.

766. PREPARE FOR AUTOLOADER MALFUNCTIONS.
Although the semiautomatic pistol is an extremely reliable tool, there is always the possibility of a malfunction. You must therefore be aware of the different types of autoloader malfunctions and know their remedies.

(1) Out of battery. One common autoloader malfunction occurs when the slide fails to go into battery after firing. To clear this malfunction, apply the following steps: a) maintain your position on your target; b) take your finger off the trigger; c) with your weak hand, slam the back of the slide with the heel of your palm; and d) resume firing.

(2) Smokestack. Another type of malfunction is called the smokestack, which occurs when a spent casing is caught in the ejection port. To clear this malfunction, apply the following steps: a) maintain your position on your target; b) take your finger off the trigger; c) with your weak hand, rake the heel of your palm along the slide and the empty casing; d) knock the casing out of the breech; e) once the casing is clear, the slide should move forward, cycling a fresh round; and f) resume firing.

FUNDAMENTALS

767. DON'T FORGET THE FIREARM FUNDAMENTALS.
If you intend to rely on a firearm for self-defense, be certain to develop proficiency in each of the following aspects of marksmanship: (1) grip, (2) stance, (3) sight alignment, (4) trigger squeeze, (5) breath control, and (6) follow-through.

768. NEVER FORGET—IT'S DIFFICULT TO APPLY THE FUNDAMENTALS CONSCIOUSLY IN A GUNFIGHT.
Firearm fundamentals must be instinctive and automatic. Keep in mind that if you have to think about them, you may lose the opportunity to fire in a timely manner.

769. AIM WITH YOUR DOMINANT EYE.
When shooting a firearm, always aim with your dominant eye. To determine which is your dominant eye, perform the following exercise: (1) extend both of your arms in front of you; (2) place

FIREARMS AND COMBAT SHOOTING

your hands together, forming a small hole between them; (3) keep both of your eyes open and look through the hole at a distant object; (4) while looking at the distant object, slowly move your hands back until they touch your face; and (5) the hole between both of your hands will be over one eye—this will be your dominant eye for shooting.

770. LEARN SIGHT ALIGNMENT.

Sight alignment is another critical component of marksmanship. It is achieved by correctly aligning your dominant eye with both the front and rear sights. To achieve proper sight alignment, first align the top of your front sight so that it is even with the top of your rear sight, and then make certain that the top of your front sight is centered in the notch of your rear sight. *REMEMBER: Correct sight alignment is the key to accuracy. Misalignment of the front and rear sights will produce an angular error that will be multiplied with distance.*

771. ACCEPT THE ARC OF MOVEMENT.

It is practically impossible to hold a perfect sight picture. There will always be some motion. Accept the fact that you will never eliminate this "arc of movement" when aiming your firearm.

772. UTILIZE FOLLOW-THROUGH.

Follow-through, an important element of marksmanship, simply means continuing to employ the shooting fundamentals throughout the delivery of your shot. This is critical because it aids in preventing any unnecessary movement before the bullet exits the barrel. Moreover, it enhances recoil recovery and provides for effective follow-up shots, if needed.

773. MASTER TRIGGER SQUEEZE.

Another important component of marksmanship is the trigger squeeze. The trigger squeeze is achieved by squeezing the trigger of your gun straight to the rear in a smooth and fluid manner without disturbing the sight alignment. *REMEMBER: Finger placement is a critical element of trigger squeeze. Prior to taking your shot, make sure the trigger rests halfway between the tip of your index finger and the first joint.*

774. CONCENTRATE ON THE FRONT SIGHT.

The human eye is only capable of focusing on one object at a time. With your dominant eye properly focused, you should see the following: (1) the front sight should always be clear and sharp, (2) the rear sight should appear less sharp, and (3) your target should look blurred. *REMEMBER: If you want an accurate shot, it's critical that you concentrate primarily on the front sight.*

775. REMEMBER THE TWO MOST IMPORTANT FUNDAMENTALS.

Never forget that the two most important fundamentals of marksmanship are sight alignment and trigger squeeze.

776. REMEMBER—GOOD SURVIVAL TACTICS ARE CRITICAL.

Although marksmanship skills are the key to surviving armed encounters, they cannot replace good survival tactics. Marksmanship ability degenerates under the stress of combat, but good tactics compensate for this.

POSITIONS, STANCES, AND GRIPS

777. MASTER THE STANDING, KNEELING, PRONE, AND SUPINE POSITIONS.

Learn to fire a firearm from a variety of combat positions and stances, including the following: (1) standing position—with or without cover, (2) kneeling position—with or without cover, (3) prone position (lying on your stomach)—with or without cover, and (4) supine position (lying on your back)—with or without cover.

778. MASTER COMBAT SHOOTING AT VARIOUS LEVELS.

Combat shooting should be practiced from the following four levels: (1) hip level—one- and two-hand grip, (2) chest level—one- and two-hand grip, (3) point shoulder level—one- and two-hand grip, and (4) sighted level (point shoulder level)—two-hand grip.

779. USE THE THUMB-TO-THUMB, KNUCKLE-TO-KNUCKLE GRIP.

Learn the proper way to grip your firearm. To achieve a proper two-hand grip, follow these guidelines: (1) fit the web of your dominant hand as high as possible on the backstrap area of the frame, (2) align your wrist and forearm with the backstrap of the frame, (3) control the pressure of the grip with your thumb and the lower three fingers of your shooting hand, (4) overlap your nondominant hand over your shooting hand (thumb-to-thumb and knuckle-to-knuckle), and grip your weapon tightly. *CAUTION: Avoid placing your nondominant index finger on your trigger guard. This positioning will affect the accuracy of your shot.*

780. KNOW THE TACTICAL ADVANTAGE OF SHOOTING FROM THE KNEELING POSITION.

Shooting from the kneeling position gives you a strong advantage in a gunfight. Here are just a few reasons why: (1) it minimizes excessive muscle tremors during a fight-or-flight situation, (2) it allows you to fire your weapon from behind a low- or high-barricade position, (3) it reduces your target exposure, and (4) it is one of the most secure combat shooting positions and can be maintained for a prolonged period.

The kneeling position can be executed by applying the following principles: (1) drop your strong knee to the ground with your weak knee pointed upward; (2) keep your weak foot flat on the ground and the ball of your strong foot on the ground; (3) keep your torso and head erect; (4) keep

Here, the author demonstrates one-handed hip-level shooting.

Here, the author demonstrates two-handed chest-level shooting.

The thumb-to-thumb, knuckle-to-knuckle grip.

Franco demonstrates the kneeling position.

When assuming the kneeling position, avoid touching your supporting elbow to your knee.

FIREARMS AND COMBAT SHOOTING

your gun arm slightly bent and pushed forward; (5) keep your supporting arm bent, pulling inward with the elbow pointing to the ground; (6) grip your handgun tightly with the thumb-to-thumb, knuckle-to-knuckle placement; and (7) to minimize recoil, lean your torso slightly forward. Develop the combat kneeling position until it's quick and natural. WARNING: When assuming the kneeling position, avoid touching your supporting elbow to your knee. This elbow-to-knee placement is slow to employ, limits your ability to traverse to your flanks, and limits your shot angle.

781. KNOW THE TACTICAL ADVANTAGE OF SHOOTING FROM THE PRONE POSITION.

Learning to shoot from the prone position is important for the following reasons: (1) it dramatically minimizes target exposure, (2) it provides the most stable firing position, (3) it provides practice in seeking cover (e.g., when faced with suppression fire), (4) it gets you accustomed to situations where you might be injured and forced to the ground, and (5) it provides the best protection when there is no cover.

To shoot from the prone position, do the following: (1) roll onto the strong side of your body while positioning your body at 45 degrees; (2) if you're right-handed, bring your weak knee up and to the left; (3) extend your gun hand straight to your target and use your weak hand for support (the knife-hand edge of both hands should be flush with the ground); (4) place your cheek on the shoulder/biceps region of your arm; and (5) relax your body and get a secure grip on your weapon.

782. USE THE AGGRESSIVE FORWARD LEAN.

When shooting with a two-handed combat stance, adopt an "aggressive forward lean." This type of body posture aids in controlling the weapon's recoil and helps maintain target acquisition and sight alignment.

The prone position.

783. MASTER THE STANDING TWO-HAND STANCE.

Work on perfecting the standing two-hand firearm stance until it is quick and natural. This stance is ideal because it's comfortable and balanced, and it controls the weapon's recoil, minimizes target exposure, and allows you to move in a 180-degree traverse.

There are several important elements to this two-handed firearm stance: (1) keep your feet approximately shoulder-width apart, with both knees slightly bent; (2) blade your stance with your strong side behind; (3) aggressively lean your body weight forward; (4) slightly bend your gun hand, pushing it forward; (5) bend your supporting arm, pulling inward with the elbow pointing to the ground; and (6) grip your handgun tightly with the thumb-to-thumb, knuckle-to-knuckle placement.

Here, Franco assumes the standing two-hand firearm stance.

784. GRIP YOUR AUTOLOADER TIGHTLY.

When holding your autoloader, always grip the weapon tightly. This is important for the following reasons: (1) it helps to control the action of the weapon, (2) it aids in controlling the recoil of the firearm, (3) it helps prevent inaccurate shooting, and (4) it prevents "limp wrist" malfunctions.

785. AVOID EXTENDING YOUR INDEX FINGER.

When holding your handgun in a stalking situation, avoid extending your index finger along the frame of the weapon. This is dangerous for the following reasons: (1) the extended index finger usually catches the trigger guard, slowing down finger-to-trigger placement; (2) it can cause an accidental discharge of your weapon; (3) the extended finger has been known to depress the slide stop stud accidentally on some autoloaders, causing possible malfunctions; (4) the anatomical placement of the index finger lacks overall economy of motion when firing becomes necessary; and (5) if your assailant attempts to disarm you by twisting the weapon out of your hand, he can easily break your index finger.

When holding your handgun in a stalking situation, avoid extending your index finger along the frame of the weapon.

The bent-finger placement is ideal because it permits quick and accurate finger-to-trigger placement, minimizes unintentional weapon discharge, and reduces the possibility of injury if a struggle ensues between you and your adversary.

To remedy the problem of the extended index finger, employ the bent-finger position. This finger placement permits quick and accurate finger-to-trigger placement, minimizes unintentional weapon discharge, and reduces the possibility of injury if a struggle ensues between you and your adversary.

786. UNIFORMITY IS CRITICAL.

One of the most important and often neglected components of a proper pistol grip is uniformity, which means that you grip your firearm the same way every time. This ensures consistent accuracy.

TARGETS

787. GO FOR THE IMMEDIATE STOP.

If you are looking for instant stopping power, aim for his head, specifically the center of the bridge of the nose or the ear for side shots. Here are a few good reasons why you should choose the assailant's head as a target: (1) if a body shot would be ineffective, for instance, when the adversary is wearing body armor; (2) if the assailant's head is the only available target during the encounter; and (3) if the assailant is high on psychoactive drugs (e.g., PCP). *CAUTION: Beware, however, because the head is a smaller and more difficult target to hit, and in some situations bullets have been known to deflect off the skull.*

788. SHOOT CENTER OF MASS.

Although the assailant's head is the most effective target for an immediate stop, the center of his body is probably your best choice. Shooting "center mass" is preferred over the head for the following reasons: (1) the assailant's upper torso is the largest target area and usually the easiest to hit in a stress fire situation, and (2) center mass also contains a large majority of your assailant's vital organs. *REMEMBER: When firing center mass, keep shooting as quickly and as accurately as possible until your assailant ceases to be a threat.*

789. SHOOT BELOW THE WAIST OF AN ASSAILANT WEARING BODY ARMOR.

Body armor will render your center mass shots ineffective. If your assailant is wearing body armor, shoot below his waist. Shooting at the assailant's pelvic area can be fatal and will certainly knock his legs out from under him.

FIREARMS AND COMBAT SHOOTING

TACTICS AND TECHNIQUES

790. MASTER TRAVERSING SKILLS.

Traversing skills are an essential component of street combat shooting. Traversing is particularly important when you are confronted with multiple assailants who try to outflank you. Traversing can be employed while standing and kneeling. However, the two key points to traversing while standing are: (1) keeping your knees bent and flexible, and (2) twisting freely at your waist.

791. DON'T BECOME DEPENDENT ON YOUR FIREARM.

A firearm is an awesome tool. However, don't make the tragic mistake of assuming that the mere possession of a gun will guarantee your safety. This erroneous assumption forms the common fallacy of dependency. Dependency is the sole reliance on a particular weapon for self-defense. Remember, no single weapon is the definitive answer to self-defense. The bottom line is that only you can accept the full responsibility for your protection, and you must have a variety of self-defense measures to meet myriad potential threats. You must be equipped and prepared to rely on all available means, but, most importantly, you must rely on your own intelligence.

792. DON'T BLUFF.

Never point a firearm at anyone unless you are technically and psychologically prepared to take a life.

793. USE THE DOUBLE-TAP PRINCIPLE.

When firing in self-defense, always assume that your first shot missed and deliver an immediate second round. This is known as the double-tap principle. Remember, it is just as easy to squeeze a trigger twice as once. The double-tap principle is important for the following two reasons: (1) it ensures more potential hits and (2) it creates greater wound damage and thus greater stopping potential.

794. DON'T MISS.

Accuracy is everything in a gunfight. Remember, it isn't the first loud noise that ends the encounter. It's the first effective round that matters.

795. NEVER SURRENDER YOUR WEAPON.

If a friend or loved one is ever held at gunpoint and you are in a standoff, never surrender your firearm. This immediately places the fate of both you and your loved one in the hands of a criminal.

796. MAKE YOUR FIREARM EASILY ACCESSIBLE.

If you own a firearm for home protection, make certain it is easily accessible in an emergency situation. Consider keeping a push-button strong box by your bed, and be capable of opening it quickly in the dark.

797. DON'T RUSH THE FIREFIGHT.

During a firefight, don't rush or give up cover. Be patient and systematic. Remember, just one tactical mistake might cost you your life!

798. MASTER THE QUICK PEEK.

The quick-peek technique is executed from a position of cover by rapidly darting out a small portion of your head and one eye to observe. It's important that you never perform the quick peek twice at the same height. If your assailant sees the first quick peek, he may aim at its last location. Therefore, if your first quick peek is high and a second one is needed, then peek low. *WARNING: Firearm position and foot placement are critical when performing the quick-peek technique. A protruding foot or firearm can give you away to the criminal.*

799. BEWARE OF THE "FATAL FUNNEL."

The fatal funnel is a danger area that is created by such openings as doorways, windows, hallways, and stairwells. These locations are dangerous because they are "choke points" that constrict your movement, and they usually provide no cover. Two of the safest methods of moving through the fatal funnel are the crisscross and button hook maneuvers.

800. MASTER THE CRISSCROSS.

The crisscross is an entry maneuver that allows you to travel across a threshold quickly while employing a correct ready-weapon position. To execute the crisscross maneuver, apply the following steps: (1) start with your firearm in the proper ready position—your gun hand should be farther away from the wall with the muzzle pointed at the door and securely tucked back; (2) place the foot that is closer to the wall forward, which permits your rear foot to take the first step across the threshold and places your body at a protective angle in the fatal funnel (or threshold); (3) maintain the correct weapon position and move quickly through the fatal funnel; and (4) clear to the corner of the room and assume a two-hand hold or kneeling position.

801. MASTER THE LIMITED PENETRATION.

The limited penetration (LP) is a corner-clearing movement performed by positioning your firearm and one eye around the corner. The tactical advantage of the limited penetration is that it offers maximum cover and provides a good observation point. The limited penetration is generally executed after a quick peek has revealed the presence of a threatening assailant around the corner. If you determine that no threat is around the corner, maintain the limited penetration to (1) observe and (2) deny mobility. If a firefight ensues, maintain the limited penetration until your immediate threat is removed.

802. MASTER THE SIDE FALL.

The side fall is an engagement technique that is executed from a kneeling position behind cover. It requires you to perform a controlled fall, allowing only minimal head and muzzle exposure around a corner. To perform the side fall maneuver, execute the following steps.

(1) Begin on one knee with your downed knee closer to the corner.

(2) Make certain your firearm is positioned on the same side as your downed knee, which will permit you to fall correctly.

(3) Always maintain a constant ready-weapon position at the corner in case your assailant should appear.

(4) From the kneeling position, drop to the side of your body, making certain to land in sequence—on your calf, hip, then shoulder blade. Keep your firearm tucked back, and during the fall thrust your arms forward in a two-hand hold. Try to prevent your elbows from hitting the ground, as this will disturb your point of aim.

(5) Engage the enemy with fire.

(6) To recover from the side-fall position, quickly tuck your lower leg under your upper leg, then perform a kicking motion with your upper leg and rock your body back to the original kneeling position. Be certain your weapon is back in the ready position.

803. KNOW THE DIFFERENCE BETWEEN COVER AND CONCEALMENT.

Make certain that you know the difference between cover and concealment. Cover is any object that protects you from gunfire. Concealment makes you invisible to your adversary and often allows you the element of tactical surprise; however, it does not necessarily protect you from gunfire.

804. BE COVER CONSCIOUS.

Always remember that your first move in a firefight is to take cover and maintain it. Cover is simply a feature or location that temporarily protects you from gunfire. Taking cover in a gunfight is important for the following reasons: (1) it protects you from the assailant's gunfire; (2) it buys you some time to identify the location of the gunfire; (3) it allows you to assess the situation from a position of safety; (4) it allows you to return fire from a relatively safe position; and (5) cover can be used to stabilize your weapon when shooting. Some of the best objects of cover include the engine block of a

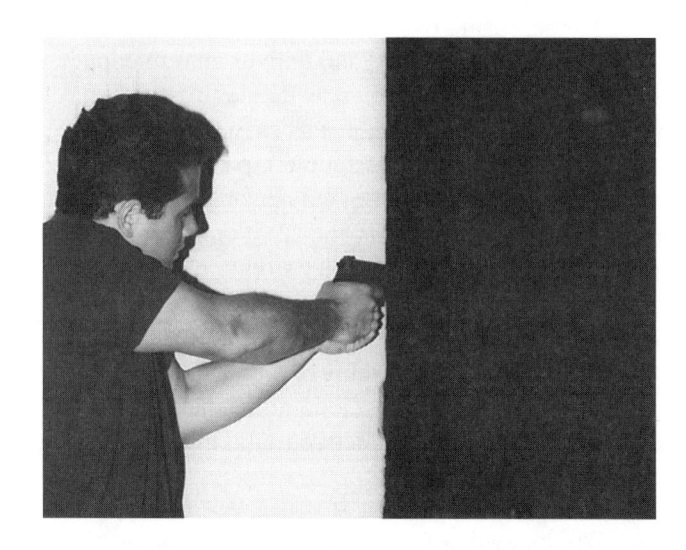

In this photo, Franco uses the corner of a concrete wall for cover.

FIREARMS AND COMBAT SHOOTING

car, a large rock, the corner of a building, a large concrete utility pole, and concrete steps. Remember, always try to question or challenge your adversary from a position of cover. This added security measure can save your life.

805. DON'T RELY ON THESE OBJECTS.

When taking cover in a gunfight, avoid the tragic error of choosing the following objects: (1) internal doors, (2) small trees, (3) car doors, (4) glass windows, (5) drywall, (6) tall grass, (7) car trunks, (8) overturned tables, (9) trash cans, (10) shrubbery, and (11) fences.

806. KNOW THAT WEAPON POSITION IS CRITICAL.

Since many firefights are spontaneous and occur at close range, don't stalk your assailant with your muzzle pointed up or down (low point hold). Furthermore, avoid holding your handgun with both of your arms extended out and locked. This positioning leaves you vulnerable to a sudden grab or disarm maneuver from the assailant. Always have your weapon in a ready weapon position that is close to your torso and be prepared for sudden engagement. The ready weapon position will facilitate immediate firing capability, maximize weapon retention, and, most importantly, allow for quick target acquisition.

807. NEVER SPRAY AND PRAY.

If you are ever involved in a gunfight and innocent bystanders are present, never fire your weapon unless you are absolutely certain that you will hit your target. Remember, precision with a firearm is critical.

808. NEVER FORGET—WHAT YOU CAN'T SEE MAY KILL YOU.

In a gunfight, just because you can't see your assailant doesn't mean that he can't see you. Always remember to find and use good cover. Until you locate your assailant, be reluctant to move.

809. USE A FLASHLIGHT WITH YOUR FIREARM.

Utilizing a flashlight in conjunction with your firearm is important for the following reasons: (1) to positively identify your target, (2) to temporarily blind your assailant as you fire at him, (3) to provide a source of illumination to see where you are going in the dark, (4) to illuminate your assailant for accurate shooting, and (5) to use as a makeshift striking weapon when lethal force is not warranted or justified.

810. BE PREPARED FOR MUZZLE FLASH.

Muzzle flash is an incandescent burst of light that is emitted from the muzzle and cylinder of your handgun. During normal lighting conditions, muzzle flash is hardly noticeable. However, when shooting in the dark or very dim light, muzzle flash can startle you and temporarily inhibit your vision. To minimize the adverse effects of muzzle flash, you'll need to get yourself accustomed to it by regularly engaging in night-firing practice.

811. EXPLOIT YOUR ASSAILANT'S MUZZLE FLASH.

When confronted by an armed assailant in a dark environment, you can exploit his muzzle flash and use it to your advantage. From behind cover, throw something (e.g., rock, bottle, stick, book, ashtray) away from your position to draw his gunfire. Once your adversary fires his weapon, watch for the muzzle flash that reveals his approximate location. Quickly counterfire where you last saw the assailant's muzzle flash. ***REMEMBER: When shooting in the dark or in poor lighting conditions, you'll have a tendency to shoot high, so aim slightly low.***

812. DEFEND AGAINST MULTIPLE ARMED ASSAILANTS.

Defending against multiple armed assailants is extremely difficult and very dangerous. Here are some tactics that you should employ to enhance your chances of surviving the encounter.

(1) Seek cover—always try to seek cover immediately (e.g., large concrete utility poles, large rocks, thick trees, an engine block, the corner of a building). This will temporarily protect you from the assailants' gunfire.

(2) Attempt a tactical retreat—scan your environment for any possible escape routes. Look for windows, doors, fire escapes, or any other avenue that will allow you to flee the altercation safely and quickly. ***WARNING: Never leave a position of cover to escape unless you***

absolutely have to and you're certain you can do so safely.

(3) Shoot the immediate threat—you must determine which assailant is the greatest and most immediate threat to you. Generally, this will be the assailant who is closest to your position of cover.

(4) Shoot sparingly—avoid running out of ammunition. Shoot only when you have to and try to keep an approximate count of the rounds that you have fired. Remember, emptying your entire magazine before you've eliminated your threat can get you killed.

(5) Be prepared to move—always be prepared to move or escape at a second's notice. When moving from a position of cover (especially in the fatal funnel), always move as quickly as possible, with your weapon in the ready weapon position. Be aware of the surface area on which you are standing. You don't want to slip or trip.

813. MASTER ONE-HAND RELOADING.

There may come a time when one of your hands becomes wounded in a firefight and you'll have to reload your weapon with one hand. Develop this skill for both an autoloader and a revolver.

Although there are several different methods for reloading an autoloader one-handed, here is one that you should master: (1) drop the empty magazine to the ground; (2) place your autoloader between your knees, and angle the gun so the muzzle is pointed away from you; and (3) insert a fresh magazine with your good hand, grip your firearm, and return to the ready position.

For the revolver, the process is as follows: (1) insert the revolver vertically in your belt, (2) open the cylinder, (3) push out the used cartridges, (4) insert new rounds, (5) remove the weapon from your belt (keep your finger out of the trigger guard), (6) close the cylinder, and (7) resume firing.

814. KNOW HOW TO CONTACT SHOOT.

Develop contact shooting (touching target) and close-to-contact (approximately one inch away from target) skills. However, be careful after executing a contact shot. Blood and human tissue have been known to obstruct the barrel of a firearm. A firearm malfunction can occur, thereby subjecting you to a greater possibility of being disarmed.

815. FORGET WARNING SHOTS.

Don't fire warning shots at your adversary. It's dangerous and risky for the following reasons: (1) firing into the air can injure or kill an innocent bystander; (2) firing into the floor, ground, or ceiling can cause ricochets and overpenetration into an adjacent room; (3) warning shots take your sights off your immediate threat (the assailant) and expose you to possible counterfire; and (4) it wastes ammunition. Remember, shoot to kill—not to intimidate.

816. TAKE YOUR HAND AWAY.

When cycling your autoloader, be certain to take your hand away from the muzzle. You don't want an accident to occur.

817. NEVER SEND A MAN WHERE YOU CAN SEND A BULLET.

Don't take chances or expose yourself in a firefight. Don't move or give up cover until you are confident that it can be accomplished safely. Establish this by conducting reconnaissance by fire. This means firing into likely cover or places where the assailant may be hiding.

818. CREATE THE FATAL FUNNEL.

If you ever have the drop on your assailant, try to take a low position of cover, preferably at the end of a hallway or a narrow staircase. Once your assailant moves forward, he will be at a tremendous disadvantage. His lateral movement will be dramatically limited, and he will be forced into your "kill zone." When this occurs, your assailant will be in your fatal funnel.

819. SHOOT TO STOP, NOT TO WOUND.

If you are legally warranted and justified in shooting a criminal assailant, shoot to stop his threatening action and not to wound him. Shooting to wound is risky for the following reasons: (1) wound targets are generally smaller and more difficult to hit in real-life encounters, and (2) wounds will not guarantee that your adversary will stop his attack.

FIREARMS AND COMBAT SHOOTING

820. TIME IS A VITAL FACTOR.
Most people don't realize that time is a vital factor in a gunfight. In many cases, you are more likely to run out of time than ammunition.

821. MOVE LATERALLY.
When under gunfire and running for cover, try to run laterally. Also keep in mind that linear movements (advancing or retreating) can be accomplished with broken rhythm, serpentine running patterns.

822. MASTER DRAKE SHOOTING.
When your assailant pins you down with suppressive fire and you cannot tell exactly where it's coming from, employ the drake shooting tactic. Drake shooting is executed by firing your weapon into places of likely cover and accomplishes the following objectives: (1) it helps identify your assailant's position of cover, (2) it helps flush your adversary out, (3) it aids in suppressing your assailant's gunfire, and (4) it denies mobility to your assailant.

823. BE PREPARED FOR THE MEXICAN STANDOFF.
The Mexican standoff is a precarious situation where both you and your adversary have the drop on each other. In such a situation, it's important to utilize either a verbal or physical distraction so that you can safely take the initiative by firing first. A verbal distraction might consist of asking your adversary a question such as, "Are you sure you want to do this?" While asking the question, shoot repeatedly at your assailant. A physical distraction might consist of quickly shifting your eyes to the side, changing the expression on your face, or smiling and looking over your assailant's shoulder. Once your assailant is distracted, shoot him repeatedly.

824. LEARN TO SHOOT AND SPEAK AT THE SAME TIME.
This tactic is especially important during a Mexican standoff with a criminal assailant.

825. SHOOT, EVALUATE, SHOOT, REEVALUATE.
When firing at your assailant, don't make the tactical error of emptying your entire magazine or cylinder. After firing a few rounds, you will need to see if your shots have been effective. You must evaluate your shots quickly or you will never eliminate the threat. Remember, when evaluating your shooting, do so from a position of tactical cover.

826. MOVE AS QUICKLY AS POSSIBLE.
In a gunfight, move from a position of cover to another position of cover as rapidly as possible. Though some situations might justify moving and shooting at the same time, it is best to fire from a stationary position of cover. *CAUTION: Never move without a plan. Moving from a position of cover without first locating another place of cover can get you killed in a firefight. Moving and firing at the same time, called "suppression fire," is only used to keep the bad guy down.*

827. KEEP YOUR GUN HAND FREE.
Whenever possible, try to get into the habit of keeping your gun hand free of food, telephones, books, flashlights, and so on. Practice using your nongun or weak hand for everything.

828. EXPECT AND SUSPECT ANYTHING AND EVERYTHING.
Don't make the fatal error of assuming anything in a gunfight. For example, don't make the false assumption that your assailant is wounded or dead just because there is a temporary pause in gunfire.

829. KNOW THE EIGHT FATAL ERRORS.
Avoid the eight fatal errors that have killed many self-defense practitioners: (1) failing to concentrate—if you fail to keep your mind on the task at hand, you will make tactical errors that can cost you and your loved ones your lives; (2) yielding to tombstone courage—if the situation allows, wait for police assistance (only under the most extreme situations should you engage in a gunfight with a criminal assailant); (3) not getting enough rest—to protect yourself effectively, you must be alert (being sleepy in a potentially threatening situation will endanger you); (4) taking a bad position—never let anyone get a better or more secure position than you; (5) ignoring danger signs—as a trained combatant, you will need to recognize danger signs (e.g., movements, strange cars, or other warnings) that should alert you to watch your step and approach with caution; (6) failure to watch the assailant's hands to see whether he is reaching for a weapon or getting ready to strike you; (7) relaxing too soon—

never relax until you are absolutely certain that danger is eliminated; and (8) having a dirty or inoperative weapon. (Is your revolver or autoloader clean? Will it fire effectively in a time of need? How about the ammunition? When was the last time you visited the firing range? Why rely on a firearm that might not work?)

830. **DON'T INTIMIDATE YOUR ASSAILANT.**

A firearm should never be used to intimidate or coerce another person. You should only display your weapon when you reasonably believe that you or another person is in imminent danger of grievous bodily harm or death.

831. **DON'T DISPLAY YOUR FIREARM IN PUBLIC.**

If you do carry a firearm on your person, be extremely careful to avoid any trivial confrontations on the street. When carrying a concealed gun, never let anyone see it until you are about to use it. The privilege to carry a firearm carries the obligation and responsibility to exercise discipline, discretion, restraint, and good judgment.

832. **DRAW YOUR FIREARM SAFELY.**

When drawing a firearm from your holster, always keep your finger out of the trigger guard until the weapon clears the holster. You don't want to shoot yourself in the process of drawing your weapon. Make it a habit to practice smooth quick-draw techniques on a regular basis. And don't practice with a loaded gun!

833. **KNOW HOW TO REHOLSTER YOUR FIREARM SAFELY.**

When reholstering your firearm, remember to keep your finger out of the trigger guard and your thumb behind the hammer. This will help minimize the possibility of an accidental discharge.

834. **BARE YOUR WEAPON AND THEN DRAW.**

When drawing your firearm from concealment (e.g., sports coat, jacket, long shirt, fanny pack, ankle holster), make certain to pull your clothes out of the way with both of your hands and then draw your weapon.

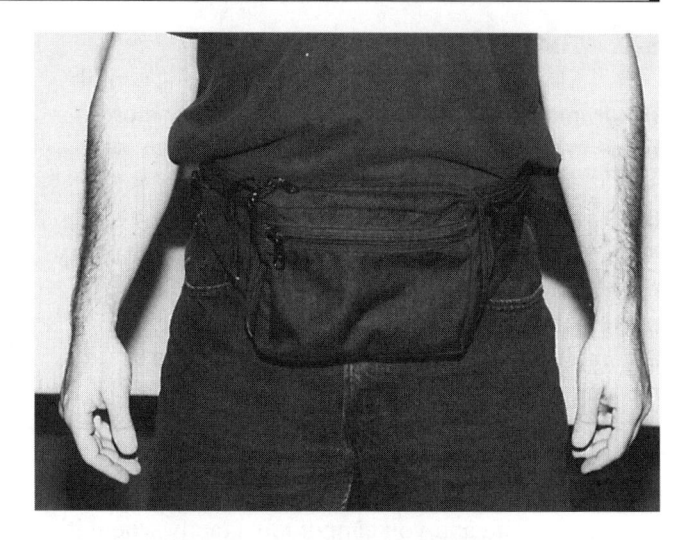

The firearm fanny pack is ideal for street concealment.

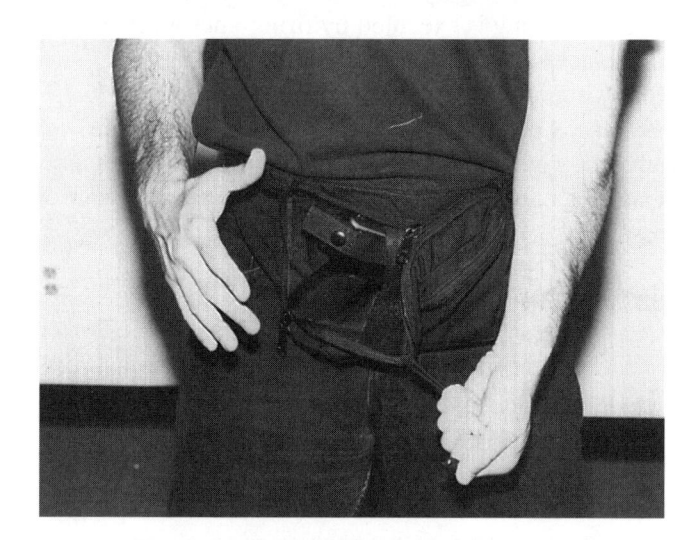

The pull string provides for quick drawing of the weapon.

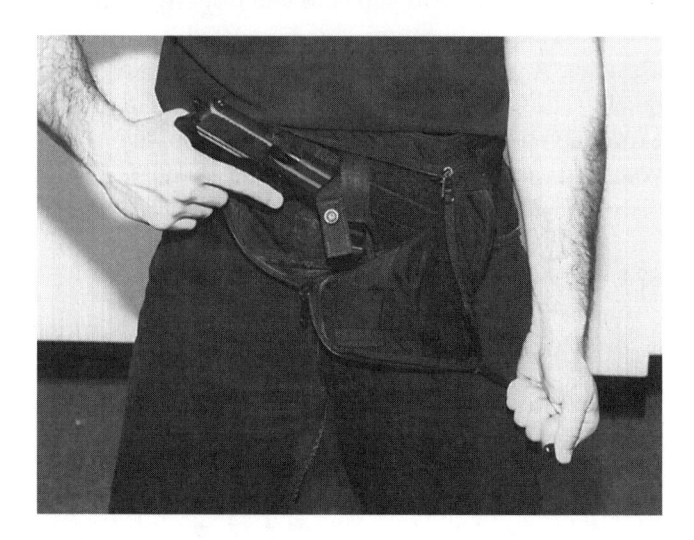

Notice how the author's finger is out of the trigger guard until the weapon clears the holster.

FIREARMS AND COMBAT SHOOTING 173

HOME INTRUSION

835. PREPARE FOR THE INTRUDER.

The serious fighter thinks nothing of spending countless hours preparing for a possible street fight. However, very few practitioners are adequately prepared to handle an intruder in their home. Richard Ramirez, the infamous "Night Stalker" who terrorized Los Angeles residents for nearly a year before being caught and convicted, was notorious for his ability to surreptitiously enter victims' homes, rob them, and, in many cases, kill or rape family members before leaving. The Night Stalker case is just one of many similar cases that occur in American homes each night. According to law enforcement statistics, there is a strong possibility such an occurrence can happen to you and your family. Yet the unfortunate fact is that criminal intrusion is a subject seldom addressed in the martial arts studio.

Ask yourself some important questions. Do you have a tactical plan should someone invade your home? Do you have the knowledge and expertise to keep both you and your family out of harm's way? Do you own a firearm, and are you trained to use it in this type of situation? Do you have a designated "safe room"? If you answered "no" to any of these questions, you and your loved ones may be at great risk.

836. ASSESS YOUR HOME.

Now is the time for you and your family to assess your home and design a tactical plan in case you are ever faced with a criminal intruder. Begin by drawing a detailed diagram of your home and discuss your safety options and the various strategies you can employ. Make certain all of your family members are familiar with the layout of your home, including all entrances, escape routes, and possible ambush zones. You must also assess your home for various points of cover in case there is a shoot-out with an intruder.

Discuss what types of makeshift weapons are located throughout the house, and make certain that everyone knows how to use them correctly. If you have a security alarm system in your home, make certain everyone is familiar with its operation and limitations.

837. DESIGNATE A SAFE ROOM.

Designate a safe room in your house in case you and your family are faced with a criminal intrusion. The safe room is a strategic location in your home where family members can escape from an intruder and wait for the police to arrive. Most people choose a particular bedroom in their house. Be certain there is a working telephone in the safe room so you can contact an emergency dispatcher during the threatening encounter.

When you and your family arrive in the safe room, do the following: (1) keep the doors locked, (2) have everyone stay away from the entrance and find cover behind a protective barrier, (3) keep your firearm pointed at the entrances, (4) stay focused and alert with your finger on the trigger, (5) if the intruder attempts to enter the safe room, tell him that you have called the police, that they are on the way, and that you are armed with a gun, and (6) if the criminal assailant still forces entry despite your warnings and he presents a deadly threat to you or your family, then shoot him. *WARNING: Before squeezing the trigger, be certain of your target.*

838. HOLD YOUR ADVERSARY AT GUNPOINT.

If you manage to capture and hold a criminal at gunpoint, stay behind cover with your gun in the ready

Are you prepared to handle these two criminal intruders?

When holding a criminal at gunpoint, be certain to keep him at a safe distance and in an awkward position.

weapon position. Keep your assailant at a safe distance and in an awkward position. You must always be in complete control of the situation! Order the assailant to do the following: (1) put his hands in clear view; (2) turn and face away from you so he cannot see what you are doing; (3) slowly raise his hands straight over his head (be certain you can see his fingertips); (4) slowly drop to his knees, without using his hands; (5) once he's on his knees, cross one leg over the other; (6) have him lie on his stomach with his arms stretched at his sides; and, finally, (7) place his hands flat on the floor with his palms facing up.

Under no circumstances should you allow your assailant to get within grabbing distance of your gun. And do not search him for any weapons. Simply keep him in this awkward position until the police arrive. *WARNING: If you do see a weapon (e.g., knife or gun) on your assailant, do not allow him to touch it or remove it. Warn him that if he makes any slight move in the direction of the weapon, you will shoot him immediately. And don't make the fatal assumption that your assailant only has one weapon. Many criminals have backup guns.*

Keep your words to a minimum. Do not engage in any conversation with your assailant. Bark out commands loudly, firmly, and confidently; let him know that you mean business. Stay focused and alert at all times. Keep your finger on the trigger and aim your gun at the center of his body. Don't take your eyes off him, and be aware that he might have accomplices nearby. If your assailant attempts to run away, let him go. Finally, if your adversary makes a move that a reasonable person would interpret as life threatening, or if he tries to take your weapon away from you, then shoot him repeatedly or until all hostile action has ceased.

839. PREPARE FOR HOSTAGE SITUATIONS.

If an intruder grabs a family member and holds him/her hostage using a deadly weapon (e.g., gun, knife, etc.), it is permissible for you to use deadly force to end the confrontation. If such a situation occurs, try employing the following tactics: (1) prevent your hostage taker from leaving the area; (2) keep your assailant contained in one area until help (the police) arrives; (3) if you have a clear shot at your assailant's head, take it (in most cases you will only get one shot); (4) never surrender your weapon to your adversary; (5) if you are unarmed and taken hostage, keep your cool and look for any possible opportunity to escape or disarm the intruder; and (6) don't make the fatal error of believing the hostage taker's assurances that he will release you unharmed if you cooperate. *WARNING: Hostage takers are characteristically unstable, desperate, and untrustworthy.*

840. KEEP YOUR FIREARM OUT OF SIGHT.

After a shoot-out with an intruder, be careful not to display your gun. Keep it out of sight when the police arrive. Never approach them with a firearm (or any weapon) in your hand. This is extremely dangerous because the police have no way of knowing who is the law-abiding citizen and who is the criminal.

If you are holding a criminal at gunpoint and the authorities arrive, immediately shout "Don't shoot!" and quickly tell them who you are. If the police command you to drop your weapon, do so immediately. Do not argue with them or offer any type of resistance. Avoid making any sudden moves, and always keep both of your hands in plain view.

841. KNOW HOW TO COUNTER GUN GRABS.

There may come a time when your assailant will try to grab your weapon when it's either holstered or in your hand. Here are some life-saving points to remember: (1) you must regain control of your weapon immediately (remember, the longer a struggle lasts with your adversary, the less are your chances of survival); (2) keep in mind that if your

FIREARMS AND COMBAT SHOOTING

handgun is a revolver (in the double-action mode) and your assailant grabs hold of the cylinder, he will prevent it from firing; and (3) if your handgun is an autoloader and your assailant grabs hold of it, it will usually fire once, but you'll have a malfunction after the first shot. So be prepared to clear any malfunctions immediately.

One of the most effective methods of regaining control of your handgun is to jerk your weapon back toward your abdomen and strike your assailant with your nongun hand. You can finger-jab his eyes, knife-hand-strike his throat, hammer-fist-strike his nose, or palm-heel-strike his chin. Once your weapon is free from your assailant's grasp, immediately clear any malfunction (if it's an autoloader) and shoot him until he is no longer a threat.

842. REMEMBER—YOU ARE YOUR OWN WORST ENEMY.

Your biggest enemy in a gunfight is your mixed-up moral conscience. Being forced to use deadly force can create apprehension during a life-and-death encounter with a criminal assailant. This is because of incorrect perceptions or misinterpretation of many religious or associated beliefs.

Our culture and system of government are both based on the Judeo-Christian ethic. With this in mind, morality issues have been ingrained in us by our parents, teachers, friends, and cultural upbringing. Therefore, such common statements as "pick on someone your own size" or "don't hit a woman" often leave you with the fatal perception that a smaller or female adversary should be treated differently, when, in reality, anyone—regardless of size, age, gender, race, or appearance—has the potential to destroy you.

The Bible can also be easily misinterpreted regarding the use of deadly force. This misinterpretation can be identified in two situations.

(1) Hesitation or failure to act—The commandment "Thou shalt not kill" can cause people to hesitate to fire. A more accurate translation of this commandment is "Thou shalt not murder" (Exodus 20:13) (murder being the unjustifiable taking of another human life). Some people feel they have no right to kill another human being. When using deadly force, your objective is not to take life from another human being, but to stop your adversary from causing you grievous bodily harm or possible death. However, the possibility of the adversary dying should be of no consequence to you. The bottom line is when warranted and justified, killing another person is permitted even under God's law.

(2) Guilt—people who justifiably employ deadly force later suffer some degree of guilt over their actions. They often question their right to take another life in defense of their own. They believe that life is sacred and that only God has the right to take it away. However, in the Bible, if someone tries to kill another unjustifiably, he forfeits the sanctity of his life, and he suffers any consequences brought on by his own actions (Exodus 21:12 and 14). God commands us to protect our lives from others who would take it away unjustifiably. At the same time, God removes the sanctity of a person who chooses to attempt to take the life of someone else unjustifiably. ***CAUTION: People must resolve any moral conflicts in their own minds prior to placing themselves and others in a situation where deadly force might be employed.***

DISARMING TECHNIQUES

843. MASTER THE NINE DISARMING PRINCIPLES.

There is always the possibility that you will be at the wrong end of a gun. Therefore, it behooves you to master gun disarming. Successfully disarming a criminal assailant involves the following nine critical principles: (1) become familiar with all types of firearms, (2) try to determine the gunman's intent, (3) determine the proximity and exact positioning of the gun, (4) try to blade your body, (5) use a verbal distraction, (6) quickly get out of the line of fire, (7) redirect and grab the firearm, (8) control the firearm, and (9) neutralize the gunman.

844. KNOW YOUR GUNS.

The foundation of learning how to disarm

someone with a firearm is familiarizing yourself with the weapon. Now is the time to eliminate the mystery and uncertainty about guns by informing yourself. Try to study the various models that are on the market. The more you know about a particular weapon, the less fear of the unknown you are apt to experience when faced with the real thing. Learn different firearm operations, sounds, ranges, accuracy, ammunition capacities, recoil, and penetration. Most importantly, you must know the general mechanical operation and nomenclature of a particular firearm if you plan to disarm the gunman successfully. Remember, knowledge is power, and power is survival.

845. DETERMINE THE GUNMAN'S INTENT.

When you encounter any gunman, assess his demeanor and pay close attention to what he is saying and doing. Find out exactly what it is he wants you to do. For example, does he just want to intimidate you with the weapon? Or is he hell-bent on blowing your brains out? Does he want you to go with him somewhere? Does he want your car or your wallet? If he wants anything material, give it to him. It can always be replaced. Never argue with a gunman or fight for your possessions. However, if you believe that your adversary is going to kill you—and sometimes it's very hard to know—then you have no choice but to attempt a disarm technique. In some situations, you may need to rely on your instincts. Remember, if something doesn't feel right, chances are it isn't.

846. REMEMBER—PROXIMITY IS VITAL.

Successfully disarming a gunman requires that you determine the proximity of the weapon. You can disarm somebody only if his firearm is within arm's reach. If a criminal assailant is 10 feet away from you, then you can forget disarming him. Instead, you should concentrate on maneuvering yourself or the assailant into disarming range. For example, during the initial seconds of the encounter, try to move slightly closer to the gunman. In most situations, the closer the gun, the better, but sometimes a little distance can be used to your advantage.

847. REMEMBER—POSITIONING IS CRITICAL.

Successfully disarming a gunman also requires that you determine the positioning of your assailant's firearm. It's essential that you know exactly where the weapon is located. For example, is the gun pointed at your face, your right hip, or your heart? Or is it pressed hard into the center of your back?

In addition to the strategic implications of the gun's position, you need to know your own target vulnerabilities for every particular disarm. For example, when you redirect the firearm, will it travel across such vital targets as your face, throat, or chest, or will the gun pass across your shoulder?

When you are analyzing the gun's positioning, it is critical to understand that your assailant can commit the assault from four sides: (1) frontal assault—the gun is pointing at the front of your head or body, (2) rear assault—the gun is pointing at the rear of your head or body, (3) right assault—the gun is pointed at the right side of your head or body, and (4) left assault—the gun is pointed at the left side of your head or body.

Each assault side can then be broken down into one of three different height classifications: (1) high—the assailant's gun is pointed at either your head, throat, or neck, (2) medium—the assailant's gun is pointed at either your chest, back, stomach, or ribs, (3) low—the assailant's gun is pointed at either your lower back, hips, waist, groin, or legs.

848. DISTRACT YOUR ADVERSARY BEFORE YOU DISARM HIM.

Assume that you have determined that disarming your assailant is your only chance for survival, you are in disarming range, you know where the firearm is located in proximity to your body or head, and you are aware of the target vulnerabilities for the particular disarm you are going to attempt. Now is the time for some type of verbal distraction. Ask the gunman a question that will require a verbal response. For example, you might ask, "Where are you taking me?" or "What do you want from me?" These questions are critical because they will distract your adversary temporarily and give you a split second to act with your disarm maneuver.

849. MOVE OUT OF THE LINE OF FIRE.

When utilizing a verbal distraction during a disarming technique, it's also important to make a nontelegraphic and lightning-quick movement. Your goal is to reposition your body or head (depending on where the muzzle is pointed) rapidly so that you are out of the line of fire. For example, if the assailant's firearm is pointed at the front of your head, quickly

FIREARMS AND COMBAT SHOOTING

slip your head sideways. Or if the gun is pointed at your torso, quickly turn and twist sideways. ***WARNING: When attempting to move out of the line of fire, do not telegraph your intentions. It could cost you your life!***

850. REDIRECT AND GRAB THE FIREARM.

At the same time that you move your body and head to get out of the line of fire, you must redirect the assailant's gun or gun hand with your closer hand and move it in a direction opposite your body or head target. Do not glance at the firearm before you attempt to redirect it. This glance will telegraph your intentions. Once you've redirected the firearm, grab hold of the barrel (revolver) or slide (autoloader) and maintain control over the weapon. Don't be afraid to grab the barrel or slide. It is not the gun or any of its parts that will kill you. It's the bullet that comes screaming out of the muzzle!

Once you grab the firearm, immediately reinforce your hold with your other hand. Literally hold on for dear life, and also be certain that all of your body parts stay clear of the muzzle. Reinforcing your grip provides greater control and leverage for the inevitable life-and-death struggle.

851. NEUTRALIZE THE GUNMAN.

With the firearm redirected and temporarily under control, attack your assailant with everything you've got. Employ vicious knee strikes to the gunman's thigh or groin. Or you may have to attack with head butts to his nose, bites to his face, or any other offensive action that doesn't diminish your control over the weapon or move you back into the line of fire. Continue with repeated strikes until your assailant releases his grip on the gun, is completely neutralized, or both. If the weapon falls to the ground, then quickly pick it up and use it to keep your adversary sufficiently incapacitated. ***CAUTION: Some firearms (especially autoloaders and shotguns) can discharge accidentally if dropped.***

852. KNOW WHAT TO DO IF YOU ARE SHOT.

If you are shot, try to stay on your feet, maintain your shooting position, and stay behind a position of cover. Do not look at your wound until your threat has been eliminated. Ignore the pain and keep shooting until your assailant has been neutralized. Mentally tell yourself that you will survive the encounter and fight back no matter what.

Expect the following symptoms: severe pain, burning sensation in the wound, breathlessness, reduced vision, potential lack of mobility, anger, fear response, and a tendency to lose your nerve.

LEGAL CONSIDERATIONS

853. DON'T SHOOT A FLEEING FELON.

Don't shoot a fleeing felon in the back unless he is still armed, dangerous, and an immediate threat to you or others in society.

854. JEOPARDY MUST EXIST.

Legally, in order for you to be justified in using deadly force, jeopardy must exist. There are three elements that constitute jeopardy: (1) ability—the assailant must have the ability to cause you or another person grievous bodily harm or death (he must have access to something that he can use to cause grievous bodily harm or death); (2) opportunity—the assailant must have the opportunity to cause you or another person harm or death (usually involving proximity or control of their chosen weapon or both); and (3) intent—the assailant must have shown a manifested intent to cause you or another person grievous bodily harm or death.

855. USE A FIREARM ONLY AS A LAST RESORT.

Your firearm should be discharged only as a last resort when you reasonably believe that there is a threat of imminent danger or loss of life or grievous bodily harm to yourself or another person, and then it should be used only to stop the threat. Because a firearm places you in the position of judge, jury, and executioner in seconds, always make certain your actions are legally justified. Remember, once you squeeze the trigger, you can never call the bullet back.

TRAINING

856. VISIT THE FIRING RANGE ON A REGULAR BASIS.

Shooting a gun is just like any other physical skill that requires practice to become proficient. The firing range is the best place to learn how to use a firearm effectively in a self-defense situation. If you do own a firearm and plan on using it in an emergency situation, then it's your responsibility to visit the firing range on a consistent basis. This is especially important for law enforcement officers.

A firearm places you in the position of judge, jury, and executioner in a matter of seconds. Always be certain that your actions are legally justified.

857. HOLD ONTO YOUR FIREARM.

Make it your business to practice firearm retention skills. This includes both holstered and drawn firearms, for both long and short guns.

858. BE INSTINCTIVE.

Take the time to develop and practice instinct shooting, loading, drawing, holstering, traversing, retention, disarming, and malfunction skills. Remember, thinking creates lag time, and lag time means loss of initiative and possibly death. Action will always be faster than reaction.

859. PRACTICE WITH YOUR EYES CLOSED.

To acquire a greater understanding of your firearm, practice field-stripping, assembly, loading, and unloading of your weapon with your eyes closed.

860. PRACTICE DISARMING TECHNIQUES IN DIFFERENT ENVIRONMENTS AND CONDITIONS.

Disarming someone with a firearm (long or short) is a very dangerous task performed under very desperate circumstances. Remember, you can't master disarming principles and techniques by reading about them. Practice with qualified instructors who know what they are doing and use mock training pistols with functional triggers. Rehearse in many different environments and conditions. For example, practice in such places as your car, stairwells, elevators, and alleys. Attempt disarming techniques when your hands are slippery and wet or when wearing gloves. Experiment under such adverse conditions as snow, rain, and in darkness or dim light. The more varied the situations and environments, the better prepared you'll be for the actual encounter. Remember, when you're disarming someone with a firearm, there are no second chances!

861. PRACTICE AND PREPARE FOR THE 12 ASSAULT POSITIONS.

When studying how to disarm someone with a firearm, you must be prepared to defend against the following 12 general assault positions: (1) frontal assault high, (2) frontal assault medium, (3) frontal assault low, (4) rear assault high, (5) rear assault medium, (6) rear assault low, (7) right assault high, (8) right assault medium, (9) right assault low, (10) left assault high, (11) left assault medium, and (12) left assault low.

862. VISUALIZE FIREARM-RELATED SKILLS AND SCENARIOS.

Practice visualizing various firearm-related skills and scenarios. For example, visualize the appropriate use of cover and concealment, immediate action drills, the Mexican standoff, disarming maneuvers, holding a criminal at gunpoint, malfunction remedies, one hand reloading skills, muzzle flash exploitation, correct shooting positions, and various other scenarios.

863. PRACTICE SPEED-LOADING DRILLS.

Reloading speed and technical fluidity are essential. Practice reloading skills from out-of-battery and in-battery positions. When reloading, always keep your finger out of the trigger guard, keep your gun on target, cant the weapon slightly, and bring your magazine to the firearm. And remember to avoid instilling bad habits (e.g., leaving empty cartridge cases or dropping empty magazines on the floor).

864. PRACTICE RELOADING BY FEEL.

Learn and practice reloading your firearm by feel. Reloading by feel and not sight is important for two reasons: (1) it allows you to keep your eyes on the assailant's location, and (2) it allows your weapon

FIREARMS AND COMBAT SHOOTING

to be aimed in the correct direction. Remember, when practicing reloading skills with your firearm, always use dummy cartridges.

865. PRACTICE IMMEDIATE ACTION DRILLS.

Here are three immediate action drills (IADs) that you should practice on a regular basis: (1) if the assailant has the initiative (gunfire), seek cover; (2) if neither you nor the assailant has the initiative, act first (take the initiative) and fire; (3) if you have the initiative over your assailant, then fire. *REMEMBER, ALL IADs MUST BE INSTINCTIVE.*

866. PRACTICE WEAK-HAND SHOOTING.

It's important to practice shooting skills with your weak hand. Ambidexterity with firearms is an invaluable skill that will set you apart from shooters who can use only one hand. Here are just a few reasons why this is critical: (1) there is a possibility that your strong gun hand may be injured in a firefight, (2) weak-hand shooting will enhance your combat confidence, and (3) your environment or position of cover may require you to shoot with your weak hand.

867. GET QUALIFIED TRAINING.

No matter what type of gun you own, it isn't going to help you unless you know what you are doing. Get trained by a qualified instructor in the following topics: (1) the fundamentals of safe gun handling, (2) basic operation and maintenance, (3) basic marksmanship skills, and (4) combat shooting skills and tactics. Ideally, if a firearm is to be kept in your home, family members should be trained as well. *BEWARE: Don't be duped by martial art instructors claiming to be firearms instructors. Most martial art instructors are completely ignorant on the subject of firearms. Always check out the instructor's qualifications thoroughly before signing up.*

CHAPTER NINE
Philosophy

"The most difficult task in the world is to think clearly."

868. REVENGE CAN BE AN HONORABLE TRAIT.

869. WHEN YOUR MIND, BODY, AND SPIRIT FUSE INTO AN EFFICIENT AND UNEMOTIONAL WEAPON, YOU WILL BECOME A WARRIOR.

870. KEEP YOUR COMBATIVE SECRETS TO YOURSELF. A CLOSE FRIEND TODAY MAY BE YOUR ENEMY TOMORROW.

871. IT IS BETTER TO DIE WITH DIGNITY THAN TO LIVE WITH DISHONOR.

872. ASIAN DOCTRINES HAVE NO PLACE IN AMERICAN STREETS.

873. THERE ARE NO REAL SECRETS IN LIFE, JUST FACTS HIDDEN BY IGNORANCE.

874. FIGHTING IS ATTRACTIVE TO THOSE WHO HAVE NOT EXPERIENCED IT.

875. YOU ARE RESPONSIBLE FOR WHAT YOU DON'T KNOW.

876. TO TRULY MASTER THE ESSENCE OF COMBAT, YOU MUST STUDY IT AS A SCIENCE AND EXPRESS IT AS AN ART.

877. APPROACH COMBAT IN TERMS OF BLACK AND WHITE, BUT BE PREPARED FOR GRAY.

878. NEVER UNDERESTIMATE THE VICIOUS CAPABILITY OF A HUMAN BEING.

879. AGGRESSIVE ACTION WINS.

880. IT IS BETTER TO BE TRIED BY TWELVE THAN CARRIED BY SIX.

881. EVERY FIGHT MUST BE WON FAST.

882. LIFE IS SHORT; BE PRAGMATIC.

883. ACQUIRE AN INSATIABLE HUNGER FOR KNOWLEDGE.

884. VIOLENCE BEGINS WHERE DIPLOMACY ENDS.

885. ALWAYS TREAT BOOKS WITH RESPECT AND VENERATION.

886. STRICT ADHERENCE TO TRADITIONAL PERSPECTIVES WILL ALMOST GUARANTEE YOU DEATH IN A REAL FIGHT.

887. REACHING THE PINNACLE OF COMBATIVE COMPETENCY DOES NOT OCCUR THROUGH SOME MYSTICAL TRANSFORMATION. IT'S ACQUIRED THROUGH DEDICATION AND LOTS OF HARD WORK.

888. BEWARE OF THE EGO. HE IS A DARK BEAST DESIROUS OF DESTRUCTION.

889. IF ANY STYLE OR SYSTEM OF COMBAT WILL NOT ALLOW FOR CHANGE, THEN IT WILL SURELY DIE.

890. NEVER SHOW AN ACT OF DEFIANCE THAT YOU ARE NOT PREPARED TO DEFEND.

891. A GREAT FIGHTER WILL ALWAYS ACT SWIFTLY AND DECISIVELY; HE DOESN'T KNOW THE MEANING OF APPREHENSION.

892. A TRUE WARRIOR IS ALWAYS ALONE.

893. SUPPORT CAPITAL PUNISHMENT.

894. NEVER TEACH SELF-DEFENSE TO ANYONE ON THE WRONG SIDE OF THE LAW.

895. FRUSTRATION AND TIME ARE THE GATEKEEPERS THAT SEPARATE THE AMATEUR FROM THE EXPERT.

896. IN A REAL FIGHT, PERCEPTION IS REALITY.

897. THE BETTER PREPARED YOU ARE, THE LESS LUCK YOU WILL NEED.

898. DESPAIR IS ALWAYS ONE STEP AWAY FROM DEATH.

899. THERE ARE NO ABSOLUTES IN COMBAT.

900. A STUPID MAN DIES A STUPID DEATH.

901. TRAIN FOR THE EXCEPTION AS WELL AS THE RULE.

902. BEWARE THE TRADITIONAL MARTIAL ARTS. THEY WILL TEACH YOU JUST ENOUGH TO GET YOURSELF KILLED IN A REAL FIGHT.

903. THROW OUT YOUR BLACK BELT.

904. ORDER AND JUSTICE CAN ONLY BE EXECUTED THROUGH A HAND OF MIGHT.

905. CHI IS A FOOLISH MYTH.

906. TRADITIONAL MARTIAL ARTS ARE NOTHING MORE THAN SOCIALLY ACCEPTED CULTS.

907. A KARATE OR KUNG-FU INSTRUCTOR IS NO MORE QUALIFIED TO TEACH SELF-DEFENSE THAN A FITNESS INSTRUCTOR AND NOT NEARLY AS QUALIFIED AS A HIGH SCHOOL COACH.

908. NOT ALL FIGHTING STYLES ARE CREATED EQUAL. THERE ARE SUPERIOR SYSTEMS OUT THERE.

909. QUESTION AUTHORITY; JUST DO IT RESPECTFULLY.

910. YOU WILL ALWAYS HAVE MORE TO LOSE THAN YOUR ASSAILANT.

911. NEVER BETRAY A FRIEND.

912. THERE IS NO HONOR IN DEFEAT.

913. NEVER REJECT A TECHNIQUE SIMPLY BECAUSE YOU DISLIKE ITS SOURCE.

914. KARATE IS DEAD.

915. HELP THE MISGUIDED BY DEMYTHOLOGIZING THE MARTIAL ARTS.

916. COMBATIVE TRUTH IS NOT RELATIVE. IT'S A FACT.

917. FOR EVERY ATTACK, THERE IS A LOGICAL COUNTER.

918. ALWAYS KEEP A MINDFUL EYE ON YOUR OWN ATTITUDE. IT IS USUALLY THE FIRST THING THAT WILL GET YOU INTO A FIGHT.

919. HUMANKIND IS GETTING MORE VIOLENT WITH THE TIMES.

920. ANYTHING NEW CREATES DISCOMFORT.

921. LOGIC CHANGES.

PHILOSOPHY

922. A WELL-SEASONED FIGHTER IS AN EXCELLENT PREDICTOR OF MOVES.

923. DON'T RESPECT PACIFISTS OR FIGHT FOR THEM.

924. TRUST NO ONE.

925. WHAT YOU DON'T KNOW CAN CERTAINLY GET YOU KILLED.

926. KNOWLEDGE IS USELESS UNLESS IT IS PUT INTO ACTION.

927. EFFICIENCY IS NOT ANYTHING THAT SCORES.

928. A FIGHT IS NEVER REALLY OVER.

929. JUSTICE IS NOT ALWAYS SERVED.

930. DISCOVER WHAT YOU DON'T KNOW.

931. THE MORE YOU KNOW, THE LESS YOU WILL FEAR.

932. SUCCESS AND FAILURE TRANSLATE TO LIFE AND DEATH IN COMBAT.

933. BLIND BELIEF AND ADHERENCE TO UNPROVEN PRINCIPLES IS PURE AND SIMPLE SUICIDE.

934. TO ABANDON STRUCTURE IS TO ABANDON THE FUNDAMENTALS OF COMBAT.

935. CONCEPTUALIZATION SHAPES AND MOLDS COMBAT CHARACTERISTICS, BUT IT BECOMES USELESS IF IT IS NOT SOLIDLY AND SAFELY ACTUALIZED.

936. CONCRETE SYSTEMS AND STRATEGIES PROVIDE EFFICIENCY AND OVERALL COMBAT DIRECTION.

937. A FORMIDABLE FIGHTER IS A COLD AND VICIOUS ANIMAL, ALBEIT AN INTELLIGENT ONE.

938. A FUNCTIONAL SELF-DEFENSE SYSTEM IS ALWAYS IN A STATE OF GENESIS.

939. ANALYZE EVERYTHING.

940. SELF-MASTERY SEPARATES THE TRUE EXPERT FROM THE ETERNAL NOVICE.

941. BEWARE OF THE CALL OF VIOLENCE AND BE EVER VIGILANT OF THE EGO'S CHARMS.

942. COMBAT FORMLESSNESS IS THE FETUS OF DEATH.

943. A FIGHTER MUST POLICE HIS SKILLS WITH A MORAL FABRIC CALLED HONOR.

944. FEAR IS ESTABLISHED WHEN IGNORANCE IS ACTUALIZED.

945. DEFEND THE WEAK.

946. EVERY MAN IS AFRAID OF SOMETHING.

947. ACQUIRE THE COURAGE AND INSIGHT TO QUESTION AND CHANGE COMBAT PARADIGMS.

948. EXPERIMENTATION IN THE FACE OF DANGER IS AN INVITATION TO DISASTER.

949. IT TAKES A LIFETIME TO MASTER A CREDIBLE SYSTEM OF COMBAT.

950. THERE IS ELEGANCE IN SIMPLICITY.

951. WHAT'S PRACTICAL ISN'T ALWAYS POPULAR, AND WHAT'S POPULAR ISN'T ALWAYS PRACTICAL.

952. THOSE WHO INSTRUCT LEARN.

953. NEVER TEACH ANYONE ALL THAT YOU KNOW ABOUT FIGHTING.

954. TACTICS CAN BE STUDIED AND TECHNIQUES CAN BE LEARNED, BUT FIGHTING MUST BE EXPERIENCED.

955. IN COMBAT, EVERYONE LOSES IN THE GAME OF CONCEPTUAL ABSTRACTION.

956. VIOLENCE IS A DARK CLOAK THAT YOU MUST WEAR EVEN IF YOU DON'T LIKE THE WAY IT FITS.

957. AS LONG AS HUMANKIND WALKS THE EARTH, THERE WILL ALWAYS BE A TIME, NEED, AND PLACE FOR COMBAT.

958. LIFE BETRAYS EVERYONE.

959. IF LUCK FACTORS INTO YOUR SELF-DEFENSE FORMULA, THEN YOU ARE STILL NOT PREPARED FOR COMBAT.

960. EVERY PROBLEM HAS A SOLUTION.

961. IN COMBAT, ANYTHING THAT CAN GO WRONG MIGHT GO WRONG.

962. THE FIRST CASUALTY OF FIGHTING IS THE EGO.

963. NEVER, EVER FORGIVE EVIL.

964. THOSE WHO SPEAK THE TRUTH ARE NEVER LIKED.

965. FEAR KILLS A MAN TWICE.

966. COWARDS MAKE THE BEST BULLIES.

967. IT IS FAR BETTER TO DIE BY YOUR OWN THEORY THAN TO DIE BY SOMEONE ELSE'S.

968. LEAVE NOTHING TO CHANCE.

969. THERE ARE TWO TYPES OF PEOPLE IN THIS WORLD: VICTIMS AND VICTORS. WHICH ONE ARE YOU?

970. A TRUE INNOVATOR CREATES FOR HIMSELF AND NO ONE ELSE.

971. THE ONLY THING THAT STANDS BETWEEN YOU AND DEATH IS YOUR ABILITY TO FIGHT.

972. YOU WILL NEVER KNOW ALL THERE IS TO KNOW.

973. LIVE EVERY DAY AS IF IT WERE YOUR LAST.

974. A PACIFIST IS A MAN WHO IS TOO COWARDLY TO FIGHT AND TOO FAT TO RUN.

975. ALL GREAT FIGHTERS ARE SLAVES OF PERFECTION.

976. MAKE SURE YOU KNOW THE LAWS AND RULES OF COMBAT BEFORE YOU ATTEMPT TO CRITICIZE THEM.

977. SELF-DEFENSE IS NOT JUST A RIGHT; IT'S A RESPONSIBILITY.

978. THE TRUTH IS ALWAYS REVOLUTIONARY.

979. IN COMBAT, IT IS ALWAYS BETTER TO ACT THAN REACT.

980. TRUTH GIVES YOU THE POWER TO MAKE THINGS BETTER.

981. TRUST IN GOD, BUT ALWAYS LOCK YOUR DOOR.

982. NOTHING IS SACRED IN COMBAT.

983. THE LONGER A FIGHT LASTS, THE GREATER YOUR CHANCES OF INJURY OR DEATH.

984. ATTACK EVEN WHEN YOU RETREAT.

985. THOSE WHO REJECT THE NECESSITY OF VIOLENCE REJECT THE NECESSITY OF PEACE.

986. ONLY FOOLS RUSH INTO COMBAT.

987. RESPECT RANK!

988. ALTHOUGH COMBAT PREPAREDNESS IS CRITICAL TO YOUR SURVIVAL, NEVER FORGET THE IMPORTANCE OF LOVE, LIFE, AND LAUGHTER.

PHILOSOPHY

989. SELF-DOUBT IS A FIGHTER'S GREATEST ENEMY.

990. TRUST YOUR INSTICTS BEFORE YOUR HEART AND YOUR HEART BEFORE YOUR MIND.

991. THE GREATNESS OF A MAN IS MEASURED BY HIS CHARACTER, NOT HIS FISTS.

992. SELF-DISCIPLINE IS THE TICKET TO SUCCESS. WITH IT YOU CAN ACCOMPLISH EVERYTHING.

993. UNBRIDLED EMOTION IS A PREREQUISITE FOR FAILURE.

994. DURING COMBAT, FOCUS ON THE OPPORTUNITY AND NOT THE PROBLEM.

995. IT IS FAR BETTER TO BE A GOOD SOLDIER THAN A POOR GENERAL.

996. WE ARE OFTEN BETRAYED BY THE ONES WE TRUST THE MOST.

997. FOR A SEASONED FIGHTER, COMBAT IS A NATURAL STATE.

998. WORKING AND SURVIVING THROUGH HARDSHIPS WILL STRENGTHEN YOU FOR ALL THE DAYS OF YOUR LIFE.

999. DON'T ASK QUESTIONS IF YOU ARE NOT PREPARED TO HANDLE THE ANSWERS.

1,000. NEVER FORGET GOD.

1,001. ? ? ?

Glossary

A note to the reader: Many of the terms in this book may be strange to the first time reader. This is because most of the argot in this text are unique only to Contemporary Fighting Arts. What follows are some important terms often used in the CFA system.

A

Accuracy—The precise or exact projection of force. Accuracy is also defined as the ability to execute a combative movement with precision and exactness.

Action—A series of moving parts that permits a firearm to be loaded, unloaded, and fired.

Adaptability—The ability to physically and psychologically adjust to new or different conditions or circumstances of combat.

Aerobic exercise—"With air." Exercise that elevates the heart rate to a training level for a prolonged period of time, usually 30 minutes.

Affective domain—This includes the attitudes, philosophies, ethics, values, discretionary use-of-force, and the spirit (killer instinct) required to use your combative tool or technique appropriately.

Affective preparedness—Being emotionally and spiritually prepared for the demands and strains of combat.

Aggression—Hostile and injurious behavior directed toward a person.

Aggressive hand positioning—Placement of the hands so as to imply aggressive or hostile intentions.

Aggressive stance—(See *fighting stance*.)

Aggressor—One who commits an act of aggression.

Agility—An attribute of combat. One's ability to move his or her body quickly and gracefully.

Amalgamation—A scientific process of uniting or merging.

Ambidextrous—The ability to perform with equal facility on both the right and left sides of the body.

Ambush—To lie in wait and attack by surprise.

Ambush zones—Strategic locations (in everyday environments) from which assailants launch surprise attacks.

American stick strangle—A stick strangle used with a hammer grip.

Analysis and integration—One of the five elements of CFA's mental component. This is the painstaking process of breaking down various elements, concepts, sciences, and disciplines into their atomic parts, and then methodically and strategically analyzing, experimenting, and drastically modifying the information so that it fulfills three combative requirements: efficiency, effectiveness, and safety. Only then is it finally integrated into the CFA system.

Anatomical handles—Various body parts (i.e., appendages, joints, and, in some cases, organs) that can be grabbed, held, pulled, or otherwise manipulated during a ground fight.

Anatomical power generators—Three points on the human body that help torque your body to generate impact power. They include: (1) feet, (2) hips, and (3) shoulders.

Anatomical striking targets—The various anatomical body targets that can be struck and that are especially vulnerable to potential harm. They include the eyes, temples, nose, chin, back of neck, front of neck, solar plexus, ribs, groin, thighs, knees, shins, and insteps.

Arm lock—A joint lock applied to the arm.

Asphyxiate—To cause asphyxia; to kill or make unconscious through lack of adequate oxygen.

Assailant—A person who threatens or attacks another person.

Assault—The willful attempt or threat to inflict injury upon the person of another.

Assault and battery—The unlawful touching of another person without justification.

Assert—To stand up for your rights; one of the five possible tactical responses to a threatening situation. (See *comply*, *escape*, *de-escalate*, and *fight back*.)

Assessment—The process of rapidly gathering, analyzing, and accurately evaluating information in terms of threat and danger. You can assess people, places, actions, and objects.

Attachment—The touching of the arms or legs prior to executing a trapping technique.

Attack—Offensive action designed to physically control, injure, or kill another person.

Attack by draw—A method of attack whereby the fighter offers his assailant an intentional opening designed to lure an attack. One of the five conventional methods of attack.

Attribute uniformity—When various combative attributes (i.e., speed, power, accuracy, balance, etc.) are executed the same way every time.

Attributes of combat—The physical, mental, and spiritual qualities that enhance combat skills and tactics.

Autoloader—A handgun that operates by mechanical spring pressure and recoil force, which ejects the spent cartridge case and automatically feeds a fresh round from the magazine (also known as a *semiautomatic handgun*).

Awareness—Perception or knowledge of people, places, actions, and objects. (In CFA, there are three categories of tactical awareness: *criminal awareness*, *situational awareness*, and *self-awareness*.)

Axiom—A truth that is self-evident.

B

Backfist—A punch made with the back of the knuckles.

Backstrap—The rear, vertical portion of a pistol frame.

Back position—One of the ground fighting positions, the back position is assumed when your chest is on top of your assailant's back.

Balance—One's ability to maintain equilibrium while stationary or moving.

Barrier—Any large object that can be used to obstruct an attacker's path or angle of attack.

Blading the body—Strategically positioning your body at a 45-degree angle.

Block—A defensive tool designed to intercept an assailant's attack by placing a nonvital target between the assailant's strike and your vital body target.

Bludgeon—Any clublike weapon used for offensive

GLOSSARY

and defensive purposes (e.g., baseball bat, club, pipe, crowbar). Bludgeons are usually heavier and thicker than sticks.

Bludgeon-defense stance—A strategic posture that a fighter assumes when confronted by a bludgeon-wielding attacker.

Body composition—The ratio of fat to lean body tissue.

Body language—Nonverbal communication through posture, gestures, and facial expressions.

Body mechanics—Technically precise body movement during the execution of a body weapon, defensive technique, or other fighting maneuver.

Body weapon—One of the various body parts that can be used to strike or otherwise injure or kill a criminal assailant (also known as *tool*).

Bore—The inside of the barrel of a firearm.

Boxing—(See *Western boxing*.)

Breakfall—A method of safely falling to the ground during a fight.

Burnout—A negative emotional state acquired by physically overtraining. Some symptoms of burnout include: physical illness, boredom, anxiety, disinterest in training, and general sluggish behavior.

Bushido—The ancient and honorable code of the samurai or warrior.

C

Cadence—Coordinating tempo and rhythm to establish a timed pattern of movement.

Caliber—The diameter of a projectile.

Cardiorespiratory conditioning—The component of physical fitness that deals with the heart, lungs, and circulatory system.

Carriage—The way you carry yourself.

Cartridge—A cylindrical case containing components of a round of ammunition: case, primer, powder charge, and bullet.

Center mass—The center portion of the torso.

Center-fire—A type of firearm cartridge that has its primer located in the center of the case bottom.

Centerline—An imaginary vertical line that divides your body in half and that marks many of your vital anatomical targets.

Chamber—1) The part of a firearm in which a cartridge is contained at the instant of firing. 2) The raising of the knee to execute a kick.

Choice words—(See *selective semantics*.)

Choke—A close-quarter (grappling-range) technique that requires one to apply pressure to either the trachea or carotid arteries.

Circular movement—A movement that follows the shape of a curve.

Classical—A term referring to the methods and techniques of traditional martial arts.

Close-quarter combat—One of the three ranges of knife and bludgeon combat. At this distance, you can strike, slash, or stab your assailant with a variety of close-quarter techniques.

Close-to-contact shooting—Discharging a firearm with the muzzle approximately one inch away from the target.

Cognitive development—One of the five elements of CFA's mental component. The process of developing and enhancing your fighting skills through specific mental exercises and techniques. (See *analysis and integration*, *killer instinct*, and *philosophy*.)

Cognitive domain—This encompasses the specific concepts, principles, and knowledge required to use your combative tools or techniques effectively.

Cognitive exercises—Various mental exercises used to enhance fighting skills and tactics.

Combative arts—The various "arts of war." (See *martial arts*.)

Combative attributes—(See *attributes of combat*.)

Combative fitness—A state characterized by cardiorespiratory and muscular/skeletal conditioning, as well as proper body composition.

Combative mentality—A combative state of mind necessary for fighting. Also known as the *killer instinct*.

Combative power—The ability or capacity to perform or act effectively in combat.

Combative truth—A combative element that conforms to fact or actuality and is proven to be true.

Combative utility—The quality or condition of being combatively useful.

Combat ranges—The various ranges of armed and unarmed combat.

Combination—(See *compound attack*.)

Come-along—A series of holds or joint locks that forces your adversary to move in any direction you desire.

Coming to a base—The process of getting up to your hands and knees from the prone position.

Common peroneal nerve—A pressure point area located approximately four to six inches above the knee on the midline of the outside of the thigh.

Completion phase—One of the three stages of a stick or bludgeon strike. The completion phase is the completion point of a swing.

Comply—To obey an assailant's demands. One of the five tactical responses to a threatening situation. (See *assert*, *de-escalate*, *escape*, and *fight back*.)

Composure—A combative attribute. Composure is a quiet and focused mind-set that enables you to acquire your combative agenda.

Compound attack—One of the five conventional methods of attack. Two or more body weapons launched in strategic succession whereby the fighter overwhelms his assailant with a flurry of full-speed, full-force blows. (See *indirect attack*, *immobilization attack*, *attack by draw*, and *single attack*.)

Concealment—Not making something visible to your adversary.

Conditioning training—A CFA training methodology requiring the practitioner to deliver a variety of offensive and defensive combinations for a four-minute period. (See *proficiency training* and *street training*.)

Confrontation evasion—Strategically manipulating the distance or environment to avoid a possible confrontation.

Congruency—The state of harmoniously orchestrating the verbal and nonverbal de-escalation principles.

Contact evasion—Physically moving or manipulating your body targets to avoid being struck (i.e., slipping your head to the side or side stepping from a charging assailant).

Contact shooting—Discharging a firearm with the muzzle touching the target.

Contemporary Fighting Arts (CFA)—A modern martial art and self-defense system made up of three parts: physical, mental, and spiritual.

Conventional ground fighting tools—Specific ground fighting techniques designed to control, restrain, and temporarily incapacitate an adversary. Some conventional tactics include submission holds, locks, certain choking techniques, and specific striking techniques.

GLOSSARY

Cool-down—A series of light exercises and movements that immediately follow a workout. The purpose of the cool-down is to hasten the removal of metabolic wastes and gradually return the heart to its resting rate.

Coordination—A physical attribute characterized by the ability to perform a technique or movement with efficiency, balance, and accuracy.

Counterattack—Offensive action made to counter an assailant's initial attack.

Courage—A combative attribute. The state of mind and spirit that enables a fighter to face danger and vicissitudes with confidence, resolution, and bravery.

Courageousness—(See *courage*.)

Cover—Any object that protects you from gunfire.

Criminal awareness—One of the three categories of CFA awareness. It involves a general understanding and knowledge of the nature and dynamics of a criminal's motivations, mentalities, methods, and capabilities to perpetrate violent crime. (See *situational awareness* and *self-awareness*.)

Criminal justice—The study of criminal law and the procedures associated with its enforcement.

Criminology—The scientific study of crime and criminals.

Crisscross—An entry maneuver that allows you to travel across a threshold quickly while employing a correct ready-weapon position.

Cross-stepping—The process of crossing one foot in front or behind the other when moving.

Crushing tactics—Nuclear grappling range techniques designed to crush the assailant's anatomical targets.

Cutting accuracy—The ability to cut your assailant with precision and exactness.

Cutting makeshift weapon—One of the four types of CFA makeshift weapons. Any object or implement that can be used to effectively stab or slash an assailant. (Also see *distracting makeshift weapon*, *shielding makeshift weapon*, and *striking makeshift weapon*.)

Cylinder—The part of a revolver that holds cartridges in individual chambers.

D

Deadly force—Weapons or techniques that may result in unconsciousness, permanent disfigurement, or death.

Deadly weapon—An instrument designed to inflict serious bodily injury or death (e.g., firearms, impact tools, edged weapons).

Deception—A combative attribute. A stratagem whereby you delude your assailant.

Decisiveness—A combative attribute. The ability to follow a tactical course of action that is unwavering and focused.

De-escalate—One of the five possible tactical responses to a threatening situation. The science and art of diffusing a hostile individual without resorting to physical force. (See *assert*, *comply*, *escape*, and *fight back*.)

De-escalation stance—One of the many strategic stances used in the CFA system. A strategic and nonaggressive stance used when defusing a hostile individual.

Defense—The ability to strategically thwart an assailant's attack (armed or unarmed).

Defensive flow—A progression of continuous defensive responses.

Defensive mentality—A defensive mind-set.

Defensive range manipulation (DRM)—The strategic manipulation of ranges (armed or unarmed) for defensive purposes.

Defensive reaction time—The elapsed time between an assailant's physical attack and your defensive response to that attack. (See *offensive reaction time*.)

Demeanor—One of the essential factors to consider when assessing a threatening individual. A person's outward behavior.

Dependency—The dangerous phenomenon of solely relying on a particular person, agency, instrument, device, tool, animal, or weapon for self-defense and personal protection.

Destructions—Techniques that strike the assailant's attacking limb.

Diet—A life-style of healthy eating.

Distance gap—The spatial gap between the different ranges of armed and unarmed combat.

Distancing—The ability to quickly understand spatial relationships and how they relate to combat.

Distracting makeshift weapon—One of the four types of CFA makeshift weapons. An object that can be thrown into an assailant's face, body, or legs to distract him temporarily. (See *cutting makeshift weapon*, *striking makeshift weapon*, and *shielding makeshift weapon*.)

Distractionary tactics—Various verbal and physical tactics designed to distract your adversary.

Dojo—The Japanese term for "training hall."

Dominant eye—The eye that is stronger and does more work and is used for aiming a firearm.

Double-action—A type of pistol action in which squeezing the trigger will both cock and release the hammer.

Drake shooting—Firing your gun into places of likely cover.

Dry firing—The process of shooting an unloaded firearm.

Duck—A defensive technique that permits you to evade your assailant's strike. Ducking is performed by dropping your body down and forward to avoid the assailant's blow.

E

Ectomorph—A body type classified by a high degree of slenderness, angularity, and fragility. (See *endomorph* and *mesomorph*.)

Effectiveness—One of the three criteria for a CFA body weapon, technique, tactic, or maneuver. It means the ability to produce a desired effect. (See *efficiency* and *safety*.)

Efficiency—One of the three criteria for a CFA body weapon, technique, tactic, or maneuver. It means the ability to reach an objective quickly and economically. (See *effectiveness* and *safety*.)

Ejector—The part of a pistol that ejects empty cartridge cases.

Embracing the range—A ground fighting tactic whereby you pull or embrace your assailant.

Emotional control—One of the nonverbal principles of strategic de-escalation. The ability to remain calm when faced with a hostile or threatening person.

Emotionless—A combative attribute. Being temporarily devoid of human feeling.

Endomorph—A body type classified by a high degree of roundness, softness, and body fat. (See *ectomorph* and *mesomorph*.)

Entry method—A method that permits you to safely enter a combat range.

Entry technique—A technique that permits you to safely enter a combat range.

Entry tool—A tool that permits you to safely enter a combat range.

Escape—Also known as tactical retreat. One of the

GLOSSARY

five possible tactical responses to a threatening situation. To flee rapidly from the threat or danger. (See *comply*, *de-escalate*, *assert*, and *fight back*.)

Escape routes—Various avenues or exits that permit you to escape from a threatening individual or situation.

Evasion—A defensive maneuver that allows you to strategically maneuver your body away from the assailant's strike.

Evasiveness—A combative attribute. The ability of avoid threat or danger.

Evasive sidestepping—Evasive footwork where the practitioner moves to either the right or left side.

Evasive techniques—Maneuvers strategically designed to neutralize your assailant's attack without making contact. Evasive techniques include sidestepping, retreating, slipping, and escaping.

Evolution—A gradual process of change.

Excessive force—An amount of force that exceeds the need for a particular event and is unjustified in the eyes of the law.

Experimentation—The painstaking process of testing a combative hypothesis or theory.

Explosiveness—A combative attribute that is characterized by a sudden outburst of violent energy.

F

Fake—Body movements that disguise your attack. This includes movements of the eyes, head, shoulders, knees, feet, and, in some cases, the voice.

Fatal funnel—A danger area that is created by openings such as doorways, windows, hallways, stairwells, etc.

Fear—A strong and unpleasant emotion caused by the anticipation or awareness of threat or danger. There are three stages of fear in order of intensity: fright, panic, and terror. (See *fright*, *panic*, and *terror*.)

Feed—(See *attachment*.)

Feeler—A tool that tests the assailant's reaction time and overall abilities.

Feint—A tool that draws an offensive reaction from the assailant, thereby opening him up for a real strike. Feints are different from fakes because they are performed through the movement of an actual limb.

Femoral nerve—A pressure point area located approximately six inches above the knee on the inside of the thigh.

Fight back—One of the five possible tactical responses to a threatening situation. To use various physical and psychological tactics to either incapacitate or terminate a criminal assailant. (See *comply*, *escape*, *assert*, and *de-escalate*.)

Fighting stance—One of the different types of stances used in CFA's system. A strategic posture you can assume when face-to-face with an unarmed assailant. (See *de-escalation stance*, *knife-defense stance*, *knife-fighting stance*, *firearms stance*, *natural stance*, *stick-fighting stance*.)

Fight-or-flight syndrome—A response of the sympathetic nervous system to a fearful and threatening situation, during which it prepares your body to either fight or flee from the perceived danger.

Finesse—A combative attribute. The ability to skillfully execute a movement or a series of movements with grace and refinement.

Firearm follow-through—Continuing to employ the shooting fundamentals throughout the delivery of your shot.

First strike principle (FSP)—A CFA principle that states when physical danger is imminent and you have no other tactical option but to fight back, you should strike first, strike fast, and strike with authority.

Flexibility—The muscles' ability to move through maximum natural ranges. (See *muscular/skeletal conditioning*.)

Fluid-shock strike—A strike that is delivered by allowing your striking tool to remain pressed into the target area for a brief but definite period of time.

Follow—A defensive technique used in the mid to long range of knife combat.

Footwork—Quick, economical steps performed on the balls of the feet while you are relaxed, alert, and balanced. Footwork is structured around four general movements: forward, backward, right, and left.

Formlessness—A principle that rejects the essence of structure or system.

Forms—Traditional martial arts training methodology whereby the practitioner performs a series of prearranged movements that are based upon a response to imaginary opponents. (See *kata*.)

Fractal cognizance—The awareness and strategic utilization of sub-combat ranges for both armed and unarmed fighting.

Fright—The first stage of fear. Quick and sudden fear. (See *panic* and *terror*.)

G

Gi—A traditional martial art uniform constructed of heavy cotton canvas material. The gi is commonly worn by practitioners of karate, judo, aikido, and jujitsu.

Grapevine—A stabilizing technique used during a ground fight. The grapevine can be applied when you have either one foot (single-leg grapevine) or both feet (double-leg grapevine) hooked around the assailant's legs.

Grappling range—One of the three ranges of unarmed combat. Grappling range is the closest distance of unarmed combat from which you can employ a wide variety of close-quarter tools and techniques. The grappling range of unarmed combat is also divided into two different planes: vertical (standing) and horizontal (ground fighting). (See *kicking range* and *punching range*.)

Grappling-range tools—The various body tools and techniques that are employed in the grappling range of unarmed combat, including head butts; biting, tearing, clawing, crushing, and gouging tactics; foot stomps; horizontal, vertical, and diagonal elbow strikes; vertical and diagonal knee strikes; chokes, strangles, joint locks, and holds. (See *kicking-range tools*.)

Ground fighting—Fighting that takes place on the ground (also known as the horizontal grappling plane).

Guard—1) A fighter's hand positioning. 2) One of the positions used in ground fighting. The guard is a scissors hold applied with the legs.

H

Hammer—The moving part of a gun that causes the firing pin to strike the cartridge primer.

Hammer grip—A hand grip used to hold an edged weapon, bludgeon, and some makeshift weapons; it is assumed when the top of the bludgeon or the tip of the edged weapon is pointing upward.

Hand positioning—(See *guard*.)

Handgun—A firearm that can be held and discharged with one hand.

Hang fire—A perceptible delay in the ignition of a cartridge after the primer has been struck.

GLOSSARY

Headhunter—A fighter who primarily attacks the head.

Head-hunting—Strategically selecting and pursuing the assailant's head as your primary impact target.

Heavy bag—A large cylindrical-shaped bag that is used to develop kicking, punching, or striking power.

High-line kick—One of the two different classifications of a kick. A kick that is directed to targets above an assailant's waist level. (See *low-line kick*.)

Hip punch—A traditional martial art punch launched from the practitioner's hip.

Histrionics—The field of theatrics or acting.

Hold—A specific manner of grasping or holding an assailant.

Homicide—The death of another person without legal justification or excuse.

Hook kick—A circular kick that can be delivered in both kicking and punching ranges.

Hook punch—A circular punch that can be delivered in both the punching and grappling ranges.

Human shield—Using your assailant's body as a shield or obstacle in combat.

I

Ice-pick grip—A hand grip used to hold an edged weapon, bludgeon, and some makeshift weapons; it is assumed when the tip of the edged weapon or the top of the bludgeon is pointing downward.

Ice-pick stick strangle—A stick strangle used with an ice-pick grip.

Immobilization attack—One of the five conventional methods of attack. A highly complex system of moves and countermoves that allows you to temporarily control and manipulate the assailant's limbs (usually his arms and hands) in order to create an opening for attack.

Impact power—Destructive force generated by mass and velocity.

Impact training—A training exercise that develops pain tolerance.

Incapacitate—To disable an assailant by rendering him unconscious or damaging his bones, joints, or organs.

Indirect attack—One of the five conventional methods of attack. A progressive method of attack whereby the initial tool or technique is designed to set the assailant up for follow-up blows.

Infraorbital—A pressure point area located above the upper lip at the base of the nose. Pressure is applied with the middle finger in an inward and upward direction.

Initiation phase—One of the three stages of a stick or bludgeon strike. The initiation phase is the initiation point of a swing.

Insertion points—Specific anatomical targets you can stab with a knife or makeshift weapon.

Initiative—Making the first offensive move in combat.

Inside position—The area between both of your assailant's arms where he has the greatest amount of control.

Intent—One of the essential factors to consider when assessing a threatening individual. The assailant's purpose or motive. (See *demeanor*, *positioning*, *range*, and *weapon capability*.)

Intuition—The innate ability to know or sense something without the use of rational thought.

Intuitive tool response (ITR)—Spontaneously reacting with the appropriate combative tool.

J

Jab—A quick, probing punch designed to create openings in the assailant's defense.

Jeet Kune Do—"Way of Intercepting Fist." Bruce Lee's approach to the martial arts, which includes his innovative concepts, theories, methodologies, and philosophies of unarmed combat.

Joint lock—A grappling-range technique that immobilizes the assailant's joint.

Judo—"Gentle Way." A Japanese grappling art (founded by Jigoro Kano in 1882) which is used as a sport. Judo utilizes shoulder and hip throws, foot sweeps, chokes, and pins.

Jujitsu—"Gentleness" or "suppleness." A system of self-defense that is the parent of both Judo and Aikido. Jujitsu specializes in grappling range but is known to employ a few striking techniques.

K

Karate—"Empty hand" or "China hand." A traditional martial art that originated in Okinawa and later spread to Japan and Korea. (See *Kung-Fu*.)

Kata—"Pattern" or "Form." A traditional training methodology whereby the practitioner practices a series of prearranged movements.

Kick—1) A sudden, forceful strike with the foot. (See *high-line kick* and *low-line kick*.); 2) The recoil of a firearm.

Kickboxing—A popular combat sport that employs full-contact tools.

Kicking range—One of the three ranges of unarmed combat. Kicking range is the farthest distance of unarmed combat, wherein you use your legs to strike an assailant. (See *grappling range* and *punching range*.)

Kicking-range tools—The various body weapons employed in the kicking range of unarmed combat, including side kicks, push kicks, hook kicks, and vertical kicks.

Killer instinct—A cold, primal mentality that surges to your consciousness and turns you into a vicious fighter.

Kinesics—The study of nonlinguistic body movement communications (i.e., eye movement, shrugs, facial gestures, etc.).

Kinesiology—The study of principles and mechanics of human movement.

Kinesthetic perception—The ability to accurately feel your body during the execution of a particular movement.

Kneeling firearm stance—A strategic stance you assume when kneeling down with a handgun.

Knife-defense stance—One of the many stances used in CFA's system. A strategic stance you assume when face-to-face with an knife or edged-weapon attacker. (See *de-escalation stance*, *fighting stance*, *knife fighting stance*, *firearms stance*, *natural stance*, *stick fighting stance*.)

Kung-Fu—"Accomplished task or effort." A term used erroneously to identify the traditional Chinese martial arts. (See *karate*.)

L

Lead side—The side of the body that faces an assailant.

Leg block—A blocking technique used with the legs. The leg block can be angled in three different directions: forward, right, and left.

Limited penetration (LP)—The LP is a corner-clearing movement performed by positioning your firearm and one eye around the corner.

Linear movement—Movements that follow the path of a straight line.

GLOSSARY

Lock—(See *joint lock*.)

Long-range combat—The farthest distance of knife and bludgeon combat. At this distance, you can only strike or slash your assailant's hand.

Low maintenance tools—Offensive and defensive tools that require the least amount of training and practice to maintain proficiency. Low maintenance tools generally don't require preliminary stretching.

Low-line kick—One of the two different classifications of a kick. A kick that is directed to targets below the assailant's waist level. (See *high-line kick*.)

Loyalty—The state of being faithful to a person, cause, or ideal.

M

Makeshift weapon—A common everyday object that can be converted into either an offensive or defensive weapon. There are four makeshift weapon classifications in the CFA system: (1) cutting makeshift weapons, (2) shielding makeshift weapons, (3) distracting makeshift weapons, and (4) striking makeshift weapons.

Maneuver—To move into a strategically desired position.

Manipulation accuracy—The ability to manipulate your assailant's limbs and joints with precision and exactness.

Martial artist—One who studies and practices the martial arts.

Martial arts—The traditional "arts of war." (See *karate* and *kung-fu*.)

Martial truth—(See *combative truth*.)

Mechanics—(See *body mechanics*.)

Medicine ball—A large, heavy ball used to strengthen and condition a fighter's stomach muscles.

Meet—A defensive technique that intercepts the assailant's line of attack with a slash.

Mental attributes—The various cognitive qualities that enhance your fighting skills.

Mental component—One of the three vital components of the CFA system. The mental component includes the cerebral aspects of fighting including the *killer instinct*, *strategic and tactical development*, *analysis and integration*, *philosophy*, and *cognitive development*. (See *physical component* and *spiritual component*.)

Mesomorph—A body type classified by a high degree of muscularity and strength. (See *endomorph* and *ectomorph*.)

Methods of attack—The five conventionally recognized methods of attacking. They include *single*, *indirect*, *attack by draw*, *immobilization*, and *compound*.

Mexican standoff—A precarious situation where both you and your adversary have the drop on one another.

Mid phase—One of the three stages of a stick swing. The mid phase is the contact or impact point of the swing.

Mid-range combat—One of the three ranges of knife and bludgeon combat. At this distance you can strike, slash, or stab your assailant's head, arms, and body with your weapon.

Misfire—A failure of a cartridge to fire after the primer has been struck.

Mobility—A combative attribute. The ability to move your body quickly and freely while balanced. (See *footwork*.)

Modern martial art—A pragmatic combat art that has evolved to meet the demands and characteristics of the present time.

Modernist—One who subscribes to the philosophy of the modern martial arts.

Modification—To make fundamental changes to serve a new end.

Mounted position—One of the five general ground fighting positions. The mounted position is where the practitioner sits on top of his assailant's torso or chest.

Mouthpiece—A rubber protector used to cover your teeth when sparring. There are two types of mouthpieces: single and double.

Muscular endurance—The muscles' ability to perform the same motion or task repeatedly for a prolonged period of time.

Muscular flexibility—The muscles' ability to move through maximum natural ranges.

Muscular/skeletal conditioning—An element of physical fitness that entails muscular strength, endurance, and flexibility.

Muscular strength—The maximum force that can be exerted by a particular muscle or muscle group against resistance.

Muzzle—The front end of the barrel of a gun.

Muzzle flash—An incandescent burst of light which is emitted from the muzzle and cylinder of a handgun.

N

Natural stance—One of the many stances used in CFA's system. You assume a strategic stance when approached by a suspicious person. (See *de-escalation stance*, *fighting stance*, *knife fighting stance*, *firearms stance*, *knife-defense stance*, and *stick fighting stance*.)

Neutralize—(See *incapacitate*.)

Neutral zone—The distance outside of the kicking range from which neither the practitioner nor the assailant can touch the other.

Nomenclature awareness—The ability to understand and recognize the system of names used in combat.

Nonaggressive physiology—Strategic body language used to de-escalate a potentially violent individual.

Nontelegraphic movement—Body mechanics or movements that do not inform an assailant of your intentions.

Nuclear ground fighting tools—Specific grappling-range tools designed to inflict immediate and irreversible damage. Some nuclear tools and tactics include: (1) biting tactics; (2) tearing tactics; (3) crushing tactics; (4) continuous choking tactics; (5) gouging techniques; (6) raking tactics; (7) and all striking techniques.

O

OC (Oleoresin Capsicum)—Also known as pepper gas, a natural mixture of oil and cayenne pepper used as a self-defense spray. OC is an inflammatory agent that affects the assailant's mucus membranes (i.e., eyes, nose, throat, lungs).

Offense—The armed and unarmed means and methods of attacking a criminal assailant.

Offensive flow—A progression of continuous offensive movements or actions designed to neutralize or terminate your adversary. (See *compound attack*.)

Offensive range manipulation (ORM)—The strategic manipulation of ranges (armed or unarmed) for offensive purposes.

Offensive reaction time (ORT)—The elapsed time between target selection and target impaction.

One-hand reloading—The process of reloading a firearm with only one hand.

One-mindedness—A state of deep concentration wherein you are free from all distractions (internal and external).

Opposite poles—One of the ground-fighting positions. The opposite pole position is assumed when both you and your assailant are

GLOSSARY

facing opposite directions. This often occurs when sprawling against your adversary.

Ornamental techniques—Techniques that are characterized as complex, inefficient, or impractical for real combat situations.

P

Pain tolerance—Your ability to physically and psychologically withstand pain.

Palming—The strategic concealment of a knife or edged weapon behind the forearm. Also known as knife palming.

Panic—The second stage of fear. Overpowering fear. (See *fright* and *terror*.)

Parry—A defensive technique. A quick, forceful slap that redirects an assailant's linear attack.

Pass—A defensive technique used in knife fighting.

PCP—A street drug known to cause extremely violent behavior, incredible strength, and immunity to pain.

Patience—A combative attribute. The ability to endure and tolerate difficulty.

Perception—Interpretation of vital information acquired from your senses when faced with a potentially threatening situation.

Perpendicular mount—One of the five general ground fighting positions. The perpendicular mount is established when you are lying on top of your adversary and both of your legs are on one side of his body.

Personal protection—(See *self-defense*.)

Philosophical resolution—The act of analyzing and answering various questions concerning the use of violence in defense of yourself and others.

Philosophy—One of the five aspects of CFA's mental component. A deep state of introspection whereby you methodically resolve critical questions concerning the use of force in defense of yourself and others.

Physical attributes—The numerous physical qualities that enhance your combative skills and abilities.

Physical component—One of the three vital components of the CFA system. The physical component includes the physical aspects of fighting, including *physical fitness*, *weapon and technique mastery*, and *combative attributes*. (See *mental component* and *spiritual component*.)

Physical conditioning—(See *combative fitness*.)

Physical fitness—(See *combative fitness*.)

Pistol—A gun with a short barrel that can be held, aimed, and fired with one hand.

Pitch—One of the four components of the human voice. The relative highness or lowness of the voice.

Poker face—A neutral and attentive facial expression that is used when de-escalating a hostile individual. The poker face prevents a hostile person from reading your intentions or feelings.

Positional asphyxia—A position that causes a lack of oxygen or excess of carbon dioxide in the body that is usually caused by interruption of breathing and causes unconsciousness or death.

Positioning—The spatial relationship you and your assailant in terms of target exposure, escape, angle of attack, and various other strategic considerations.

Positions of concealment—Various objects or locations that permit you to temporarily hide from your adversary. Positions of concealment are most commonly used to evade engagement with your assailant, and they permit you to attack with the element of surprise. Positions of concealment include trees, shrubbery, doors, the dark, walls, stairwells, underneath cars, large and tall objects, etc.

Positions of cover—Any object or location that temporarily protects you from the assailant's gunfire. Some positions of cover include large concrete utility poles, large rocks, thick trees, an engine block, corner of a building, concrete steps, etc.

Post traumatic syndrome (PTS)—A group of symptoms that may occur in the aftermath of a violent confrontation with a criminal assailant. Common symptoms of post traumatic syndrome include denial, shock, fear, anger, severe depression, sleeping and eating disorders, societal withdrawal, and paranoia.

Power—A physical attribute of armed and unarmed combat. The amount of force you can generate when striking an anatomical target.

Power generator—(See *anatomical power generators.*)

Precision—(See *accuracy.*)

Premise—An axiom, concept, or rule; any valid reason to modify or go beyond that which has been established.

Pressure point—A point on the body where a nerve lies close to its surface and is supported by bone or muscle mass.

Probe—A offensive tool that tests the assailant's combative abilities.

Proficiency training—A CFA training methodology requiring the practitioner to execute a specific body weapon, technique, maneuver, or tactic for a prescribed number or repetitions. (See *conditioning training* and *street training.*)

Progressive indirect attack—(see *indirect attack.*)

Prone firearm stance—A strategic stance you assume when lying down with a handgun.

Proxemics—The study of the nature and effect of man's personal space.

Proximity—The ability to maintain a strategically safe distance from a threatening individual.

Pseudospeciation—A combative attribute. The tendency to assign subhuman and inferior qualities to a threatening assailant.

Psychoemotional training—Combative training conducted when you're experiencing different types of emotional states.

Psychological conditioning—The process of conditioning the mind for the horrors and rigors of real combat.

Psychomotor domain—This includes the physical skills and attributes necessary to execute a combative tool, technique, or maneuver.

Psychopath—A person with an antisocial personality disorder, especially one manifested in aggressive, perverted, criminal, or amoral behavior.

Pummel—A flurry of full-speed, full-force strikes delivered from the mounted position.

Punch—A quick, forceful strike with the fists.

Punching range—One of the three ranges of unarmed combat. Punching range is the mid range of unarmed combat from which the fighter uses his hands to strike his assailant. (See *kicking range* and *grappling range.*)

Punching-range tools—The various body weapons that are employed in the punching range of unarmed combat, including finger jabs, palm-heel strikes, rear cross, knife-hand strikes, horizontal and shovel hooks, uppercuts, and hammer-fist strikes. (See *grappling-range tools* and *kicking-range tools.*)

Q

Qualities of combat—(See *attributes of combat.*)

GLOSSARY

Quick peek—A technique which is executed from a position of cover by rapidly darting out a small portion of your head and one eye to quickly observe.

R

Range—The spatial relationship between a fighter and a threatening assailant.

Range deficiency—The inability to effectively fight and defend in all ranges (armed and unarmed) of combat.

Range manipulation—A combative attribute. The strategic manipulation of combat ranges.

Range proficiency—A combative attribute. The ability to effectively fight and defend in all ranges (armed and unarmed) of combat.

Ranges of armed combat—The various distances in which a fighter might physically engage with an assailant while involved in armed combat, using knives, bludgeons, projectiles, makeshift weapons, and firearms.

Ranges of engagement—(See *combat ranges*.)

Ranges of unarmed combat—The three distances in which a fighter might physically engage with an assailant while involved in unarmed combat: kicking range, punching range, and grappling range.

Reaction dynamics—The assailant's physical response to a particular tool, technique, or weapon after initial contact is made.

Reaction time—The elapsed time between a stimulus and the response to that particular stimulus. (See *offensive reaction time* and *defensive reaction time*.)

Rear cross—A straight punch delivered from the rear hand that crosses from right to left (if in a left stance) or left to right (if in a right stance).

Rear side—The side of the body farthest from the assailant. (See *lead side*.)

Reasonable force—The degree of force that is not excessive for a particular event and that is appropriate for protecting yourself or others.

Refinement—The strategic and methodical process of improving or perfecting.

Repetition—Performing a single movement, exercise, strike, or action continuously for a specific period.

Research—A scientific investigation or inquiry.

Rest position—A relaxed posture you assume (when holding a stick or bludgeon) during idle periods in class (i.e., talking to another student, receiving instructions, etc.).

Reverberation path—The path in which your stick or bludgeon can bounce back at you.

Revolver—A handgun consisting of a cylinder that brings several chambers successively into line with the barrel of the gun.

Rhythm—Movements characterized by the natural ebb and flow of related elements.

Right to bear arms—A provision of the Second Amendment to the U.S. Constitution that prohibits our government from interfering with the right of the people to arm themselves.

Rimfire—A firearm cartridge that has its primer located around the rim of the case bottom.

Round—1) A period of time. 2) A single unit of ammunition. (See *cartridge*.)

S

Safe room—A strategic location in your residence where you and family members can escape from an intruder who has entered your home.

Safety—One of the three criteria for a CFA body weapon, technique, maneuver, or tactic. It means that the tool, technique, maneuver, or tactic presents the least amount of risk for the practitioner. (See *efficiency* and *effectiveness*.)

Scissors hold—(See *guard*.)

Secondary hand—A close-quarter technique used in both knife and bludgeon fighting whereby you temporarily hold your assailant's weapon hand in place after you have employed a defensive maneuver.

Secondary weapons—Various natural body weapons that are applied during armed combat.

Selective semantics—The selection and utilization of strategic words to de-escalate a hostile person. Also known as *choice words*.

Self-awareness—One of the three categories of CFA awareness. Knowing and understanding yourself. This includes aspects of yourself that may provoke criminal violence and will promote a proper and strong reaction to an attack. (See *criminal awareness* and *situational awareness*.)

Self-confidence—Having trust and faith in yourself.

Self-defense—The act of defending yourself or one's family. (Also called *personal protection* or *self-protection*.)

Self-enlightenment—The state of knowing your capabilities, limitations, character traits, feelings, general attributes, and motivations. (See *self-awareness*.)

Semiautomatic handgun—(See *autoloader*.)

Sensei—Teacher.

Set—A term used to describe a grouping of repetitions.

Setup tool—A tool used to throw the assailant off balance and/or open his defenses.

Shadow fighting—A CFA training exercise used to develop and refine your tools, techniques, and attributes of armed and unarmed combat.

Shielding makeshift weapon—One of the four types of CFA makeshift weapons. Any object that can be used to effectively shield oneself from an assailant's attack. (See also *distracting makeshift weapon*, *cutting makeshift weapon*, and *striking makeshift weapon*.)

Shooting accuracy—The ability to shoot a firearm with precision and exactness.

Shot—A package or wad of metal balls that vary in size and spread out as they travel away from the muzzle of a shotgun.

Shotgun—A single- or double-barreled, smooth-bore firearm used for firing shot or slugs at a relatively close distance.

Shoulder roll—A defensive technique that rocks your body away from a punch in order to nullify its force.

Side fall—A firearm engagement technique that is executed from a kneeling position behind cover.

Sifu—(See *sensei*.)

Sight alignment—A component of marksmanship whereby you correctly align your dominant eye with both the front and rear sights of your firearm.

Sights—Various electronic, optical, and mechanical devices used to aim a firearm.

Single attack—One of the five conventional methods of attack. A method of attack whereby you deliver a solitary offensive strike. It may involve a series of discreet probes or one swift, powerful strike aimed at terminating the encounter. (See *compound attack*, *indirect attack*, *immobilization attack*, and *attack by draw*.)

Single-action—A type of pistol action in which pulling the trigger will release the hammer.

Situational awareness—One of the three categories of CFA awareness. A state of being totally alert to your immediate surroundings, including people, places, objects, and actions. (See *criminal awareness* and *self-awareness*.)

GLOSSARY

Skeletal alignment—The proper alignment or arrangement of your body. Skeletal alignment maximizes the structural integrity of striking tools.

Slash—One of the two ways to cut someone with a knife or edged weapon. A quick, sweeping stroke of a knife. (See *stab*.)

Slipping—A defensive maneuver that permits you to avoid an assailant's linear blow without stepping out of range. Slipping can be accomplished by quickly snapping the head and upper torso sideways (right or left) to avoid the blow.

Snap back—A defensive maneuver that permits you to avoid an assailant's linear and circular blow without stepping out of range. The snap back can be accomplished by quickly snapping the head backwards to avoid the assailant's blow.

Somatotyping—A method of classifying human body types or builds into three different categories: *ectomorph*, *mesomorph*, and *endomorph*.

Speed—A physical attribute of armed and unarmed combat. The rate or a measure of the rapid rate of motion.

Spinning kicks—Kicks delivered with a spin of the body.

Spinning punches—Punches delivered with a spin of the body.

Spiritual component—One of the three vital components of the CFA system. The spiritual component includes the metaphysical issues and aspects of existence. (See *physical component* and *mental component*.)

Sprawling—A defensive technique in grappling range accomplished by lowering your hips to the ground while simultaneously shooting both of your legs back.

Square off—To be face-to-face with a threatening assailant who is about to attack you.

Squib load—A cartridge which develops less than normal velocity after the ignition of a cartridge.

Stab—One of the two ways to cut someone with a knife or edged weapon. A quick thrust made with a pointed weapon or implement, usually a knife. (See *slash*.)

Stable terrain—Terrain that is principally characterized as stationary, compact, dense, hard, flat, dry, or solid.

Stance—One of the many strategic postures that you assume prior to or during armed or unarmed combat.

Stance selection—A combative attribute. The ability to instinctively select a stance appropriate for a particular combat situation.

Standing firearm stance—A strategic stance you assume when standing with a handgun.

Step and drag—Strategic footwork used when standing on unstable terrain.

Stick block—A defensive technique that stops your assailant's stick strike.

Stick deflection—A defensive technique that deflects and redirects your assailant's stick strike.

Stick twirl—A dexterity exercise performed with either one or two sticks.

Stop-hit—A method of hitting the assailant before his tool reaches full extension.

Stopping power—A firearm's ability to stop an assailant from continuing any further action.

Strategic leaning—A defensive maneuver that permits you to evade a knife slash while remaining in range to counter.

Strategic positioning—Tactically positioning yourself to either escape, move behind a barrier, or use a makeshift weapon.

Strategy—A carefully planned method of achieving your goal of engaging an assailant under advantageous conditions.

Street fight—A spontaneous and violent confrontation between two or more individuals wherein no rules apply.

Street fighter—An unorthodox combatant who has no formal training. His combative skills and tactics are usually developed in the street through the process of trial and error.

Street smarts—Having the knowledge, skills, and attitude necessary to avoid, defuse, confront, and neutralize both armed and unarmed assailants.

Street training—A CFA training methodology requiring the practitioner to deliver explosive compound attacks for 10 to 20 seconds. (See *conditioning training* and *proficiency training*.)

Strength training—The process of developing muscular strength through systematic application of progressive resistance.

Striking accuracy—The ability to strike your assailant with precision and exactness (this includes using natural body weapons, bludgeons, and some makeshift weapons).

Striking art—A combat art that relies predominantly on striking techniques to neutralize or terminate an attacker.

Striking makeshift weapon—One of the four types of CFA makeshift weapons. Any object that can be used to effectively strike a criminal assailant. (See *distracting makeshift weapon*, *cutting makeshift weapon*, and *shielding makeshift weapon*.)

Striking shield—A rectangular-shaped shield constructed of foam and vinyl used to develop power in most of your kicks, punches, and strikes.

Striking tool—1) A natural body weapon that impacts with the assailant's anatomical target. 2) A hand-held implement that impacts with the assailant's anatomical target.

Strong side—The strongest and most coordinated side of your body.

Structure—A definite and organized pattern.

Style—The distinct manner in which a fighter executes or performs his combat skills.

Stylistic integration—The purposeful and scientific collection of tools and techniques from various disciplines, which are strategically integrated and dramatically altered to meet three essential criteria: efficiency, effectiveness, and combative safety.

Surface area—(See *terrain*.)

System—The unification of principles, philosophies, rules, strategies, methodologies, tools, and techniques of a particular method of combat.

T

Tactical calming—(See *de-escalation*.)

Tactical option selection—A combative attribute. The ability to select the appropriate tactical option for any particular self-defense situation.

Tactics—Applications of tools and techniques.

Tactile sight—A combative attribute. The ability to "see" through tactile contact with your assailant.

Takedowns—Various grappling maneuvers designed to take your assailant down to the ground.

Target exploitation—A combative attribute. The strategic maximization of your assailant's reaction dynamics during a fight. Target exploitation can be applied in both armed and unarmed encounters.

Target impaction—The successful striking of the appropriate anatomical target.

Target orientation—A combative attribute. Having

GLOSSARY

a workable knowledge of the assailant's anatomical targets. Target orientation is divided into five different categories: (1) impact targets—anatomical targets that can be struck with your natural body weapons; (2) nonimpact targets—anatomical targets that can be strangled, twisted, torn, crushed, clawed, gouged, broken, dislocated, or strategically manipulated; (3) edged weapon targets—anatomical targets that can be punctured or slashed with a knife or edged weapon; (4) bludgeon targets—anatomical targets that can be struck with a stick or bludgeon; (5) ballistic targets—anatomical targets that can be shot with a firearm.

Target recognition—The ability to immediately recognize appropriate anatomical targets during an emergency self-defense situation.

Target selection—The process of mentally selecting the appropriate anatomical target for your self-defense situation. This is predicated on certain factors, including proper force response, the assailant's positioning, and range.

Target stare—A form of telegraphing whereby you stare at the anatomical target you intend to strike.

Target zones—The three areas in which an assailant's anatomical targets are located. (See *zone one*, *zone two*, and *zone three*.)

Technique—A systematic procedure by which a task is accomplished.

Telegraphic cognizance—A combative attribute. The ability to recognize both verbal and nonverbal signs of aggression or assault.

Telegraphing—Unintentionally making your intentions known to your adversary.

Tempo—The speed or rate at which you speak.

Terminate—The act of killing.

Terrain—The type of surface that you are standing on. There are two classifications of terrain: stable and unstable. (See *stable terrain* and *unstable terrain*.)

Terrain orientation—A combative attribute. Having a working knowledge of the various types of environmental terrains and their advantages, dangers, and strategic limitations.

Terror—The third stage of fear. Overpowering fear. (See *fright* and *panic*.)

Throw—Grappling techniques designed to unbalance your assailant and lift him off the floor.

Timing—A physical and mental attribute of armed and unarmed combat. Your ability to execute a movement at the optimum moment.

Tone—The overall quality or character of your voice.

Tool—(See *body weapon*.)

Traditional martial art—Any martial art that fails to evolve and meet the demands and characteristics of the present time. (See *Karate* and *Kung-Fu*.)

Traditional style/system—(See *traditional martial art*.)

Traditionalism—The beliefs and principles of a traditional or classical martial art.

Traditionalist—One who subscribes to the principles and practices of traditional martial arts.

Training drills—The various exercises and drills aimed at perfecting combat skills, attributes, and tactics.

Training methodologies—Training procedures utilized in the CFA system.

Training zone—The training zone (or target heart rate) is a safe and effective level of physical activity that produces cardiorespiratory fitness.

Trapping—Momentarily immobilizing or manipulating the assailant's limb or limbs in order to create an opening for attack.

Trapping range—The distance between punching and grappling range in which trapping techniques are used.

Traversing skills—Pivoting and twisting laterally. Traversing skills can be used for both armed and unarmed combat.

Trigger squeeze—A component of marksmanship. Trigger squeeze is achieved by squeezing the trigger of your firearm straight to the rear in a smooth and fluid manner, without disturbing the sight alignment.

Troubleshooting skills—A combative attribute. The ability to immediately diagnose and solve problems when engaged with an adversary.

U

Unified mind—A mind that is free and clear of distractions and focused on the combative situation.

Uniform Crime Report (UCR)—A nationwide cooperative statistical compilation of the efforts and reports of 16,000 state and local law enforcement agencies that voluntarily report data on crime.

Unstable terrain—Terrain that is characterized as mobile, uneven, flexible, slippery, wet, or rocky. (See *stable terrain*.)

Unstructured modernist—A martial artist who adheres to the abstract principles of combative formlessness.

Use-of-force response—A combative attribute. Selecting the appropriate level of force for a particular emergency self-defense situation.

V

V grip—A strategically defensive grip used to defend against an edged-weapon attack.

Vertical trapping—Trapping techniques that are applied while standing face-to-face with your adversary. (See *immobilization attack*.)

Viciousness—A combative attribute. Dangerously aggressive behavior.

Victim—Any person who is the object of a particular crime.

Violence—The intentional utilization of physical force to coerce, injure, cripple, or kill.

Visual monitoring points—Specific points or locations on your assailant that you should look at during an emergency self-defense situation.

Visualization—The purposeful formation of mental images and scenarios in the mind's eye.

W

Warm-up—A series of mild exercises, stretches, and movements designed to prepare you for more intense exercise.

Warrior arts—(See *martial arts*.)

Weak side—The weakest and most uncoordinated side of your body.

Weapon and technique mastery—An element of CFA's physical component. The kinesthetic and psychomotor development of a weapon or combative technique.

Weapon capability—An assailant's ability to use and attack with a particular weapon.

Weapon hierarchy mastery—Possessing the knowledge, skills, and attitude necessary to master the complete hierarchy of combat weapons.

Weapon uniformity—Gripping or drawing your hand-held weapon the same way every time.

Western boxing—A Western combat sport that only employs punching-range tools.

Y

Yell—A loud and aggressive scream or shout used for various strategic reasons.

GLOSSARY

Z

Zone one—Anatomical targets related to your senses, including the eyes, temple, nose, chin, and back of the neck.

Zone three—Anatomical targets related to your mobility, including thighs, knees, shins, and instep.

Zone two—Anatomical targets related to your breathing, including front of neck, solar plexus, ribs, and groin.

Zoning—A defensive maneuver designed to negate your assailant's stick strike through strategic movement and precise timing. Zoning can be accomplished by either moving in the direction of your assailant's strike (before it generates significant force) or by moving completely out of his stick's arc.

Suggested Reading and Viewing

SUGGESTED READING

Franco, Sammy. *Killer Instinct: Unarmed Urban Combat for Street Survival,* Boulder, Colorado: Paladin Press, 1991.
____. *Street Lethal: Unarmed Urban Combat,* Boulder, Colorado: Paladin Press, 1989.
____. *When Seconds Count: Everyone's Guide to Self-Defense,* Boulder, Colorado: Paladin Press, 1994.
Tzu, Sun. *The Art of War*, New York: Delacorte Press, 1983.

MAGAZINE ARTICLES

Franco, Sammy. "Prerequisites to Innovation." *Inside Karate*, December 1989.
____. "Shadow Fighting," *Inside Karate*, October 1989.
____. "Do Bruce Lee's Theories Work in the Street?" *Inside Karate*, August 1989.
____. "Training and Conditioning for the Martial Artist," *Inside Karate*, April 1989.
____. "The Heavy Bag," *Inside Karate*, December 1988.
____. "The Three Ranges of Unarmed Combat," *Inside Karate*, October 1987.
____. "Analytical Street Fighting," *Inside Karate*, February 1987.
____. "Training and Conditioning for the Martial Artist." *Inside Kung-Fu*, March 1991.
____. "The Focus Mitt," *Inside Kung-Fu*, March 1991.
____. "Low-Line Kicking," *Inside Kung-Fu*, September 1990.
____. "Training and Conditioning for the Martial Artist." *Inside Kung-Fu*, December 1989.
____. "Aerobics for the Martial Artist," *Inside Kung-Fu*, April 1989.
____. "Home Invasion," *Black Belt Magazine*, November 1994.

SUGGESTED VIEWING

CFA Tape 1: *Fundamental Techniques*, Panther Productions. Videotape.
CFA Tape 2: *Kicks, Punches, & Conditioning,* Panther Productions. Videotape.
CFA Tape 3: *Grappling & Defense,* Panther Productions. Videotape.
CFA Tape 4: *Street Self-Defense Techniques,* Panther Productions. Videotape.

About the Author

Over the past 20 years, Sammy Franco has emerged as one of the nation's leading experts in the field of self-defense and martial sciences. Highly regarded as an innovator and teacher, he has authored numerous magazine articles and several best-selling books, as well as a series of instructional videotapes.

Mr. Franco's experience and credibility in the combat sciences field is unparalleled. He is a Law Enforcement Master Instructor who regularly teaches and supervises defensive tactics training for local and federal law enforcement agencies, including the U.S. Border Patrol. He is a member of the American Society of Law Enforcement Trainers (ASLET) and is listed in the *Who's Who Directory of Law Enforcement Instructors*. He is a nationally certified police instructor in the following curriculums: PR-24 Side-Handle Baton, Police Arrest and Control Procedures, Police Personal Weapons Tactics, Police Power Handcuffing Methods, Police Oleoresin Capsicum Aerosol Training (OCAT), Police Weapons Retention and Disarming Methods, Police Edged Weapon Countermeasures, and Use of Force Assessment and Response Methods. He is also a nationally certified firearms instructor (police and civilian) who specializes in firearm safety, personal protection, and advanced combat shooting.

Mr. Franco is perhaps best known as founder and creator of Contemporary Fighting Arts®, a highly scientific combat system that has been featured in newspapers, on the radio, and on television—including CBS' *48 Hours*. His previous books, *Street Lethal*, *Killer Instinct*, and *When Seconds Count*, have been acclaimed as "field guides for those fed up with the fear of becoming one of tomorrow morning's statistics."

Mr. Franco holds a Bachelor of Arts degree in criminal justice from the University of Maryland and regularly conducts exciting and informative seminars on the martial arts, self-defense, firearms, and the growing problem of violence in America.

To contact Mr. Franco for interviews, seminars, or personal appearances, write him in care of the publisher.